FOURTH CITY

FOURTH CITY

ESSAYS FROM THE ————
PRISON IN AMERICA

EDITED BY
DORAN LARSON

MICHIGAN STATE UNIVERSITY PRESS
East Lansing

☻ The paper used in this publication meets the minimum requirements
of ANSI/NISO Z39.48-1992 (R 1997) (Permanence of Paper).

Michigan State University Press
East Lansing, Michigan 48823-5245

Support for work on this volume was provided by the Digital Humanities
Initiative (DHi) at Hamilton College and the DHi-Supported American
Prison Writing Archive. The DHi is funded by Hamilton College and
the Andrew W. Mellon Foundation.

Printed and bound in the United States of America.

19 18 17 16 15 14 13   1 2 3 4 5 6 7 8 9 10

Library of Congress Cataloging-in-Publication Data

Fourth city : essays from the prison in America /
edited by Doran Larson.
    pages   cm
Includes bibliographical references and index.
ISBN 978-1-60917-397-5 (ebook)—ISBN 978-1-61186-107-5 (pbk. : alk. paper)
1. Prisons—United States. 2. Prisoners—United States. I. Larson, Doran.
HV9471.F638 2013
365'.973—dc23   2013014959

Book design by Walton Harris
Cover design by Gregory Lord

Michigan State University Press is a member of the Green Press Initiative and
is committed to developing and encouraging ecologically responsible publishing
practices. For more information about the Green Press Initiative and the use of
recycled paper in book publishing, please visit www.greenpressinitiative.org.

Visit Michigan State University Press at www.msupress.org

TO ALL AMERICANS WHO BEAR NUMBERS FOR NAMES

CONTENTS

ACKNOWLEDGMENTS

Thanks first to Olivia Wolfgang-Smith for her invaluable assistance in editing this volume; to Rory Pavach for the groundwork involved in getting the call for essays into as many prison facilities as possible; and to Nora Grenfel and Maeve Gately for their readings and clerical work. Thanks are due to Robert Ferguson for his advice about the shape of this book. Thanks to the members of "English 442: Booked, Prison Writing," of Fall 2009 at Hamilton College, for their diligent typing; to Jill Schoolman of Archipelago Books for her generous insider's guide to likely editors and publishers; to Pamela Fadem of the California Coalition of Women Prisoners; to Jeffrey Williams and William Billiter; to Hamilton College, which recruits extraordinary students and is always ready to support faculty initiatives in teaching and research; to Angel Nieves and Janet Simons of the Digital Humanities Initiative at Hamilton College, with generous support from the Andrew W. Mellon Foundation, and to Hamilton Dean of Faculty Patrick Reynolds; to Greg Lord for the cover design; to Julie Loehr, Kristine Blakeslee, and the whole team at Michigan State University Press for their faith in and commitment to this project. Finally, I want to thank the members of the Attica Writers Workshop, inside Attica Correctional Facility. They have shown me that human beings who have made fatal mistakes, and who endure terrible conditions, can also be very fine, generous, and wise people. At every meeting they renew my faith in both the human spirit and in its singularly American permutations..

PREVIOUS PUBLICATION ACKNOWLEDGMENTS

Danner Darcleight's "Concrete Carnival," Peter Mehmel's "A Hidden Cost," and A. Whitfield's "JCF Welcome" appeared in *the minnesota review*; Linda Field's "Life Without Children," Running Water's "Prison or Kids: It's Not a Joke," and the anonymously authored "Mother-Daughter in Prison" appeared in *The Fire Inside: Newsletter of the California Coalition of Women Prisoners*; Intelligent Allah's "Bread and Water Vegan" appeared in *American Vegan*; Markeithia R. Reevez's "Inmate Jane Doe" and Chastity C. West's "Left Behind" appear on the PEN Prison Writing Awards website; A. Whitfield's "It Could Be Me" and Robert F. Piwowar's "A Lesson in Language" appeared in *Stone Canoe* 4 (2010) and 6 (2012).

INTRODUCTION
THE AMERICAN PRISON WRITER AS WITNESS

Fourth City: Essays from the Prison in America presents the widest sampling to date of first-person, frontline witness to the human experience of mass incarceration in the United States. Pushing back against the monstrous caricatures of prisons and prisoners in popular film and television, these essays offer direct engagement with life as it is lived every day by the American citizens held inside state and federal institutions. If we aspire not only to practice equal treatment before the law but also to mete out only humane and constructive forms of legal justice, we need to know what these Americans have witnessed of life on the receiving end of legalized punishment. These writers alone can testify to whether the largest prison system on earth doles out punishment in the service or at the expense of justice.

The United States imprisons a greater number and percentage of its own citizens than any other nation on earth: greater than Russia or China, Cuba or Iran. Although we make up only 5 percent of the earth's population, we lock up 25 percent of the world's incarcerated people. If gathered together in one place, incarcerated Americans would constitute the nation's fourth largest city—a city larger than Houston, Philadelphia, or Phoenix.[1] In the face of American claims to practice exceptional respect for human liberty, such facts are widely cited with shock and lament. But shock is not insight. Lament is not understanding. And statistics alone cannot convey the nature of life inside the world's leading prison state. *Fourth City* bears witness to life as it is lived every hour of every day, at the end of the forty years since the American prison began to grow out of proportion to both crime rates and international norms.[2] These essays by incarcerated Americans show us the roads that lead to prison, the damage done inside, and why so few return from prison to live as fully enfranchised citizens. Together they form a chorus bearing witness to the failures of an institution that claims to serve us all. It remains for us to choose to listen. But the stakes involved in this choice cannot be fully weighed without some understanding of the U.S. prison's unprecedented growth.

Social scientists have worked for years to explain the exponential growth of the American prison—growth accelerated and sustained since 1973 despite stable and sinking rates of crime.[3] The picture is now clear. Once a necessary evil linked to crime rates, the prison has become the catch-all answer to social, public-health, and economic problems whose constructive remedies we have abandoned, failed to maintain effectively, or legally barred. These more benign remedies include social welfare that enables work rather than punishing unemployment amid a globalized labor market; evenly distributed, quality public education; affordable physical and mental health care, including effective drug and alcohol treatment; even-handed police enforcement; and, when all else fails, manageable case loads for public defenders working in courts where judicial discretion can fit measured punishment, public service, treatment, or restorative acts to crimes and their perpetrators. In the name of getting Big Government out of the lives of private citizens, we have deregulated the economy and dismantled public supports, while shifting government resources into an equally large, equally costly, and deeply interwoven "penal state" that polices, prosecutes, and punishes those abandoned by labor markets, public assistance, and due process.[4]

To give these changes in public policy the gloss of upholding American values and defending public safety, politicians—voicing white unease over the changes in racial order brought about by the Civil Rights movement, and aided by popular media and victims' rights groups funded by prison guards' unions[5]—have demonized the entire prison population as a threat to public order. This has been accomplished by highlighting the most gruesome cases of violent crime even as violent crime continues to shrink and prisons fill with nonviolent offenders.[6] Today, after four decades of bipartisan "tough on crime" politics and militarized domestic Wars on Crime and Drugs, American prisons hold their wards for numbers of years out of all proportion to the rest of the industrialized world, and focus the prison's mission on punishment and suffering rather than treatment, education, or training.[7]

The result is arguably the world's largest state-run system for recycling human misery: among the more than six hundred thousand Americans released from prison each year, two-thirds emerge less equipped and less able to secure places in free society than when they entered, and return within three years.[8] In the past, American prisons offered a necessary service to citizens who deserve security in their persons, homes, families, and communities; with a range of other options available to police and courts, locking up citizens was a last resort.[9] But the American prison has cancerously outgrown its service to public safety. Today it does less to resolve the problem of crime than to sustain a multibillion-dollar industry[10] built on translating the failures of civic and economic community into new and overfilled criminal categories. What this means is institutionalized marginality for the seven million Americans marked by (and cycled through) probation, jail, prison, and parole, and effectively premarking their millions of children and dependents for further suffering.[11]

So now we have a choice. With 2.26 million Americans incarcerated in prisons and jails,[12] we can choose to see this Fourth City as an insuperable problem. We can continue to take satisfaction in the thought that convicted people are suffering, and we can continue to pay for that satisfaction in tens of billions of dollars dedicated to ensuring that prisoners will be made unable to return to lives outside as productive, tax-paying citizens and contributors to the revitalization of the communities where they committed their crimes. Or we can search for ways to create prisons committed to the restoration of persons and communities—a search that can begin by choosing to listen to what the men and women living inside the American prison today can tell us about what is wrong with prison practice. We can acknowledge this Fourth City as the dwelling place of the Americans who are best positioned to understand what our prisons do, to whom, and to what practical purpose. We can take the unprecedented step of welcoming their witness into our efforts to understand, and to begin dismantling, the prison we have built. Doing so not only would be a practical step toward smaller and smaller prisons that do socially constructive work but it could also serve as the first step toward making American criminal justice less criminal and more just.

In separating men and women from their homes and families, restricting their movement, and stripping them of selected civil and property rights, the police, courts, and prisons carry out the violence that law sanctions the state to practice against the state's citizens.[13] Policing, courtroom procedures, and prison practices are thus symptomatic sites for judging any state's legal integrity, its commitment to equal treatment, and its overall moral health. We make these connections wherever camps and prisons emerge under tyrannous configurations of power: judging Stalin by his gulag, the Reich by its death camps, apartheid by Robben Island, and Iran by Evin. We are certainly right to condemn such regimes, but we do so on the assumption that the full implementation of American legal rights, even-handed police enforcement, and courts that make no practical distinctions based on race or class have effectively isolated the prison from judgments upon the moral integrity of the state. The prisoner thus becomes the rightful victim of his or her own actions; the prison becomes a quarantined space for punishment of private, moral ills, and nothing in this complex bears significance for our assessment of the nation's legal health and democratic integrity. This is the working assumption in the United States today. And it is at least forty years out of date. As sociologist Bruce Western observes, "Convict status inheres now, not in individual offenders, but in entire demographic categories."[14] In turn, as the essays in this volume suggest, the violent dysfunction inside American prisons may be less the effect of whom we lock up than of institutional practices veiled by the sanction of law.

Fourth City seeks to break this quarantine and pull back this veil. Its premise is that American prison writers—like those who have written from Siberia, Auschwitz, South Africa, and Tehran—remain our permanent vanguard in understanding whether the violence meted out by the law achieves order in the name, or at the expense, of justice. *Fourth City* provides a venue for the vital work that only American prison writers can perform: the work of helping us understand whether prison practices in the United States might indeed challenge our claims to respect human rights even where we agree to suspend selected civil rights; and the equally important (and deeply linked) work of authentically representing the lives of the 2.26 million American citizens whose public images are almost exclusively created by free-world makers of film and television who have never done time inside, and by local and national for-profit news organizations that prosper by producing a narrow repertoire of monsters that thrill our fears and fantasies of what goes on inside.[15] If we rely on such images to tell us what the prison is and what incarcerated Americans are, and then sanction judicial and prison policy in response to such images, we fail to differentiate ourselves from Soviet citizens convinced that the gulag held only "anti-revolutionary deviants," Germans who believed that the ghettos and camps kept the *volk* safe from a lethal scourge, or white South Africans who never doubted that Apartheid was the only safeguard against chaos. The writers in *Fourth City* test such complacency. Whatever presumptions about prisons and prisoners the reader might bring to this volume, those presumptions can now be tested in the light cast by incarcerated Americans themselves.

Among the writers in this volume, the reader will find no Solzhenitsyns, no Frankls or Levis, no Mandelas. Yet these writers not only retain the right to document their experience; we need such documentation in order to know whether the American prison today is an institution dedicated to justice, correction, and the rule of law, or solely to what prison writer and reformer Kate Richards O'Hare called "social vengeance."[16] These writers have apologies to give. None is apologetic about the state of the prison in America. We cannot afford to ignore a consensus this widespread among a body of Americans this large and living inside the steel and concrete evidence of exactly how our prisons fail their charge of correction so badly as to sustain a national recidivism rate of 67.5 percent.[17] The writers here report on a system that is not only badly broken, but *will* not take the steps these writers know are needed in order to turn concrete warehouses into sites of restoration. They also provide evidence that convicted citizens retain a deep sense of right and wrong, of what is just and unjust, of what works and does not work, and of their own roles as prison and American citizens, and they show us that the institutions that oversee them too often lose sight of these differences. Few other groups of Americans can bear such direct witness to the institutionalized practice of our values. No others live in a place where those values, poured in concrete, have shaped such a peculiarly American community.

The initial working title for this collection was *Voices through the Wall: Prisoners Write about Prisons*. But this title quickly proved overly generic as essays arrived from prisons across the

United States and fell into categories that mapped out the roles of civic constituents: journalists, chroniclers of daily life, legal investigators, health-care workers, community activists, teachers, church members, cooks, artists, and common citizens pursuing personal happiness.[18] From an archipelago of razor-wired neighborhoods, writers from Alabama and Washington, from California and Missouri and Massachusetts, politicized prisoners, those convicted of violent and nonviolent offenses, men, women, straight, gay, transgendered, Black, white, Hispanic, and Native American, repeat and one-time offenders . . . virtually all report on similar problems, and issues, and sources of hope. However differently states and facilities take on the jobs of self-policing or rehabilitation, each of these authors feels caught inside *one* institution. Even in writers who have known only a single jailhouse, there is an abiding sense of authority to speak of "the prison system" as a whole. These writers see themselves writing from, of, and for *a single community under hostile supervision*—an experience more homogeneous than that borne by inhabitants of Albuquerque or Memphis, Boston or L.A.

The title changed to *Fourth City* in order to begin the work these essays demanded: to modify our collective imagination of the prison to reflect the prison to which its inhabitants bear witness.[19] By envisioning the prison as the nation's Fourth City, we gain a tangible image of the sheer size of this population, we begin to appreciate the cohesiveness of the punishment regime that incarcerated Americans undergo, and we take these steps without allowing this institution's inhabitants to sink into a faceless mass. In granting the individual lives lived inside this Prison City the recognition they deserve as the lives of American citizens, we begin to understand that they are simply too many to be dismissed as an unfortunate liability of liberal democracy. They are as integral to any assessments of the nature of contemporary American life as the lives unfolding at this moment in New York, Los Angeles, or Chicago. The exception is that the conditions endured in this Prison City devolve directly from laws, policies, and practices determined by the state and maintained by public compliance expressed in the taxes collected to run a metropolis of cages. Responsibility for mass incarceration reaches into the same corporate and political boardrooms that claim to serve us all. It is ingrained in a peculiarly American history of racialized class relations. It is fed by mediated fears of the poor and disenfranchised. With numbers high above those of any other nation today, the roots of the American prison reach down into the full depth of our history. As the one city in whose maintenance every voting and tax-paying citizen bears a hand, our Fourth City speaks more directly than all others to the values practiced in America today. Whatever these writers may have done to hurt others and themselves, we all bear the weight of the consequences of what occurs next.

In order to enlist imprisoned people's help in the task of shrinking and dismantling the prison complex, we must first try to understand who they are. At the same time that *Fourth City* helps us gain a tangible grasp of the scale of incarceration in the United States, it prepares us to take the first step back down from these conspicuous heights by helping us decipher the faces inside this confined city. Reading through these essays, we begin to get some sense of how its inhabitants fill the aggregate shape and bear the real effects of the world's largest punishment regime.

Though incarcerated in twenty-seven different states, the writers in this volume impress upon us that walking the streets of America's Prison City is as distinct an experience as walking Sunset Boulevard, Michigan Avenue, or Broadway. Yet no single image will ever announce this Prison City as the palm trees lining Hollywood Boulevard announce Los Angeles, as the Sears Tower viewed across Lake Michigan announces Chicago, or as the Empire State Building announces New York. It is simply the *other* to life in the free world. An archipelago city spread across every state, we can picture it only in generic fragments: walls, razor wire, watchtowers, bars, and concrete—fragments of the apparatus of containment, holding equally fragmented clichés and stock images of those inside. The writers who live there, however, report from one place: from the frontlines in the civil class and race war carried in from outside and raging day by day between convicts and state employees (*all* of whom suffer this war's dehumanization) and between convicts themselves. Yet amid these scenes of uniformed occupation, these writers want to imagine real civic involvement in civil lives. We see this explicitly in the essays gathered under "Community Activists" and "Civic Dysfunction and Its Critics." It is implied in every essay that critiques policies and practices prohibiting acts of agency that would allow these writers to assume institutional responsibility for themselves. It is evident in the frustration of writers whose best energies and intentions are consumed by the daily labor of self-defense inside prisons that exercise little responsibility beyond warehousing bodies. The desire to make responsible choices as members of professionally regulated communities is implicit in every lament over acts of humiliation, dehumanization, and brutalization experienced at the hands of, or tolerated by, state employees. Yet despite these conditions, the desire to be of benefit to others, even from inside, is explicit throughout this volume, and especially in the two categories of essays placed as solos between the themed choruses of this volume: under "Ticket In" writers tell stories of the lives that led them to prison, thus warning others of the hazards that brought them here; under "Kite Out" imprisoned people address the young outside and inside in order to help them toward better paths.[20] These essays convey the good civil will of a population larger than fifteen states but that has no vote and no representatives. If New York is a city of breakneck ambition, Los Angeles the city of stars, and Chicago the city of big shoulders, Prison City may best be understood as the city of violent longing.

The authors gathered in *Fourth City* are neither the caricatured monsters touted by popular film and staged for ugly sensation in so-called reality TV, nor the faceless statistics generated by social science. These are Americans whose lives and voices are as singular as any in the free world. Here the reader will find humor, love, defiance, resilience, and determination against the worst imaginable odds; s/he will find endurance, pathos, aspiration, calm, self-analysis, and reflection, along with anger and resentment. Prisons are not happy or safe places. But we damage the very texture of democracy if we shrink so large a segment of our population to the images that fill our TV screens every night. Such images blind us to the effects of a prison whose failures institutionalize the suffering and criminality of whole categories of citizens. They prejudge for failure men and women who, though they may have damaged, might also in future contribute to the restoration of our most troubled communities. And they absolve us of collective responsibility for what goes on inside and for its effects outside. Incarcerated Americans lead morally and emotionally complex lives—lives animated by conscience, outrage, guilt, shame, and fear; by joy, hope, and love. *Fourth City* grants its citizens the authority they have earned: to witness the full gamut of social, moral, emotional, and psychological experiences walled up and disappeared inside American prisons. Needless to say, what such witness brings to light is not always pleasant to look at.

Whatever we might think of the wars on crime or drugs, they feed another civil war that rages every day, in every state in the union: the civil war waged by the disenfranchised, working-class and working-poor, predominantly white men and women hired from the rural regions where we plant prisons, and the predominantly poor Black and poor Latino men and women taken from parts of cities where the police wage war against civil failure, against abandonment by the state—

except from behind shields. The irony is that the cause of economic loss among these warring parties is the same: the deportation of decent paying jobs—in factories and on farms—that once meant that poor urban people of color could look forward to a wedding band and a union card as rite of passage, rather than to a Department of Corrections number and decades of time inside; and also meant that rural and semirural people could aspire to similarly productive rites rather than to a prison guard's uniform, a nightstick, and equally long and dehumanizing years inside.[21] We need to dismantle the demeaning popular images on either side of this confrontation.

For every act of rape, for every act of cruelty that occurs inside a prison—whether perpetrated by staff or convicts—there are untold numbers of men and women on both sides of this war that bear the human weight of witnessing such acts.[22] There are indeed people in our prisons who have become so hardened that the suffering of others is one of their few sources of pleasure. But these are only a fraction of the convicted population; and such personalities are found in disturbing numbers among state-salaried employees who usurp the authority of courts, judges, and juries each time they exercise arbitrary powers of punishment—employees who themselves suffer twenty-five-year terms in eight-hour shifts.[23] The stories of these employees also need to be told, and they deserve their own volume.[24] *Fourth City* begins the project of opening up this walled city; it begins to dismantle the myths projected upon those walls from the outside, allowing us to see that among convicted Americans there are human beings who have been brought to a place of self-reflection, self-questioning, and self-awareness that few of us will ever have to explore. Equally significant, though they report on a prison that has become the repository for the failures of social and economic community, the writers here are disproportionately drawn from among those depicted by the media and other profiting parties as those of whom we should be most afraid: the men and women convicted of violent crimes, of murder or manslaughter. To anyone who works inside American prisons, this makes perfect sense: long-term prisoners are typically the leaders, the stabilizing forces, and elders of the prisoner population; they have less to lose by telling their stories and more to gain by telling them (in hopes that their writing might someday change their conditions), and, in order to maintain life and sanity, they are the most invested in making prisons into more humane institutions. In direct contradiction of the depictions on the outside, long-term prisoners are the prisoners from among whom the prison's best thinkers and writers have typically emerged. These writers live in a place where turning away—from others, and from one's own past acts—is always the safer path. Yet they have decided to write about what they have seen, what they have felt, what they have done, and the toll that seeing and feeling and their own past actions have exacted. In obvious ways, these essays confirm popular images of the prison: the cruelty, the inhumanity, the violence. But they also show us the human faces and hearts and minds that endure these conditions, and show us that the American prison is a place where the courage of humane conscience can and does survive.

We should not be surprised that these writers are able to reflect deeply upon their condition. They write at their risk. The institutions in which they live do not want to see broadcast what their wards have witnessed. Such conditions select out for those to whom writing, at whatever cost, matters deeply. Whatever actions brought them there, the men and women who dare to write from this metropolis deserve our recognition. If we grant it, we will find a prison bearing two sets of roots: one set is dry and withered, retracting from a founding faith in the redeemability of all human beings; the other set has regained vitality with the prison boom since 1973. These roots developed in the penal plantations, factories, and mines that relabeled the Black bodies of slaves as the bodies of convict labor, from the Civil War to World War II (and beyond).[25] Our prison today is simply more inclusive in holding the bodies of poor Black, poor Latina/o, poor Native American, poor Asian and Pacific Islander, and poor white Americans. The Philadelphia Quakers who invented the penitentiary imagined it would better those that it held. Today, in face of the prison's size and abject failures, it is we on the outside who need to know what the incarcerated are thinking. We need to understand how our Fourth City judges us.

These writers document, reflect on, critique, and condemn an institution whose successes and failures speak directly to our successes and failures as a civil society. This is the burden that prison witness has borne since Socrates chose to accept the death sentence announced by the judges of Athens; since St. Perpetua recorded her thoughts in the days preceding martyrdom for refusing to deny her Christian faith; since Martin Luther King wrote a letter from a jail cell in Birmingham. Each of these writers turned collectively sanctioned captivity into a platform to speak back against unjust laws or the unjust practice of law, and we are all their beneficiaries. The writers in *Fourth City* are not Socrates, or St. Perpetua, or Dr. King. Many are in prison because they are poor, and of a hyperpoliced and legally unprotected race. Many represent the failures of civic society to support families and schools on the very uneven playing field that is the United States today. A few claim innocence. But whatever the causes and collective failures that stand behind their acts, and whatever faults in fair policing and criminal justice procedures sent them to prison while others go free, most are there for what they have done, for the damage they have perpetrated against others and against themselves, and not for the nobility of their beliefs. Yet whatever paths brought them to Fourth City, these writers are virtually all committed to documenting the destructive effects of the prison as a public institution. They remain our sole frontline witnesses to what the conditions of the institutional captivity we sustain today may say about how true we are to our own most noble beliefs. As long as we continue to allow criminal culpability to discount all claims to credibility in witnessing the workings of this institution, so long as we allow mere passage through the prison to relegate men and women to a class to which we do not listen, we will continue playing a moral shell game with ourselves: convinced that we need only be concerned with equal protections before the law, while ignoring the need for protection from actions taken behind the veil of law.

The writers in *Fourth City* both are and represent the only documentarians, journalists, philosophers, and policy critics that we have who can tell us what our criminal justice system looks and smells and feels like from the receiving end. Without reading these writers, we might feel better about our civil and criminal justice practices. But we would remain what we are today: a body politic on painkillers, smiling while the rest of the world smells something rotten. The essays in *Fourth City* bring light and air to a morbid wound that too many on the outside have come to accept as natural, and those inside as inevitable.

Prison critic Michelle Alexander writes that "criminals today are deemed a characterless and purposeless people, deserving of our collective scorn and contempt"—a "'they' [who] are no longer part of 'us.'"[26] *Fourth City* is an occasion to reconsider such comforting demarcations. It is a place to begin developing healthy suspicions about the convenience of such seemingly clear distinctions, and what they say about our will and ability to practice our own most noble values. While imprisoned Americans live removed from us, *Fourth City* demonstrates that they remain of us, with character, and, if we will listen, with purpose.

NOTES

1. Tyjen Tsai and Paola Scommengna, "U.S. Has World's Highest Incarceration Rate," Population Reference Bureau, August 2012, www.prb.org/Articles/2012/us-incarceration.aspx; "Incarceration," The Sentencing Project, www.sentencingproject.org/template/page.cfm?id=107; "Criminal Justice Fact Sheet," National Association for the Advancement of Colored People, www.naacp.org/pages /criminal-justice-fact-sheet.

2. Marc Mauer, "Comparative International Rates of Incarceration: An Examination of Causes and Trends," The Sentencing Project, June 20, 2003, www.sentencingproject.org/doc/publications/inc _comparative_intl.pdf.

3. "Crime—National or State Level Data with One Variable," *Uniform Crime Reporting Statistics*, U.S. Department of Justice, www.bjs.gov/ucrdata/Search/Crime/State/TrendsInOneVar.cfm.

4. See Loïc Wacquant, *Punishing the Poor: The Neoliberal Government of Social Insecurity* (Durham, NC: Duke University Press, 2009); Bruce Western, *Punishment and Inequality in America* (New York: Russell Sage, 2006); Jonathan Simon, *Governing through Crime: How the War on Crime Transformed American Democracy and Created a Culture of Fear* (New York: Oxford University Press, 2009).

5. Simon, *Governing through Crime*; Western, *Punishment*; Christian Parenti, *Lockdown America: Police and Prisons in the Age of Crisis* (New York: Verso, 2000); Marc Mauer, *Race to Incarcerate* (New York: Free Press, 2006); Michelle Alexander, *The New Jim Crow: Mass Incarceration in the Age of Colorblindness* (New York: Free Press, 2010); "Prison Guards Back Victims' Groups," *American Radioworks*, http://americanradioworks.publicradio.org/features/corrections/slide3/slide1.html; Joshua Page, *The Toughest Beat: Politics, Punishment, and the Prison Officers Union in California* (New York: Oxford University Press, 2013).

6. U.S. Census Bureau, "Crimes and Crime Rates by Type of Offense: 1980 to 2009," www.census .gov/compendia/statab/2012/tables/12s0306.pdf. Alexander, *The New Jim Crow*.

7. Mauer, "Comparative International Rates of Incarceration"; "Trends in U.S. Corrections," The Sentencing Project, December 2012, www.sentencingproject.org/doc/publications/inc_Trends_in _Corrections_Fact_sheet.pdf; Marie Gottschalk, "Days Without End: Life Sentences and Penal Reform," *Prison Legal News*, 2013, www.prisonlegalnews.org.

8. "Recidivism," U.S. Department of Justice, http://bjs.gov/index.cfm?ty=tp&tid=17.

9. David Garland, *Punishment and Welfare: A History of Penal Strategies* (Aldershot, UK: Ashgate, 1985).

10. Estimates run toward $80 billion per year; see John Schmitt, Kris Warner, and Sarika Gupta, "The High Budgetary Cost of Incarceration," The Center for Economic and Policy Research, June 2010, www .cepr.net/documents/publications/incarceration-2010–06.pdf. "If you had a dollar to spend on reducing crime, and you looked at the science instead of the politics, you would never spend it on the prison system. There is no better example of big government run amok"; Dr. Michael Jacobson, criminologist and former head of New York City's correction and probation departments, and now the president of the Vera Institute of Justice, quoted in John Tierney, "Prison Populations Can Shrink When Police Crowd the Street," *New York Times*, January 25, 2013. For a powerful study of the industrialization of incarceration and the false promise of prosperity it offers to rural regions, see Ruth Wilson Gilmore, *Golden Gulag: Prisons, Surplus, Crisis, and Opposition in Globalizing California* (Los Angeles: University of California Press, 2007).

11. Laura M. Maruschak and Erika Parks, "Probation and Parole in the United States, 2011," Bureau of Justice Statistics, November 29, 2012, http://bjs.ojp.usdoj.gov/index.cfm?ty=pbdetail&iid=4538;

Alexander, *The New Jim Crow.* On the children of prisoners, see Jeremy Travis, Elizabeth Cincotta McBride, and Amy L. Solomon, "Families Left Behind: The Hidden Costs of Incarceration and Reentry," Urban Institute Justice Policy Center, October 2003, revised June 2005, http://www.urban.org /UploadedPDF/310882_families_left_behind.pdf; see further references in the introduction to the section "Family Life In and From Prison City."

12. Lauren E. Glaze, "Correctional Populations in the United States, 2010," *Bureau of Justice Statistics,* December 15, 2011, http://www.bjs.gov/content/pub/pdf/cpus10.pdf.

13. See Robert Cover, "Violence and the Word," *Narrative, Violence, and the Law: The Essays of Robert Cover,* ed. Martha Minow, Michael Ryan, and Austin Sarat (Ann Arbor: University of Michigan Press, 1992), 203–38.

14. Western, *Punishment,* 31. Western makes this statement specifically about the life trajectories of poor, urban Black men without education. Social scientists such as Western and Wacquant thus lend contemporary credence to the argument raised by Black Power writers in the early seventies, that the American prison is simply the latest installment in the history of slavery and Jim Crow. See Alexander, *The New Jim Crow.*

15. See Michelle Brown, *The Culture of Punishment: Prison, Society, and Spectacle* (New York: New York University Press, 2009).

16. Kate Richards O'Hare, *In Prison* (Seattle: Washington University Press, 1976), 49.

17. "Reentry Trends in the U.S.," Bureau of Justice Statistics, http://bjs.ojp.usdoj.gov/content /reentry/recidivism.cfm.

18. I detail the practical steps by which *Fourth City* came together in its present form in the Afterword.

19. The use of *Fourth City* as the title was first suggested by incarcerated writer Kenneth E. Hartman, in correspondence about the size of the prison and jail population; that this population is larger than America's fourth largest city is also noted by Wacquant, *Punishing the Poor,* 114–15.

20. "Ticket" is prison jargon for the written report of a rules violation. "Kite" is prison slang for any unofficial, written communication.

21. See Western, *Punishment;* Wacquant, *Punishing the Poor;* and Gilmore, *Golden Gulag.* On the conditions that exacerbate tensions between prisoners and corrections officers, see John J. Gibbons and Nicholas de B. Katzenbach, "Confronting Confinement: A Report of the Commission on Safety and Abuse in America's Prisons," The Vera Institute of Justice, June 8, 2006, www.vera.org/pubs /confronting-confinement (esp. parts 2 and 3); see also Kelsey Kauffman, *Prison Officers and Their World* (Cambridge, MA: Harvard University Press, 1988), esp. ch. 9.

22. The *National Prison Rape Elimination Commission Report* (June 2004–June 2009, http://nprec.us /publication/report/executive_summary.php) documents that nearly half of the sexual assault committed in American prisons and jails is perpetrated by staff. This fact, when paired with evidence that corrections officers suffer a life expectancy well below the national average, should make clear that everyone living or working inside is damaged—morally, psychologically, and physically—by the American prison as it operates today.

23. See the following articles on the effects of the stress borne by correctional staff: "Prisons: Correctional Officers—Correctional Officer Stress," http://law.jrank.org/pages/1791/Prisons -Correctional-Officers-Correctional-officer-stress.html; F. Cheek and M. D. S. Miller, "Reducing Staff and Inmate Stress," *Corrections Today* 44, no. 5 (October 1982): 72–76, 78; Tracy E. Branhart, "Mandatory Overtime = Sleep Deprivation," Corrections.com, January 11, 2010, www.corrections.com /news/article/23187-mandatory-overtime-sleep-deprivation.

24. *Fourth City* begins the process of building the American Prison Writing Archive online, a digital repository for nonfiction writing by imprisoned people, corrections officers, prison staff, administrators, volunteers, and others who work or live inside American prisons.

25. See Mary Ellen Curtin, *Black Prisoners and Their World, Alabama, 1865–1900* (Charlottesville: University of Virginia Press, 2000); Douglas A. Blackmon, *Slavery by Another Name: The Re-Enslavement of Black Americans from the Civil War to World War II* (New York: Anchor, 2009); Matthew J. Mancini, *One Dies, Get Another: Convict Leasing in the American South, 1866–1928* (Columbia: University of South Carolina Press, 1996); Alexander, *The New Jim Crow*.

26. Alexander, *The New Jim Crow*, 138, 139.

LIFE ON THE STREETS OF PRISON CITY

The Life

INTRODUCTION

The essays in this first section offer an introduction to the life lived every day on the streets of Prison City: a city with its own language, culture, social hierarchies, currencies, and codes of conduct. Each essay peels back the stock assumptions about prisons (about violence, rape, etc.), revealing the human experience that stands behind popular images of prisoners and prisons. Several portray the supportive relationships that incarcerated people wrest from the day-to-day weight of life in overcrowded cages as they attempt to make this life into one worth the name. Each testifies to the fundamental fact from which life in Prison City devolves: this is the life that occurs when personalities as varied, distinct, and multifaceted as those of people on the outside meet the standard operating procedures of a mass-scale prison that takes little, if any, account of the fact that it houses individual human beings rather than numbered bodies.

In "Concrete Carnival," Danner Darcleight assumes the guise of a carnival barker leading a picaresque tour of many of the institutional characters, issues, and themes that follow throughout these pages. His title suggests what results when troubled men are left to pursue their needs and desires inside cement boxes. The dexterity of his prose alone suggests the potential that these boxes contain. Yet in the very exuberance of Darcleight's writing, we sense the effort required to counter the weight of a decades-long sentence to this life.

Once we step off of Darcleight's carnival ride, we get down to sober facts in Michael Beverley's "A Perspective on Prison": a practical explanation of how prison hierarchies work, how position and rank are established, and the consequences of violating prison codes. Beverley portrays a prison run with malign neglect, and in which the incarcerated are free and actively encouraged to create their own systems of violent discipline. Between this essay and Darcleight's, the underlying reasons for the prison's failures begin to emerge: Prisons remain indifferent when not openly hostile to individuals, and official discipline is arbitrary at best.

For many years now, the rate of increase in the numbers of women entering jails and prisons has surpassed the rate for men.[1] Part of the reason may be found in Markeithia R. Reevez's "Inmate Jane Doe." Reevez offers an overview of the unsuitedness for women of prisons and programs designed for the management of male prisoners. Reevez adds more light to our deepening image of the prison's failure to prepare its inhabitants for life back in the free world. We see women given no more motivation *not* to game the system, or to seriously reconsider their behavior, than when engaged in the lifestyles that brought them to jail. If prisons fail to account for the needs and personalities inside the bodies they hold, Reevez makes clear that this failure is compounded for incarcerated women. She helps us to understand how women are affected by a prison that may be more a cause of, than an answer to criminal behavior.

If men fare badly and women worse in prisons that treat all of their wards as though there were in fact a single, incorrigible "criminal type," the lives of gay and transsexual people surely represent the worst of both prison worlds. Catherine Lynn Quick contributes a telling exposé of the potentially fatal challenges facing such prisoners. In "Transsexual in Prison" she writes of the brutalization and use of gay and transsexual people inside prisons that collude in their abuse.

Yet she also offers insight into the unexpected ways that—despite the violent pecking order described by Michael Beverley, the haphazard violence depicted by Danner Darcleight, and the gender myopia decried by Markeithia Reevez—even those marked as weak and vulnerable can offer crucial emotional comfort within this environment. As long as prisons house prisoners according to flat-footed distinctions of biological sex, transsexual and gay people will be horribly victimized inside;[2] but Quick also points out that even this policy can be made to yield—and gay and transsexual people should be credited for creating—unexpected benefits when prison staff and prisoners treat each other like the needy people they are. Her essay introduces two others showing that despite fostering dehumanization, Prison City is a place where the inhabitants also manage to discover comfort, friendship, even love. These essays make clear that if incarcerated people are not crushed by the prison, this has much less to do with prison policy or practice than with the resilience of incarcerated people in maintaining their humanity despite the ways prisons work.

Freedom affords us the luxury of letting relationships come or go, often fading simply because sustained contact can prove inconvenient, or relegating these relationships to "liking" another for one's Facebook page. But in a place where a single relationship can offer the spark of hope that keeps one alive, the stakes, rewards, and pain of losing contact are very high indeed. In "Friendship," George Whitham describes what it meant to meet a man with a similarly brutal background, facing similar time, and to develop and lose a depth of friendship that most of us might hope for. Corey John Richardson's "How Some Men Find Love" tells the story of finding love for the first time in prison, and the virtually inevitable loss that concludes prison relationships. In these essays we see again that the prison is the cumulative experience of distinct individuals facing and sometimes meeting the challenge of retaining a hold on their humanity inside institutions that treat humanity as contraband.

We need to attend to what prison writers have to tell us that disrupts self-serving ideas of prisons and those who live there. But popular images of the prison are not entirely misrepresentative. They are simply reductive, cartoon versions of The Life actually lived in Prison City. Jose Di Lenola's "The Art of Aggression" brings home these facts. Prisons are violent places in part because people acculturated to violence live there. They are also violent because prisons do too little—if anything effective—to change the habits, cultures, and desperation carried from the street. The result is that violence spreads like a communicable disease: men and women with no desire to engage in violence must do so in order to secure their own lives and the reputations upon which the quality of those lives will depend for years. And how each person deals with the violence in prison is as singular as his relationship to his own mortality and the circle of friendships, support, and backing he can create. "The Art of Aggression" demonstrates that prison violence involves people weighing their fears against the costs of failing to secure their lives.

As the reader works through these first essays, s/he will begin to learn the language, the recurrent challenges, and the structures that bind this archipelago city into one massive accumulation of singular Americans. This segment offers seven first steps inside Prison City: a place that we may begin to think and speak about and thus reconsider in ways that reflect the prison we have built and filled, rather than the one we have invented to comfort ourselves with images of how unlike "us" "they" are. Here we begin to see how the largest of any nation's gathering of incarcerated people actually live from day to day, on the tax dollars every free-world reader pays to keep the lights on in Prison City.

NOTES

1. "Hard Hit: The Growth in the Imprisonment of Women, 1977–2004," Institute on Women and Criminal Justice, www.wpaonline.org/institute/hardhit/index.htm.

2. Gianna E. Israel, "Transsexual Inmate Treatment Issues," 2001, http://www.firelily.com/gender /gianna/inmates.html; Oliver Libaw, "Prisons Face Dilemma with Transgender Inmates," *ABC News*, January 22, 2013, http://abcnews.go.com/US/story?id=90919&page=1; Patrick Letellier, "Court Rules Against Trans Woman over Sexual Assault in Prison," *Lesbian News* 33, no. 2 (September 2007): 13; Alexander Lara, "Forced Integration of Gay, Bisexual and Transgendered Inmates in California State Prisons: From Protected Minority to Exposed Victims," *Southern California Interdisciplinary Law Journal* 19, no. 3 (2010): 589–614; see also Regina Kunzel, *Criminal Intimacy: Prison and the Uneven History of Modern American Sexuality* (Chicago: University of Chicago Press, 2008).

DANNER DARCLEIGHT, *New York*

CONCRETE CARNIVAL

Step right up to the show that never ends . . . come inside, come inside . . .

'Tis quite a ride, this life inside. One of the scariest shows on earth. A carnival of the bizarre in a fairground of bars and steel, bricks and concrete. Save for the sporadically flickering fluorescents, there are no flashing lights, but we have our bearded women, games of chance, and hustlers lurking around every corner. The rides are painted in institutional grays, browns, tans, and greens; their scariness warranted, their destination nowhere good. The bells don't indicate a winner, but alert us—losers to a man—when we're to be counted, leave our cells, when to return; sometimes they signal a dangerous breakdown in the established order.

Our admission fee is paid in years. In lieu of ticket stubs, rap sheets condense all the victims robbed or raped, hurt or killed into a burst of penal code. We pays our money, we takes our chances.

I'm your carnival barker, a hooker with a heart of fool's gold. You, reader, are a townie, a citizen strapping in for this ride of mine. Mind you, my peers don't fully accept me; they sense that I came from the right side of the tracks. But the world makes little distinction among us. So you see, I don't belong, yet I do belong here.

I'll lead you around, try to keep you safe, introduce you to the oddities. I speak the language, know how to move. But I try to believe that it's all a ride that ends in eighteen more years if I'm a lucky boy and I retain a tenuous grip on my sanity, which is the best I can do. So don't look for a through line. Like the rest of us, you'll have to take it day by day, scene by scene. Since I'll be your guide, you can call me Odi.

Enough talk, let's begin. Keep your arms inside the ride at all times. Don't make any sudden moves and I'll return you in one piece, scout's honor.

GAMES OF CHANCE

I went to chow on Sloppy Joe night. The sloppiest Joe in the state, slopped over undercooked fries, served in a cavernous mess hall half-filled with two hundred diners.

After eating, my group was lined up at the exit. The large exit door swung open as we held our spoons at the ready to toss into the bucket upon leaving. We were just about to be given the *Go!* command when a fight broke out in one of the sections still eating. The door slammed shut, and with it our chances of getting out without a headache.

We're ordered up against the wall; our escort officer unsheathes his nightstick and runs toward the melee. Fights in the mess hall have the potential to turn into riots in the mess hall, so the ten ridiculously outnumbered cops treat it with called-for seriousness. Our escort officer, a huge country boy reliving his high school football-glory days, subdued—nay, sent flying—the fighters with a running tackle. And then things took a horrible turn.

A newly minted sergeant panicked and gave a signal to the officer in the gas booth. Forty feet overhead three slots opened to disgorge three spinning canisters of teargas that dropped to the floor and bounced.

The mess-hall tables were enveloped in a sinister cloud. Time compressed. Memory spooled: Fire Academy when I was a seventeen-year-old volunteer firefighter: an ex-Navy SEAL lecturing us on things gaseous after our stay in the smoke room: *Your first reaction to tear gas is to rub your eyes—avoid doing so at all costs.*

The gas stung every pore of my recently shaved face; my eyes and mucous membranes felt like they were being seared raw; tears and snot streamed uncontrollably. But I didn't touch my face. I was more worried about the screaming throng of flailing inmates running in my direction, for we were standing in front of the exit. This way to the giant egress, folks.

A sympathetic door suddenly swung open, my two friends and I linked arms, and we ran out into the corridor. To our left were bars, to the right a wall of cops three deep, all holding nightsticks that would randomly swing out for our heads. Straight ahead an open door led to an evacuation yard. We made for this door while I cringed against a headshot, then poured down the couple of stone steps into the welcome fresh air.

I turned and saw an old man who had tripped down the steps and lay helplessly on the ground as others stepped on or over him. I ran and grabbed the oldster. Got him away from the steps and kept dragging him, using a cross-body carry that I'd never attempted out of water; then a flood of inmates, the mob proper, burst through the door. Out of the crowd's reach, I brought the old man to his feet and shouted, "You okay?!"

"*Si, si. Gracias, mi hijo.*"

"*De nada, viejo.*"

He held tightly to my arm and looked up at me with rheumy eyes. "*Gracias,*" and some more in Spanish too fast for me to understand.

Then I noticed his shaking hand going for his face.

I grabbed it and leaned my face close to his. "No, uh, *no toca sus ojos.*"

Nodding and attempting to smile, he said in heavily accented English, "Yehs, ohkay, ohhh-kay." Holding his arm, I escorted him to an *amarillo* crew of Latin Kings and left him in their charge.

The sun was beginning to set; underfoot the ground was muddy in spots, with islands of old snow. There were guards with assault rifles on the rooftops, one of whom aimed playfully down on us. A stiff wind blew. A flashback to a war I'd never been in.

My friends and I huddled close for warmth and, at my urging, found an available spot against the wall. The trigger-happy camp guards were three stories straight overhead. Our position was moderately safe. The hours passed in relative silence, the cold and tear gas residue putting a serious damper on an otherwise rowdy bunch.

It grew dark. No one knew how long we'd remain outside. We watched the corridor windows. An hour passed. Then two. My face stung, my extremities were numb. I kept my hands under my pits. The three of us each took turns being the warmer middleman.

It was nearing nine P.M. Judging by the flurry of activity in the lighted hallways, our stay was drawing to a close. Guys dropped shanks and used their dirty sneakers to surreptitiously bury them in the mud. I was surprised to see how many guys were packing.

Some four hours after the shit hit the fan, the door opened and a bullhorn announced that we'd be called in by company. Naturally, my company was one of the last to be called. Never have the hallways been more inviting; the heat was a pleasant welcome, even if the fluorescents were harsh on inflamed retinas. Dull-eyed and stiff, we walked through a gauntlet of angry cops. We filed past a nurse who was accompanied by a sergeant, and were asked if we needed medical attention. The sergeant's glare might as well have been a recorded message: *You really don't want to request medical attention.*

Down another hallway, we stripped for cops who checked us for weapons and marks of having been in a fight. I shook as I got dressed, not entirely from the cold. In my cell ten minutes later, I removed tear-gas infused clothes and threw them all in a plastic bag. Then I filled my sink with cold water and washed the pain away as best I could.

Managerial statistics was the bane of my existence junior year. Paying no heed to the law of averages, I never go to dinner on Sloppy Joe night.

It was my first week in prison. Granted, I'd done a year in county waiting for the media to die down and move on to their next murderer of the month so as to cop out in peace. Then there was reception, where I was officially brought into the state prison system: stripped, deloused, shaved, assigned a number, IQ-tested, physician-prodded, warehoused until a suitable home could be found for me. I was in reception for six months before being transported to the place that would be my home for a couple of decades. Eighteen months earlier I was, as they say, a free man, and, as we say, one could still smell the street on me.

This was my first week; I was double-bunked in a cell designed for one. At eight A.M. I came out for breakfast and waited on the company with the rest of the guys. Turning around to address someone, I saw a tall Black kid with wild eyes, his hair twisted into tiny braid-like offshoots, slowly walk up behind a guy called Moonie, nonchalantly withdraw a jagged tuna-can top, and rip Moonie from the corner of his mouth backwards, stopping at the ear lobe.

This isn't really happening.

Moonie's earlobe dangled precariously from a piece of twisted skin. His Black flesh parted ungracefully, the white cheek meat splayed open to the world, the blood flowing. (So much blood from cuts to the face.) All the idle chatter ceased as Moonie mechanically walked a few steps and grabbed the handle of a metal mop wringer sitting nearby. The two now square off, the kid with his bloody can top, Moonie with his cudgel. This isn't the movies; there's no hooting and cheering. We watch quietly, pretending (at least me) not to see anything. A cop sits on a desk on the other side of a gate, twenty feet away. It's the morning and he's probably hung over, but I can't believe he lets this behavior go on.

The boys bob and weave, no strangers to this bellicose dance. The blood pours into Moonie's mouth; the reptilian brain takes over, swings the wringer straight for the opponent's face. Whoosh, it misses. The kid has parried well, and with a hungry grin he now looks to move back in, to tag the other side of Moonie's face. The kid advances, but Moonie draws on reptilian strength and delivers a sick-sounding blow to the kid's head. The kid's knees give a comical shake, he falls backwards, his head hits against a metal tray slot welded to the front of a cell.

Whack-a-mole.

He's probably concussed before he hits the floor. The kid drops in a pile against the cell bars and floor, folded over.

The smell a second later, bludgeoning, indicates that this bloody, unconscious pile of human has just auto-evacuated.

The cop's attention is finally piqued. He bangs his nightstick on the ground in an alert for backup, then yells, "Drop the fucking mop wringer!" and to us onlookers, "Up against the wall! Now!"

Following the others' lead, I place my palms on the brick wall and stare. Behind us, the mop wringer drops noisily to the terrazzo floor. I'm shaking, but probably not as violently as I imagine. Moonie's told to lie on the floor and he complies.

The cops tramp noisily up the stairs: jangling keys, clanking nightsticks, bad haircuts. The company's gate slides open with a whir; cops snap on rubber gloves, handcuff Moonie, and take him away. We remain, as directed, on the wall. The kid's dragged away by his feet.

The company officer mills about with his coworkers, makes small talk, jokes to the sergeant, "I knew they were fighting 'cause I've never seen Moonie use a wringer. You know how hard it is to get him to clean the stairway."

This is met with laughter. Dark humor is oddly reassuring at times such as this.

I suppress a chuckle and remember what my grand-pappy told me when I was just a pup: Never bring a can top to a mop-wringer fight. Believe you me, there is no humor like gallows humor.

We're locked back into our cells as the blood trails are covered with bleach and mopped away. I want off this ride.

I looked for the ride jock to tell him that I wanted off, that I was going to be sick. He was probably goldbricking behind the funhouse, eating a pink cloud of cotton candy. The thought occurred: This kid just had the shit kicked out of him. To this day, when told that someone got the shit kicked out of him or was the one doing the shit-kicking, I always inquire: Seriously? Literally? Real-life shit in the pants?

In the days that followed the incident, I learned that Moonie had shorted the other guy out of five dollars on a bag of weed. Five dollars. And to make matters more interesting, the kid had offered to sell me a bag of weed at reduced price the night before the fight. I turned the offer down because, being new, I wasn't comfortable enough to begin breaking the rules, and the half-priced offer sounded too good to be true, like some type of setup.

In retrospect, I see that he knew exactly what he'd be doing the next morning and wanted to sell off his wares before he was carted off to the box. The kid had done what he believed necessary. Me, I'd have eaten the five bucks and never again done business with Moonie. These were the stakes now, the new ground truth. I could be cut over five dollars. This logic was completely foreign to me, remains so, but I act as if . . .

I still want off the ride.

THE TUNNELS OF LOVE

Cheri had legally become Cheri at some point in his life. He's a young Puerto Rican pre-op trannie who's quite "passable" as a female—which is, I'm told, the standard to which trannies aspire—and all the more passable to the incarcerated and sex-starved.

We were in the same block a few years back. An unredeemable flirt, I'd make nice enough that Cheri would steadily gift me joints, but not so much so that he'd think me a potential John. We were roughly the same age, frequented some of the same mega-clubs back home, and reminisced about the different name-brand hits of ecstasy from the nineties. We'd discuss different club DJs until he inevitably began voguing in the middle of the yard, and I'd say, "You're embarrassing me."

Cheri made cuckolds of more than a few men. The amused cops would bring him makeup and lip gloss and panties; the cons would give him all manner of drugs. The latter in return for some sexual service—a rough trade the likes of which I didn't need, but was curious to know about.

He was protected, because the things Cheri got away with in here would land someone like me in the box. One autumn night in the yard, Cheri stumbled up to me and latched onto my arm. "Whoa," says I. "Had a few too many, did ya?"

"Ohhhhdeeeee, it's my birthday."

Cheri was playing a role I remember well from my youth: Sloppy Drunk Girl. A potent odor of alcohol wafted off him. Not the shitty grapefruit hooch we brew in garbage cans, but honest-to-goodness hard liquor. From *the world*.

"Happy birthday, Cheri."

I looked, and hoped, for a water bottle filled with some clear liquid other than water. Looked to no avail.

"Odi, you . . . are . . . sooooo . . . cute."

This accompanied with the look: I'm going to throw up soon.

"Thanks, Cher."

We were walking again, me playing my role: He Who's Trying to Avoid a Scene.

Between hiccups, Cheri said, "Lemme blow you."

"Well, it sounds like fun, but why don't we try to get you a nice sit."

We walked past my crew's table. Although empty that night, I couldn't deposit Cheri there; protocol and table politics forbade bringing a chump to sit alone with me. Cheri made a sickening burp, one that portended a watery finish, a vurp. I spotted the table at which Cheri and the other 'mos were known to dole out handjobs, and hoped that we'd make it there before Cheri popped all over the side of my body he was using as a crutch.

Without looking too obvious, I deposited Cheri into the bench seating, propping his back against the wall. "Thaaata girl," I might have said, relieved that the hardest was over. Standing with my back to the wall, I instinctively reached for Cheri's wrist and took a pulse: Concerned Friend Who Happened to Be a Former EMT.

While I maintained a coolish gaze towards the horizon, Cheri stuck his head under the table and sprayed steaming vomit. When he was done, I helped him back up, gave him a Starburst, made sure he was okay, promised to return, then left to spin the yard's perimeter.

I realized that I forgot to hit him up for a joint, but let it stand; Cheri might be able to get away with such drunken theatrics, but I worried I'd be scooped up from the yard, brought in for pat-frisking, and didn't want to smell like a roach clip.

Ten minutes later, when I returned to where I'd deposited Cheri, he was gone but easily enough spotted on the lap of some guy a few tables down, and no longer my problem.

Several nights later I sat at the table with my best friend, Ant, a tough, streetwise, blond-haired, blue-eyed Italian kid a couple of years older than me. Cheri swished by and I told him he could sit. So long as certain protocols were followed, Cheri was welcome, however briefly. In the land of the thuggishly insecure, appearances are everything, and people-watching is elevated to high art. The 'mos gossip like high school girls; the message gets distorted and travels like a brushfire. If I was sitting alone, I wouldn't have invited Cheri over, but having Ant with me provided heterosexual cover. Cheri was conscious of keeping his hands above the table, something that was done for our sake. Most importantly, he was getting us baked, and that could be used in response to any of our crew who wanted to know why we allowed a chump to sit at the table. This protocol isn't discussed, it's just understood at a perception-equals-reality level.

After smoking, Cheri, seated at my side, leaned into my ear and in a breathy, sexy, black-and-white-movie-starlet way, said something about how much I'd like a blowjob from him or how quickly he'd make me come. Then he was standing. I looked across the table to Ant—who, like me, is a *Seinfeld* watcher—and said, à la George Costanza, "Jerry! It moved, Jerry!" We laughed tears through bloodshot eyes. Dare I admit that I wasn't lying?

My cousin J. came to visit. Great conversation as always. Mountain Dew and an inhaled cheeseburger ensuring I'd fly all over the map. Word soup. Spraying monologue, losing the plot, discussing his forays into plotte (kooch). While he got me food from the vending machines, I scanned the room from the back corner. A sixty-something with the slight headshake of early Parkinson's played cards with his incarcerated son (grandson?); this made me sad. I perceived the old guy as ex-military, a civilian having to be subjected to this life inside. Like me. And the rest of my family.

The old guy left and, in so doing, gave J. and me an unobstructed view of the next table: Hispanic with dreads, with his heavyset, middle-aged woman. J. was describing some concert. Her abdomen was shaking like she was laughing. But she wasn't laughing.

The dread was dry humping her. With his knee. Her face was red and splotchy, her hair thin, unlike her frame. She had the Linda Lovelace type of Fuck-Face: tightened mouth, scrunched-up brow. Lamaze-class breathing.

We'll call her Helen because that's nice and she looked like a Helen. Helen probably works as a lunch lady or a librarian or a DMV clerk, and says things like "You can't do that." No, "We can't do that," and "It's against company policy." She probably takes particular delight in saying, "I'm sorry, sir." When she sits in the lunchroom at work and describes to her coworkers her man doing time—the gentleman fucking her with his knee—Helen uses words like "caring" and "romantic" and "kind." She probably mules drugs for this mug.

I show J., who cautiously looks; still facing me, his eyes scan rightward, the pupil replaced by white. We continue talking, but he's visibly shaken. Oh, the fucking humanity. Reality so real it becomes unreal.

Minutes pass and conversation continues. I periodically check back, unable to help myself. Why couldn't she be hot? Like the girl at the soda machine with the improbably perky tits who must be pregnant.

The dread slowly licks fingers that surely ventured south of her border. I tell J., and we both pretend to swallow back impulsive vomit. Ten minutes. Twenty. "J., she's about to come." We watch her face get redder, her breathing become more frantic. And then it's over.

I tell J. that if he gets drunk that evening, he's got to recount that scene for his friends. Before leaving, I helped him paint it in his memory: red-faced, porcine lunch lady getting a knee job, her belly jiggling.

Waiting to go back, the knee-fucker asked if I wanted a Jolly Rancher. I said Sure, held up my hand, and Jedi-willed a good catch. He threw from twenty feet away. I made it look easy, unwrapped the grape candy and lolled it on my tongue. Smacked it around, then thought of him licking his fingers. Spit out the candy into its wrapper and tossed it in the garbage. Getting strip-searched on the way out, I drew the short cop who I'd seen before but never heard speak. He looked and sounded like the wise scientist ubiquitous in japanime. He called my sneakers "neakeys."

I got naked, lifted up my junk for his gander, turned around, raised my feet, and wiggled my piggies. I waited for him to say "Bend and spread"; instead, he said, "Waiting for a drum roll?" His delivery was comical, not malicious. I bent and spread. He said, "Therrrrre's a happy face. Get dressed," and walked out as I giggled to myself.

LOSE YOURSELF IN THE FUNHOUSE

We don't really discuss our crimes; it's gauche. The "So whatcha in for?" line standard in most Hollywood depictions of prison just isn't kosher. Many men have appeals currently in the courts, and snitches abound. And asking such a question, if answered, would lead to "And you?" and who wants to invite a public airing of their worst.

Still, I'd found out that Aaron had a dirty case, a rape charge, and while that was supposed to mean the end of my talking to him, my feelings didn't change. I'd found it out in an amongst-friends deal, from a guy who also had a dirty case.

This was our second meeting since my finding out. Yom Kippur in the mess hall. Nation of Islam fifty feet away, the other side of the mess—fifty of them, fifty of us. NOI celebrating Ramadan, peppering their sermons with angry rhetoric. Aaron and I laughed at the dark irony of it all. Aaron, the observant Jew: Puerto Rican father, Jewish mother. Quite a *simpatico* character: thin build, dark features without the swarthiness, calm, quiet, smart.

Since he's two months away from the end of his sentence, he worried aloud about civil confinement, a policy whereby, if deemed a threat to the public, an ex-offender can be held indefinitely. This is a new policy set at the very top, and local management is scurrying to handle the logistics. Guys are being held until the policymakers can designate a civil confinement facility for them to be housed in.

I reassure Aaron that civil confinement is only for the worst of the worst. He describes his crime. An entrapment along the lines of a *To Catch a Predator* series. He doesn't defend it. He was up to no good and got caught. Disowned by his mom. A *shondeh*, a disgrace, just like me.

I asked if he's okay, if anyone's fucking with him. "Thank God," he said, "I'm okay."

"How about the cops?" I said. This was the point in my life when I began asking questions even if I feared the answers.

"When I first got here, in the reception room, a guard slapped me really hard in the face." I cringed, said, "Ooof." Then, for no apparent reason, I imagined that the person with whom I was speaking was my brother, not Aaron.

The person sitting next to me, Aaron, my brother, described his stay in one of the rougher blocks. I began to cry, just a gentle trickle of tears. I looked to the NOI guys. Tears made everything blurry. He recounted his first night. His gate cracked, two massive cops walked in, called him a "rape-oh," smacked him around, stuck his head in the toilet.

I think of my brother again, maybe to torture myself, upping the emotional ante. I focus on my breathing so as to check the tears. I hear myself saying: "Look at me. Look at me. Whatever you need, whatever you fucking need, you let me know."

Across the table from me at chow sat a bearded Hispanic bug, the kind of guy whose psychiatric chart probably reads like a cut 'n' paste of the DSM. His eyes remained almost closed as he shoveled food into his gob, his neck cocked at an odd angle, alternately staring off toward the ceiling or the floor, smiling at times, mumbling continuously. Occasional facial tics and rubbery smiles. I glimmed the nametag on his state shirt: *Trescabeza*.

A Korean friend once told me that in his country, weird dreams are referred to as "dog dreams." These dreams cross-pollinate with my waking life, making it weirder 'round the clock. In a recent dog dream I was actively concentrating on conjugating Spanish verbs, leaving out the *vosotros* because there's no place for it in the dream world.

Trescabeza. Three heads. Was this some bizarre joke played by a booking officer with a sense of humor? Was I dog-dreaming? Or was this a perfectly apt name for a schizophrenic? And anyway, all of us here need a couple of spare heads in order to survive.

The thing is, I see faces and animals in the painted cement. In this regard, *Trescabeza* and I are quite *igual.* But I know they're random chips of paint, an opportune juice stain, not some supernatural force. Pattern-recognizing animals, we humans are. I see a bus, a ship, a hippo. Hamlet suggests to Polonius what any child can see in passing clouds.

Over time we learn to turn that feature off, lest we become too engrossed, to the detriment of our daily functioning. The key is to understand that the ability lies dormant in us. One simply should not speak to the patterns, unless one wants to be referred to the washed-up social worker who passes for a mental-health professional. I make the patterns work for me. I amuse myself when bored by finding figures, faces in the floor. Take it a step beyond gazing and note the patterns, the timetables, say, of the cellblock rounds man. (If you're into sucking down joints in your cell and don't feel like being interrupted by a crewcut cop making a round, this type of pattern recognition is for you.)

Tease out the patterns to the big-picture flow of life inside, and you can learn how to avoid much of the bullshit. You can pay your drug bills in full and not in flesh, and steer clear of other extracurriculars.

Then there's everyone's default fantasy, a place where you can lose at least one head for days: Escape.

Every prison movie deals with it in some fashion, because the nicest thing about prison is leaving. It makes for a nail-biting plot arc as our protagonist hatches his plan, keeps it mum from guards and snitches, digs and tunnels, evades the bloodhounds, and spends the rest of his days lambing it on a white sand beach, frosty beer in one hand, foxy blonde in the other. This is why drugs are so popular in prison, for drugs are ultimately about escaping your life, and no one wants to escape their life more than one doing time.

I've mellowed a great deal, but am still known to wet my beak from time to time. If the authorities were cool with it, I'd smoke a fat joint every night and melt away into scrumptious slumber. But, alas, they're not, and I stand to lose what few perks and privileges prison has to offer.

The tunneling and climbing have been tried before me. The System always learns from its lapses and immediately plugs the hole. You'd be foolish to assume I've given serious thought to escaping. I have a room with a view to a guard tower, and a guard with a high-powered rifle. I have a room with a view to someone who's been trained to kill me if I venture anywhere too close to the wall.

A good book provides a few hours of daily escape as I roll toilet paper into my ears and paint the scenes of, say, Dickensian London while the barely muffled idiots to my left and right shout along with *Jerry Springer* or BET.

Seeing as how I have no appeal before the court, I'm trapped in this funhouse for the time being. Maybe the best I can do is record the experience, step outside of it, break my bid into a series of daily journal entries and occasional essays—a load I'm more able to bear on a day-by-day basis. Yes, that shall allow for brief respites as I crawl into my shell and chronicle this chaotic freak show.

I'll die behind the wall, or I won't. I'll taste the sweet air of the unincarcerated, or I won't. And this, too, shall pass; act as if. Make the adage a Jacob's ladder that leads over the wall of Painfuck, and into the heady mental state called Acceptancefreedom. The Gordian knot of Hard Time shall gradually untie itself, until one day it becomes the piece of rope I'll use to hold up the pants I'm given upon release.

This way to the GIANT EGRESS, ladies and gentlemen . . .

As promised, I've gotten you through this shithole, hopefully not too much the worse for wear. You can find your way out from here. I can't leave with you. Yes, I can see your car, your regularly scheduled life, just past that last paragraph. Please remember me to the beach, to the bar that sits poolside.

P. T. Barnum once remarked that the entire world's a circus, people the clowns. I'll put on a funny hat and dance to that tune. Prison is a shitty, diet-cola version of the world, so we're the carnies to the world's clowns. And what's a carnival but a poor man's circus? We're misfit toys, wayward boys, sad jesters, maniacal clowns. In my darker moments, I dream of donning my clown outfit, painting tears on my face, and taking a rusty razor to my throat. No need for a melodramatic suicide note; I'd probably fuck that up, too. Let the tears speak for themselves.

MICHAEL B. BEVERLEY, *New Hampshire*

A PERSPECTIVE ON PRISON

When I was a boy, my mother often said that one day people would no longer have names, we would be known only by number. I know she didn't mean what I would bring upon myself, yet it is not entirely disingenuous to say I am now known as 78552. That is my inmate ID within the New Hampshire state prison system. However, I would rather be remembered as Michael.

Though I am now a felon, this wasn't how my life began. I was the third of eight children. For the first nine years of my life, I lived in welfare housing in Brockton, Massachusetts. In the second half of my childhood, I lived in a quaint rural community. Though our family wouldn't have been considered devout, we maintained a moderately religious home. And many of the teachings I didn't receive by attending church more regularly were taught in our home as a simple matter of piety and decency.

In my teen years, I was an industrious boy. In addition to the projects my father demanded of me, I had my paper routes and a job at a caterer. At the age of fourteen, I started my career in computers. Throughout my adult years, I was either operating computers or programming them. The field seems to be as easy for me as breathing. I can't say I love the work—I would rather it was a hobby as opposed to a career—but I am good at it, so it was a natural direction to pursue.

Now, I am a father of four, divorced, and forty-seven years old. I am short-statured (5-foot-zero), 128 pounds, brown eyes, and balding dark hair with a slow invasion of grays beginning to make their mark, though I generally keep my head shaved.

In December 2005, my life took an abrupt turn when I was incarcerated. And in spite of years living in the projects and having been exposed to abuse and violence throughout my childhood, I was not prepared for this. In the nearly seven years I've been down, I've begun to question whether anyone, regardless of their life experiences, can say they were prepared for prison the first time they came in. It's true, some adapt much more readily than others do, but none of us have ever had to live like this before.

For the dynamics of prison are not those faced by the common man, not even by the street thugs and hustlers. Certainly, within society there is aggression, in the workplace, in school, and on the field: rivalry and competition, or the more insidious behaviors like bullying, backstabbing, nepotism, and discrimination. However, behind bars the politics and psychology of living take on a far greater significance. The subtle nuances of the pecking order seen in the business world, in the gym, or in competitive sports become vocal and often violent. The slightest fault, sign of weakness, misspoken word, or unmanaged body language can invoke the need to reestablish pack position or capture an opportunity to rise in the ranks. This is not optional; it is the law in this community. These are the protocols of survival.

This might mislead one to think that a street thug or gang member would fit right in. They do tend to learn the ropes more quickly, but they also experience a learning curve, especially if they were accustomed to being a predator or an alpha dog on the outside. No matter who you were when you came in, now you are prey. Though not every inmate is a predator, any one of us can become a target. If someone who has lived predating on others turns his back, loses a sponsor (an inmate that vouches for another), offends the wrong man, or violates a code, then he will without exception be taken advantage of, and few if any will care.

The crime that landed you in prison becomes an integral part of day-to-day life behind the walls. It reminds me of the identification the Jews were made to wear in Germany, the specialized license plates some states are considering for drunk drivers, and the sexual offenders registration—each purported, by its endorsers, to protect citizens, but which become labels to justify ostracism, continued punishment, and in some instances violence. Though nothing in prison approaches the abomination that happened to the Jews, there is a very real segment of the prison population that would (if the consequences were removed) act on their desire to maim or kill those they deem less deserving. Their views of human life are distorted and judgmental. The security in prison does not prevent them from violence, ranging from petty name-calling to shankings (knifings.) Because of this, each inmate must quickly learn his place and the means of maximizing his safety.

The types of crimes are informally scaled according to a hierarchy of perceived severity. As in militant and gang structures, the strongest and most violent define the scale. At the top are the "solid" crimes. These include murder, assault, drug use, and the like. Those at the bottom are domestic violence, baby killing, rape (rippers), and child molesters (skinners).

However, having a solid crime does not assure you that accolade. How you handle yourself after your arrest, during prosecution, and ultimately after you are behind the walls will affect your status. A man who has turned state's evidence becomes a rat, a title that puts him in the ranks of a rapist. Entering and leaving a gang, failing to follow through on a gang order, sporting a controversial or restricted tattoo, not defending yourself in a fight, and reneging on a debt are a few of the many other ways to violate the convicts' code. Likewise, there are many means an inmate may choose to establish himself or rise within the pack. There are limits, however; a person who is in on a non-solid crime can never become truly solid. If he handles himself smartly, at most he may reach the place where it is said of him, "He's in on a bad crime, but he's solid." Which means: you can't socialize with him, but you can do business with him.

Ultimately, the world we call prison functions differently than any of us knew or could imagine before we arrived here; and so each of us must acclimate to the new culture. Unfortunately, acclimation does not necessitate a change in motives or underlying behaviors. And so, if an inmate is inclined to criminal behaviors, his methods may change, but he will act out and predate on the system and other inmates. Because such types compose a significant majority of the population, it is their behaviors that tend to govern how the system responds.

For all inmates, when we enter prison we find ourselves assaulted on three fronts: the Department of Corrections (DOC), the other inmates, and ourselves. The degree of impact that each one of these has on us is individualized. There are too many variables related to our tolerance of authority and controls, life experiences, and self-image to make an accurate prediction of how any particular individual will respond and manage (or not) to survive.

THE DOC

Our first battle is the DOC staff, and like any other group, they form a bell curve in how they do their jobs, in this case managing and relating with inmates. A few see inmates as humans that have made a mistake or functioned from flawed thinking that harmed one or more individuals, or society. These staff members use and guide the system to promote caring treatment and rehabilitation of inmates, with the aspiration that they can help the inmate return to society as a healthy contributor.

There is a similar number of DOC staff that see inmates as a disease of society and so deserving of nothing but scorn and abuse. They twist and corrupt the system to humiliate and punish the inmates at every opportunity. Whether they are sadistic or simply disillusioned and cynical, they cannot be convinced that inmates are redeemable, and so they justify their abusive actions.

The majority of the staff fall in the large middle range: from reserved optimism to bitter skepticism, rational compromise to punitive correction, individualized guidance to mass punishment. In various fields, they land in various places on the continuum and respond to the complexity of rehabilitating inmates who also have varying degrees of remorse and ability to reform.

Because an inmate's management in the system is dependent on the thinking of the staff they encounter, the success or failure of the inmates' treatment is inexorably linked to staff behavior. This does not mean that staff holds the ultimate responsibility for the inmates' rehabilitation, for each inmate must (if he is ever going to be a healthy member of society) take personal responsibility for his own rehabilitation. Yet, because inmates also form a bell curve in openness and preparedness for correction, the majority of inmates exist within the range that will be influenced in one direction or the other based on the experience and opportunities they are exposed to within the prison. How the inmates are treated by the staff and the culture of the environment will, without exception, either contribute to or detract from the efficacy of the rehabilitation process.

It is evident American correction officers (COs) are not educated in rehabilitation. Their training in security and safety is critically important, and is plainly visible. Yet, without training specifically in correction they are unable to facilitate behavior changes in the inmate population. They know only one tool: punitive treatment. The often excessive misuse of negative reinforcement, the absence of a reward system, and retaliation for an inmate filing a grievance against an officer's misconduct distort whatever value this tool might have and undermine its effectiveness.

This challenging dynamic between the staff and the population is inescapable. Very often the decisions of the DOC appear to the inmates as though the DOC is unaware of the implications for, or is at odds with, rehabilitation. We inmates must continually adjust to the behaviors and atmosphere imposed by the staff. As each man chooses for himself, a few will express their discontent with violence; most will gripe; and some tend to reflect, then find a healthy outlet for their frustration. I, for example, attempt to capture the moment in words.

A recent example involves a change in our housing situation. In an effort to save money by cramming more inmates into limited space, the facility decided to remove tables from our dayroom area and install bunk beds. I have no doubt the administrators see their action as reasonable. For us inmates, we went from forty common-space seats for sixty-eight inmates to twenty seats for seventy-eight. Common space was reduced by nearly half, noise volume increased, and being ousted from a two-man cell and put in an exposed bunk on the dayroom floor became a threat. This did more than change the physical aspects of our housing area; it created a "haves and have-nots" struggle. This divide, between the DOC's operations and the inmates' concerns, was palpable. As I listened to the grumbling and fears, I too became concerned about the impact.

The very simple act of swapping out five tables for five bunks appears minor on the surface, but it is only one example of the ongoing changes. Generally speaking, the conditions of our confinement never improve and progressively worsen. Instead of two gyms, we now have one. We've gone from six hours of daily gym time to half that, and gym is now offered only three or four days out of seven. Holiday parties are no longer permitted. Religious groups have been so strongly opposed and constrained as to make them nearly nonexistent. Education has been trimmed to scarcely more than provision for a GED. Vocational opportunity is available for only one-quarter of the population, and the financial incentive for working has been reduced from fifty dollars per month to three dollars for the first six months and twenty dollars per month following that.

The challenges of working through the DOC system, relating with a staff that is (not always, yet) often confrontational, and an environment that seems increasingly dehumanizing are hurdles that too many inmates find insurmountable.

OTHER INMATES

The second battle each inmate faces is the other inmates. It is critical that each inmate quickly comprehends that he is housed with other convicts, many of whom have finely tuned criminal thinking and behavior.

Many inmates will banter about the expression "doing your own time." Ideally, this means an inmate is socially responsible to his peers, addresses the programs ordered by the court or recommended by the DOC, and serves his or her time without getting involved in any other inmates' business. In reality, this doesn't happen. And ironically, those that tend to throw this expression around the most are the same ones who put themselves in other inmates' concerns. In spite of that, it behooves each inmate to try to adhere to the idea. Failure to do so will more often than not turn physical. For example, if an inmate steals from another, you don't ask questions. Nor do you talk about it with names, even if you were witness to the event. If you observe an inmate pass another inmate a kite (note), you don't inquire about it. If you notice an inmate sporting a new tattoo, you don't ask who did the work. Essentially, in prison, we keep our eyes open and our mouths shut.

When an inmate violates the convicts' code, it is considered the responsibility of the offended man to retaliate. Failure to do so marks him as a "punk" and invites further and escalating abuse. Even if the offended is sure to fare the worst in a fight, it is thought better to fight and lose than not to fight at all. Even though one-on-one is the expected convict code, gangs (crews, boys, brotherhoods, etc.) will often attack as one to show their bond and instill fear in individuals and smaller gangs. Any inmate who is at risk of being assaulted must be prepared to act or react accordingly, or enter PC (protective custody).

Because inmates don't often do their own time, an inmate's reputation becomes critical and bears upon his rehabilitation process by both direct and indirect means.

By direct means, I am referring to actions an inmate takes that reflect his personal values or state of mind. For instance, there is a stigma associated with compliance with the system, or getting help through mental health services. Either of those may be regarded as sullying an inmate's reputation. If an inmate attends programs without some degree of contempt, he is perceived as weak-minded and conforming to the brainwashing by "the Man." So, while the majority of inmates are attending programs, they will do so not to be educated or helped, but to receive the required document needed at their parole hearing. Their attitudes during the program sessions are usually disrespectful and confrontational. This allows the inmate to maintain the image of a convict. Fewer inmates will attend programs that are only recommended. However, there again, the majority even of these attendees are only doing so to persuade the parole board. Often after returning to housing, they will deride the value of the programs to keep face among their peers. Collectively, between the misbehavior in the sessions and back within the population, their actions reinforce the community's contempt for the programs. Those that have no reputation to protect, or are able to subordinate reputation to rehabilitation, are far more likely to attend programs with an aim toward self-improvement.

Mental health services and groups are an even greater threat to an inmate's image. The fear of possible perception that he is crazy, weak, or not in complete control of his choices becomes an obstruction to the inmate getting the help that he needs.

Indirect affronts to a reputation come by association and refer back to the prison hierarchy. Those at the top of the hierarchy are generally tolerated by all inmates, whereas those on the bottom by very few. Those at the top form gangs, and those on the bottom become isolated. And though those on the bottom don't ostracize each other, neither do they defend one another, since they fear bringing attention to themselves. This tendency leads the shunned into becoming more alone and defenseless. Thus their needs for mental health services are more evident. Given that their social position has already placed them outside of peer acceptance, they readily seek and receive mental health treatment. Undesired inmates join treatment groups, while those at the top of the hierarchy (though in equal need of mental health treatment) are far less likely to join.

One result is that prison can worsen an inmate's mental and moral state through interaction with other inmates. The temptation to adopt criminal thinking is pervasive and compelling. If you want to learn how to be a criminal, go to prison. A shoplifter might learn to become a home invader, a drug user to become a drug dealer, or a man in on simple assault may become more violent, risking a future manslaughter or murder.

Though the potential for physical violence of all kinds is very real, it has less of a lasting impact than the threat of violence. This brings me to the third battle each inmate engages in: the battle within his own mind.

THE BATTLE WITHIN

In addition to dealing with the DOC and its staff, as well as with other inmates, the prisoner must gain a clear understanding of the environment he is imprisoned in, while addressing his rehabilitation and healing needs. It is difficult for any man to wrap his thoughts around these facts, especially while coming to grips with the loss of his freedom, and what it means for him and about him. The profusion of lawfulness and lawlessness in such close proximity is unmatched in civilian life. An inmate who fails to recognize his own limits and how power operates frequently learns the hard way.

For example, it is important for inmates, sex offenders particularly, to understand and accept that whether they are guilty or not does not matter; if they were convicted, the courts, the cops, and the convicts all see them as guilty, and no one is interested in hearing their side of the story.

One time (in a not uncommon occurrence), a new man came onto our housing block; he had not assimilated himself to his environment, and became an example of how a man can make his situation worse. He had been sentenced on the crime of molesting a little girl, with some exceptionally heinous acts that resulted in the girl needing corrective surgery.

He started his time here by lying about his charge: stating he was in on murder. He had failed to accept and learn where he was. We live in the information age. Between the law library and friends or family with Internet access, people can find out exactly why a man is in prison; and his face had been plastered on the TV, and so he should have known better. He was quickly made aware that his charges were no secret. So he reverted to talking about them and recycling the defense he had presented to the courts. He falsely believed that an argument could be persuasive. He was angering the other convicts, sex offenders and non–sex offenders alike.

When sex offenders come in, they are mercilessly harassed. This is the time when they should find the lines they shouldn't cross, places they should not go, postures they should avoid, and above all, to keep their mouths shut. This inmate not only defended himself when spurned, he exacerbated his situation by bringing the subject up.

He didn't see or accept the lines in the sand, and it cost him. It is possible he was destined to be smashed from the start because of his case. However, his naiveté and his misdirected grasping to overcome his shame and acquire companionship sealed the deal.

These events are seldom protracted. They occur and are over within a matter of minutes. This is as it must be. Surprise is used to capture the advantage, and speed to avoid being caught. The apparent spontaneity is misleading.

By evening chow, the day following his arrival, his charges and housing were known throughout the facility. There are many inmates that believe it is their right or obligation to harm other inmates. So word was passed, placing a price on this man's life. This established motivation. As anyone who reads crime novels or watches TV is aware, this is one of the three pillars in committing a crime: motive, opportunity, and means.

Opportunities are many, even more so since they removed the officers from direct supervision positions. (Direct supervision places correction officers in positions to monitor inmates without the use of cameras or other visual aids.) The sally ports, bathrooms, cells, stairwells, and the yard give ample options with hardly any waiting. Some convicts are motivated without being concerned with being caught. They are aware they can accomplish their goal of hurting someone before the cops can intervene, and so they will strike as soon as a target is within reach. And then regard the discipline report and talk of the event as a badge of courage.

Means is the most difficult of the three and more complex than it appears at first. Though the most common weapon, one's own hands, is readily available, physical measures aren't enough. There needs to be political backing as well. A convict does not want to become known as someone who bangs out weaker inmates. With sex offenders this is usually overlooked, yet it is still better if there is, or appears to be, obvious justification.

This sex offender provided it: He lied about his charges, failed to take responsibility for his conviction, and he put himself in harm's way by trying to appease the solid convicts. When the event went down, the politics was, "He asked for it." In prison, ignorance and stupidity have a price. It should be noted, however, though the politics were clearly met, the inmate that did the smashing provided himself cover; he said, "You called me a bitch!" This kind of disrespect circumvents the hate-crime charges and the fallout for banging out a weaker inmate.

An hour later, this kid put himself in protective custody. It has been nearly a year, and when I see him, it is obvious he hasn't yet been able to disappear into the shadows. If you imagine a dog hanging his head, his tail between his legs and trailing a streak of urine, it is a fair description of him. When I see him at mealtimes, it doesn't matter where he sits; he is kicked out of his seat repeatedly.

I pity him and imagine him going through an emotional struggle that is drowning him: His face healed many months ago, and the verbal bullying is leaving no marks on his body, but the war that must exist within his head is dangerous. If he is ever going to return to society, he is going to need to come to grips with his guilt and conviction, and to rediscover himself and a reason to be alive tomorrow.

His story is not unique. All the inmates that are in on charges of harming women, children, or the elderly experience similar threats and oppression to varying degrees. Several walk the halls with their heads held low, hoping to pass unnoticed.

This kind of abuse of inmates is not only committed by inmates. I have witnessed it multiple times: prison cops humiliate inmates because of their charges, or advertise them to other inmates, specifically to encourage this kind of treatment. This also further distorts the attitudes the solid inmates have toward their own crimes. They perceive that there is such a thing as a good crime. I once witnessed an officer tell an inmate that he was the kind of inmate he likes and that the prison needed more like him. What other conclusion could be expected from this inmate except that his crime is acceptable? There are many times when a staff member's behavior, if it isn't actually criminally wrong, is morally wrong. The structure and culture of the system provides no redress for this abuse, and the abuse will continue until there is.

Although the above example centers on a sex offender, the mind battles are not limited to them. Every inmate fights to some degree with culling his thoughts and behaviors. While inmates on the bottom of the hierarchy are struggling with psychological issues such as persistent hatred and self-loathing, those on the top are burdened with breaking away from the pressures to remain criminals. Though some continue to be sociopathic, the majority truly feel regret and shame for who they've become. Many can't conceive of ever being different—either because they've never known otherwise, or have become so habituated, they don't know where to begin. I hear it in the confrontations, in their frustration and in their tears; they want a different life.

In addition to the physical separation from society, there are the social and emotional separations. The likelihood of this divide adversely affecting the mental and emotional health of the inmate is significant.

Those in on solid crimes are apt to have come from a social structure that included other criminally minded people. Many of these people will drop away for obvious reasons; those that don't may undermine the inmate's correction. However, some family and friends may remain in contact; provided they aren't contributors to the inmate's criminal thinking and behavior, they can augment the rehabilitation process.

Conversely, for the non-solid inmate, his crimes are as much of an assault on the sensibilities and morals of society as they are on the other inmates, very often resulting in most, if not all, of his friends and family disassociating from him. He is not likely to have people defending his criminal thinking and behavior, and it means he has little to no support structure.

Finally, when one regards the successes and failures of the prison system, or if one desires to reduce recidivism, one must address all the needs of the inmates during their incarceration. If one accepts that there are moral minimum standards that must undergird the treatment of inmates, then one must address the ongoing violations of those standards. Prison inmates are people who have made legal and moral mistakes, but they are worth rehabilitating and giving a second chance at being productive members of society; if we believe this, we must endeavor to change the current system.

If one considers inmates as throwaways, blights excised from society, then nothing need be done; continue on the present course. But we should see that increasing prison populations, parole violations, and recidivism are not testaments to the degradation of society; they are testaments to the failure of the prison to value, educate, and transform its inmate population.

I've heard many shallow and mindlessly glib remarks such as "If you didn't want to be here, you shouldn't have committed the crime." If the issues were that simple, the prisons would be nearly empty. Without dismissing the culpability we must own, our choice to commit our crimes, the environments, psychology, sociology, and behaviors leading to the committing of crime are far more complex, and unplanned. To assume it can be said to an offender, "Go forth and sin no more," and expect that to be sufficient to rehabilitate him is pedantic and naive.

In the years I've been down I've talked with, or listened to, a few hundred inmates, and not once have I heard one say that as a child, he looked into his father's eyes and said, "One day, I want to be a criminal. I want to be removed from society and made to live in a six-by-ten cinderblock bathroom. I want to shame you, Mom, and all of my family. I want to hate myself for the harm I've caused, and what I've done with my life." What I have heard is that at points in their lives they were victimized, or exposed to experiences, temptations, or environments they didn't know how to, or couldn't find the restraint to, process healthily. Fortunately, when most people reach these points they make the right choices. These men and I, we chose wrong. But why did we choose wrong?

It would be nice if the simple answer "Next time, choose right" were enough. In truth, for some, it will be. For most, their psychology and habituated behaviors demand more out of the system. Without it, they will continue to fail.

I happen to be an independent, well-educated man with a strong survival instinct. I have managed to make significant progress in my mental and behavioral rehabilitation, in spite of the three battlefronts. But I am an exception to the norm, not the measure of it. My hope that I will continue to avoid inmate-on-inmate violence, and find staff that will work with me, is tenuous.

My education is not in criminal psychology or correction; it's not even in humanities—I wish it were. I would gladly participate in any effort to improve the success rate of the prison system. For the sake of avenging their victims, mothers, fathers, siblings, children, and communities are losing their men to crime, and far too often not getting them back.

It's not enough to put us behind bars. We need a path to rehabilitation that is clearly navigable. We need staff that aids the process and does not impede it. We need a means of confronting inmate politics and violence so that those who seek personal change can overcome those very real challenges. We need ample psychological and behavioral therapy to be certain we've addressed what is abhorrent in our thinking and behaviors, so that we may one day return to society: healthy, happy members of families and the community.

MARKEITHIA R. REEVEZ, *Virginia*

INMATE JANE DOE

If one were to believe all the reports that the media broadcast or print, one would think that 99 percent of all offenders were male. With the exception of a few high-profile crimes committed by women, a lot isn't really known about women in prison, and this is where the misconceptions begin. Being an offender within the Virginia Department of Corrections for the last nineteen years,

I've seen a population explosion that does not appear to be slowing down. Not only does society in general not understand why this phenomenon is happening, but apparently the Virginia Department of Corrections doesn't know how to address this issue, or maybe they understand it and are exploiting this explosion to create jobs for Virginians. The Virginia Department of Corrections generally makes decisions, policies, and procedures based on the behaviors of the male population, which immediately puts the female population at a disadvantage when it comes to how they can get decisions, policies, and procedures changed or adjusted to address their specific needs.

Many people are not aware that the female offenders within the Virginia Department of Corrections do not have the same rights as the male offenders, especially in a system that is predominantly geared towards male offenders. For example, programs formatted to give offenders job skills, with which they can obtain employment after release, are basically geared towards the males. This in turn increases the recidivism rate for female offenders. But don't get the impression that the female offenders are totally victims of this system. In fact just as they adapted to survive on the outside, many enter the prison system only to use it to their advantage in money, sex, and scandals.

Many come into the Virginia Department of Corrections without job skills and leave with many skills they have no intention of ever using, because as mothers with children waiting for their return, they most often leave the prison system for the social services system. Is this the average image of the female offender? Yes. A majority of the female population dropped out of school to have children and have never worked because they relied on the welfare system to provide for their families. The average female offender is no different from your mother, sister, friend, or neighbor; she just happens to live in prison with restrictions that cause her to adapt and survive until she is home again, where she adapts again to survive through the services offered on the outside. A minority of female offenders are high school graduates who had a steady work history before incarceration. Then there are those who are college graduates faced with how they will adjust to employment-seeking with criminal histories.

POPULATION EXPLOSION

The female offender population within the Virginia Department of Corrections (VADOC) has increased 500 percent since I entered it in 1991. When I entered the VADOC there was only one state institution for female offenders. Today there are five, and there is a need for more beds every day. This explosion has various explanations, but the main causes from my point of view are recidivism, the lack of equal rights for female offenders, the lack of programs appropriate for female offenders, lack of drug rehabilitation programs (the VADOC is designed for punishment, not drug rehabilitation), and, of course, the main reason many women are in prison today: codependency.

So how did the VADOC make room for this population explosion? They just turned a few of the male institutions into institutions for women, not designed with the female in mind. In 1997 the VADOC finished building the Fluvanna Correctional Center for Women (FCCW), an institution for women in Troy, Virginia, which was to house the female population with long-term sentences and be a facility to address medical needs. The FCCW opened in 1998, and since changing wardens in 2003, the powers that be have been trying to make this institution a maximum-security institution; but most of it is not designed to house maximum-security offenders as specified by the VADOC and the Justice Department. Mainly this institution lacks the wet cells that maximum-security institutions require to keep maximum-security offenders locked down on a 23:1 basis. For example, the administration at FCCW has a new policy of making us keep our doors locked, with the exception of five minutes every half hour during the dayroom hours. Not only is this a security risk for us if we are caught outside our cells while a fight is in progress, but this is unrealistic for the female offender because we have different bodily issues than the male population. Maybe we can make our bladders adjust to this type of strict schedule, but no one can absolutely control intestinal functions or biological issues unique to only the female population. This is also causing problems with our sleep patterns; many are caught behind a locked door after waking up to find that they missed the "cell break" period. This frustrates those in authority who greatly desire to make FCCW a maximum-security prison, which in turn frustrates the female population here because of the constant changes in decisions, policies, and procedures that violate our rights. There is an ongoing battle between the FCCW administration and the female population. When changes are made, we complain; the administration says they have the right to make changes; we in turn write the VADOC; and some officials will deny that those changes were made, or take sides with the administration, thinking that that will stop the complaints. Our last resort is the media, on which we and our families have come to rely a great deal lately, because the moment the media exposes any complaints about unfair changes in decisions, policies, or procedures, the FCCW administration denies the charges and then quietly changes back to old policies until they come up with another bright idea.

NOT ALL ARE EQUAL

Many don't understand the great disparity of rights between the male and female populations. The male offender pay scale goes far beyond what a female is allowed to earn. Most vocational programs offered to female offenders are geared more towards the male population. Yes, we have Software, Cosmetology, Printing, and Computer Aided Drafting. But other programs such as Electrical, Plumbing, HVAC (Heating, Ventilation, and Air Conditioning), and Building and Maintenance require women to complete a two-year apprenticeship program before they can join a union. This is unrealistic for women who have to return home to a family they will have to provide for. FCCW offers employment through the tailor shop, but it does not compare to the employment opportunities offered to the male population. The male institutions offer employment in welding, tailor shop, upholstery, forklift licensing, construction work with outside contractors, and other various employment opportunities. These in turn allow the male offender to make as much as $1,000 or more a month, whereas the females are allowed to make up to $400 a month at most. And there are only a handful of those who do make more than $300 a month, because there aren't that many jobs for the female population compared to those offered to the male population.

Another example: when the male offenders hid weapons in their hair, the VADOC decided to make all offenders cut their hair, even though there has never been an incident of a female offender hiding a weapon in her hair. When it comes to recreational rights, male-offender rights are never violated. Our rights to recreational programming are violated on a daily basis. We have the right to have (not scheduled and then canceled) recreation three hours a week, but this rarely happens. We have a weight room that is constantly closed to us. We have exercise equipment which is closed off to us because no one wants to pull this equipment back out after visitations on the weekends and holidays. We only have access to playing basketball, volleyball, softball, or walking during recreation, even though offender funds were used to pay for other equipment and for games we are no longer allowed to access. Our aerobics classes, which were in high demand and ran successfully for two years, were discontinued because our recreation supervisor is "on military leave"; however this is just an excuse that this administration uses to justify not allowing us to have aerobics, because our recreation supervisor actually switched from reserve status to active status to become a recruiter. Did I mention that this is also a medical facility in which there are a high number of offenders with medical issues related to obesity? These are just some of our rights that are constantly violated.

PROGRAM UTILIZATION

Many think that offenders sit around playing cards, watching TV, and drinking Coca-Cola all day. This is true for many, but not the majority here. Most work or go to school because such work is the only form of financial support they have. Most with long terms work to break the monotony. For the most part, many sign up for any educational program to support themselves while incarcerated. But this system is flawed. Many should not be paid to get a high school education, because many exploit this system by continually failing the LIP (Literacy Incentive Program) or the GED (General Education Development) tests. Why? Because it's easier to attend a class than to work, especially if you never plan on establishing a work history. Once you obtain your GED, you'll have to get a job, and many don't see that as an option. It's easier to stay in the LIP class for fifteen or seventeen years. Yes, we have women here who've been in the LIP program for more than seventeen years. This is a sad statistic for us. Women who relied on the welfare system before incarceration will think of the LIP or GED program as an easier way to obtain financial support than to actually work.

This brings me to the issue of the vocational programs, which need to be adjusted in the VADOC for female offenders. For one, there should be more than one software program to facilitate a greater turnaround rate. Skills obtained through this program are more realistic than others for females. They can go right out and obtain employment with these skills. No offender should be allowed to enter a vocational job until they obtain their GED. There is currently a policy stating that an offender must be in LIP to obtain employment, but it is not enforced. As for other programming, the female population usually exploits these as a way to see their "girlfriends." The VADOC has to realize that the only way to slow down the recidivism rate is to offer more programs that will assist the female offender immediately upon release. There have to be more housing programs for females upon release also; most of the housing programs only take male offenders. They also have to make decisions, policies, and procedures for the female institutions separately from the male institutions. Maybe more female offenders will appropriately utilize programs if they are realistically designed to address their needs after release.

RECIDIVISM

The recidivism rate among the female population increases every year. This is largely due to the VADOC focusing primarily on punishment instead of drug rehabilitation. A lot of women come to prison as drug addicts. They are given a sentence, and then most return because they go right back to abusing drugs. The sad thing I've come to realize is that most women leave here with the false impression that they are drug-free because they've been incarcerated for years. The reality is that they were probably arrested during the addiction, and with no access to drugs in the VADOC (for the female population anyway) they build this belief that they have kicked their habits. They fail to realize that they had to cease using because of force, not choice, so when they return home, they go right back to taking drugs—because it was not their choice to stop; they were just arrested.

The other cause of recidivism is the lack of financial support. Most are expected to earn a living after living off the welfare system all their lives. When faced with having to seek employment (something most have never done) and businesses that do not want to hire ex-offenders, this becomes a big issue. Many cannot live off the minimum wages most ex-offenders are offered, so they go right back to committing crimes. Once an offender has paid their debt to society, many people would think society would want these individuals to come out and become contributing members of society, but this is far from the case. Many don't think that ex-offenders deserve a second chance. Either way, society is going to carry the burden of providing for these individuals, whether it's through taxes for the prison system or for social services.

FINAL WORDS

While the complaints I've written about in this article are of importance, there are many other issues that the VADOC should address when it comes to the female population. It must be able to provide adequate medical services to us without denying us the right to be active members of our treatment option selection. For women and men, the VADOC has to be more considerate when serving food that is often spoiled because of improper storage practices. Improper storage practices are just as much a money-mismanagement issue as serving food that is inedible. Stop denying that this institution does not serve spoiled food. It does! Find a more efficient way to store food properly. This is a total waste of money, especially in an environment where many don't have a choice of what food is served. The VADOC must provide better recreational programming, especially in an institution that is considered a medical facility. The obesity, hypertension, and diabetes rates are increasing at an alarming rate at this facility. That alone should warrant yoga and aerobics classes to defray the cost of medical services provided. The medical services within the VADOC need to be more preventive then reactive. In closing, my opinion is that the Virginia Department of Correction has to find a way to ensure the security of their institutions and society while ensuring the safety and rights of offenders, especially female offenders. They can achieve these ends without violating the civil rights of female or male offenders.

CATHERINE LYNN QUICK, *Arizona*

TRANSSEXUAL IN PRISON

There is a lot to talk about when it comes to prison(s) and the way a person is treated there. This is just one subject of many, by one person of many, with no guarantee that you will ever see these words anyway; but here goes.

You see, I belong to a minority within the prison system, and yet we are one of the groups most abused and mistreated by both convict and guard.

I am a forty-six-year-old pre-hormone, pre-op, MTF (male to female) transsexual; but within the prison system, we are grouped with the gay(s) and that is how we are seen.

A prison environment is already a very rough situation; when you come in you are checked out by every type of predator known to man, and let me tell you that you know the second you hit the yard that you have life-and-death choices to make, and it will be the next few minutes that will decide whether you live or die.

There are things here to understand, as the dynamics of prison are not in any way similar to the dynamics of the outside. The rules and morals of the outside do not apply within the prison walls; that is why everyone is subject to assault, rape, and death. Those that are transsexual and even gay are those that receive from those categories on a regular basis.

But along with all the threats and dangers one must face, there is an advantage to those who are strong enough to hold to their standards, and YES you can even find love in prison, which to many may seem weird if not impossible; but if you truly look at the situation, you will see that a large majority of those in prison have been misused and abused throughout their lives, and when you have those in need of love meeting those who are in need of love, the dynamics can work out so that both can have what society and family have denied them to date.

Now on the flip side of all this, you have those who really were nobodies out on the street—or he's a gang leader, and he becomes somebody, or thinks he or she is somebody, on the inside. And they cause most of the violence that is perpetrated on other people in the system with the help of guards and staff that think it is their job to harass and torment you and not just keep you locked up.

If a guard does not like you (which is usually the case with any gay or transsexual), they will put you in a dangerous situation (such as in the same cell with a known rapist, or a person who is homophobic, or just a person who likes hurting other people) and then pretend that they had no clue about what was going to happen.

As for your fellow convicts . . . well everyone that I have ever met has a point where they will leave their own norm and seek the comfort that you (the transsexual) have to offer. The problem is, until they can actually own up to their needs, they will blame YOU and hurt you after having sex with you, 'cause they can't face the fact that they chose to be with you, and, even worse . . . *they enjoyed it!*

But here is one basic fact that most people do not realize. Those who are gay and transsexual save guard and convict lives on a regular basis. No one can argue that prison is not a very stressful environment; it is even more stressful than war, and it is the gays and the transsexuals that help ease the stress and paranoia of prison, and help bring the high levels of violence within a prison down to a level that is livable. But again, that is only in a prison environment where the guards understand that and protect us from just being raped and beaten every day. I have been lucky enough to have found several of these places while doing time. Now don't get me wrong: if I am caught, they have to do their jobs; but they usually apologize for having to do so. The usual unsaid agreement is, keep it out of my supervisor's face and there will be no problems . . . And then sometimes they can even let you know that they may have heard that so-and-so has had a really bad day, or that a family member died or whatever, and that allows you to make arrangements to ease that man's tension and pain.

Like it or not, world, gays and transsexuals ARE the sex therapists of the prison world. We are not the garbage that you would like to make us out to be, and you should show some of the heart that you all claim to have, and make laws and prison policies to help those that, whether you know it or not, help you.

And for those of you that are gay or transsexual and may be heading to prison, understand that there IS such a thing as being independent and free within a prison so that you are *not* the property of anyone or a gang. But you have to work for it from the start; don't let prison or convicts or guards control you or your body. *You* control it, and if you do, then you can use it at *your* discretion for the greater good of all.

GEORGE WHITHAM, *Massachusetts*

FRIENDSHIP

This is a story about prison, friendship, and love. You certainly never see prison as a place where one would expect to find friendship and love. Prisons are designed to punish and tear apart the human soul. From my point of view, prisons for the most part are not fit places for dogs, let alone human beings.

This is a true story about two men, myself and my friend Billy, who I affectionately called Mr. Bill. Actually I really enjoyed calling him Mister, because I truly respected him that much. I was a person who never respected anyone. Both Billy and myself had much the same childhoods: we both were abused in the home. I was born into a family of alcoholics. There are no pretty words to describe my parents; they were drunks. My dad would come home from work, see me, and decide it was time for his workout. His workout consisted of beating on me. From the age of five to sixteen, I was beaten almost on a daily basis. Twice I was beaten so badly that I almost died. As a child I always tried to figure out what I had done wrong, so that I could change it so the beatings would stop. When I talk about being beaten, I'm talking about a 200-pound man hitting a 40- to 50-pound boy with a closed fist. It got to the point where most times I no longer felt the punches. My mother was no saint; she would often get in a few kicks when my dad was finished. The most vivid memory that I have is of my father telling me, "Stop your crying; real men don't cry." It was a lesson I learned well; I carried it inside me till late in my life.

Billy's abuse was far different and more painful, as well as destructive. Billy was sexually abused and raped by his stepfather, who made Billy feel like it was all his fault. Billy was ten to twelve when this took place. By the age of thirteen and fourteen Billy was shooting up heroin, and was a full-blown junkie by the age of sixteen. I would often tell Billy I wish we could have changed places. Not that I would have liked being raped. But because I wanted to spare him the pain. Being raped, especially when you're a child, brings with it a kind of pain that most people don't know, and they should be thankful for that.

Billy and I met in 1975. Billy had about eighteen months in on his natural life sentence, while I had about nine months in on my life sentence. At first I didn't like him. It took about a year for us to start building a friendship. Like I've said, prisons are not about making friends and building up trust. Especially when it's two murderers. At that time the prison system saw us as mad-dog killers. We were no longer human beings. In fact, the prison system's point of view was that the moment we picked up our con numbers, we no longer existed as humans; we were now the sum of our con numbers. I deserved being in prison because I beat a man to death and I had no right taking that man's life. But Billy, on the other hand, was involved in an armed robbery that went bad. Billy's partner stabbed a man to death, and Massachusetts, like most states, has the felony murder rule. If a person dies during a felony, then all who are involved get charged with the murder. I always felt bad that Billy got caught up in that kind of crime. Although I was convicted of second-degree murder, I was eligible for parole after serving fifteen years. Not once was Billy ever jealous or envious of my possible release.

Billy and I spent nearly eleven years together before I was classified to another institution. Because we are not allowed to write to other prisoners, we could not stay in contact with one another. It would be another eleven years before we'd end up in the same institution again. But during those eleven years we thought about one another. There were times during those years when someone I knew would come up to me and say, Do you know Billy so-and-so? and my heart would actually skip a beat, and I'd always say, "Sure!" and I'd get a full report on what Billy had been up to. Those were the few times the prison grapevine worked. (The prison system has men so scared that they won't deliver messages like that.)

Then I was classified to come to this place, and I did not want to come here, because at that time it was a prison just for lifers and we had heard that if you came here you died here. So I came here kicking and screaming, but once I arrived here, to my complete surprise, Billy greeted me in the yard. As a prisoner I had believed that I was never to feel or experience real joy. But seeing Billy was a real bucketful of joy for me. The first few minutes I was horrified, because he had aged beyond what I felt he should have—but then again, I too had aged badly. The prison system takes its toll on you one way or another. But Billy had changed in other ways. He was more relaxed; he seemed to have a kind of peace that all men search for but rarely attain. I liked what I saw, and to be honest, I was finally in a place where I wanted a change. I was too old to continue fighting the battles I had going on inside me. So I started going to the different programs that Billy was attending, and slowly I too began to change. In the years I hadn't heard from Billy, he had gotten married to a wonderful woman who didn't even live in this state. I myself had met a woman, and we shared a wonderful friendship for twenty-five years. Pam had always wanted more than a friendly relationship, but I was always telling her she could do better than me. I did care for her, but I was truly afraid I'd hurt her and I didn't want that. In 2005 Pam passed away. For the first time in my life, I had to deal with the death of someone dear to me.

For the first time in my life, I felt a kind of pain that no pill could relieve. It was my good friends here who propped me up and carried me through the toughest period of my life. Billy was right there every inch of the way; without their help I don't know where I would have been. I did contemplate suicide, but I was smothered with love from Billy and my friends. Not once did the system give a rat's ass about my inner pain and torment.

It was a group of men who society deemed unworthy to be on the streets who nursed me back into a functioning human being.

Billy got me and himself enrolled in college, and I'm talking about one of this state's most prestigious colleges, where students pay up to $40,000 a year. At first it was tough going. I wanted to quit that very first semester because I didn't think I was smart enough to be in those classes. But I have done well, whereas Billy began to falter. Right from the start, I tried my best to encourage him; he hung in, and he was beginning to do well. Then the unthinkable happened: Billy got sick. At first we thought it was just a stomach thing. The food here isn't always the best. He couldn't keep anything down. He put in sick slip after sick slip. Their answer was antacid tablets. But he kept getting worse. I try not to be critical of the medical staff here, but they really dropped the ball on this one. They finally did some blood work and they saw many things wrong with the samples. This all took months before they realized something was wrong.

They finally started taking Billy to the outside hospital, where, after months of tests, needles, and MRIs, they determined he had cancer tumors in his liver and there was no cure. The only thing that might have helped him would have been a liver transplant. Inmates are barred from such things. Our lives are less valuable than others'. From time of diagnosis until he passed away was less than two months. Some people will read this and say that I'm pretty lucky because I had time I could spend with him before he died; but I say, bullshit—because my life was turned into a living hell. I want to hear one person say it's easy to watch someone die. I watched my friend die on a daily basis, piece by piece, cell by cell. I kept myself in a constant state of denial. Billy was not going to die, he was going to beat this dreaded disease. I saw him lose most of his body weight. I witnessed his voice become a tiny whisper. He lost his ability to speak because he constantly threw up and his own stomach acids ate away the lining of his throat. The times when he could barely walk, they would take him to the outside hospital, where they put him on meds and IV's and he would rebound. We would go through this process half a dozen times. Each time the pain got worse for me. Just before they took him out for the last time, I got to walk in the yard with him; I got to tell him the things I needed to say. I even got to tell him that I loved him, which he just kinda waved off with a weak smile.

When I found out they would be taking Billy out for the last time, I ran down to our HSU (hospital) so that I could see him one last time. I had one last thing to tell him. I got there just minutes before they took him away. I gave him a hug. I didn't care what others thought. Love and compassion are not common sights in this place. While I was hugging him I whispered that I was sorry that I hadn't been able to comfort him and ease his pain. In a soft whisper he said, *You've been a good friend.* That was the last time I saw him and it's the last word that keeps echoing in my head. On December 5, 2008, my friend Billy Simpson passed away.

When I was told of his passing, it brought me to my knees. I have always been a strong man. I have always been able to take a punch or to take a beating without a whimper. But the death of my friend hurt me in ways I couldn't prepare for. Then I had to do the hardest thing I have ever had to do: I wrote to Patty, Billy's wife, to tell her what had happened. I must have written ten letters before I got it right. Now I have a true sense of what a commander goes through when he has to write a letter to the family of a soldier, letting them know of their child's passing. Luckily when I heard back from Patty, she told me she had come to Massachusetts to spend the last days with her love. She took his body back to New York for burial.

I am still in mourning over the loss of my friend. There are still times when I run to my cell so that I can cry; that's the only place where I have enough privacy to let it all out. In writing this I have had to stop a few times to cry. My voice still cracks when I try to speak of Billy. When I started writing this it was just fourteen days shy of the first anniversary of Billy's passing. When I look back over this past year, it's like looking at a train wreck. I'm the train wreck. But the one good thing is that I have friends who have helped me get through the tough times. I even have friends, from the various programs I have attended, who also knew Billy, who are there for me when I need them. I also get to see their grief and sorrow, which is important to me. In this year I have spoken to Billy often. Some will think I'm nuts, but I keep a conscious link with my friend. I know that wherever he may be, he is at peace; his torment is over with. And I have asked that when it's my time that he come to get me and help me with the process. I have been in prison for almost thirty-five years, and not once in that whole time have I ever ridden such a rollercoaster ride of feelings and emotions. I never thought that I'd ever care so much for another human being.

In the years since Billy's passing much has happened. I still deal with the emotional loss daily. I have continued on with college. I'm a little over halfway to getting my degree. I'm going to get that degree for Billy. Patty and I write regularly and are becoming friends. Billy would have liked that. I have thanked some of the people who have propped me up and supported me through this whole process. (I have also put on thirty pounds because I have been using food to give me comfort and that's not good for me. After New Year's it's diet, diet, diet. To shed this extra weight.) I finally recognize myself as a caring human being who's not just a con number or a statistic. I now try to help others the way Billy helped me.

The prison system still grinds its slowly turning wheels. It treated Billy's death as just another change in the prison count; someone will take his place, his bed will be filled. All's back in balance once again. There is one thing the system never figured on, and that was that one of its occupants, one of its numbers, would become a human being who feels and cares.

COREY JOHN RICHARDSON, *Kentucky*

HOW SOME MEN FIND LOVE

We don't always do the right things. For me, I rarely did the right ones. A few years ago, I was facing a lot of prison time for a rather atypical white-collar crime . . . and my codefendant had just taken a deal in the middle of our joint trial. For those of you who do not know about the system, this ensured that I would be the one to go away for quite a while.

I was paralyzed with fear. Surely, I would be a target, and not just because of my rather obvious middle-class demeanor or my high-profile case. I am gay. Not in an overt way. I never immersed myself in Gay culture. I am just gay. As I waited for that day to come when I would be transported to a concrete world behind razor-wire fences, the prison-violence documentaries on A&E were foremost in my mind—not my favorite Jeff Stryker videos from college when he made all his sexual conquests in the local county lockup.

Oddly enough, I developed a fantasy of meeting someone in prison. Certainly not some gangbang, rapefest fantasy, but maybe some strong young soul who needed love just as much as I did. The world had thrown me away. In prison, the Land of the Throwaways, there's much hunger for love (and for food and money and freedom), and it mutates into behaviors difficult to explain.

I have heard that the Roman armies, the Spartans, and other cultures of the ancient world embraced homosexuality. When you lock men up for decades at a time, it is quite easy to figure out why it becomes natural to seek the arms of another man. Just men, men, and more men, year after long year. It was just as natural for the ancients with their long campaigns to conquer distant lands. Perfectly straight men become situationally gay, at least for a time. Homosexual acts in prison facilitate the sexual release and sometimes salve the need for love.

After I unpacked the little bit of property I had, I walked around the prison. I tried to look natural, but surely my eyes were as big as half dollars. I know that my nerves were shredded. It did not take long to see a few "sissies," a few "punks," and a few "boys" (common prison nomenclature), all walking with their respective "friends"—gay men in quite larger numbers than I had expected in prison. How could this be? Had drinking, drugs, or just plain stupidity brought them to prison like they had me? It seemed so.

Gay men in prison are an unusual bunch. Some are undercover and some are proud, tough queens. Some are just rather average. Many gay men in prison distinctly assume female affectations. They aren't transgendered, though prison has plenty of the transgendered also. To some gay men, female attributes are bait, and many straight convicts are more open to sex with another man when they perceive a female illusion orchestrated with shaven legs and plucked eyebrows. I was lonely, but that just wasn't me.

In a few weeks it was overwhelmingly clear to me that prison (at least in this state) was a 24/7 meat market. This is what had terrified me? And while several hundred men were trying to figure out if I was merely a "fish" easily tricked or perchance gay, I had already decided to plant myself in the path of the biggest, most beautiful young man this world has ever known. Eventually, he sat down beside me and said hello.

As a gay man I had often felt, underneath the surface, rejected and alone, but now I felt utterly destroyed. I hoped to find some companionship. I hoped he would be the one. It was more than I could have ever dreamed possible. It was instant. He loved my knowledge, my worldview, and our multitude of differences. He dragged me to the weight pile, took me to the chow hall, and even hopelessly tried to teach me basketball. We shared meals in the dorm, watched movies on the weekend, and, well . . . we didn't just screw. This man made love to me like no one else ever has. It was wonderful each and every time. This was a man so straight that I was terrified to even kiss him that first time. This straight man completely, unreservedly, met every need that I had sexually and otherwise, and found several that I had not known even existed. No man that I have ever known was stronger, or more tender and sensitive.

Then he was gone. It was about a year that we had shared, and then he made parole. As much as I thought I had appreciated him, it was only a fraction of what he deserved. He held me in his arms as I cried real, honest-to-goodness tears. This man loved me as I was, never asked for more from me than my time and love. I still do the same workouts. Still cook the same meals. Still run the same track. I still smile when I think about his beautiful face laughing in the summer sun as we walked together across the prison yard.

Prison is still a 24/7 meat market, but I never found love again. As I edge closer toward release, being pursued has lost its luster. When my love left, I began to discover more of myself. I still see men—gay with straight—finding comfort in each other's arms. Don't think, though, that corrections administration is accepting of homosexuals, or that prison is safe. Neither is true. A fight in prison may cost you fifteen days of segregation, but get caught in the arms of another man and you will spend ninety days in "the hole" and you will get six months added to your sentence due to loss of good time. Purchasing condoms on the black market is nearly impossible, and the medical departments are loath to offer expensive HIV testing. Think of this: "Barely Legal" porn mags showing clearly underage girls are permissible, but a gay political or literary magazine is considered contraband and therefore not allowed in the institution. Allegedly it "promotes homosexuality." Serving ten, twenty, thirty years or longer promotes homosexual acts—not a magazine.

Straight men in prison do not see their partners in a particularly male way. These couples still fight like couples in the free world. Some are even abusive. Some cheat. Many people outside scam lonely gay men through pen pal services. Gays need to fight sometimes, like everyone else. Everyone, gay or straight, misses their families, misses their freedom. It is still prison. But one thing is certain: I grew into the man I always wanted to be in prison, but not because of prison—in spite of it.

When my friend left, he went to live with his parents, who were raising his twin sons. In his enthusiasm over us, he told his mother the whole truth. Maybe I was merely part of his prison experience as well. We often joked, "What happens in prison stays in prison"—like some ad for corrections. Maybe when he shed his prison attire, he shed me too, but I hope not completely. I pray that part of what we were lingers still. He said before he left that I had changed him forever. I felt the same, and still do. After having truly been loved for the first time in my life, I found that I was finally proud to be myself without reservations; I was glad to have been born gay, and maybe now I could find real love once again upon my release, but this time with another gay man.

Mother Theresa said once that we humans are angels with only one wing, and that we need each other to fly. He helped me get from that place of loss and confusion to the sure-footing of where I am today. I hardly knew that it was happening. What an odd place for it all to have occurred.

JOSE DI LENOLA, *New York*

THE ART OF AGGRESSION

I swerve. Pursued. Fear compels me forward through the milling chaos of prisoners. Recreation has ended. Men exchange last minute goodbyes and fist bumps.

I glance over my shoulder. Still following—gaining.

To my left stretches a row of thirty-eight dimly lighted five-by-seven-foot cells. On the right, a wall of paint-chipped bars. The gallery is over a hundred feet long, but barely twelve feet wide. A cramped space for the seventy men to jostle about. The stench of festering winter and unwashed bodies saturates the air. At the end, the guards are too blinded by the mass of bodies to notice anything suspicious. So they search for unusual movements: rapidly parting crowds, a sudden hush of noise in an otherwise constant din, and the obvious, flying fists.

I snatch bits of conversation as I career past. I have never been more focused in my life. I assess every hand gesture, arm movement, and eye glance for indications of danger.

He's still there. A pressure below my ears speaks anxiety, fear.

Chiprock, a 6'3" 240-pound man, has been chasing me since we came in from the yard. He's always there, towering over my 5'7" 140-pound frame. I adjust my course to the left, away from a prisoner's flailing arm and another's hand in pocket. I weave, and weave again. Slowly I'm shunted close to the cells where one could reach out from the darkness to grab and stab. But I stay close to the bars. Chiprock's right-handed, my mind warns—give him no room.

Making my move, I edge to the right. Too late. In my peripheral I see a flash over my right shoulder. A hand rapidly descends toward my face. My mind slows to a crawl. Men walk in an exaggerated, silent display of movement. Laughs and conversations ribbon out in no-time.

Finally, my muscles respond. I shift my weight to the ball of my right foot. First my head, then a desperately long turn. A strike upon my shoulder. Then, time comes crashing back to speed. Walking backwards now, my pursuer is just six feet away, face twisted with menace, his two gold fronts gleaming. The prisoners around us part into a gladiator circle, all while we move inexorably toward the COs.

My eyes dart to his hands. A razor blade, blood dripping from its gleaming edge. It doesn't register to check my face for the gaping tear.

This is a common occurrence in prison. Cut from behind, never from the front. Enough to make a movie gunslinger turn over in his grave with disgust. This is the story of how I learned the art of aggression.

Before I came to Great Meadow (Comstock) I was in Elmira "reception." A stopover point between county jail and a correctional facility "upstate." My days were spent walking the recreation yard. Several guys and I would talk of the prisons we could be transferred to. Such places as the fabled Attica, said to be the most violent. Coxsackie, a prison where adolescents are sent, and rumored to be just as violent as Attica. Comstock, nicknamed "gladiator school," and many others, shrouded in second-hand information. I was an adolescent then, just seventeen years old, and knew deep down which places I feared to go.

Up to this point in my incarceration, I hoped prison would be like reception. Confined movement, twenty-hour lockdowns, and relative stability in the daily routine. Every time I stepped out of my cell, not sure of what violence the day might bring, I was scared and nervous. Yet, by some freakish streak of luck, there was not one fight during my time in reception. Even with the fear and uncertainty of what prison I'd be transferred to, I blocked most of the feelings out. I lived each day as if transfer would never come—playing basketball, cards, and writing letters to my family.

I wasn't the praying type, but I prayed every day to be sent to a "safe" prison, if such a place existed. In reception you have no choice where you go. When you're told to go, you go—no questions asked.

The transfer day eventually arrived, snapping me back to reality and sending a chill over my skin. After packing my scant belongings into a burlap sack, shackled and handcuffed, I still didn't know where I was heading. Only on the bus did the CO inform us: Comstock, Gladiator School. During the seven-hour drive I imagined mayhem: stabbing, cutting, rape, extortion. I was in for a re-education into the "upside-down kingdom."

The first week in Comstock, while waiting in line to go to dinner, I saw a prisoner stabbed four times, his lung punctured twice. The next day in the yard, while sitting on the concrete bleachers, a guy came and sat near me. At first I didn't notice anything amiss, until he turned his head. From temple to lips, a jagged rip spewed blood down his neck and shirt; he'd been cut with a can lid. I was astounded by how a can lid could cause so much damage. I got up and walked away. The first lesson you learn in prison is mind your own business. I'll never forget the looks of horrified panic on those men's faces.

It was there on the bleachers that I realized how much I didn't know and had to learn fast if I wanted to survive, uncut and without holes in my lungs.

So there I was, fresh upstate, at an age when the average boy just gets his driver's license, begins to date seriously, and is planning for college. I would be earning a master's in Prison Survival: etiquette, weapon smithing and smuggling, group dynamics, armory, fear and aggression. All of which trumped everything I had come to know about prison from TV, movies, and reception rumors.

For instance, gate etiquette. Yelling on the gate of your cell is like shouting in the schoolyard—two boys taunting each other while a jeering crowd circles. The tiers in Comstock are open from the first floor to the fourth. On the first floor (the flats), I can call up to the fourth and be heard clearly. So when a prisoner is talking on the gate, everyone can hear what's said. In most cases this is not a good thing.

A couple days ago, two guys from the floor above me were arguing. Back and forth they traded insults, punctuated by "Suck my dick," and "You's a bitch." No one jeered; silence spoke louder. For an hour and a half this went on, until both became hoarse. They moved on to blasting tape players and violent hip-hop lyrics. Later that day, one of the men ended up with a knife in his neck. The gate is a stage, and once you put it out, there's no getting it back.

I've lived on this tier for six months, and because of my location and age, I have formed a tight friendship with several of the men around me. Goldie, an African American named after a pimp, locks on my right side. He's a few years older than me and also from Rochester. We hit it off right from the start.

I first saw Goldie when we were going to lunch. Exiting his cell, the 6'2" man ducked so as not to hit his head on the door frame. Wearing glasses, he greeted me with his ubiquitous smile and a head nod.

"What chu plan on doin' tonight?" said Goldie.

"Probably call home, or some shit," I responded. "Why, what you gonna do?"

"Hit the weights, you heard. You?"

"If I got time." Thinking of something to occupy myself with until recreation: "Ay yo, Goldie, got somethin' I can check out?"—the something is pornography.

"Naw. All mine's out."

"Does Carlos got?" Carlos is another guy close to my age who I hang out with playing handball, dominoes, and cooking meals.

"Naw. But Chiprock does, you heard."

Raising my voice from the gate, I called down the nine cells, "Chiprock." A couple seconds passed.

"Yo yo yo, what up son?" said Chiprock.

"Got somein' I can check out?" I said.

"What you want?"

He must have the mother lode of stashes: "Don't really matter—got some Tabitha?"

"A'ight. What you got?" he shouted back.

Confused by his question: "Nottin' right now."

"Well I ain't got unless you got somein' for me, you heard. I don't let my shit out like that."

"Damn man, can't get nothin'?" I responded with disappointment.

"What I just said? Give me somein' and I give you somein'."

Giving up: "Yea a'ight. I don' wanna talk. Goldie, see you when we come out. Gonna do some reading."

Turning to my locker, from a stack of magazines I picked up a *Scientific American*, laid down, and waited three hours for recreation.

After calling home and having my collect call refused, I walked to the yard with Toño. Of all the guys that lock near me, Toño is the oldest. A 5'3" Puerto Rican with a ponytail. He wobbles slightly side to side when he walks, as if his feet constantly hurt; but I'd never tell him that to his face. After a few weeks, observing him interact with others, I noticed how respected he was. Toño was the first person I began to trust. Much of our time walking the yard was spent enlightening me as to the ways of prison. I asked questions and he gave me answers, honest answers. He explained the gangs, COs, gambling, drug use, how to sharpen metal into wicked knives . . . everything I wanted and needed to know.

The yard in Comstock is often referred to as the "parking lot." A blacktopped space large enough to hold three football fields. The concrete gray wall surrounding the prison is part of the yard. Stretching along two sides are courts for playing handball. There are three TVs, a baseball diamond, volleyball court, two basketball courts, a soccer field, cement bleachers, twenty-five phones, steel tables scattered around, and plenty of walking space.

It must have been the second or third week into the snowfall of winter when I noticed something peculiar. The snow remained pristine white. Because there were no exhaust fumes, mud, and other such muck, the snow remained white. Always white. A stark contrast to the clothing the prisoners wore. Brown, burgundy, green, and yellow jumpsuits appeared drab in the snow. It's an eerie sight.

Even with winter in full swing, there were plenty of men outside. Close to 350 prisoners walked the compacted snow trails crisscrossing the yard. Occasionally someone would slip on a patch of ice. Some found their balance, others fell hard.

As we walked I constantly surveyed the groups of men. Most hung out in their staked-out territory: the Latin Kings, Bloods, Crips, Five Percenters, Ñetas, Christians, Muslims . . . everyone had a place.

Toño and I approached the "hole." The spot farthest from the officers' station one can get. A choice place for men to fight, get their "shit off, gun-to-gun," that is, knife-to-knife.

When Toño and I were as close as the snow-trodden path allowed, I saw Chiprock and fifteen or so men. Talking, huddled in a tight circle. Chiprock glanced up as we passed.

I turned to Toño: "Yo, Chiprock's bugged out, you heard," then proceeded to tell him about our earlier conversation.

"Word to mother son, dat's the way he is," Toño explained. "Keep people from keeping his shit, jackin' pages, *oíste*."

"Yeah, I hear you."

As we reached the side of the yard opposite the hole, my neighbor Goldie approached. "Yo dude, I need to holla at you."

"Go 'head."

"Over here," he indicated a patch of vacant snow. "Watch you back. Word is Chiprock gonna try cut you."

"What! Man you trippin'. What the hell for?" I struggled to bury the panic in my voice.

"Remember when you asked to see some books? And you said, 'I don't wan' talk.'" He shook his head, shrugged his shoulders. "He got offended."

"When did you hear this?" Toño asked.

Goldie thumbed over his shoulder to the Rochester area of the yard. "My peoples told me."

"That's the dumbest shit I ever heard. Just for sayin' that?"

Goldie raised a fist. "Man, those fightin' words, you heard. Specially on the gate. His homez might be ampin' him to do it, that's the word." He looked around cautiously. "You ain't heard it from me, you heard."

I clapped Goldie on the shoulder. "A'ight, good lookin' for the heads-up."

As Goldie walked away I turned to Toño: "Can you believe that?"

"Chiprock's got a complex, *oíste*. And he got position wit' Bloods, reputation, face, all dat shit." He nodded toward a neutral place by the wall. "Let's play the wall and wait for the yard to close. Too cramped to be walkin' 'round this bitch."

Great, I thought. Not only is it my first prison beef, it was with a Blood—one of the nation's most violent gangs. This situation had gone from bad to seriously messed up.

Exasperated, Toño said, "It's the gate dude. Chu gotta watch what you be sayin', peoples listenin' all the time." He went quiet for a moment.

As we stood by the cold gray wall, stomping our feet, fighting Old Man Winter from biting off our toes, I watched the yard. Men walked in protective groups of threes and fours. Other prisoners stood watching a volleyball game, Buffalo vs. Brooklyn. Bright floodlights spaced around the yard and wall cast long shadows that followed the men at their heels. The night sky hung dark gray, starless above the prison's bright lights. And as each group passed by, I imagined eyes buried in winter hoods watching me. Speculating, weighing.

Toño said, "Think he's gonna try cut chu on the flats, *oíste.* So when we line up I be behind you. Keep movin', don't stop."

"I got it. Move, get to the cell, then tomorrow see what's up."

I hope I sounded sure, unafraid. I was petrified.

A CO called over the PA system, "*Yard closed!*" and instructed everyone to line up by blocks. Toño and I walked over to the area designated for A-Block.

I made sure to look out for Chiprock. I spotted him, twenty feet behind me. Toño tapped me on the shoulder. "Remember, move."

My heart began to race when we were ordered to return to our cells. With dry mouth, jittery hands, and numbed feet, I swerved through the line, closer to the front. Every so often I glanced over my shoulder, checking Chiprock's progress.

Still there.

The line of prisoners entered through a side door next to the mess hall, then turned down the main corridor. Security cameras are evenly spaced along its length. I wondered what the CO saw at that moment.

I checked over my shoulder. Is he gaining? My mouth dry, saliva thick as cotton.

When we reached the flats, men broke from formation and scattered about while walking the narrow tier. I picked up speed, focused, and occasionally bumped a prisoner as I passed, leaving him with a pardon and excuse me.

I looked. Fifteen feet away now, gotta keep moving.

So this is how I find myself on the flats, face-off with Chiprock, his hand holding a razor, blood dripping from its edge. My ears ringing, through a red haze of rage I peer into Chiprock's eyes and release the animal within me. I look at Toño: "Fuck it, let's get 'em."

I move toward Chiprock. But to my astonishment he hands the razor off to Carlos, then melts into the crowd. Two Blood cronies take point, preventing me from getting to Chiprock.

"Hey, keep it movin'," a CO yells.

The circle breaks up and we move on again, as if nothing happened. That's when it occurs to me to check my face. With a trembling hand, I touch my check. Nothing. I rub the rest of my face and expel a sigh of relief. Did he cut himself when he hit my shoulder? A minute later, I'm in my cell.

I don't pace or sit, just stand at my gate fuming. I can't believe this motherfucker tried to cut me. I want to get him—get a knife, forget a razor—and put a hole or two in his lungs.

I'm not sure how much time passes. The only stimuli registering in my mind are the sounds of men in their cells shuffling about, and the aroma of cooking late-night meals of fish and meat.

Toño calls, "*Se*"—the shortened form of my name.

The suddenness of his voice causes me to flinch. "Yo." My hearing so acute it's as if he's in my cell.

A green knit hat lands in front of my cell with a thunk. I snatch it up, knowing exactly what it is. Untying the string holding it closed, reaching inside, I grasp the warm blade; the hat falls to the floor. Fluorescent light gleams along its edges from tip to hilt: eleven inches of chrome-plated steel. It takes me six long hours, grinding on the concrete floor, to hone the double edges. Toño and I rotate nights holding, so there's a better chance the COs won't find it.

Bright red electrical tape serves as a grip, complete with a strap to fit around the wrist. That's

Toño's idea: "There a lot of blood when you stab someone. You fucked if you drop it and you enemy get it and stab you."

Made sense to me.

I'm not calm, nor panicking, merely quiet. This situation has come to a place of no return. What can I do? There's only one choice. Carefully placing the knife under my pillow, I move on to cook a meal of rice and beans. It's amazing I have any appetite at all.

With the lid from a can of beans, I chop onions, garlic, and green peppers. An exercise in distraction. But still, fear and anticipation worry my mind. By two-forty in the morning, my body is wracked with fatigue; I fall into a restless sleep. Under the pillow lies the first shank I've ever made.

I wake not in a gentle rousing, but startled from a nightmare I can barely recall. The lingering memory is of shouting on the fringes of dream and wakefulness—I hope it was only in my dreams. My eyes open; steel bars and concrete walls greet me. I hate this stinking place.

By the light of a gray dawn I retrieve a small wash-bucket, fill it halfway with winter-cold water, drop in a heating coil, and wait. The morning is silent. An occasional flush of a toilet scatters the stillness. Blazing steam pipes sap moisture from the air and wreak havoc on my nose. It is dry and raw and oozes blood. As a child I can remember being plagued by bloody noses, once having to be taken to the hospital for hemorrhaging.

After the bleeding stops, I make my bed, straighten the cell, and wash up with warm water. Boiling water in a small hot-pot, I nurse a cup of instant coffee. I stare at the pillow, mindful of what lies beneath it. With a hand-held mirror I peer down the gallery, checking for COs, though there's still thirty minutes till the count. I have a program today, and the thought of waiting until two-thirty for my confrontation with Chiprock unnerves me.

I reach beneath the pillow with a shaky hand and grasp the blade. As my fingers meet metal, a vision emerges of thrusting wildly, recklessly, through a world of red, bloody red—liquid fire splashing the pristine snow beneath my feet. I release the blade like a hot iron, unable to reconcile necessity with fear and doubt. I sit on the edge of the bed, sipping coffee, staring at the stack of magazines, desperately trying to figure a way around this insanity.

A conversation Toño and I had a few months ago comes to mind.

"Chu know what a vest is?" asked Toño.

"What, like a bulletproof vest?"

"*Sí.* You can make one. Get magazines and tape dem 'round you chest, stomach, and back." He banged a fist along his torso. "That way it harder to stick you, *oíste.*"

I grab some magazines and line the elastic waistband of my pants, testing the range of motion and bulkiness beneath the hooded sweatshirt. I wonder if I can pass the numerous checkpoints to get to program. Hastily pulling out the magazines, tearing covers, I put them away. I can't do it. Sure, I can pass the COs, but it feels like a silent affirmation, acceptance of the dark road I'll have to travel. I see knives and blood, and suddenly the idea of having to stab Chiprock leaves me despondent.

Sitting on my bed, the only sound is the thundering of my heart. As the blood courses through my veins, doubt races through my mind. The bars close in around me. I can't take this silence anymore, and reach for my favorite Nine Inch Nails tape, *Broken*, then wait ten minutes till the count.

Just before the doors open for breakfast, I check the blade again, secured in a cardboard sheaf tied to my left forearm. Two escort officers pass my cell heading to the back of the gallery, wave all ready, and the doors open. Extending my neck, I peer to my right towards Chiprock's cell to see if he's going to breakfast. I don't want him to catch me off-guard. I don't see him. To my left, Toño steps out nonchalantly, dressed in a brown hoodie and green army jacket, and greets me with a smile. "You got it?"

"Yeah," patting my forearm.

"Good, I see you in *la yarda*, meet at the volleyball court."

Toño and I line up with the other prisoners for breakfast. I feel a looming danger. Recalling my first few weeks here—the prisoner stabbed in the lung twice, the guy cut with a can lid—I see enemies in the faces I examine as we wait. My unease mounts with each passing second. As we walk to the mess hall, I keep an eye out for metal-detector checks. The COs try to keep prisoners off-guard by randomly administering a check just before entering the mess hall or yard. Today I pass by unexamined, still in possession of my gun.

Entering the mess hall, the noise, and my paranoia, picks up considerably. Glances from men seem to say, good luck, hold your head, or, you're going down. In this place news travels fast.

After breakfast I exit the building into the cold winter wind. Frigid air numbs my lips and sets fire to my lungs. The sky is azure and a light breeze stirs the snow. As I walk to the vocational buildings, I check the men around me. When none are looking, I pull the blade and stash it in a snowbank. I can't take it with me to welding. Prior to leaving, all the prisoners are sent through a metal detector.

For six and a half hours I mindlessly work my projects. Welding pieces of metal together, not caring how well the beads are placed. Tension builds, fear slowly takes over, and that old mechanism, fight or flight, wants to kick in. Where can I run to? I could tell the COs about Chiprock, but I'd have to sign into Protective Custody (PC) and that would make me a rat. Something like that never leaves a man. No matter what prison you transfer to, or how many years pass by—you'll always be remembered as a rat. I have to face this situation, no matter the outcome. For the rest of the day the other guys in welding give me space. Alone with my thoughts, I recall going to trial and worrying about the verdict. This waiting is worse.

Two-thirty arrives. Shivering in the icy wind, I stand under a leafless tree in a small patch of snow-covered grass. It is not the cold that has me shaking. I'm hopped on adrenaline. The CO calls recreation and I walk back along the frozen sidewalk. Not caring who sees me, I quickly find the knife stashed in the snowbank. When I grab the blade it feels warm, and I wonder if that's possible after all this time lying in the snow.

As I enter the building, eight COs line up to my right and Toño's instructions come to mind. Don't look at them, walk like you're supposed to be here, as if you run this place, but never look at them. Over and over I repeat his advice and pass by, like I'm supposed to be here, it's perfectly natural to have a chrome-plated knife tied to my forearm.

I realize this is my way out. All I have to do is look nervous, make eye contact, anything to draw attention, and I won't have to worry about Chiprock. But I can't do it. How could I live the next twenty-six years behind the wall with that following me around? Guys have done just that; it's called "pulling a stunt." Instead of carrying out a beef, they conveniently get caught by COs. By the time their disciplinary sanctions are up, the situation has cooled off. I pass, and the COs don't give me a second glance.

Exiting the yard door, I head straight toward the volleyball court. The sun reflects glaringly off the white snow. As my eyes sweep the yard, I'm taken aback by the number of men. There must be four hundred. I wonder if they all came out to watch the spectacle. There is a cruel fascination in watching a prison beef transpire, like driving by a car wreck. You can't avert your eyes. Toño and a group of guys are huddled in a circle. They look up as I approach. Some slip away.

"*Oye*, it all good?" Toño asks.

"All good. What up wit' Chiprock?"

"I talk wit' him and leader of Bloods." He nods in the direction of the hole. "Says he leave you alone, but you gotta pay 'em a hundred dollars a month."

"Get the fuck outta here, you serious?" The idea of paying him anything offends me, and in that moment anger kicks in, the best counter to fear. "I ain't payin' shit."

"I know that, an' wouldn't let chu, *oíste*. How you live if you did?" With hands in pockets he shrugs his shoulders. "What chu wanna' do?" The look in his eyes and tone of his voice says it all—there is no choice.

I look around at the men assembled on the volleyball court. They watch, weighing, examining me. I finally realize what this is really about. I'm new, and they don't know what I'll do. So they maintain a safe distance. I'm sure some want to help, but if I won't fight my own battles, stand up for my respect, I'll be a liability to their reputations.

Toño asks, "What you thinkin'?"

"You know. Go tell 'em to meet me in the hole."

Is that satisfaction I see in his eyes?

As Toño walks to the hole, I notice two groups of Puerto Ricans shadowing him a short distance away, like an army force securing the perimeter. It seems Toño's safety is threatened as well. I notice other groups of Latinos gathered. Some wearing the yellow hoodies of the Latin Kings. While others are Ñetas, and neutrals, those not affiliated with any of the gangs. What's their interest in this fight?

While I wait for Toño to return, I check the tension of the yard. It is visible. Too many men are playing the wall. Cliques are gathered in their designated turfs; the Rochester crew has gathered to see what will happen to one of their own. The usual noise is controlled in anticipation. That's when I notice something else—where are the COs? They usually walk the yard in groups of threes. I spot them gathered at the entrance of the tower. Twelve guards, gloved and gripping their batons, watching the yard. They feel it too. Ready to move suddenly and violently.

After a ten-minute wait, Toño returns. "He say okay, meet at the hole." He grabs my arm, looks me in the eye with resolve: "Keep the wrap 'round you wrist. Stab up to his chest or face. He got lot of clothes on. But if he don' come in *cinco* minutes, come back." That last part is strange, but I don't say anything.

"Okay," is all I can muster. Gripping the blade in my army-coat pocket, I make my last walk to the hole—the farthest spot from the tower. I pick out a place undisturbed by tracks; the snow, almost knee deep, fills my boots. I am hot, sweating, oblivious to the cold. When I reach the wall, I lean against it, right foot propped up, and wait.

In this moment a thought occurs to me. I should be home, not in prison. Not in this crazy place. I should be playing on my ice-hockey team, at prom with my girlfriend, having fun with friends. I may not live past seventeen. I could die today, in this yard. The heartbreak would surely destroy my aunt. She's barely holding on now.

Five minutes pass. I don't see Chiprock anywhere. Every eye in the yard is trained on me, waiting, anticipating a gladiatorial event. From deep within I muster up courage, or insanity, and wait an extra five minutes.

When I look over in Toño's direction, he flags me to come back. I reach him and he pulls me aside. "I'll go see what up, *oíste*." He walks to the assembled Bloods. In the group I spot Chiprock dressed in a red hoodie, green army coat, and red sweatpants—he doesn't look my way. After a few minutes Toño returns.

"Dis mother-fucker's a cower. Chu know he go home in two weeks? He don' wanna figh' chu." He laughs, "Said it no fair cuz you too small. Hey, I tol' you come back in five minutes."

"I heard you, but I felt like waiting."

"Chu crazy, but that was good, it show *cajones*, you got *cajones*. I think it scare him a little." He laughs again. "Okay. Bloods say you gotta fight one they people."

Shaking my head, on the verge of growling, "Hold on. My beef's wit' him. Fuck these dudes gotta do wit' it?"

"I know, but dis the way it is." Hands and shoulders shrug in one motion: What can you do?

"This is crazy." But I have committed myself. My anger drives me further down this rabbit hole. I need to send a message—violent as possible—that I won't be anyone's victim. I have to prove that in this upside-down kingdom I can get just as crazy as the next guy. "Fine, who?" I ask Toño.

"Day say a guy in a purple hoodie will come. Remember everythin' I say"—his eyes gleaming.

For the second time I make my way to the hole. A little calmer, my heart beats a little slower, soothed by necessity and anger. I lean up against the wall and wait: a posture of violence in check. Men gather in their areas, the guards by the tower. To my left I see a purple hoodie approach. I will do this. Then three more men in purple hoodies join him. My body stiffens. I hear a grinding in the distance and realize it's my teeth. Slowly I unclench my jaw and tighten the grip upon my knife. I'm not going to live past the next few minutes; I have never been more sure of anything. I should have known it wouldn't be a fair fight.

As the purple hoodies approach, they look in my direction, glaring and eyeballing me. But they continue on past, around a bend, and head back to the group of Bloods. Confused, I look over at Toño. He shrugs his shoulders. He's just as confused. As the purple hoodies join the group of Bloods, I check my watch—five minutes. I decide to leave, not wanting to press my good fortune. I don't know what happened and I don't really care. I thank God, the gods, and all the sacred beings in the universe.

Walking up to Toño, I catch myself from slipping on a patch of ice. "What the hell happened?"

"*Yo no se*, but I find out." He wobbles over to the group of Bloods. His waving hands tell me he's not happy. After ten minutes he returns.

"Beef's off. You did it, faced 'em, an' he wan' no *problemas*. Oh yeah," he laughs, amused, "he cut he's thumb last night when he try cut you."

I nod. I feel the pent-up anger, fear, and anticipation straining for release. Outwardly, for those who are watching, I act as if it doesn't matter that the beef is off. Inside I feel like Rocky, like jumping up and down with both fists in the air atop the steps of Liberty Hall.

Toño continues, "But don' sleep 'round Chiprock. They could be tryin' to fool you into believin' all's good."

"Yeah, I know. Rockin' me to sleep and get me when I ain't lookin'."

"Yo, po-po commin'," someone says.

A group of COs are heading in our direction. Toño reaches his hand out to me. "*Dame esa pistola.*"

I pass him the knife, and he passes it off to another Puerto Rican who sticks it into a nearby snowbank.

"Everyone stay where you are," one of the guards shouts, while another points to me: "You, get on the ground now, asshole!"

Quickly I lie on the ground while four COs approach with handcuffs. The others sift through the snowbanks. A warm blanket of relief envelops me. I have survived; that's all that matters. I stood up for my respect.

The COs found the knife and I was "keep-locked," confined to my cell pending a disciplinary hearing. Charged with passing a weapon, I escaped a possession charge because I wasn't the last person to have it. I received sixty days keep-lock, the regular time for first possession. It was a small price to pay for my respect from the other prisoners.

Before I was released from keep-lock, Toño had a beef with another Blood on the gallery. On his way to breakfast he stabbed a guy in the face and neck with two pens.

Goldie got into an argument in the yard over a basketball game. In classic prison style he got cut from behind. It would be twelve years before I saw him again. He passed away a month ago.

Chiprock pulled a stunt and received three months keep-lock. He did it so he wouldn't have to leave his cell before going home.

Over the next year and a half, I had many more situations. The last earned me a ten-month keep-lock for weapon possession. Transferred again, I was sent to Attica. On the bus ride, my mind reinvented the mayhem: stabbing, cutting, extortion. A few weeks prior to my arrival, a prisoner had been stabbed to death in a stairwell—a portentous note to arrive on.

I emerged from keep-lock emotionally and psychologically shut down. Waiting all those months, day after day, for release back into general population created an irrational fear of violence lurking around every corner. I expected all-out war. However, the COs run Attica with an iron fist. More confined and controlled, there is the usual stabbing and cutting, but it's not as frequent. A prison's reputation has a way of growing larger than life.

I never expected to see anyone from Great Meadow again. Prison is like that. You meet guys, make friendships, or enemies, but in the end everyone either goes home, dies, or transfers to another prison.

I was surprised to see Toño in the yard one day, walking toward me with that wobbling gait. It was good to see a familiar face, but a cloud of violence followed him and I worried about its shadow. Toño and I caught up. He told me about Chiprock: two weeks after his release he was gunned down.

Toño didn't last long at Attica. An enemy from his past caught up with him. While he was at lunch, his cell was set on fire. Prison security placed him in Involuntary Protective Custody. I haven't seen him since.

With the constant problems I was having with prisoners and COs, I knew two things with certainty: one, I would not survive another extended keep-lock; and two, by the law of averages, it was only a matter of time before I killed a prisoner—or was killed.

Even understanding that, I failed to notice the cloud of violence I had gathered over my head—until it rained down upon me. After getting into an argument with another prisoner, he attempted to stab me in a shower stall. Somehow I managed to escape unscathed and the COs none the wiser. Thankfully several influential prisoners mediated the beef. One happened to be a Blood. (Go figure.) That was the last straw. I had enough of constantly looking over my shoulder for enemies, new and old.

Since this last incident I have been—to use a phrase from my peers—on some "Chuck Chillout shit," staying out of fights. Still, I know I'm never far from the next beef. And the descent into savagery is swift.

Ticket In

JULIUS KIMYA HUMPHREY, SR., *California*

THE SHAPING OF A CONVICT

"Boy . . . what'cha doin' back there?"

"Nuttin' mama," I yelled in response to her call from the living room that also served as her bedroom. This was an arrangement made in 1961, when I was four years old. In a jealous rage, my father shot my mother several times one night at a club, leaving her paralyzed and with two options: she could either lie in her bed or sit in her wheelchair. Unfortunately for my siblings and me, her disability would eventually open the door for pimps, prostitutes, addicts, and hustlers to waltz into our lives.

In the club that night in Stockton, California, the moment my father pulled the trigger, the possibilities for who I could be shifted in a new direction. He was born in 1912 or 1914 in the Deep South, at a time when Black men were still being brutally murdered for looking at white women. I can imagine anger rooted in his heart long before he met my mother. He didn't realize it then, but the decision he made that night began the process of me being shaped into a convict. It wasn't long before I became a criminal, and in 1979, when I was twenty-one years old, I found myself in Soledad State Prison, serving a five-to-life sentence. Considering all the wrong I had done, any number of things could have sent me away, but in the end it was my addiction to drugs and alcohol that would begin my decades of incarceration, and in 1998 lock me in a cell forever under California's "Three Strikes" law. When my father injured my mother, he created situations, circumstances, and a lifestyle for me and my siblings that injured us both physically and mentally, and the only rehabilitation the system gave us was incarceration.

While my mother lay in a rehabilitation center in Lodi, California, recovering from her injuries, my siblings and I were sent to live with other family members, who wanted nothing to do with us because we were Black. My mother was Miwok Indian, born on the reservation near Angels Camp, California, in 1921. I remember she told me that she had very little schooling, and I wonder if that played a role in her decision to place my siblings and me in the care of her first son from an earlier marriage, along with his wife, who were both Indian. They became our first foster parents, and the things we experienced while we lived with them have haunted me my entire life, and some things are still too painful to speak about. I remember when one of us would wet the bed while sleeping, in the morning we would be marched out on the back porch, naked. No matter what the condition, cold, fog, or rain, we would stand there holding hands, cuddled together. I vaguely remember the way the events unfolded because I could not have been more than six years old. I believe that the only reason some events remain woven in my thoughts today, unforgotten and so strong, is because the experience was never treated professionally. The system failed because it never asked us, "How do you feel?" Writing about it now is my rehabilitation. I remember standing on the old wooden porch with no shoes or socks on, feet cold, shaking, looking through the railing down at the growling pit bulls that patrolled the back yard.

The Indian woman who should have been caring for my siblings and me while our brother

54

was at work beat and abused us daily. When Child Protection Services (CPS) finally came to our rescue, we were so malnourished, with sores covering our heads, we had to be hospitalized. Then things began to change and we were placed in our first and only real foster home, there in Stockton, owned by an older Black couple named Mr. and Mrs. Jackson. It was there that my siblings and I fully recovered and started looking like human beings again. Then after a few years passed, our mother arrived and moved us a couple cities away from Stockton to Sacramento, and as a youngster I learned things that under normal conditions I would not have known anything about until I entered my teens.

When I think back to my youth, I see that I had many adult responsibilities before even grad-uating from grammar school. I recall coming home from Del Paso Heights Elementary one day, and having my mother appoint me to cook our Thanksgiving turkey. So I tied my wagon to the back of my Stingray bicycle, both of which I built from discarded used parts, and off to the store I went. Once there, all alone, I shopped. I bought one fat twenty-pound turkey, cornmeal, lard, and a few other items before heading home.

In the living room my mother sat up in her bed, looking into the kitchen where I stood at the table, and through the noise of my siblings she shouted at me how to prepare our turkey. Following her instructions, I separated the long neck, heart, and liver that were neatly wrapped and tucked safely inside its hollow body. I boiled them and added some diced parsley, celery, oregano, and a pinch of salt and pepper in one big pot to make the dressing. I carefully chopped up the neck, heart, and liver and mixed everything together with the fresh baked cornbread. Then I heated the lard until it melted, added a small amount of salt and pepper before it could harden, and bathed the turkey with it. From that year forward I was the one who cooked every turkey that came into our home, and it felt good to receive all the accolades for my cooking, es-pecially at such a young age. Each of us children prepared something: one of my brothers boiled potatoes while another baked the ham, but my youngest sister who still lived at home was the best cook. My mother had turned her into a master chef.

During that time in the '60s, my siblings and I grew up fast in Sacramento, and many who read this will agree that we grew up too fast. I was no more than seven years old when I discov-ered what "going all the way" meant. Our home had become a hangout for all the criminals that infested our neighborhood streets after the nightclubs closed. Unable to sleep, I would watch one sex scene after another in the bed across from mine. The box springs squeaked loud and fast, keeping pace with the foot-stomping James Brown tune that blared from our one-speaker record player. The streetlight found its way through the torn sheet that hung as a curtain in front of the window, exposing the unknown prostitute with her legs pinned back against the wall, moaning out loud while a desperate man pounded in and out of her. Neither one of them was concerned that I, a little boy, lay only a few feet away. But it was those events that would arouse my curi-osity about sex. What a way for any child to learn about the "birds and the bees." It tarnished my concept of sex with a woman when I became active. What I saw when I was a child did not teach me to respect women, so I didn't value a woman's love.

Some nights I would get out of bed and maneuver my way through the uninvited guests who would be partying at our house, and through the smoke-filled rooms until I reached my mother's bed. There I would sit on the floor beside it while she patted my head. I would sit there and watch the strangers dance while the masquerade of faces slipped in and out of my bedroom. I knew no one. I often sat there until the sunlight reached over the horizon, embracing me with its warm rays.

Many mornings our family's refrigerator and kitchen cabinets would be empty because of a wild party the night before. With no food to relieve the hunger in my stomach, I would walk through the rooms and collect the beer, wine, and whiskey bottles, and empty their contents into a tall mayonnaise jar and drink it. Then after kissing and saying goodbye to my mother, I would go to school and play marbles in the dirt with the other kids, drunk. What I didn't know then was that I had laid the foundation for my first addiction. This is one of many things that until now I've told no one. But I know, at the same time, the experience was shared silently by my siblings, who also hold untold secrets in their hearts.

It was nice being back with my family in Sacramento, but life was hard. There were times I wished I had been back in the huge soft bed I slept in all alone when I lived at the Jacksons' foster home, waking up knowing that I would eat breakfast every morning. The smell of the fresh homemade biscuits that flowed from the oven down the hall, under the bedroom door, and into my nostrils made me hungry. I would lie in bed and envision my foster mother, "Mama Jackson," spreading butter on the hot biscuits. It melted and ran down the sides. I felt safe lying in my bed at the Jacksons' home. The sound of birds chirping outside my window comforted my young heart and made it hard for me to pull the covers back and crawl out of bed, but the smell of the biscuits was irresistible. I didn't know then that my life was about to head downhill again. Living in Sacramento with my mother, I stayed in trouble; so did some of my brothers, and it wasn't long before our bad behavior made us wards of the court. We didn't realize it, but we were already being shaped into convicts. The juvenile court system knew it. It just had other names it used to describe us. And all this happened before I turned ten years old.

The neighborhood my family settled in when we moved to Sacramento was Del Paso Heights, and it quickly pulled us into a life of crime and incarceration. I was around ten when school began to no longer hold any significance for me, though I cannot say with certainty that it ever did. I do believe that because of the way my brothers and I were behaving, the juvenile court was preparing to place us back into foster care. Then a small-time hustler from Chicago, who my siblings and I came to know as "Uncle Bob," rose up out of the group of people who would invade our home with their all-night parties, to help our mother raise us. When my brothers and I would get in trouble and find ourselves sitting in front of a judge, Uncle Bob would be the one there to support us because our mother's condition left her unable to attend.

"Okay!" the judge shouted, his voice roaring like the wizard in *The Wizard of Oz*. "I've been told that you want to assist in the care of these children, is that correct, Mr. . . . let me see here—Mayhew . . . yes, Mr. Mayhew?"

"Yes, your honor, that's correct."

"All right then. I'm releasing them into your custody. Maybe you can make a difference in their lives. Good luck."

"Thank you, your honor."

I don't know how many times Uncle Bob came to our rescue, but he kept coming, and the years kept passing. Then I turned fourteen years old, and the juvenile court started sending my brothers away. One at a time I watched three of them sent to the Carson Creek Boy's Ranch to serve time. Uncle Bob continued to lend his support, but by then we had strayed too far from his reach. Our way of thinking and surviving in the world had already formed. We had become criminals in every sense of the word, and it wasn't long before I ended up at the Boy's Ranch too. I was out of control and did whatever I wanted, and I no longer listened to my mother or Uncle Bob. By then I had already spent most of my life in the custody of the juvenile system, and in the back of my mind I was visualizing myself in the penitentiary. After all, I was the big fourteen. My experiences up to that point told me that I was already a man. I had convinced myself even more by spending that summer with my girlfriend in the back seat of her parents' car, practicing everything I saw in my bedroom in earlier years. Then, after another all-nighter, early one morning she hit me with the news.

"'Em pregnant," she whispered.

With the car windows fogged from heavy breathing, we laid there sweating while our hands and arms slipped from each other's bodies. Lying there in love or lust, it made no difference to me, and after the rush from the sex high began to subside, I remember saying, "Pregnant! Girl . . . yoe mama gunna kill you." Then, already addicted to heroin and drowning in alcohol, I was finally sentenced to serve time at the Boy's Ranch. My whole life had grown to be centered around hustling, getting high, and sex, and no, I had never been faithful to my girlfriend, and she knew it. Days after being released I became a father, and I was only fifteen, desperately needing one myself. My heroin use had only gotten worse while incarcerated, so after arriving at my mother's house I unpacked and made love to my girlfriend, and then out the door I went. A young sista who had worked the streets for me before my incarceration was waiting on me. I simply ventured deeper into the criminal activity I had been a part of before. I hustled hard and manipulated every young woman who listened to me, and before too long my criminal behavior was at full speed again.

During the day I would take the young sista shoplifting at the malls in Sacramento, and at night I would take her to one old-timer's house after another, so she could trade sex for money in order to keep our addiction under control. Many times during the day she would team up with one of my brother's girls, and when they returned they would have thousands of dollars worth of merchandise to sell. None of us ever used our earnings to rise above the poverty we lived in, because we were ignorant in the lifestyle we lived, and everyone in our circle was using heroin and cocaine, and drinking alcohol all day.

My life continued down the same road of addiction and criminal activity uninterrupted for the next four years, and then my older brother from my mother's first marriage was murdered. He had been rising as a drug dealer after he separated from the Indian woman who abused us, and moved to Sacramento. A few of his own childhood friends were later convicted for taking his life. The police had been called to a remote area on the outskirts of Sacramento, where a smoldering car was found by morning workers on their way to the hop fields. After a long and grueling investigation, it was determined that the motive was robbery. When my brother was finally buried, I could see my mother's own life coming to its end every time I looked into her eyes, but I didn't want to acknowledge the inevitable. My brother's murder broke her heart, and she lay there wounded by her loss, unconcerned with the world around her. My attempts to cheer her up were ineffective, and she appeared to be disconnected from the reality of everyday life. It was as if she had already crossed over to wherever our souls go when we die, and closed the door behind her.

One morning after arriving home around 2 A.M. from a party, I sat by my mother's bed, on the floor, the same way I did when I was a little boy, and we spoke about our lives, past and present, as well as our good and bad times. Before retiring for the night I gave her her medication, along with a tumbler of ice tea, which she loved. Then I kissed her goodnight and walked into my bedroom to the crib where my son lay sleeping. I stood there looking down at him, and I heard his mother call my name, almost at a whisper. As I turned around, the dim light cast from the lamp on a nightstand next to our bed allowed me to see her beautiful Black body lying there on top of the blankets, waiting for me. Every night was the same. She never went to sleep without us making love. We were each other's first lovers, and when it came down to us having sex, enough was never enough.

"JuJu . . . wake up. Sump'in wrong wit yoe mama," my girlfriend shouted. I opened my eyes to find the morning well upon me, but I wasn't rested. The night before, my girl had proved to be more than I expected. Still, like I had grown to see in my mother and other women, she rose with the dawn every morning with a certain resilience and determination to do all the amazing things that women do.

Jumping out of bed I ran to my mother's side and found her unresponsive to my efforts to wake her. Did she purposely fall to sleep without taking her medication? She knew the consequences.

Once at the hospital, I looked down upon my mother with eyes filled with tears. The doctor standing in the room calmly informed everyone present that she was comatose, and most likely would not recover. A few months later she died without ever regaining consciousness. She passed away a few weeks after my twenty-first birthday. I spiraled out of control even more. I believe my mother gave up her will to live. Losing her first-born child, witnessing the bad lives the rest of us were living, and considering her own condition, she must have decided not to take her medication. The unusual conversation we had the night I returned home late from a party was her way of saying goodbye. Afterwards, she just closed her eyes and rode out the storm that she had too long lived in.

It was 1978, and another winter was approaching as I sat alone in my mother's house. My entire family, including the young women who had been a part of my brother's and my life and used to roam the hallway, were all gone. Every move I made echoed off the walls of the empty rooms, the silence my only company. Even my girlfriend had packed up and left, disappearing with our son while I was away one night. It was just my addictions and me, sitting in the house that morning. Neglected bills after my mother's death caused the cold from outside to wrap around me like a blanket. The only insulation I had to protect me was the heroin and alcohol that flowed in my veins. Then, just when I began to feel like I had nothing to live for, God blessed me. Another beautiful Black young woman, who would also be the mother of my youngest son, came into my life. I didn't recognize it as a blessing at the time—drug addicts rarely do. Still, she helped me pack up my personal belongings, and moved me in with her and her young son. She became the love of my life. After my addictions destroyed our relationship, my feelings for her never faded, and to this day she remains rooted in my heart.

I stayed semi-drunk, never sober enough to realize I was an alcoholic. It wasn't long before I found myself back behind steel bars. But after everything I had been through, prison was right where I wanted to be. I was who I wanted to be; I was a convict. Everything that had happened in my life up to that point, beginning with the night my father shot my mother, shaped me more and more each day into a convict. As a young man I had looked forward to graduating from high school and joining the army.

So here I am in Soledad State Prison, lying on the bunk in the single cell that's assigned to me. With my feet crossed and hands folded behind my head, I take a deep breath. In reality I am incarcerated. But here, away from the everyday drug and alcohol use that came along with the lifestyle I had lived before coming to prison, my incarceration makes me feel more free than I have felt in years.

Coping with Life in Prison City

INTRODUCTION

The next two clusters of essays—"Coping with Life in Prison City" and "Seeking Peace in Prison City"—may seem so closely related as to collapse into one. But in allowing them to do so, we would fail to appreciate the important difference between the labor required to survive life inside, and efforts to give that life some meaning. The life inside Prison City may be different from life elsewhere, but one constant binds us: we endure each day from inside our own minds, attempting to manage the things over which we have some control—thoughts, memories, emotions, attitudes—in order to make better lives for ourselves. As "The Life" has shown, Prison City carries the peculiar challenges of an environment filled with troubled and often hostile men and women (both incarcerated people and staff) living in conditions bound to multiply the chances for open conflict, and certain to impose less visible but no less debilitating psychic wear. In these circumstances, the resilience that incarcerated Americans show in coping with their circumstances might teach us all things worth knowing about the weight that people can bear, and how, and for how long.

A. Whitfield's "It Could be Me" is a deeply sober meditation inspired by news of the killing of one prisoner by another. This act of violence sets off thoughts that the author must both engage and tightly control in order to retain hold on the self-understanding and resolve he has earned by accepting the weight of having taken a life—work carried out despite living among callous men in a callous institution. Here as elsewhere in this volume, we see the seriousness with which some men and women enter into self-searching in order to retain a hold on whatever constructive parts of themselves they can salvage under the weight of their crimes and the life that prison offers as a result of those crimes.

Robert F. Piwowar's essay, "A Lesson in Language," is ostensibly about learning foreign languages in prison and learning the language *of* prison; but beneath its good humor, the essay also shows that part of the labor of coping with life inside means simply paying attention to where one lives, accepting the lessons this environment has to offer rather than regretting what one may be missing from a former life, and retaining a quiet intellectual curiosity even as the chaos of Prison City rains about one's ears.

Incarcerated people must cope as they can with the psychological challenges of life in prison. They are also too often confronted with the unwillingness of prison staff to allow the practical necessities to make this life safe and an experience that will aid return to a constructive life outside. As Martin G. Gann describes it in "One Small Voice through the Wall," this is a particularly acute challenge for men and women managing physical handicaps—in this case severe hearing loss: a loss that puts Gann in real danger from day to day, and directly affects his ability to communicate with family, whose support is vital to any man or woman hoping for a successful life outside prison walls.

In "Food for Thought," B. G. Jacobs revisits his childhood memories of helping his Puerto Rican grandmother cook *pastelios* in the company of his extended family. He then describes the difficult and risky work required to reconnect with that time inside his cell. In this essay we get a hint of the ingenuity and creativity that incarcerated people must exercise in pursuit of the simplest goals. Jacobs also demonstrates that in prison, one must learn to find pleasure in the very thought of a reward and the work required to achieve it, because no results are ever sure in the face of the exercises of power and control under which the incarcerated live.

Stephen Whetzel witnesses the life-changing power of the relationships that can be created between incarcerated people and those on the outside who know each other only through letters. The events in "A Renaissance" begin with the goodwill and advice offered to Whetzel by a prison counselor, who insists that the author make contact with the world outside. Here, as in B. G. Jacobs's essay, we see the extraordinary lengths to which incarcerated people are willing to go in order to create some semblance of the lives and relationships they need in order to resist institutionalization.

Dean Faiello's "Impermanence" starts with a description of the author's work in a discussion group, with outside volunteers, that helps prisoners work through the issues they face while enduring incarceration. His essay offers a sampling of how various men in a maximum-security prison cope with this life. Faiello must also negotiate with his own reactions when the unpredictable jealousies and resentments carried by men who have nothing else to hold onto slap back his efforts to help others as well as himself. This essay presents a man coping with the material, social, and psychological challenges of prison. In addressing them, he attempts to take the next step, to seek an abiding peace amid the madness of prison life.

In all of these essays, we see again the labor required to make life inside America's most debilitating city into a life in more than name; and we see that each incarcerated person must do this in his own way.

A. WHITFIELD, *New York*

IT COULD BE ME

There was a young man killed in here a couple of days ago. A gray day, like any other day in the joint. A-Block, where the killing took place, is one of five cold, dark, dank cellblocks in Antioch. The soft beige of the surrounding walls, the polished terrazzo floors, and pale windows belie the character of those within. A is notorious for housing the most violent and callous among us—gangbangers, chicken hawks, the indifferent, and, unfortunately, many arriving straight from reception: lambs staked in the middle of the wolves' den. When the A.M. chow bell rings and you step from your cell onto a company that seems to stretch on endlessly, forty-four killers step out with you, and you'll never feel more alone. That's how this young man got it: stepped out the morning after he arrived and bang, right in the heart.

That same day I was standing in line, waiting to place my weekly phone call home, and I remember thinking, "Some mother woke to some awful bad news this morning."

In all of the talk I have heard concerning the stabbing—the boy, twenty, was dead before he hit the ground—I have yet to hear any concern for him or his family; no sympathy, no anger. At afternoon chow I heard an old-timer, covered with inked skulls and twisted barbed wire, wax philosophical to another illustrated con, "Well that goes to show ya—Ya snooze, ya lose." In the prison library a young, fresh-faced kid, probably no older than the dead kid, whispered to another in a tremulous voice; he'd heard it was a case of mistaken identity—the killer thought he was someone else. Most conversations center on who did the stabbing and how much time he might get in the box.

We identify with perpetrator rather than the victim, even though the victim is one of us. It scares the hell out of me to think this. But then I ask myself, "What do you expect?"

I have been moldering away in one prison or another since 1985, and have seen too many die, both young and old. I can no longer envision myself waking up in the morning, brushing my teeth, dressing (can I wear these socks a second day?), stepping out of my cell, and driving a piece of steel through a man's chest. There was a time, not too long ago, when I could have done it without a second thought.

Now I find myself contemplating the feeling this young man had as that steel pierced his heart. What were the last thoughts that passed through his mind? Did he know he was dead before he was dead?

His last thoughts, if he had time for them, must surely have been of his son or daughter, for the mother who gave him life. Or are these just the thoughts I would have; was he so different from me that his last thoughts would be of something I cannot comprehend? I'm sitting here in my cell as I write this, staring at a paint-chipped yellow wall alive with pictures of my daughter's childhood, years that I've known only through pictures and an occasional letter or phone call. She's twenty now, and I try to recall what the world looked like to me when I was that age. Even through a drug-addled mind I rarely thought of death—I enjoyed a young man's promise of long life, not a life sentence. Now, in my fifties, I'm fast approaching the end of the latter. I've read that once one reaches fifty or thereabouts, the thought of death begins to occupy one's imagination more often. I know I think about it all the time.

I can't help but wonder how awful those last few moments must have been for the man I killed. (I have long since accepted responsibility for the act.) The thought is repugnant to me, and I tell myself with conviction and sincerity that the creature I was then is not the man I am now. I am more of a human being for detesting and condemning my actions, yet less of a human being for having committed the act.

I struggle. Transformation is difficult in any environment, but in prison the helplessness and hopelessness can be overwhelming. I am often beset with feelings of doubt and guilt and pain and fear. I sometimes doubt not only my ability but my resolve to make the right choices in life. It pains me at times to confront what I could have been and what I have in fact become. And I have to face the fear that my newfound concept of what it is to be human is an illusion, that it is fostered by mistaken beliefs, that I will be forced to confront obstacles too large for me to overcome, and not have the moral strength to sustain my humanity. I'm scared I'll wake up one morning to look in the mirror and see the monster that was once me staring back, ready to devour me.

Some would say that I should let go of the guilt so the healing process can begin. But I don't want to heal. I deserve to carry this guilt around with me until the day that I die. I refuse to be consumed by it, but it is part of me, as big a part as any virtue or conscience I may now possess. It serves as a reminder of what I was then and what I never want to be again.

The sky is burning into a purplish-orange twilight as the evening-count bell rings, pulling me to my feet to stand as I have stood thousands of times before. All is quiet but for the jingling of keys and padding of shoes as the guards make their way up the company, lips silently moving as they pass by one inmate after another. When they have gone, I pour a cup of coffee and return to the cooling sheets of my bunk. Soon I'll hear the dull, metallic clunk-clank signaling the opening of the cell gates for the evening rec', but I won't stir. I take a sip of cold coffee. In the last few years I venture from my cell less and less. Watching other men pass, sliced up by the bars of my cell, I know that I won't find the solace I seek by walking circles around the prison yard.

ROBERT F. PIWOWAR, *New York*

A LESSON IN LANGUAGE

Incarceration has forced me to postpone my plans for traveling to the continents of Europe and Asia. Six years into a twenty-year sentence, watching *Globe Trekker* on PBS or flipping through vacation mags in the prison library is the closest I get to real travel. But I try to pay attention to where I am, and I've found that prison is its own foreign land, complete with its very own language.

My travels to Quebec and Mexico taught me that every street sign, television or radio program, menu, and all product packaging provide lessons in language. Simply going about a regular routine in a foreign land, the language teaches itself to you. This form of pedagogy may not be as systematic as buying a Rosetta Stone DVD or enrolling in a Finnish 101 course, but it gets the job done. Infants learn to speak a language in a similar way, interacting with the people and world immediately around them.

My ideas about what constitutes language have changed greatly in the harsh environs of a maximum-security prison. Body language reveals mood and character more than the spoken word. It's important to observe, and express oneself with care. Being marked as a tourist here can be costly.

Facial tics, clenched jaw or fists, a cold stare, even a wave of the hand can convey meanings that lead to violence. I've learned the art and science of reading people, how to listen intently even when not being addressed, how to discern silent signs of anger, fear.

Yet even behind thick, thirty-foot-high concrete walls and razor-sharp concertina wire, conventional foreign languages are also available. Spanish *novellas* or variety shows on Univision provide daily opportunities to learn juicy phrases such as *Tenga cuidado!* (watch your step) or *buena suerte* (good luck) or *No hay vida sin fatigas* (there's no life without hardships).

For those truly motivated and fortunate enough to receive a call-out to the library—the equivalent of winning the daily lotto numbers—one can check out a beginner's Spanish or French textbook.

Speaking with my friend Max, who grew up in Colombia, has accelerated my understanding.

Max is in his mid-fifties and enjoys a calm, friendly disposition. Gray hair and round glasses give him a scholarly look. He's been "down" (in prison) over twenty-two years. Young Latino prisoners address him as "*Viejo.*"

I often engage him in Spanish while we sit in the dayroom, waiting to go to program or to the yard.

"*Buenos días, Max. Como está?*"

"*Muy bien, Bobby. Está bien?*"

"*Así, así, otro día en la vecindad.*"

(So, so, another day in the neighborhood.)

We have acclimated ourselves to the neighborhood of prison and its language. Correction officers are referred to as "COs," "hacks" or "police" when they're not present. A prisoner despises the term "inmate," preferring "convict" or "prisoner." A prison sentence is a "bid." Anything modeled into a weapon is a "shank" or "gun." A "bug" or "bug-out" is a crazy or insane person. A bug-out with a shank is a dangerous combination.

The dayroom we sit in is a twenty-five by twenty foot area at the front of two galleries in honor block. Furnished with black vinyl couches, overstuffed chairs, round Formica tables, and a large color TV, it's a casual place to converse. The concrete floor is painted a rustic red hue.

About ten people sit waiting for the hall captain to call for honor block yard over the squawk box inside the CO's bubble. Honor block is a small section of the prison reserved for those who have demonstrated a pattern of good behavior during their bids. It accommodates roughly seven percent of the population. Honor block affords us privileges: larger cells, more time out of our cells, unlimited showers, cooking facilities, refrigerators, and a private yard. The rest of the prison populace get two showers a week, no access to cookware or refrigerators, and far less movement from their cramped cells.

Max is speaking to Shabib, a fortyish, balding man from Turkey. I've learned some Turkish and Arabic from him, but nothing of any consequence. I've found that unless I practice a language frequently, I tend to forget it. Shabib speaks in a clipped, distorted English, often blurring pronunciations. He often asks me to help him.

"I have a new stragedy to work out," he says to me and Max.

"What's your new tragedy?" I ask.

Max laughs heartily.

Shabib says, "What, I say something wrong?" exchanging glances with us.

"The correct word," I say, "is strat-e-gy. So, what's your new workout plan?"

"Yes, yes, my plan. Thank you very much Bobby. Now I do light weight, many, many reps. No heavy, only light, much reps."

Our conversation is interrupted by two short rings of an alarm bell. A fight has broken out somewhere in the prison. We return to the gallery—a security routine that everyone knows. The rumor mill begins immediately. I hear someone say it's a fight in C-Block, while another insists with vehemence that it's in D-Block. I think about Seneca's essay "On Noise," where he speaks about empty vessels and mindless chatter. From our vantage point in front of long windows and bars that border our gallery, I can see COs moving quickly through the corridor toward A-Block.

"They don't call A-Block Afghanistan for nuthin'," Panama says. "Shit's always poppin' off."

Panama is a short Spanish kid (under twenty-five) with spiked hair. He goes by "Panama" because he says he was born there, but he doesn't speak a lick of Spanish. Most of us doubt that he's from Panama. Prisons mirror society's deceits. Prisoners alter their history, pad their exploits, embellish stories, outright lie. We have our own language for this too. We call it freestyling, fronting, being a stunter, or truth-twister with lip blisters.

Everyone on our gallery is looking out the windows, trying to figure out which gallery in A-Block the fight is on. Jorge, a rotund fellow, emerges from his cell. His bleary eyes tell us he just awoke. Bumping into Max in a groggy state, he asks, "*Que paso?*"

"*Tontería!*" (foolishness) Max snaps. "*Acuéstate!*" (go back to bed).

Laughter erupts.

"Yeah man, take yo' ass back to bed," his neighbor says.

A running commentary evolves around the bells breaking our routine.

"People be wilyin', son."

"Problee the po-lease beatin' on someone for nuthin'."

"This shit is crazy."

"Another day in the neighborhood," I say.

Everything will be on hold until the "all clear" is given. This could be in as few as twenty minutes for a minor skirmish, or as long as all morning in a rare major fight.

"Man, my stragedy is messed up," Shabib says.

Prison language transitions over time. Some terms endure while others fade away. Recently I heard an antiquated yet accurate word to describe some prisoners. An old-timer told a friend, "That guy Sonny is really 'chateauing' up in honor block." Then he added, "Yeah, he's 'stretching out,' let me tell ya." Both terms mean someone who's relaxing during their bid, more concerned with personal comforts, food, and leisure than anything else.

The flipside of chateauing in honor block is "the box," officially known as special housing unit (SHU). Fighting with a weapon or getting a dirty urine test are the two most common routes to the box. There, nearly all privileges are stripped away, personal property is denied, any belongings confiscated. You spend twenty-three hours a day in a rancid cell, most likely next door to a bug-out. The incident we're waiting on is likely to send someone to the box.

Thirty minutes have passed since the bells tolled. A steady rain begins to descend from dark gray nimbostratus clouds. They nix my plans to work out in the yard. Seagulls bleat noisily while perched like sentinels on the A-Block handball-court wall. They're angered by the deluge as well.

I return to my cell, gathering clothes to wash and iron. I expect a visit tomorrow, so I select my best items: long-sleeve, cotton Nautica button-down shirt, white Hanes tee, Nike socks, and standard-issue green pants. The latter provided by the state.

While washing clothes in a five-gallon bucket in a slop sink on the backside of a prison gallery, I learn from the tag on my Nautica shirt how to say, "Machine wash, cold, gentle cycle, tumble dry, warm iron" in French. I can hear the mellifluous sound of a nylon-string acoustic guitar floating from Max's cell. He plays to relax. I imagine being on the Pacific shore of Colombia, watching cobalt blue waves gently blanket the white sand. The ocean is swallowing a burnt-orange orb as I sip a mimosa.

A stream of people flowing off the gallery into the dayroom tell me that the "all clear" has been given. Routines begin anew. I can feel the tension and anxiety begin to subside. Pent-up tension leads to bad things in prison.

Last week, waiting in the humid corridor in two-by-two formation, a CO barked on the guy in front of me.

"Who you eye-ballin', asshole?"

The guy kept staring, did not flinch. The CO stood there for a moment, then, obviously intimidated by the guy's stature, turned away. The line proceeded to the academic building. About thirty minutes later, the CO, accompanied by a sergeant and another CO, stood outside the prisoner's classroom. From the office I work in, I could see them take him out of class into the hallway staircase. Within five seconds I heard the thumping and pounding before the bells chimed.

After washing and hanging my clothes to dry, I return to my cell. I pick up a pen and notebook from my desk. Looking out past the windows and bars, I write a haiku:

> Cold Steel Prison Bars
> Twenty years to pass behind
> Rain falls, Hope must rise.

I return the notebook and pen to their place on my desk. I take my silver and blue Bulova wristwatch off its clear plastic stand. It's a Rolex by prison standards. Miraculously, it slipped through property room scrutiny. According to written directives regulating property, watches are limited to a value of fifty dollars. The watch's instruction pages contain a plethora of languages. I try to read how to set the stopwatch and activate split-time measurement in Korean, German, Chinese, and Norwegian.

If I had been born in Helsinki, I would master at least three languages and serve only one-third of my sentence with good behavior. In the U.S., however, English remains the standard. Xenophobes view prisoners with the same disdain as immigrants. Learning foreign languages continues to be as eccentric as drinking absinthe or listening to a polonaise.

The following day I prepare early for my visit. On my thin mattress, I neatly lay out the clothes I will wear. My mood is happy, upbeat. A sonata plays quietly from my radio. When we were children, my brother and I would attempt to decipher the Polish that our parents sometimes spoke. They used it to veil their meanings. Our grandfather, who was born in Krakow, Poland, had a Polish dictionary that we'd use in our investigations. When our translating hit a wall, we asked our grandfather directly.

"*Dziadek* (grandfather), what does *spokojne* mean?"

"It means quiet."

"What about *Soboto*?"

"Saturday."

"How 'bout . . ."

"*Dzieci spokojne*." (Children, quiet.) "Get the dictionary; I'm trying to read the paper."

The visiting room is vastly different from any other part of the prison. Brightly colored murals of Niagara Falls, downtown Buffalo, and lower Manhattan cover the walls. Women and children's voices are a welcome, pleasant change. Tall, clear windows allow natural light to fill the room. Walking through the entrance door after being pat-frisked, I quickly spot my brother Martin, his wife Kristen, and their two-year-old daughter, Jenna. After checking in with the CO at the front desk, I approach their table with excitement. I embrace all of them individually. Sitting, talking with family during a visit is the closest to freedom a prisoner experiences. It's an escape, briefly, from confinement.

During our visit, Martin brings up a phone call he was expecting from me last weekend that I didn't deliver on.

"Oh, we got burned on Saturday and stalled on Sunday," I say.

Kristen looks puzzled. "You got burned?"

"Yeah, that means the CO didn't let us out at night to use the phone. And he stalled us on Sunday, didn't let us out at the proper time."

I realize that I've learned a language from a foreign land, developed over years by the denizens of IncarcerNation.

As I hold Jenna on my knee, she smiles, places her tiny hand on my bearded chin, and says, "Hi, Unka Bobby."

A lesson in language.

MARTIN G. GANN, *Washington*

ONE SMALL VOICE THROUGH THE WALL

I hope to convey my experience dealing with a disability and trying to survive or exist in the Washington prison system, where neither empathy nor compassion exist. The second experience I want to write about being the most important thing to me while I serve my time, and that is my family.

I preface this writing with a short background of myself for a better understanding of who I am, where I was, and where I find myself now.

I fell two years ago at the age of fifty-six. I was at the time married, am still married, and have now been married for eighteen years to a wonderful wife who has remained spiritually and mentally by my side. We both have children from previous marriages, but have none together. We love each other totally, and she is the only stable element and most important person in my life.

I had always been a contributing part of society. I started working when I was fourteen years old and had never been unemployed until I fell. I have been a property owner and taxpayer. I served my country in the U.S. Navy during the last years of the Vietnam War. I have been a member of several fraternal organizations and was an active member of, and participant in, our church.

During my lifetime, I have worked and played around very noisy equipment. In the Navy, I worked on and around jet aircraft. I ran chainsaws for many years cutting firewood. I fired many guns for sport. In my many years in the hydro industry, I worked around extremely loud equipment. All of these combined have resulted in a profound loss of hearing. I was fortunate enough to be working for a responsible employer who was able to provide me with good quality hearing aids a few years prior to being incarcerated. Without using my hearing aids it is very doubtful that I would hear well enough to understand what is being said to me. Because I had never been in any correctional system, I was not, and could never have been, prepared for what I am now experiencing. That brings me to the first of two subjects: living (or existing) in a correctional institution with an extreme hearing disability.

Being hard of hearing is tough enough for anyone, anywhere, anytime, but being hard of hearing in jail or prison is enough to drive a person into a constant state of nervous fear. If you don't hear or if you misunderstand something said by a fellow inmate or a corrections officer, it can result in immediate reprisal or unexpected discipline. In county jail, I was denied batteries for my hearing aids. They "allowed" me to keep my hearing aids, but refused to give me any new batteries when the ones I came in with went dead. I was finally allowed to have batteries, but only after my wife supplied batteries to be passed on to me. I then had to give up the old set of batteries and wait sometimes more than twenty-four hours for someone to bring me the new batteries from the properties room. During those times without batteries, I am at the mercy of those around me to know and/or remember that I am unable to hear. I made the choice, out of fear, to mostly keep to myself, to the extent I could, in a small confined area, designed for two, with the three people assigned to my cell.

Even now, in state prison, I find myself without the use of my hearing aids. Prison policy does not allow me to keep a spare set of batteries. When hearing-aid batteries go dead, there are but a few minutes' notice (unlike flashlight batteries that gradually dim). A spare set of batteries only makes sense. That way, I could hear even while I awaited the time for battery exchange. Before incarceration I carried spares in my wallet, my vehicles, and in my wife's purse. I have been told that I cannot have spare batteries because a person can get a high from ingesting the contents of the batteries, and someone could use the batteries to energize a tattoo gun. I personally believe neither of these to be the true reason. My batteries are a mere 1/8th of an inch wide and only last five to seven days. It is my opinion that it's nothing more than a power and control decision that no one on the staff is willing to question.

At this time, I am allowed to exchange old batteries for new batteries at the pill line at noon or six P.M., Monday through Friday, provided the line is not too long and I am not at work, visiting, or programming. Outside of these times, I am also allowed to make the exchange in the normal pill line on Saturdays or Sundays.

There are other times that I am unable to hear. I remove my hearing aids when I'm in bed and when I go to the shower. If an emergency occurs during these times, I can only hope that someone will let me know what is going on, or that a corrections officer does not speak to me and assume by my lack of response that I am being disrespectful, for which I can be punished.

When I became a ward of Washington State I was issued a picture ID, and the words "HEAR- ING IMPAIRED" were printed clearly and visibly on the bottom. This was great in that both inmates and correctional staff were aware of my disability. I have been told that the facility I am currently assigned to will *not* add anything like this to my new ID when my original ID is no longer usable, leaving me without this simple means of notification.

The personalities of the officers and staff range from the power-hungry and the narcissistic on one extreme, to somewhat compassionate and caring on the other. The majority of the officers and staff are heavy on the power-hungry end. I must say I am fortunate, for my assigned coun- selor is caring. For this I am grateful, and it has made a difference. Recently the block I am in had a fire drill. This counselor made it a point to go to everyone's cell that had a hearing disability to make sure we were aware of what was happening. It never even occurred to the corrections officers to facilitate something like this.

I now move on to the second, and the most important, subject of my writing: my wife, my family, and my friends. Visit days are what I live for. I am blessed in that my correctional center is only about a twenty-mile drive for my wife. Here, the inmates are allowed to have a 3½-hour window of time for visiting each Friday, Saturday, Sunday, and Monday.

When my wife and I first began visiting, we found that I could not hear or understand most of what she or my other visitors were saying due to the volume and constant chatter of the other visitors that completely surrounded us. Hearing aids are not selective in what they amplify. They amplify all voices on all sides. The visiting room is exactly like a very loud restaurant environment.

On our second or third visit, we were placed at a table in a corner where there were other people on only two sides. We found that being seated in this area made all the difference in the world, and we were able to carry on a somewhat normal conversation. My wife began requesting this type of seating from the assigning officer. This was accommodated several times. Then she was told by a different officer that they don't take requests for seating. After explaining the hearing situation, my wife was then told it wasn't a medical reason and that there was no difference in hearing ability wherever we were placed.

I then sent written communication to the visiting Sergeant explaining the situation, and for the next three or four visits we were placed in seating that affords better hearing due to a lower ceiling, acoustical tiles, and no other visitors on two sides. This was great until the visiting lieutenant got word of this accommodation and put a stop to it. The reasoning was that no one could receive special seat assignments except for medical reasons. We explained that lack of hearing is a medical reason, to no avail. At the time there was a sign at the assigning desk explaining that a medical reason would be if a visitor or inmate had an allergy to someone's perfume. Immediately after questioning this, we began being seated directly in the center of the visitors' room.

After attempting communication with the facility superintendent, my wife was so frustrated with the situation that she went directly to the Washington State head of the prisons, the Secretary. Her correspondence was directed to a designated family visiting advocate. After several weeks of discussion between the facilitator and the institution, we are now seated in the area where hearing is best. This entire process took almost five months. During this process we felt the family visiting advocate actually cared, and her actions on our behalf made this apparent. It was not long after these events that another lieutenant was assigned to Visiting and she did everything possible in her short tenure (she has recently been transferred to another facility) to make the visiting environment more efficient and friendly for all. My wife currently serves on the local facility Visitors' Committee and is working directly with the staff in attempting to improve not only the atmosphere in visiting, but all aspects of maintaining the inmate and family connection during incarceration.

A couple of months ago, another situation related to family and visiting came about and is still ongoing. I am employed in a corrections industry job, making eyeglasses. Until a couple of months ago I was also attending college-credit classes, studying interactive multimedia and the three other required support classes, and maintaining a 4.0 average for these classes. Once I began working, the I-media class available to me was Monday through Friday evenings from 6:20 P.M. to 9:15 P.M. I had been regularly excused from Friday evening class by the teacher to go to my regular visits with my wife and friends, as the visiting time and class time on Friday coincided. I never missed an assigned deadline despite attending these visits.

One day an internal memo went out to all work locations and schooling advisors stating that inmates could not be excused from "programming" to attend Visiting. At this time, my class instructor regretfully informed me that if I did not show up for class on Friday evenings that I would suffer the consequences of an "infraction." Since this class was not required, I was forced to drop the class in order to keep my record clean from any infractions. I was put in the situation of making a choice, and naturally my family comes first. I am still actively pursuing my return to this educational class, but on a Monday through Thursday basis. This is a cumbersome and time-consuming grievance process for something that seems such a no-brainer. Let an inmate, who is not only working full-time but is also using his down time to further his education and nurture his family relationships, continue to accomplish all these things.

My wife and I continue to work toward improving these situations not only for ourselves, but the others that find themselves in similar circumstances. If only a few individuals could be moved to positions where they couldn't abuse their power to control efforts by inmates to improve themselves, the outcomes of incarceration would be much better.

B. G. JACOBS, *New York*

FOOD FOR THOUGHT

Lying on an uncomfortable two-inch vinyl mattress, in a stifling prison cell, I was at peace for the first time in a long time. Eyes closed, my mind was centered on one thought: what can I use for an ersatz flour to make dough? (*Pastelios* were in my immediate future.) I was finally away from the stress and madness of prison and safely locked away in thoughts of food.

Cooking is a way for me to both relieve stress and express myself. One of the few pleasures I can still get out of life is to cook a dish, then share it with people. It's heartening to hear how much they've enjoyed something that I've created using my hands, mind, and heart.

Currently I am doing time behind the walls of a maximum-security prison, so as you can imagine, pleasure is rare; but when I am either by myself thinking up new dishes or actually putting them together in my cell, I go to a much safer, happier place than reality usually allows.

My memories of cooking go back to when I was a child. My family and I used to go to my grandmother's house at least once a week for dinner. I would stay in the kitchen when she made something I really liked—cutting here, stirring there. When my Aunt Milagros visited from Florida, my brother and I would really be put to work. These two ladies are the sweetest, funniest Puerto Rican women you could imagine. My aunt's accent was so thick I had a hard time understanding her as a child, but my grandmother was always in a good mood. When my aunt was visiting, we would all get together and cook. Assuredly, when my aunt went back to Florida, we would have a freezer full of *pastelles*, Puerto Rican–style *tamales.*

My brother and I would be given the job of grating hundreds of green bananas into a paste-like dough. My grandmother did not waste any food, so if either of us tried to throw away the last quarter of the banana because we were scared of grating our fingers, she would say, "There's plenty more left; you two better use all of that." So we would grate them all the way down to our fingertips. The four of us would be at the table for hours, working, laughing, and eating together. My grandmother's kitchen was filled with all sorts of bric-a-brac, pictures, and flowers. Her countertops were red, which matched her brick-patterned linoleum floor. She usually had a plastic sheet covering a red and white tablecloth, but what I most vividly remember were the aromas. The smells of garlic and onion sautéing in olive oil, pork slowly roasting in the oven, and my favorite smell of all, *pastelios* frying away on the stove. The little pockets of dough filled with heaven itself smelled utterly divine. Your nostrils would flare and your stomach immediately grumble in anticipation of these little Puerto Rican treasures. Those *pastelios* were my real reward after a hard day of banana grating.

While my brother and I busily worked away at the grating, my grandmother and my aunt would be at the stove making the filling for both the *pastelles* and the *pastelios*. This consisted of a combination of pork, onions, garlic, peppers, tomato sauce, and various seasonings.

To construct the *pastelles*, you get a banana leaf—you can also use wax paper—and lay down the banana dough. Next you put some of the pork filling in the center and cover with some more of the dough, enclosing the filling in between the dough like a sandwich. Fold in the ends of the banana leaf and wrap it up nice and tight. Once you have two of the *pastelles* done like this, you stack one on top of the other, and using twine, bind the two of them together. All that is left to do now is to boil them and enjoy.

Once all of the dough was used up, there was always a pot of the filling left over. While we cleaned up, Grandma would make dough using flour and water, roll it out on the counter to about a quarter-inch thick, then place the meat filling on the dough and begin to form patties or *pastelios*, which she would immediately begin to fry. The *pastelios* only took about 30–45 seconds per side. (Just remembering the smell of dough frying in oil, and the sizzling, popping sound it made, has my mouth watering.) She kept a plate next to the stove with paper towels to stack them on as they came out of the hot oil. As fast as she made them, we ate them, never giving her a chance to stack them up. She would try to chase us away, but with no success.

Lately, with the way stuff has been going on inside here, I needed to recapture a little piece of my childhood. In here, we all need to journey back every now and then. Can you fault us for our nostalgia? Where you're from, do people get cut for playing handball on the wrong court? Do they hang themselves because a girlfriend didn't come over? And then there's the cops. Constantly harassing people just to amuse themselves and pass the time. They act like adolescents, like the cretins in high school chasing the scrawny kid down the hall to give him the dreaded wedgie. When too much negativity starts to surround me, I try to counter it with something positive. I will call to speak with my loved ones, or write home, read a good book, or cook.

As simple as any of these things sound, everything that I do in prison is ten times more difficult than in the comfort of my own home. In order to make a phone call, I have to have my phone numbers approved by the administration, and they're placed on my allowed calling list. Phone calls can only be made collect, so if the phone does not accept collect calls (say, if it's a cell phone), then I can't call. If I am fortunate enough, however, to be able to call home, then I am only permitted to do so at designated times, such as in the yard when I am allowed out for recreation, or on my gallery every other night for ten very strictly limited minutes.

To read, if I do not have books in my cell, I can either wait to be put on a call-out for the prison library, or I can borrow one from someone I know—but then my choices are limited. If by chance I am locked in my cell, and the person with a book is some cells away from me, I can "fish." (Fishing is taking a line—usually a sheet ripped into long strips and fastened together— then anchored with some kind of weight that can be thrown from one cell to the other—usually with the help of convicts in between—until it reaches the intended destination.) The recipient will then tie whatever item it may be to the end of the "fishing line," which is then pulled back to the cell. If an officer happens to walk by while this is going on, usually he will confiscate the item(s) and line, leaving the convict to destroy yet another sheet and make more line. The other convict will lose whatever it was he was trying to pass.

Cooking is also a challenge. Prison has a canteen (more commonly known as a commissary) where we are allowed to purchase items such as tobacco, toiletries, stationary, and food, provided we have money in our accounts. We can either earn money through various prison jobs (which average 22¢ an hour) or money can be sent to us by family and friends on the outside. Commissary runs on a two-week rotation. If the commissary is out of a particular item when your turn comes around, you either wait another two weeks, or try to make a deal with someone to pick it up for you when they go.

Once you have all of the items needed, there are two main methods to cook. You can use a plastic hot-pot (purchased through commissary), or remove the metal coil from that hot-pot, discard the remains, and get hold of a large, restaurant-sized tuna can. This can be obtained from someone working in the prison kitchen. Through a series of convicts, you have the can smuggled out of the kitchen, through the facility, and delivered to your cell for a couple packs of cigarettes or stamps, the coins of the realm.

Whenever I cook—usually because whatever the state is providing that day is inedible—it takes place in the same 6' x 9' box that also holds my bed, sink, and toilet. So, the same place I use to cook, I will also use to eat, wash my dishes, use the toilet once the food finishes its course, and then sleep once I'm so stuffed I can no longer move.

Using my bed as a table, I set up my makeshift stove: a metal coil perched atop an emptied can of beans, and my tuna can used in place of a frying pan (a far cry from my grandmother's GE stove and nonstick frying pans). When it comes to frying, there are certain ingredients needed, such as oil and flour, which those housed in general population (such as myself) are not allowed to buy in the commissary. These specific items are only available to those confined in the honor block of the prison; these are men who have not been in trouble for some time, so they have earned certain privileges that the rest of us are not granted. When someone in general population (GP) wants to obtain these items, it is much like getting the tuna can. Locate someone with access to these items, make some kind of deal for him, then using those same channels, have them brought to your cell.

This is usually how I get my flour and oil, but the last person I had bringing me my stuff was stopped and pat-frisked, and my merchandise was confiscated—which undoubtedly was sold to someone else by that officer—and I was left with nothing but a pissed-off transporter.

To avoid a repeat of this fiasco, I decided to come up with a substitute flour for the dough. The oil was easy because I can purchase butter, which once melted down can be used to fry. The flour was a different story. This took more creative thinking on my part. So, as I lay there in my hot, stifling cell, I came up with an idea. Using items I had stored in the plastic bin under my bed, I took a box of macaroni and cheese, emptied the noodles into a bowl, and filled it with cold water. I let the pasta soak for around half an hour, checking every ten minutes, until I got my desired texture (think Play-Doh). Then I drained the water and grabbed fistfuls of pasta, squeezing them through my fingers by opening and closing my hand until I had a mound of wet, doughy pasta. But the dough was too sticky. I took some Cheez-It crackers and placed them inside of an empty potato-chip bag. With an unopened can of beans, I crushed the crackers into dust. I slowly incorporated it into the dough. This made the dough more pliable (and added a hint of cheese flavor to the dough). Now, with the dough complete, the work began.

I made the filling for my *pastelios* using all of the necessary ingredients, with one change. Instead of pork, I used chicken. Once that was all done, I cleared an area on the floor and laid out a large plastic garbage bag. I placed the dough in the middle and, using a tightly rolled magazine wrapped in plastic wrap, I rolled the dough out until it was the thickness of piecrust. Using a small bowl as a cookie cutter, I cut out several circles of dough. Then I placed a pile of the filling in the middle, folded it over until the two ends met, and sealed them using a plastic fork, meshing the two ends together. Once I had them all assembled, I melted down a stick of butter inside of the tuna can to use as a thick oil, and began to recapture my childhood. Because of all the obstacles that stood in my way—the jerry-rigged "kitchen" and the limited space—the whole process took me about six hours. But for those six hours, I was in complete and utter serenity. When I'm like this, nothing can bother me—provided I don't have a random cell search and watch my can and coil be confiscated, earning me a misbehavior report (or ticket).

As you can see, doing something as simple as using a phone, even reading a book or cooking—things I never before gave a second thought about—can become problematic and tiresome, which requires ingenuity and creative thinking. The next time you find yourself at your stove, in your big kitchen with counters, a table, utensils, and a refrigerator, try to picture me in a space probably no bigger than your walk-in closet, and a bed taking up almost half of that space, cooking out of a tuna can. Picture me picturing myself at my grandmother's house, remembering the good times that I took for granted.

STEPHEN WHETZEL, *Indiana*

A RENAISSANCE

It started with a visit to the psychologist.

Behind the ominous gray concrete wall surrounding the Indiana State Reformatory, not many areas existed where one could escape the late summer heat. That old maximum-security prison, a place born of a harsher time, was never known for comforts. Whether or not I felt the need for a counseling session with Eric, my psychologist and substance-abuse counselor, I looked forward to the soothing sting of cool, dry air on my skin as I melted into one of the padded chairs in his air-conditioned office.

Every week, I visited the "nut-doctor," as the prisoners around me would say. It didn't matter to them that I was taking my rehabilitation and recovery seriously. Most of the people around me had sentences of sixty years or more. They saw no need of exhausting energy to better a life that couldn't be salvaged. As far as they were concerned, only the mentally disturbed saw a "shrink" once a week. Their opinions meant nothing to me, but in a way, they were right. Prison has a way of disturbing one's sensibilities. During my incarceration, I realized that if I ever wanted to experience happiness in my life, I had to get to work on fixing myself. Eric was just as eager to help me as I was to help myself. After enduring so many cold, stoic years in close quarters, it was refreshing to open up to another human being. I enjoyed a sense of freedom at the psych office that was well worth the jeering I endured from other prisoners.

One memorable day, I entered Eric's office and didn't receive his usual jovial welcome. I could tell that something was bothering him. He was all business from the time I sat down. In a serious tone, Eric explained that he had spent part of the morning reviewing my case and my mental health record. My progress was outstanding. My psychiatric therapy involved working out the bad and replacing it with the good. His goal, and mine, was to develop a complete, functional person. Eric expressed concern that as I continued to mature mentally and emotionally, prison culture was hampering my progress. He feared that I was in jeopardy of becoming institutionalized. To support his claim, he pointed out two things: I had no outside contact with the world, and I had recently averted yet another conflict with a prisoner.

I worked hard to stay out of trouble, but in a place where many men are embittered and hardened with the sick prospect of never seeing freedom, confrontation was impossible to avoid. Violence was an integral part of the prison landscape, the way trees define a forest and water defines the ocean. Eric was insightful enough to understand that he was limited to snapshots of my warped existence, while I was bombarded with a streaming video. When Eric spoke about prison as an animalistic environment, he was referring to my home sweet home.

As part of a plan to have me reconnect with the outside world, Eric wanted me to write to a pen pal, and with the aid of the Internet, he intended to help me find someone. From a pen pal website, I had to select three addresses from people in Indiana. (He hoped that I would get a pen pal who would come visit me.) The other two could be from anywhere else in the world. The opportunity to make a friend on the outside excited me. It seemed like an eternity had passed since I had interacted with people not associated with prison.

With curious enthusiasm, I watched as Eric logged onto his computer and conjured a pen pal website. As he scrolled through the many screens of addresses, I noticed that all but a few were labeled "No Prisoners." I had no idea that so many people were against receiving mail from prisoners. While looking at addresses, I felt sick with the thought that no one would want to write to me. Fortunately, before the session ended, I had scribbled down three addresses in Indiana, one in North Carolina, and one in Canada. I believed that people on the outside didn't care to write to prisoners, but the moment I was back in any cell, I went to work writing a brief introduction letter.

When I received my first letter, I was overcome with happiness. It had been years since I received any personal mail, so the arrival of my first letter was something to celebrate. Only someone who had been abandoned and alone for a long time could truly appreciate how I felt. The prisoners around me noticed my delight and asked about my mail. When I mentioned "pen pal" they became interested and wanted to know how they could get someone to write to. I had promised Eric that I wouldn't say anything, so I told them that "my family" had set it all up. Besides, I didn't want to share my pen pal connection with anyone else. It could have jeopardized everything.

The first person to respond was Amy from North Carolina. She was a nice, young, newly married woman with a supportive husband and toy poodle. Her husband spent a lot of time on the road for his job, and she thought it would be nice to have some pen pals help her pass the time. The next week, I received a letter from Sonia in Edmunston, Canada. She was a single woman with a son and an American boyfriend. She lived a blessed life of travel and extravagance. Every so often, Sonia rotated new pen pals into her life. She loved to hear stories from people all over the world.

I didn't receive a letter from anyone in Indiana.

Amy wrote every week. Her southern charm appealed to me. She was a sticker fanatic who always put bright, puffy stickers on the envelopes. Sonia preferred to write once or twice a month. Her life was exciting and filled with adventure. Her boyfriend was a wealthy executive in the automotive industry. While Amy stayed home and cooked recipes out of cookbooks, Sonia traveled. Amy sent pictures of her poodle and her quaint country home. Sonia sent me pictures of her vacation in the Bahamas and her trip to the Detroit Auto Show.

My pen pals didn't seem to mind that I was writing from prison. While prison life bored me, Amy and Sonia found it fascinating. I equally enjoyed hearing about their life outside in the real world. In a short time, I opened to the reality of life outside prison. During the first six years of incarceration, I had subconsciously blanked out any idea of what the real world was like. I disconnected from most prisoners, whose idea of conversation consisted of crime tales and crying about their bad luck in life. To me, they were part of the prison, like the metal fixtures in a house.

Unexpectedly, my clockwork life flourished with excitement. I had been doing the same things for so long that the introduction of a simple letter into my life completely turned my world upside-down. I had things to do now. Each letter was a project. I consumed every word and phrase before drafting and writing a response. I replied to every bit of news they had shared with me, and I gave them news about my life in prison. I was no longer on the sidelines of life. I was a participant.

Just as soon as I had developed an appreciation for life, it all began to unravel. After Christmas, Amy wrote that her husband didn't like the idea of her contacting a prisoner. Unbeknownst to me, for some time, she had disobeyed her husband and had continued to be my friend. They had a terrible fight after her husband discovered one of my letters in the mailbox. At first, I was shocked, and that shock soon turned to hurt for both of us. She was such a great person to share her life with me. I had imagined her surrounded by like-minded people who supported her in everything. There was nothing for me to do but write a final parting letter.

Trouble didn't end there. Two months later, my world plunged into darkness.

Sonia, my sole connection to the outside, wrote that she could no longer be my pen pal. Her boyfriend didn't want her writing to a prisoner. Hurt swelled as I read her heartfelt apology. Everything had been going so well. Why did it have to fall apart? I felt so depressed that I was sick. I didn't want to go to work or go to the gym. I slept for a solid week. As with Amy, I wrote a composed goodbye letter.

I didn't dare tell anyone that I had lost my pen pals. I said I must have come down with the flu. That would keep them away long enough for me to regain my composure. If they knew that I had just been abandoned, they would have attacked like a pack of wolves. They would have enjoyed heaping salt into my wounds and watching me squirm, reminding me that I was no better than the rest of them. That's just the way many people are in prison, purveyors of misery. Misery loves company, especially when Misery has no reason to live.

Unexpectedly, I received one more letter from Sonia. It was a warning. She explained that one of her acquaintances, Bette, was going to write to me. She described Bette as a longtime associate who was a drug user, thief, and liar. While visiting, Bette had copied down my address without

Sonia's permission. Since Sonia had abandoned me, Bette thought she would befriend me. Sonia thought I already had enough problems in my life, and the problems her associate would heap upon me would make my life even harder. On top of it all, Bette was a French Canadian and not good with English.

Of course, I used Sonia's letter as an excuse to write to her. Perhaps she would keep writing to me. But although she cared enough to give me a warning, she had still abandoned me. The mystery woman, trouble and all, seemed better than nothing.

Two weeks later, I received a letter from my new pen pal in Canada. The letter was written in blue ink on colorful stationary. I was immediately drawn to her artistic flair, which was quite disarming. The letter was written in a mixture of French and English. The words were put together in such a way that I could barely understand the message she was trying to convey. It was like reading an entirely new language.

I concluded that Bette was infinitely more comfortable communicating in French. Her English was terrible. She used a dictionary and picked out certain words to string together to form sentences. It was a decent effort, enough to convey that she wanted to be my friend. I imagined her spending many hours just to get the one letter completed. That was the best example of patience and dedication I had experienced in a very long time. She had done it for me, and this intrigued me. I decided that, despite Sonia's warning, it was better to have a messed-up friend than no friend at all. Besides, I wasn't confident that I would be able to keep a pen pal for more than a few months anyway. The language barrier would be an issue, but I wasn't completely ignorant of the French language.

During my junior year of high school, I trudged through a year of French, because it was a requirement for college. My friends suggested that I take Spanish, which was becoming prevalent throughout the United States. The thing everyone was doing never seemed to appeal to me. Besides, nothing sounds sexier to me than the French language.

By the end of the school year, I wished that I had taken Spanish. The teacher had such a disagreeable disposition, to put it lightly, that I hated attending class. I was a good student and aced the class, but I saw no point in forcing myself to endure another year with that horrible teacher.

After Bette's first letter, I scrambled to find a French-English dictionary. I sent word throughout the prison. Money meant nothing as long as I got a decent dictionary. Of course, everyone wondered why I needed a French dictionary, and I was all too proud to explain that I had just met a new pen pal from Canada who didn't communicate well in English. It felt good to be "that guy with the French pen pal." Within a week, a friend of a friend found a small travel dictionary misplaced in the library, and it didn't cost me a cent.

It was my turn to summon the patience and determination required to construct a letter in a foreign language. I did my best to write whole sentences in French. A few sentences were a mixture of French and English. I promised Bette that if she continued to write, I would learn her language and stay in contact. She did not have to worry about writing in English, unless she felt compelled to try. It was a cry for interaction from a lonely man who had recently discovered the value of having a connection on the outside.

After sending my first letter to Bette, I anxiously awaited her reply. Just as I had given up, I received my second letter from her. It was a two-page letter written completely in French. Bette was excited to have found a friend in me and promised that we would go a long way together. I had heard so many empty promises over the years that I was expert at shrugging them off. I would appreciate the moment as long as it lasted.

Bette found constant occasion to express her care for me, often communicating how much she wished I were out. It was nice to be missed and wanted. Her words moved me to the point where my separation from the real world disturbed me. I wanted to be free, even if it were just for her sake. She couldn't wait to show me around Edmunston, and I daydreamed about seeing her town. The more time passed, the more my incarceration caused her pain. I told her that Canada did not allow American ex-cons entry. Bette didn't care. She would help me sneak across through Maine. She wanted to introduce me to all her friends at the hair salon where she worked. Little things like that touched me. For example, I found it interesting that a woman would be so excited about the arrival of moose hunting season. It was charmingly odd, yet addictively appealing. I had heard that Canadians were the nicest people on the planet. Bette made a believer out of me.

Sometimes, Bette's writing would remind me of Sonia's warning. For example, she would explain that why I was in prison wasn't as important as what I was doing with my time in prison. I would describe a violent incident, and she would merely urge me to avoid the troublemakers around me. She seemed familiar with drug problems, running up debts, and other aspects of prison culture. I never confronted her about the things Sonia had written, because I didn't want to back her into a corner. Her past didn't matter to me. I didn't need to know more than she wanted to share with me. Perhaps that was something she needed from me—to be able to live freely and express herself openly as the woman she wanted to be. Bette sent me the most incredible handmade cards. They were made of thick textured paper decorated on the outside with ribbons, tiny roses, baby's breath, glitter, cloth, etc. Inside were smooth stationery and her carefully scripted words. She wrote me that I was a man with a very good heart. (In the eyes of everyone else, I was just another convict, a waste.) Oftentimes, she referred to me as her angel. I never would have thought that of myself, but Bette had a way of expressing her insight that made her reasoning seem logical. For her, I wanted to be better. I wanted to be that good person, her angel. I vowed to learn as much as I could about French and Canada and prove to her how much her friendship meant to me.

The Reformatory had no foreign language resources, so I had to build my own French resource center. I wrote to several places across the United States that offered free books to prisoners. It was incredible what one could find. One place in particular, Books Through Bars in Bloomington, Indiana, sent me French dictionaries, French language books, and French literature. Their remarkable generosity made it possible for me to quickly immerse myself in the language. When I could afford it, I would order books from bargain catalogues. After an upgrade to the prison cable TV system, I watched IFC, the Independent Film Channel, which often showed foreign films. Hearing the language spoken only reinforced my desire to learn it.

My quest to learn French elevated me to a higher existence. I read to fill my mind with knowledge instead of merely finding escape from empty days. The more I learned, the more I wanted to learn, to grow, to evolve. Over the next years, I went to college to study psychological science and I graduated with a bachelor's degree. I learned to read, write, and speak Spanish. I completed vocational training and became a vocational carpentry tutor. Somewhere along the way, I began to work on my writing.

My adventures with French inspired me to teach the language to a group of prisoners. I benefited just as much as they did. The group helped me to explore deeper into the language. They tested me constantly. The study group started with eight people. Over the period of a year, nearly all my students left; either they were moved to a different part of the prison, to a different facility, or they gave up on the language altogether. At the end of a year, I had a single eager student, Damon.

Damon and I worked together for over two years. While others were playing cards or watching TV, we were studying. As we grew together in the French language, we grew as friends. It has been years since I've seen Damon face to face. We were transferred to different minimum-security prisons. Nevertheless, we continue to be the best of friends and have maintained close contact through his mother, who forwarded our letters. The amazing part is that we communicated exclusively in French.

I talked about Bette constantly. I wanted everyone to know about her and Canada. My friends poked fun at me about my infatuation with anything Canadian. I eagerly showed off pictures of Bette and Canada. During the Olympics, I openly rooted for Canadian athletes. I sang along with the Canadian National Anthem. The more I connected with Canada, the more I felt connected to Bette. I couldn't think of a life without her.

Bette supported me through some significant times in my life. When my sister, Misty, contacted me for the first time in many years,[1] Bette was there, eager and excited to give advice. When I rekindled my relationship with my father, Bette was there, urging me to focus on building family. With her support, I learned to forgive. Through the best and worst of prison, Bette was with me, sharing laughter and tears and teaching me how to truly live, encouraging me to strive to be a better me.

Her father's death was our first challenge. For a while, Bette was upset, but I thought she seemed to deal with it well. I consoled her through her grief, sending extra letters and cards. I wanted her to feel as if I were there with her. It took a lot of work on my end, and together, we pulled through this hardship.

Just as we had cleared one hurdle, we came upon another. A year after losing her father, her grandmother passed away. Bette's grandmother had practically raised her and had been her sole source of support for most of her life. It was a huge chunk of life that was ripped from her. For months, she was inconsolable, and I, unable to alleviate her pain, felt helpless. My support never wavered, but I knew that she wished I were actually there.

Bad luck continued to batter her. She fell and broke her arm, which required surgery that put her out of work. We continued to stay in contact, but life was a constant struggle for her. All I could do was send her as much support as possible, as she had done for me over the years. Bette's arm healed and she returned to work. We had been through a lot together and had grown closer in spite of our trials.

Then one day, Bette informed me of the worst news. Her son had died. Throughout the years, she wrote about Ian, her pride and joy, the culmination of the goodness in her life. He was proof that she was capable of bringing good into the world. I struggled to formulate words that would even begin to penetrate the shroud of pain that enveloped her and held her prisoner. Although I continued to reach out to her, she stopped writing. Bette, as I had known her, died with the passing of her son.

I knew that feeling of giving up, how even death can seem like an inviting friend. I too had suffered irreplaceable loss. Alone, under horrible conditions, I had fought my case for two and a half years. One day, it dawned on me that everything that had meaning in my life was gone. I had forgotten what I was fighting for in the first place. It didn't matter if I lived or died, but I just couldn't bring myself to end it all.

In the end it did matter—everything matters. Things happen for a reason. I no longer believe in coincidence. As a teenager, I endured a miserable year of studying French. Six years into doing the 18½ years I expected to do on a 45-year sentence, I was set on a mission by a psychologist who believed that I was a better person than even I believed. I met some amazing friends who helped me change my mind about people and life. A woman I had never met, in a country that I had never visited, writing in a language I educated myself to understand, helped me to realize my worth. It all happened the way it was intended to happen, so that I would suffer and endure, experience a remarkable renaissance, and share the story of a woman who introduced me to a wonderful life.

I didn't know the woman Sonia had warned me about. The Bette I knew was my personal angel. She was the dearest friend to bless my life, and I will always love her. I followed up with several more letters to her, sending all the love and support I could muster, but she had to be the one to accept it. Sometimes, I prayed that she wouldn't do anything to hurt herself. I had to believe that she was stronger than I was.

A few months later, I received a letter from Bette. Upon seeing the envelope, I was relieved, glad to have finally gotten through to her. Unfortunately, my joy was short-lived. She was still writing from a dark place. Her grief had not diminished. It was then that I believed we would not recover from this loss.

I never heard from her again.

We were together for over seven years, and there was no goodbye.

It just ended.

NOTE

1. The reader will find Whetzel's essay about this incident under "Family Life In and From Prison City," in this volume.

DEAN FAIELLO, *New York*

IMPERMANENCE

I sat in my cell, dressed, caffeinated, and anxious, waiting for my gate to open. The squawk box instructed inmates with 9:00 A.M. call-outs to proceed to the first floor. But my gate remained locked. The officer on duty was in the COs' galley cooking his breakfast. The aroma of bacon, mingled with French toast and vanilla, wafted onto the company. I was getting annoyed. I didn't want to miss the Cephas meeting. I had spent most of the last two days, the weekend, locked in my cell with little to do. It was Monday morning, and I needed to vent. I always felt better after attending Cephas. The group genuinely cares about us—our lives, our frustrations, our future. In prison, concern and empathy are rare. Most of the correctional staff despise us. COs usually get our attention by shouting, "Hey, stupid," or "Yo, asshole." The Cephas volunteers call us by our first names.

As the minutes ticked away, I felt my face getting hot. If I missed the meeting, there wouldn't be another for a week. And I would be stuck in my cell for four hours, until the yard opened. But the prison yard is not a place to talk about emotions. The air is filled with testosterone, not sympathy. I'd rather sit in my cell and read. J. M. Coetzee's *Waiting for the Barbarians* sat on my steel locker.

The gate cracked open with a jarring bang. I quickly covered the 240 feet between my cell and the stairway, passing the CO who had spent the last hour cooking his breakfast. He poured maple syrup over his French toast without looking up.

As I emerged from the stairway into the lobby, a phalanx of officers, each with a thick wooden baton gripped tightly in both hands, greeted me with cold stares. I kept my head down, looking at the floor as I got in line with thirty other inmates. An officer slammed the stairway door. I exhaled, and steeled myself in preparation for clearing the next five checkpoints.

The escort officer barked, "Forward." Two by two, in silence, we walked the brick passageway, like Carthusian monks heading to vespers. The only sound in the corridor was the clomp of our state-issued boots. Robotically, we stopped at each yellow line painted across the concrete floor until instructed to proceed.

The Transition Center was then a relatively new section of the prison. Its linoleum floor was still shiny. As I entered, an obese officer demanded, without even looking at me, "Call location," then instructed me to "Sit in the bullpen." It was a holding cell, devoid of air and light, where minutes could become hours. It contained only narrow wood benches and a toilet visible to all.

Of the two thousand inmates in the jail, only fifteen at a time could attend a Cephas meeting. Like nearly every prison program, there was a long waiting list. For the jail's addiction program, the list contained over one thousand names. Most would never participate.

As the officer barked, "Cephas," the bullpen gate cracked open. I walked down a well-lit corridor with painted sheetrock walls. Each meeting room had wire-glass observation windows instead of the typical barred openings. As I entered the meeting room, I shook hands with the volunteers and bumped fists with the inmates. Some of the guys called out, "Hey, yo, John, wassup?" Each week, we shared frustrations, talked about the mistakes we'd made, and struggled with change. As the weeks passed, I watched guys open up and share their pain and deal with their issues. Some progressed more quickly than others. It took work. But the rewards were tremendous.

At one meeting, a guy was pissed at his coworkers. While he had been at the law library working on an appeal, they rearranged their work area and got rid of his desk. He felt betrayed. Sitting in the meeting, agitated and angry, he told us, "I just wanna break their fuckin' faces, every fuckin' one a them." We listened, gave feedback, talked about the consequences of his choices. By the end of the meeting, he was laughing and joking. He was still mad at his coworkers, but had no intentions of hurting them.

One guy had finally divorced his wife after six years of legal wrangling. Rather than sell their house and split the proceeds, as a family court judge had ordered, she burned it to the ground. He planned on getting revenge. There was no easy solution to his intense anger, but he took our advice and joined AA. I later edited a story he wrote about the incident, and published it in the AA journal. I like to think it brought him some closure on his loss.

The Cephas meeting room was light and airy with windows on three sides. About twenty plastic chairs stood in a large circle. As I looked at the volunteers, I thought of their dedication. Inmate faces in the group often changed, but the same volunteers were there every week. Some had been attending meetings for twenty years. They showed far more commitment than we did. Despite our difficulties in getting from our cells to the meeting, it was only a fifteen-minute trip for us. Many of the volunteers drove hours to and from the prison. Once there, they waited, just like we did, to be cleared by the COs to enter the meeting. Sometimes they received a hostile reception—rudeness, even name-calling. I had heard stories of some officers calling them "tree huggers" or "mud lovers." (We are the mud.) But the volunteers always walked into the meetings with smiles and optimism. I envied their patience.

Slowly, the meeting room filled up as inmates from each block arrived. One of the volunteers, Iris, in a denim skirt and white blouse, signaled to get everyone's attention.

"OK, I think everyone's here. I see some new faces. Welcome. Would somebody like to explain what Cephas is, and what the rules are, to the new guys? Billy, you've been coming to the meetings for a while. Why don't you explain to the new guys the history of Cephas?"

Billy, just like the word Cephas, was a rock or foundation for the meetings. Incarcerated for over forty years, he had been attending Cephas meetings for eighteen of those years. Sitting with one leg crossed and his hands serenely folded over his large belly, he pursed his lips.

"OK, well, let's see. Cephas was started at Attica in 1971, right after the riot there. It was one of the programs that came about in response to prisoner issues. Later, they added the program to other prisons, including here. The meetings are a support group, you know, a place where we can deal with our issues. Like anger, or loss, being locked up, getting hit at the parole board. Boy, do I know about that." Billy's chin rested on his neck. He had been denied at the parole board twelve times.

The guy next to me snorted and muttered, "Motherfuckers."

Billy looked up. "We look at the ugly stuff, you know, our actions, the choices we've made. We try to learn from them. There's no easy solutions. You get out of these meetings what you put into them. You gotta do work if you wanna see results."

Iris neatened some papers on her lap and flipped back her long, black hair. "Thanks, Billy. OK, who wants to get started?" She looked around the circle, eyebrows raised.

I announced that the meditation class had started up again. The previous instructor had moved to Colorado. I was happy for him, but disappointed that the class had ended. Meditation taught me how to release anger. As worry, anxiety, or thoughts of revenge came to mind, I learned to let them go. As they vanished, I caught glimpses of serenity. I also learned not to dwell on others' criticisms of me. I came to see that their rejection was their loss, not mine. Meditation took practice and concentration. It wasn't easy. But it worked. I told the group to just write to the deputy superintendent of programs if they wanted to go.

Sitting next to me, a guy in a thin state tee shirt, grayed from laundering, said, "I got an anger problem. Real bad. I got mad time in the box. You think meditation help me?"

Billy answered. He looked into the center of the circle, at the floor, not directing his comments at anyone in particular: "I don't know. It taught me to not let others control my thoughts, make me react. Sometimes 'cause of what someone says, you think you gotta do something. But you really don't. Give the class a try. If you don't like it, you don't have to go. It's voluntary."

His hands still lay folded over his belly. The pant cuff of his crossed leg rode high, exposing varicose veins and mottled skin. "I used to let others make me react, you know, push my buttons. I had a real bad temper. Someone would say something slick to me, you know, disrespect me. I could feel the anger surge and take over my body, like the reaction was so fast. I had no time to think. I was just an observer, you know, watching the events take place. By the time I realized I was out of control, it was too late. I was surrounded by carnage. Things were broken; there was blood all over. I didn't even know whose blood it was. I would go into a blackout."

I thought of my first, and only, prison fight. I remembered the events leading up to it, but the actual fight I had no memory of. Only by talking with guys who witnessed it did I find out what happened. My brain had stopped.

A guy sitting across from Billy in a red sweatshirt and a red kufi said, "Hey, yo, Billy, I ain't never seen you in the box. I just done six months straight in the snake pit. When's the last time you got into a fight?"

"Oh, it's been years, lotta years. But it took me a long time to realize I could control myself. I had to change the way I thought. Which was not easy. I had to stop and ask myself, is this really a threat? Is it a threat to *me*? To my safety, to my well-being? Or am I mad just 'cause someone disagrees with me? Once I learned to answer those questions before acting, you know, just take a couple of minutes before doing anything, then I saw things different. I could feel the rage subside. I could feel myself returning to normal, you know, my brain thinking logically again."

The room was quiet for a moment. Iris readjusted her seat. I wanted to know how Billy learned to rewire his brain. "Billy, lemme ask you something. What brought about that change? How did you learn to do that?"

"Hah. That's a good question." Billy uncrossed his legs and leaned forward in his chair with his elbows resting on his knees. "When I was at Auburn, there was this support group—Adult Children of Alcoholics. It was a program the volunteers there set up. It was like AA, but they weren't alcoholics. They all had alcoholic parents. That was a real wake-up for me. I realized my anger came from my childhood, from watching my parents fight, the drunken violence, from the fear, my frustration with trying to keep my family together. You know, fixing everything. Cookin' and cleanin' when my folks was sleepin' with hangovers, or passed out. But I was just a kid. I couldn't fix everything. I didn't know how. The room in Auburn was filled with guys who had gone through the same thing. It dawned on me that I wasn't crazy. It was my childhood that was crazy. My insane, alcoholic parents."

A sadness came over Billy. He fell silent and stared at the floor. His large ruddy ears and pouty lips made him appear childlike, helpless.

Drama, who had been silent and was sitting across from Iris, asked, "Billy, they got a program like that here?"

"Nah, it was a special program volunteers had set up in Auburn. I've never seen it at any other facility."

I looked around the room at the fifteen guys seated in the circle, wondering how many of them had no idea where their anger came from. Like a fog, it constantly surrounded them, poisoning all who encountered it.

I was just beginning to look at my own anger issues through my writing. I had spent over twenty years medicating myself rather than confront my pain. I guzzled vodka and blew coke up until I forgot who I was, forgot the anxiety that pervaded every cell of my body. I was frightened of my feelings, of my anger, of the anger I inherited from my father. Drugged oblivion calmed me, comforted me, making me feel safe.

In prison I was unwillingly subjected to sobriety. I was terrified. The intensity of my emotions, in addition to the brutality of my environment, seemed overwhelming. I had no crutch to support me, to dull the pain. Sobriety made the learning curve steep. But because I was fully aware of my emotions, I dealt with my problems head-on, with a clear mind. With both hands tightly gripped on the steering wheel, I braced for a teeth-rattling ride.

In the third year of my incarceration, I found writing about the events smoothed the pavement. It gave me the ability to slow the action and view it from an observer's perspective. Clarity and peace developed. My actions and my choices came into focus. I began to see the sources of my pain, instead of being blinded by their intensity. At Riker's Island, awaiting trial, I played the tapes over and over in my mind, wallowing in my own filth, rubbing my face in the guilt. Once I arrived in prison, I joined my first volunteer program—creative writing. The teacher was a college professor who recognized the value, and importance, of prison writing. I began the process of focused writing, reconstructing the details, the dialogue, and the actors. Embracing the pain, I accepted it, and the festering wounds, exposed to air, slowly began to heal.

Cephas meetings helped me to look at other issues I had avoided—like my relationship to the word *No.* That two-letter word infuriated me. I perceived it as a locked door obstructing my way. I had mentioned during a meeting how mad I would get when officers burned me on call-outs, preventing me from attending a volunteer program. It usually happened at night. Sometimes the CO simply didn't feel like escorting us to the school building—an exhausting walk of 300 feet (roundtrip). Some COs just didn't want to take time away from watching sports on TV to open cell gates. It infuriated me that I was trying to change, as the Department of Corrections required me to do before being eligible for parole, yet the DOC, in effect, was blocking my efforts.

The Quakers offered an anti-violence program called AVP: Alternative to Violence Project. It was a nationally recognized program offered in prisons from Auburn to San Quentin. I had been on the waiting list for nine months. The day before I was to attend the program, I returned to my cell from work. I had to ask the CO to open my gate. Standing at "the bubble" waiting to speak with the officer, I glanced at his name tag. I like to address officers by their names—Mr. Miller, for example, rather than just "CO." As I stood there, he looked up from his clipboard.

"Why you lookin' at my name tag? Don't choo ever look at my name tag! You got me? Where you lock?"

I stood there, wide-eyed. "37 cell."

"Then lock in, and don't come out!"

He didn't open my cell for two days—no AVP, no yard, no chow. I ate ramen instant soups and did crossword puzzles until the regular CO came back to work three days later.

I had to wait a year before finally attending AVP. Once there, I realized why the waiting list was so long. It was only a three-day program, but it was an intensive twelve hours per day. The volunteers, some of them Quakers, all of them kind and empathetic, took care of our every need. Sated with food, coffee, and donuts, we participated in community-building exercises, laughed, and shared our personal stories. We also took a good look at our anger issues, our frustrations, the old habits that led to arguments and fights. Eating, sharing stories, communicating, I felt like I had been adopted by a normal family.

The steel door swung open. An officer stuck just his head in the room and said, "Go-back." The meeting was over. Smiling, shaking hands, we thanked the volunteers, telling them, "See you next week." We filed out of the room, returning to the bullpen. It was full of guys from other programs, mental health appointments, and parole officer interviews. I sat on a crowded wood bench. The air was stagnant and fetid.

Someone asked, "What's for chow?"

A wise guy answered, "State food."

As the calm from the Cephas meeting enveloped me, conversations in the bullpen got loud. Guys with self-esteem problems shouted at each other.

"Yo, homie, you's losin' your swag, son."

"Yo, quit playin'. I ain't losin' nothin'. I's from the Bronx, son."

Façades and masks fell into place. Tough guys resumed tough-guy images. The same guys that only minutes ago shared their pain now stuffed their feelings. Real change required more than one meeting.

Changes in my own behavior took place slowly, over the course of years. Often, others noticed a change before I did. I had been attending AA meetings religiously, twice a week, for three years. I managed to get five years of sobriety under my belt, all while incarcerated. Alcohol is rarely seen in prison, but drugs are widely available. Guys often go to the box for dirty urine. I had successfully passed numerous urinalyses. That was a big change. I used to break out in a sweat at the mere mention of a piss test.

But the biggest change I exhibited was in sharing my feelings, talking about what was going on down deep. My father had taught me to keep my mouth shut. Expressing my emotions resulted in swift retribution, usually a slap or a kick. Over the course of my three years in AA, I conquered my fear of opening up. I talked about my drug use, my behavior that led me to prison, and my faults—stubbornness, egotism, and low self-esteem. In AA, we had an expression for that—an egomaniac with an inferiority complex. I laughed, and through tears shared my secrets: lies, deceit, abusive behavior. I admitted that I stole painkillers from my mother as she lay dying of cancer. I revealed my HIV status, learning that exposing secrets took away their power.

However, not all the inmates in the programs were seeking change. Some were just looking to continue their sick behavior. Some had their own private agendas. As my participation in volunteer programs increased, so did my visibility and authority. I was elected to service-board positions in AA: co-chairman, editor of the newsletter. My dependability led me to become influential with outside volunteers and civilian staff who coordinated the programs. I was invited to the volunteer-recognition dinner each year, an inmate-catered affair packed with volunteers and administration officials. But as my influence increased, I became a target for those who were envious.

At first, I dismissed the idea that guys would be jealous of what little I had. I was subject to the same rules, and abuse, as others. I got screamed at and burnt on call-outs just like everyone. I thought it ludicrous that guys would be jealous of my involvement in the same programs in which they could participate. But I had to learn the hard way that guys who had little of value on the streets placed great value on things I took for granted—a good vocabulary, a nice smile, acceptance by my peers. The image I present—organized and confident—was perceived as a threat by those with self-esteem issues.

When my coworkers first explained this to me, I laughed. "The way I talk? I gotta change the way I talk?" "My shirt, somebody's jealous of my tee shirt?" I thought that was silly. I learned otherwise.

At the center where I worked, a facilitator was fired. I was blamed for his termination simply because I was influential and well-liked by the staff—the implication being that I was a rat. The nonsense got even crazier. A fellow member of AA sent a "kite," a jailhouse letter, to the AA staff advisor. In it, I was accused of leaking information shared at a meeting to a district attorney. I was labeled a jailhouse snitch, and with the snowball rolling, administration officials were warned my life was threatened. The advisor had no choice but to remove me from the meetings for my safety. The untruth of the accusations was irrelevant.

At the first AA meeting I missed, another member was elected to my position as newsletter editor. He had been a frequent critic of the newsletter, having run against me before and lost. I was bitter. I had developed the newsletter from a one-page mimeographed sheet into a respected and popular journal. Rumors about me spread throughout the jail. Guys that used to see me in programs, smile at me, and bump fists now averted their gaze. At times, I was greeted by icy stares. While I wasted much time ruminating about who could be my unnamed enemy, I eventually resigned myself to moving on.

As I sat on my bunk at night, stewing, I could see the chapel through the barred openings of my cell. The chapel doors were open, indicating an AA meeting was taking place. The broad arched windows glowed softly. Narrow black mullions, outlining panes of translucent glass, formed a thin latticework. As my fellow addicts congregated in the chapel, I fantasized about revenge. How could they have done this to me? Which ones spoke against me? But as the anger slowly subsided, my own words came back to me—advice I often gave out while teaching my orientation class to guys just arriving. "It's all about change. Embrace it, don't fight it. Nothing is permanent." How annoying, what a blow to the ego, to know the answer but also be blind to it. All the volunteer programs were geared to teach us how to deal with change. Sure, it's uncomfortable, aggravating, maddening. But if I could just let go and surrender, I would find glimpses of serenity in acceptance.

In meditation class, the instructor often told us, "Suffering is caused by desire, wanting things we don't have, or hanging onto things we do have and want to lose. That's foolish, because eventually, all of it vanishes. If you can accept that loss now, you will be free of suffering."

It was impractical to try to hang onto anything in prison. What little property I held, a few canvas sacks of "things," I retained only at the state's discretion. One infraction could result in the loss of it all. My prison job, the programs I attended, the positions I held in those programs . . . they were all temporary, fleeting things. The clothing I wore: state property. I thought of Viktor Frankl imprisoned in Auschwitz, stripped naked by his Nazi jailors—his family, his reading glasses, even his gold-filled teeth taken away from him. Yet he never gave up, turning his suffering into wisdom and strength. He didn't let his circumstances defeat him. He adapted and conquered, declaring, "The last of human freedoms is the ability to choose one's attitude in any given set of circumstances."

I continue to support volunteer programs, generating interest about them in the orientation class I teach, getting guys in my block to attend. But it's a struggle. Many guys try programs for a while, but give up in frustration, fed up with the hassles from guards, and intransigence on the part of the administration.

I try to help in other ways. As word got around my block that I was an aspiring prison writer, a few guys came to me for help with their own writing. They had tried attending the prison's creative writing class, but couldn't due to its limited size. I edited their work and encouraged them to persevere, sharing what I had learned from the volunteer who taught the class. I found it rewarding when guys took my writing advice and incorporated it into their work. I struggled with my own writing. We sometimes took our work into the yard, forming a picnic table of inmates with pens and writing pads. (I fancied us at the Algonquin Round Table, trading quips and barbs, filling the air with smoke and profanity.) On the days when my energy waned, they motivated me to keep going, slogging it out, one word at a time.

Letting go, I resolved to explore the path ahead, and accept what came my way. After sixteen months on the waiting list, I was offered a cell in the honor block, a privilege for those who had avoided trouble. I had been hesitant to apply for the move because I had no idea what it would be like. Once I made the move, I was relieved. Afforded more freedom, I now spend less time in volunteer programs, and more time in solitude—reflecting, writing, and meditating. An essay I wrote about my life on the streets gave me some clarity on the events that led me to prison. I plant basil and oregano in the honor-block garden. With the herbs, I make tomato sauce using the recipe my Italian grandmother taught me on her white-enameled Hobart stove. As I pour the thick, garlicky sauce over *rigatoni al dente*, I practice mindfulness—being present in the moment, accepting what is. I try to not label events as either good or bad. I try to accept them as they are, without judgment.

Ticket In

STEVEN KING AINSWORTH, *California*

LESSONS IN STUPIDITY

How does a criminal find value in his life? Is it the lesson he can give about stupidity? Or is it in some other niche that he serves his fellow man? Am I to remain a pariah? Perhaps you should decide after perusing this bit of personal history, which I offer for your benefit.

I first entered the California state prison system in 1968 at age twenty-three with an indeterminate sentence of five years to life for my part as the wheelman (getaway-car driver) in the armed robbery of American River Junior College in Sacramento County, California.

At the time, the northern California Reception and Guidance Center (RGC) was located at the California Medical Facility (CMF) in Vacaville, California. Two sheriff's deputies drove me there in a squad car. It was a short trip. Even now, forty-three years later, I can still hear the solid *thunk* of that gate slamming shut behind me!

After testing and examination by various correctional experts at RGC, I was transferred to Deuel Vocational Institution (DVI) near Tracy, California, to do my time as a young first-termer. DVI housed a majority of young first-termers that the California Department of Corrections (CDC) hoped to rehabilitate and return to society as law-abiding citizens.

The Classification Committee noted that I did not have a high school diploma and suggested I attend Tracy Adult School in the prison. I only needed the senior-year courses to graduate, despite the fact that I had completed the GED tests successfully in 1961 while serving in the United States Army. (I had joined the Army with my parents' permission three days after my seventeenth birthday, after being expelled from high school in May 1961 for possession of alcohol.) I followed the committee's advice and completed the required courses in six months and received a formal high school diploma while at DVI.

Besides the teenage abuse of alcohol, my military career was peppered with violations of the Uniform Code of Military Justice—violations that resulted in some incarceration in military stockades. I was also introduced to the family of opiates that bring a profound sense of well-being. An unauthorized trip to Baltimore, Maryland, with a fellow junkie resulted in my first felony conviction for possession of a bad check (an altered money order). The Maryland authorities suspended a prison sentence and turned me over to military authorities. After being held in the stockade at Fort Meade for a few months, I was discharged from the U.S. Army in 1964 as an undesirable.

While I was in the Baltimore City Jail, a chaplain had come by my cell to tell me that my father had committed suicide on Christmas Day, 1963. After my father made two serious attempts on my life in my teenage years, "estranged" might be the best term to describe our relationship. My mother and sister met me at the airport upon my return to Sacramento. I questioned them about my father's death, but neither could provide a rational explanation for his act. (My mother did indicate that he was unaware of my jailing in Baltimore and my discharge as a criminal.) Suicide is a very selfish act, and its effect on family survivors is piercing.

One of the consequences of my criminal discharge was my inability to get a decent job with any company that had contracts with the federal government. For instance, I applied for one of two jobs that were open at the Union Carbide plant in Sacramento, which produced rocket fuel for Aerojet General, another local company. I placed number one on the written test and number two in the interview portion. A cinch domino for hiring. Unfortunately, I was told by the personnel manager that they could not hire me due to my undesirable discharge.

The difficulty in finding gainful employment was coupled with the difficulty I had in finding a heroin connection. While I searched for someone willing to sell me some scag, I turned to codeine, a mild opiate. In the mid-sixties you could buy codeine cough syrups over the counter by signing a drug registration book. I had used codeine cough syrup and paregoric (tincture of opium) to ease the pangs of addiction in the past between fixes of horse. My favorite syrup was the ugly-tasting but potent terpin hydrate with codeine. I would make the rounds of several drug stores, buying three or four bottles at each stop. While the codeine kept the edge off my desire, it did not have the call of smack. I needed the euphoric comfort heroin held for me.

Without a job, I turned to burglary for bread to fulfill my daily needs and desires. This vocation was not without risk. Between my bust in Baltimore and my arrival at CMF in 1968, I fell thirteen times, with twenty-two charges involved. Out of four years and forty-five days between 1963 and 1968, I spent 650 days in county jails. The charges were mostly misdemeanors, sprinkled lightly with a felony here and there. The days in jail were mostly dry-outs for me and opportunities to meet hopheads, connections, and other outlaws.

As soon as I hit the bricks after a jolt in the county cooler, I would do a burglary, or hook up with some boosters and do some high-end shoplifting to obtain goods and swag that the local fence would accept and pay cash for. Within hours after leaving the hoosegow, I would be at the pusher man's pad scoring some quarter bags of heroin. Soon thereafter I would rent a motel room and slam some of the potent Mexican brown dope. Uhmmm!

This cycle continued until I quit doing burglaries and boosting, which were labor-intensive and took a lot of time with little return. I then turned to armed robbery. The proceeds were immediate! With no middleman to cut in, the cash was quickly spent as my original crime partner and I ran amok. We did many heists and took up with a trio of ladies called "The Red Gang" for their penchant for Seconal and other barbiturates. We would rent a hotel or motel room for a few nights after a decent score and invite the ladies to party with us. As my partner and I mainlined heroin or some other opium-based drug, the girls got rowdy on reds. He was the gunman in the robbery of the college that sent me to the pen in 1968. He ended up committing suicide in the hospital at San Quentin (SQ) in 1969.

So, back to DVI: After graduating from Tracy Adult School, I was advised to take a vocational trade. I chose machine operation and was assigned to the Vocational Machine Shop. I became proficient in the operation of various metalworking machines and ended up in the Prison Industry Authority's (PIA) metal fabrication machine shop.

By this time, I realized the parole board would need a little more progress in self-directed rehabilitation. I joined the Gavel Club, sponsored by Toastmasters International. It taught me the art of public speaking . . . and gave me an "attaboy" chrono for the parole board.

My next move was to formulate a parole plan to present to the board. One of the education instructors at DVI tipped me off to the Project Rebound at the state college in San Francisco, which assisted ex-cons in gaining a college degree. I was accepted for the fall semester of 1971, should I be granted a parole date in time to enroll with the freshman class.

The parole board gave me a 1971 parole date just three days before enrollment. I left DVI on a Friday, met my parole agent in San Francisco that afternoon, and met with John Irwin, a professor at San Francisco State College who headed Project Rebound. Professor Irwin was also a successful ex-con. The Project had arranged a room for me in one of the dorms. I was also introduced to an ex-con who counseled the newly enrolled ex-cons at the college.

My sister and mother visited me at the college that weekend, and Monday I registered for classes. My first three classes met the following day. I was on my way to a better life, albeit in a bit of culture shock! I was released with a good attitude and meant to do well in my classes. I was also given a work-study grant, which provided me with a job in the dorms.

Unfortunately, the ex-con who counseled the ex-cons in Project Rebound supplemented his income with some drug dealing. He had jars (1,000 doses) of mini-meth tablets and cocaine, which he shared with me for a bit of labor. I was given a jar on consignment to sell, and did some deliveries for him. I even acted as the heavy in a few buys of coke in kilo weight for the dude. I used quite a bit of the product and lost my focus on college classes.

Needless to say, I ended the first year of freedom as a parolee at large, packin' a piece and back to my criminally ways . . . slammin' smack and doing holdups. The Man ran me to ground in the parking lot of a drugstore I had just robbed in Olivehurst, California. I was sent back to prison with a new beef and two 5-to-life sentences running concurrently, in late 1972.

As a refresher, they ran me through CMF so I could hear that solid *thunk* once again. I did a few days at RGC and caught the grey goose (CDC bus) up to California Conservation Center at Susanville, California, for processing as a parole violator with a new beef. From there I was sent to Soledad-North (CTF-N) for a year or so. Then I moved over to Soledad-Central (CTF-C) to work in the wood-manufacturing plant. After a year or so of that, I went to work in the kitchen as a second cook. I did make a couple of parole-board appearances while at CTF-C, with negative results. I really did not expect a parole date; after blowing the higher-education route to freedom, I would have to come up with some other plan.

In 1975, I was transferred to Sierra Conservation Center (SCC) at Jamestown, California. I was working my way to a minimum-custody assignment, to one of the Conservation Camps as a member of a fire-fighting crew. In early 1976 I went through the physical-fitness course and fire-fighting course and passed both with flying colors. I was assigned to the Miramonte Conservation Camp in the Sierra Mountain Foothills east of Fresno, California. I lasted one day!

An upper-echelon administrator at SCC realized that because of the violence and seriousness of my two armed-robbery convictions, I had to go through a Category-D psychological program (stress test) and should not be in a forestry camp. My criminal career, as measured by contact with law enforcement, began with vandalism at fifteen and progressed in seriousness and violence from there. The camp guards transported me to the Fresno County Jail for pickup by a transport team from SCC. I returned to SCC for several weeks and caught the grey goose for the ride to San Quentin State Prison for assignment to a Cat-D program.

Upon completion of the Cat-D program, I was scheduled for a parole-board hearing. At the hearing, the board felt I was ready for parole. I told them not to release me until I had a job to go to. They took me at my word and denied me a parole for ninety days, with a recommendation I go through a pre-release program and be given a seventy-two-hour pass to secure employment.

I was given the pass and found a job with a body shop in Walnut Creek, California. I returned to San Quentin and soon went to a parole hearing. The board gave me a release upon approval of parole plan: a RUAPP. After five years inside, I was out again. I would discharge this parole in

STEVEN KING AINSWORTH   89

July 1978 . . . while awaiting judgment in the San Mateo County Jail on an assault charge that was dropped soon after my discharge and release from CDC clutches.

From my release in 1977 to my discharge off parole the following year, I tried the Joe Lunch Box routine. I was being tested every month for narcotic use (but not for alcohol), and worked several jobs through Manpower, Inc. Most of the jobs were physical and menial jobs with no upward mobility. I had taken up with a New Zealand woman with an interesting accent who I met during my ill-fated attempt at college six years earlier. Her folks were good to her and helped her buy a new car and a home in Union City, California.

I drank beer and wine for breakfast and during the commute to a job across San Francisco Bay from Union City. As soon as CDC cut its leash on me, I started to do heroin again. I felt hemmed in by my relationship, and frankly was not up to the responsibility of life as John Q. Citizen. I began to have an affair, and after a five-day absence from my companion in Union City, she found me in Redwood City, recovered her car, and threw my belongings into the street.

My reaction was both typical for me and tragic for an innocent human being. I got drunk, I got high, and I found a gun. By my thirty-fourth birthday I was running from the law once again. This time, in a bungled car-jacking, I killed a human being. The law caught up with me in May 1979. I was tried, convicted, and condemned to die in San Quentin's gas chamber.

By February 1980 I was on death row at SQ. California law required that a capital case go through an automatic appeal that cannot be waived by the condemned. By the time my appeal was over, I had decided to play the hand I was dealt. Three execution dates would be set and stayed. I had come close to execution, but survived. Twenty-two years later my death sentence would be set aside, and on May 7, 2002, I was sentenced to life without parole (LWOP), which in reality is another kind of death sentence. I sit here writing this narrative in a maximum-security prison, searching for forgiveness and some value to my life.

If only I had quit my criminal life. If only I had taken advantage of the chances given me. If only I had not taken the life of another human being.

I am a pariah. Is there some value in this lesson in stupidity? Is it my niche in life to support a vast network of civil servants? I think the reader can decide.

NOTE

I would like to dedicate this essay to John Irwin, who gave me a chance to save myself from myself. John Irwin passed away January 3, 2010, in San Francisco.

Seeking Peace in Prison City

INTRODUCTION

Despite the extraordinary challenges inside Prison City, every man and woman here wants to do more than simply survive their time inside. This collection of essays is called "Seeking Peace" because every author has managed to find ways to do just that—to discover through meditation, religion, art, or other practices, a way to push back against the predictable hostility of the prison and create pockets of inner calm. What is striking here is the unaided initiative required by incarcerated people to achieve ends that we might assume the prison would take on as its primary charge: to help people who have damaged or ended the lives of others to become people we might welcome back among us. These writers bear witness to the capacity of incarcerated people to seek and secure the changes in themselves that *should* model for Prison City what that city is all about.

Diana Waggy's "Inspiration" describes the change the author has achieved: once a mentally ill, violent woman, she finds a place of peace, tranquility, humor, and quiet remorse. Waggy's transformation was aided by one of the thousands of unpaid civilian volunteers who go into American prisons every day to give their time, care, and skills to those struggling to find peace inside.[1] But no transformation this drastic can occur without the dedicated effort of incarcerated people to make something positive of the mistakes that brought them to prison. Waggy also sees firsthand the difference between politicians who stump for tough-on-crime policies, and the quiet, daily work actually required to make real changes in convicted felons—work that makes both prisons and the streets that incarcerated people will return to someday truly safer for everyone.

Terrence Sampson was jailed at age twelve and sentenced to 30 years in prison at the age of thirteen. He became what one might expect a child to become in order to survive inside. But today he writes, "In order for my life to be meaningful, I have to have a positive impact on as many people as possible. Yes, that is what will give my life meaning." Like others in this volume, he writes to make his time inside into something positive after the destruction wrought on his own and on others' lives. "The Evolution of a Dreamer" presents yet another incarcerated American pushing on despite the daily humiliations and dehumanization that prisons are intent on meting out to their wards, and despite the anger and violence that these writers face among the most successfully dehumanized of their peers.

Shelley Mac's "Beginnings" traces the path that many convicted people discover, from lives consumed by drugs, alcohol, and the next escapist thrill, to deeper self-understanding through their first embrace of a spiritual life. The detachment and self-reflection that set the tone here are virtues that have been grasped by an author willing to engage in levels of self-assessment that few of us will ever face, let alone confess in writing; and in the peace that comes from that process, we see what real growth and maturation look like. In this way, this and other essays in this volume are not simply about life in prison, but about how any life can be conducted, by the person living it, into its truest and most fulfilling path.

Many prisons offer what they imagine are means to let prisoners work off the energy and emotions that are bound to accumulate and turn ugly among men and women living in cages: weights, gyms, recreation yards, training programs, etc. But as Michael Crawford's "The Therapeutic Nature of Art in Prison" shows, the constructive, legal means that will always serve best are those that the incarcerated discover for themselves, in which they can both invest and discover creative curiosity and expression. Crawford describes how deeply he becomes enveloped in the world of his art, and the benefits it brings both to himself and to others. His essay suggests that alongside whatever programs state and federal institutions might mandate, the incarcerated should also be encouraged to develop the constructive gifts they bring with them into the prison: gifts that should be supported as they work to make prison life a viable staging ground for lives on the outside.

We can hardly help admiring those who pursue the formidable internal labor required to discover some sense of peace and tranquility inside prisons rife with violence and the violent, and where official and unofficial staff practice is often willfully destructive. We can only wonder how it is that anyone engaging in such pursuit manages to do so in the face of outright ridicule and institutional barriers, and then goes further, to help others discover a similar path to peace. In "Bread and Water Vegan: Struggling for Health and Humanity inside Prison," author Intelligent Allah documents his efforts to do all these things in spreading the word for a vegan lifestyle committed to the health and well-being of human beings and animals alike. Like many others in this collection, he reveals the irony of the public's writing off convicted criminals as no more and no better than their crimes, while the very weight of these crimes so often inspires a transformative will to serve the common good that many on the outside never find in themselves.

Steven F. Lomas's "Meditation" completes this gathering of men and women writing about how they manage, first, to hold up and hold themselves together within the environment of the prison, and then to seek calm and tranquility in this most uncalm and untranquil place. Lomas's essay brings us back to the fundamental truth that Viktor Frankl discovered in the Nazi death camps: our last freedom is the freedom to control how we will respond to our circumstances, for "in the final analysis it becomes clear that the sort of person the prisoner became was the result of an inner decision, and not the result of camp influences alone."[2] Through a regular meditation practice, closely coupled with questioning his own motives and desires and resulting actions, Lomas, like Allah, discovers that peace is often most directly pursued by the seemingly indirect route of being better to and for others.

These essays remind us that despite how badly we manage the job of running and overseeing prisons, there will always be incarcerated men and women who will find a way, in spite of that environment, to become peacemakers—for themselves and for others. Prison City would surely be an even more violent, debilitating, and costly enterprise without their work.

NOTES

1. See Richard Tewksbury and Dean Dabney, "Prison Volunteers: Profiles, Motivations, Satisfaction," *Journal of Offender Rehabilitation* 40, no. 1/2 (2004): 173–83; Richard Shelton, *Crossing the Yard: Thirty Years as a Prison Volunteer* (Tucson: University of Arizona Press, 2007).

2. Viktor Frankl, *Man's Search for Meaning*, trans. Ilse Lasch (1946; Boston: Beacon Press, 2006), 66.

DIANA WAGGY, *Alaska*

INSPIRATION

Everyone talked quietly amongst themselves as we waited for her to arrive. Two hundred women were seated in the gym, with a dozen guards stationed around the perimeter. Long, gray curtains partitioned off part of the room—the old creaky bleachers and various cabinets, athletic gear, and other detritus usually found in the prison's gymnasium. I knew this because I was in charge of getting everything moved and cleaned in preparation for the ceremony. I felt a tinge of embarrassment because the gym floor looked filthy. No matter how many times we sweep and mop it, the ground-in dirt won't come off.

"I hope she comes soon," someone said; "my butt's getting sore."

Finally, Governor Palin arrived. The room fell silent as she and her entourage walked in. I started to rise, and then realized I would be the only one doing so and remembered the instructions given to the inmates. No standing, no approaching her, no talking to her, stay in your seat.

I was shocked at how tiny she was, how thin and fragile she looked as she walked to the front of the room, her shoulders slightly rounded and bent forward. She didn't look so delicate on television. But here, in person, she looked like a little bird in a bright red skirted suit. Someone introduced her and everyone applauded politely.

I listened intently to the governor's speech, as I wanted to hear everything she had to say to us. I was also star-struck, though this was *before* she was chosen as John McCain's running mate. Now, in 2010, she can raise $300,000 in a single evening's speaking engagement. I got to hear her for free! Wow! Imagine that.

The governor and the inmates were brought together at Hiland Mountain Correctional Center that day because of Wyatt, the first service-dog graduate of our dog-training program. Wyatt was being presented to a wounded Alaskan veteran. Besides Governor Palin and the Department of Corrections VIPs, there were officers representing every branch of the military, plus members of the wounded soldier's family and Army unit. It was a happy but stressful event because of all the important people there.

The previous day, when I learned that Governor Palin was going to come to my humble prison home, I told my job supervisor, Sgt. L., "I want to meet her. I'd shake her hand and say, 'Hi, I'm one of the people you want to kill with the death penalty.'"

"You better not!" Sgt. L. said. She knew I was joking and I would not really say that to Governor Palin. That year one of our Alaska state legislators wanted to introduce new death penalty legislation, and it had been reported that Governor Palin said she would support it if it came to her desk. In reality, it wouldn't apply to me, because my case had been closed and dispensed with, but the death penalty was still a scary thought.

Governor Palin delivered her speech, and although I could barely see her from where I was sitting, there was no mistaking her voice. She sounded just like she sounded on TV: confident and feminine with a lilt of laughter or irony or sarcasm, or whatever you want to call it that makes it Sarah Palin's unique and recognizable voice.

She talked about strength, perseverance, and overcoming obstacles so that we could achieve our "God-given destiny." *God-given destiny?* She used that phrase at least twice. I've thought a lot about God, fate and destiny, choice and free will during my fifteen years in prison. Was it my victim's God-given destiny to be murdered by me through no fault of his own? Was it God-given destiny that I be stricken with mental illness? Was it God-given destiny that my daughter become, in effect, an orphan? No. I do not believe that.

What I do believe about what happens in any person's life is in the words of a 1980s pop song: "One thing leads to another." That's it. We're all connected. We think or say or do something and that sends ripples of influence all around us. One thought causes something, which leads to something else, which leads to something else, which leads to a victory or a meltdown, depending on which direction we're going.

I was very mentally ill before I killed that poor man, and I begged anyone and everyone for help. I went to a large Anchorage church for help. An assistant pastor spoke with me for fifteen minutes, told me I wasn't resisting the devil strongly enough, then dismissed me. Did the devil make me do it? Please. I'll tell you exactly what happened. One thing led to another, which led to another and another, which led to the present moment.

I was in the hole for most of the first three years I was in prison—"the hole" meaning locked in a small cell for 23 hours a day. One of my current wingmates recently asked, "Diana, do you remember when you used to stand in your cell at Sixth Avenue jail and rock side to side and growl?"

"No!" I said with a laugh. "I remember rocking back and forth and walking in circles, but I don't remember growling."

"You sure as shit did! You were scary back then. You were off the chain!"

There's a lot I don't remember about that sad and frightening time of my life. Was it God-given destiny that I end up in that dark, lonely cell? Or was it God-given destiny that I live a completely different, wonderful life, but then I just screwed it up?

Luckily for everyone, we *can* change direction. Unfortunately, *I* didn't change direction until after I murdered someone.

What finally pulled me out of the darkness that had become my mind and my life? Medication helped significantly. Still, I struggled. One day in 1999, two years after I got out of the hole, I was agitated and couldn't calm my mind. I knew I was having a spiritual crisis, but didn't know what to do. A thought occurred to me. *Buddhists always look calm. Maybe that can help me.* I ran to my wing and looked up Buddhist groups in the phone book. There was only one listed, the Anchorage Zen Community (AZC). I called and left a voice-mail message. A few days later the phone rang in the main dayroom. It was a woman calling from AZC for me.

You have to understand that we are almost never allowed incoming phone calls. I never found out who let that call through, but I will be thankful for the rest of my life for that kindness.

Because of my call, two women from AZC, Judith and Karen, became religious volunteers and began teaching Zen meditation and Buddhist philosophy to inmates hungry to make changes in their lives. Judith has continued coming for the last eleven years and has become my mentor. The lovely, intelligent blue eyes behind her glasses show her genuine interest in inmates' lives when we talk to her. We can tell she cares by her thoughtful answers to our bewildering problems. She willingly shares her life experiences with us.

When Judith and her husband drove up to Alaska in the 1960s, they picked up a hitchhiker and delivered him to where he was going. At this man's house they met his roommate, another young man who was Buddhist. Judith watched him as he sat on a cushion in his bedroom and meditated. All of his belongings consisted of a bed, a cushion, and a few clothes. This man's aura of peace, in spite of his lack of material possessions, profoundly affected Judith, who soon began her own study and practice of Buddhism because of this encounter. She told me that man had no idea how much he influenced her—so much that it eventually led to the establishment of the Anchorage Zen Community, and in turn, led to her teaching us out here. She taught us that it was an example of how we're all connected and we don't always know exactly what or who our actions will influence.

In the beginning, when I complained about being in prison, her answer was, "There is no alternate universe where you're not in prison. You're here. You have to deal with what's happening right now."

When my mother died, I called Judith and wailed, "She died before I could forgive her!"

"Diana, guilt is useless," she assured me, in her calm and loving voice.

At one Buddhist meeting, I complained about someone intentionally bumping into me numerous times on the walkway. Judith asked me, "Is there a rule against people touching each other?"

"That's a stupid question," I snapped.

Tears began to silently fall from Judith's eyes.

"Oh great, now I made you cry."

"No, Diana, *I cried.*"

She had just come from a retreat and was emotionally raw and vulnerable. I had treated her unfairly, but she didn't say so.

Over the past eleven years, my friend and mentor took a sad, angry, self-centered, and mentally ill woman under her wing and helped her become compassionate, grateful, and at peace.

After one of our meetings, I was troubled. I told her, "I don't even have anyone to claim my body when I die." Without batting an eye, she said, "I will." And I know she will, if I need her to.

Through Zen Buddhist meditation and contemplation, I have learned about myself—all the ugly, dark, and scary stuff: the fear, self-pity, anger, and deep sadness; and, surprisingly, some good stuff too: a sense of humor, intelligence, compassion, and true remorse.

Judith has told me more than once that we are a lot alike. This is a compliment to me and gives me hope. When I'm trying to decide what to do in a given situation, I often think, WWJD? What would Judith do? What would be the *unselfish* thing to do right now? When I think of Judith I always imagine her smiling, dressed as always in blue, asking me thoughtful questions and giving me helpful advice. Was it God-given destiny that I meet Judith? I don't think so. I think one thing led to another, choices were made, and here we are.

Has Judith inspired me? Definitely. Did Governor Palin's speech that day in our gym inspire me? Not really. Of course, Judith has been coming here for eleven years and Governor Palin was here for only an hour. On the other hand, Sarah Palin has inspired thousands of other people around the country.

What's the difference between these two inspirational women? When Sarah Palin speaks to people, she walks out to jubilant applause. When Judith comes to prison, we all take off our shoes, plop down on the floor, and she says, "Okay, let's start with ankle rolls, first the right, then the left." Sarah Palin gives speeches to her fans. Judith rolls up her sleeves and does the dirty work. Palin talks about what other people should do. Judith does what she can to help other people. She comes to prison and she teaches and loves murderers, bank robbers, and chronic alcoholics. Palin mocks others who are trying their best to make positive changes in the world. Judith listens quietly as women such as I selfishly rant about our situation in the world, and then helps us become calm, grateful, and willing to comfort others who are suffering.

Judith, my friend and mentor, is enthusiastic about life, her spiritual practice, and helping people. She once sent a card to me in which she wrote, "I'm here through heaven and hell." And I know, *I know* she will be.

That's the difference between talking the talk and walking the walk.

I wonder what would happen if people just helped each other and stopped mocking personalities and arguing about ideas. There is a time and place for debate, but there is so much hostility and bitterness among people right now that it sometimes looks hopeless. Nevertheless, I can tell you that there are Judiths in this world who *are* making positive changes—men and women who will never give speeches to thousands of people and will never get media attention, but who can take a hopeless woman or a hopeless situation and transform them.

TERRENCE SAMPSON, *Texas*

EVOLUTION OF A DREAMER

It seems that all I've known in life is adversity and perseverance. Adversity has come as a result of my own choices, which have also caused adversity in the lives of people I've hurt. I regret the pain caused to others. But in some ways I am thankful for *my* adversities, for were it not for the struggle and the pain, I wouldn't be the man I am today. I could have wilted, I could have crumbled, I could have succumbed to the storms that rained continuously on my life, but I didn't, I persevered, and now others will have the choice to reap the benefits of my struggle through learning from my mistakes. In that I find gratification and a sense of meaning for the choices I made that once seemed meaningless.

My life ceased to be my own when I chose to take the life of another. I was so young, so lost, and so angry at what I couldn't understand, but the consequences and repercussions of my actions at that one moment of insanity will last a lifetime.

I always feel sad, guilty, and frustrated whenever I think about the beginning of this journey. I feel sad because of the reality of it all—I committed murder; I feel guilty for the pain that I have caused others; and I feel a sense of frustration for what can never be changed, for as badly as I want to change my past mistakes, I simply can't. I can only control the course of where my life goes from this point forward. That is now my focus.

It is time for my irresponsibility, my foolish choices, and my struggles to come to the forefront. It is time for exposure, with the hope that others will look and learn. Someone will be affected in a positive way. In order for my life to be meaningful, I have to have a positive impact on as many people as possible. Yes, that is what will give my life meaning.

A LOST SOUL

I was a twelve-year-old kid, standing in the shower area of a juvenile facility in central Texas. I was naked in front of a male juvenile staff member and tried to look tough, but in reality I was deeply afraid and confused. I was afraid of the unknown, and I was confused as to why I was standing naked in front of a stranger. That instance turned out to be the first of many strip searches that I have endured over my now twenty-plus years of incarceration.

At that time I had no idea of what lay ahead of me. I only knew the destruction that lay behind me, a vicious moment of rage that was still freshly embedded in my mind. I was in need of answers, but I didn't know where to begin my questioning. The situation seemed surreal. I was living in a haze. I was in denial and disbelief, not wanting to believe that what happened had actually happened. I didn't know it at that time, but denial, disbelief, and continuous attempts at repression of what was real would hamper my growth and development and any understanding of why I did what I had done. Living in a distorted reality had gotten me to that juvenile facility, which would turn into an adult correctional facility five years later.

My journey was just beginning. I had no way of knowing the hardship I would have to face. My focus was not on others or the pain I had caused others, my focus was on me, and it would remain that way for a long time.

Being separated from my parents was a new experience for me, but in actuality I was always separated from my parents from an emotional standpoint, until my situation brought us closer together.

I didn't know it at that time, but I had just entered a "concrete jungle"—a jungle devoid of the compassion and understanding needed for natural growth and development from childhood to manhood. I would learn the adopted attributes of the many animals that roamed the jungle, transposing their shapes over a period of time to meet the particular challenges at hand. I would learn over twenty years.

In the beginning my greatest enemy was myself. Images of my youth from ages six to twelve haunted me, along with the very terrible event that had me at that juvenile facility. I saw images of my father in an enraged state over and over again. He came for me each night, and my victim came for me as well.

I felt the punishment my father dished out over and over again, and I saw my own actions, me doing unto others what had been done unto me. I remembered fearing to leave my bedroom at night when I was living at home. I was so afraid to bump into my father at night that I would get up and urinate in the far corner of my room.

The worst times of my life had always seemed to be at night, and after I was incarcerated it seemed that my senses were heightened even in sleep, for I would be on constant alert. In my mind I thought that retribution would come in the form of my father's punishment or my victim reaching out for me, and as a twelve-year-old, I didn't know if that retribution would come as I was sleeping or when I was awake. I just always felt that it would come.

Confusion was also a part of my everyday existence. I was confused about a lot of things: Why had I done what I had done? Why didn't my parents love me? Why didn't my mother show me any affection? Why was my father so cruel to me? What had I become? I had many questions, but no way to find answers. I was just simply lost.

I spent most of my time in a state of confusion and fear. I was a twelve-year-old kid trying to figure things out, and I really had no help because I was looked upon with disdain by everyone from the very beginning. Although I didn't know exactly what people's intentions were around me, I knew they didn't wish me well, and that went for authority figures as well as my youthful fellow prisoners.

For the most part I went into a shell, and I would stay in that shell for about eighteen months until God saw fit to send someone into my life that looked at me beyond the label I wore as a murderer. Up until that time I put on the front of a hardened criminal, but I was just a confused and scared kid. I was a lost soul in a world I didn't understand.

I was sentenced to 30 years in prison when I was thirteen years old. What would I do? Where was I going? How would it all end? I had no clue. I only know that I had recurring dreams of all that was bad in my life, both the things that were dished out to me, and the things I had dished out to others.

I had no identity, no confidence, and I had no sense of direction. I was suicidal at the age of thirteen. I just didn't have the courage to follow through with an attempt. Once I was sentenced, the reality of jail weighed heavily on my shoulders, and that increased my desire to die. The only jail reality I knew consisted of what I saw on TV, and that was terrifying to me, but terror is what I dished out, and I couldn't help but think that terror was what I would receive upon entering the system.

The next four and a half years of my life were filled with disappointment, discrimination, and an unyielding storm of trials and tribulations. But through those trials my character was being shaped and molded by an unseen hand.

Even at a young age I knew I was blessed. I had made terrible mistakes in my life, but I was never without remorse. I've always felt that God saw the trueness of my heart, the trueness of how I felt about the things I had done, and because of the trueness of my heart he put people in my life to assist me through my hard times.

I had been a child monster, but I would grow into a man of character, a man of integrity, and a man with a purpose.

LESSONS LEARNED

My growth into adulthood took place in prison. I had not been exposed to the street life or the conniving nature of hardened adult criminals. At the age of seventeen, I entered into a jungle that would truly shape the core of my being. My lessons came quickly, and most came with a price.

To be seventeen years old in the prison system in Texas during those times was to be a sheep among wolves. I had gotten over my fear of the unknown—as it related to serving time—in the Texas Youth Commission for four and a half years, although struggles at the juvenile level and struggles at the adult level were totally different. People didn't die because of a conflict at TYC. People died in prison because of a conflict, and this was a lesson I learned quickly.

I had somewhat of a cocky attitude when I first arrived at prison. I was physically fit and I was ready to prove myself on all fronts. I had a sense of fear, but I already knew how to make my fear work for me instead of against me. I was not afraid to fight, and I vowed to not let anyone take advantage of me. The rites of passage for a young teenager at that time were clear: either you showed you would stand up for your manhood, or you would become a victim in more ways than one. I showed that I would stand up for my right to be called a man, but I was never seriously hurt. I was indoctrinated into the violence very quickly. In my mind I only had one choice: adapt to survive.

It's said that God watches over babies and fools, yet looking back I don't know which category I was in. I was a baby amongst men, but I also had a foolish pride that almost cost me my life twice during my now fifteen-year stay in prison. At any rate, however God viewed me, a baby or a fool, I'm thankful for it.

I had not yet been in prison for six months when I witnessed a man killed. I watched seven Hispanics stab and beat to death another Hispanic male. It was a gang hit, a deadly gang hit.

My whole concept of serving time changed at that point, and that one instance started a cycle of terrible decision-making on my part for a period of about twelve years. I felt I had to adapt to my new environment, and I made wrong choices in the beginning because I was focused on survival. After being subjected to so much violence at the very beginning of my prison stay, I made the choices I felt necessary.

Prison is a very destructive environment for the most part, and it took me about twelve years to learn the *power of choice*. I made choices to hang around with a prison gang my first three years in prison. I then made choices to participate in the "prison street life" for another nine years. Some prison units aren't as violent and rugged as others, but some units are the worst places in Texas to be. I myself have been on two such units.

I have encountered gang wars, prostitution, minor drug selling, *major* drug selling, extortion; seen men stripped of their manhood; and I even saw men smoking crack cocaine and shooting heroin for the first time in my life—all during my prison stay.

At one point the prison street life fascinated me, and again I lost remnants of my soul. I quickly embraced the prison "game" and I accomplished every goal I set for myself. I learned about treachery and how to be both a snake and a snake handler. I learned about deceit and how to engage in the "long and short con." I learned about dishonesty and how to lie to get what I wanted. I embraced all of these attributes because my life then seemed meaningful. I had a purpose in life, and *most importantly* this new life allowed me to run from the reality of pain, guilt, and shame that up until that time lived at the forefront of my mind.

Nine years seemed to fly by once I entered the prison streets. I became totally institutionalized and stopped having contact with the outside world. I had outstanding support from my parents, but I retreated even from them so that I could focus fully on making my life as comfortable as possible in prison. Because of the circumstances surrounding my crime and the response from the public, I believed that I would be in prison for the rest of my 30-year sentence. Resigned to my fate, I chose the fast life to make time fly.

My parents came to visit me once a month, and during my visits I often boasted about my exploits. What I deemed a look of fascination turned out to be shock and pity for their only child. They both knew I was headed for rock bottom, but they allowed me to continue my course, to get my lessons.

Sometimes there are periods in life when we truly lose focus on what's important and our choices lay the foundation for true disappointment and destruction. I was living like prison was all that I had to live for, believing that there was nothing else to live for except the completion of my 30-year sentence. I made up my mind to make the best of it while I was here. I gave all my time and energy to the "game" and I loved every minute of it.

My father was a violent man turned minister, who is now the pastor of his own church. During my years of growth in the ways of institutionalized living, my father—a man I blamed for creating the twelve-year-old monster I became—was growing in a different way. His spirit glowed every time I saw him, and whenever he asked what my relationship with God was like, I shrugged him off. I was the prodigal son embarking on my own journey through a world I had created for myself.

Each time I left visitation, I enjoyed going back into the jungle and taking my place among the vines. Most men in prison take the form of one animal or another. Only here would you see the attributes of lions, wolves, jackals, and hyenas coexisting at the same time, and for many years I lived among them, became an example of each one of them, and I didn't believe I was susceptible to any other kind of change.

For eighteen years of my life, I sheltered myself from the uncertainty and adversity that existed all around me in this concrete jungle. I switched into a different animal to meet the need at hand: cunning like a fox, assertive and aggressive like a wolverine. I traveled on the ground for many years, sometimes as a sole figure with a single purpose, other times as a member of the packs of hyenas and wolves that roamed and hunted relentlessly. Survival instincts caused these changes in my mentality and my form, for only the strong survive here. This was the life of the penitentiary streets that I embraced.

But everything is susceptible to change, and I was no exception.

ENLIGHTENMENT

We all travel on our own unique and distinct roads paved with our own unique and distinct challenges. At some point in time, people grow into a level of maturity that allows them to recognize nonproductive ways of living, but I believe most people incur change in their lives as a result of powerful experiences, which are often *painful* experiences.

I believe the signs of the need for change surround us. But people often prefer to make their own personal journey up "fool's hill." I too traveled up fool's hill, only to be spared time and time again. If a person keeps playing with fire, they are sure to get burnt, and at one point, the flames finally caught me.

I sat staring in disbelief at a deep cut in my left forearm that was about three inches wide. I was amazed that I was still conscious, and the nurses and physician assistant were amazed at my consciousness as well.

I sat in a prison infirmary, receiving twenty-nine stitches for a cut that nearly cost my life. The losing battle that I had endured that day changed the way I would view that and all previous lessons before that.

The assistant pointed to an artery beside my cut and said that if that had been cut, I could have lost my life from the blood loss. I took that information with a laugh until I saw the very serious look on the assistant's face. I asked him if he was serious, and he told me that he was very serious. I immediately began to reflect on the situation that led to my cuts—three cuts in all—and all I could think was: foolish pride, and *God watches over babies and fools.*

I was taken to an isolation cell and would remain there for the next thirteen days while there was an investigation into my near-fatal accident. I didn't know it at the time, but this would be the most important date, until then, in my life. I would never be the same after that thirteen-day stay, and it was during that time that I believe a divine presence spoke to me, through past images of what had been, and images of what could be—what *would* be.

I never saw myself as anything more than what I was at that point in time—a lost wanderer. The storms in my life had defeated me. I had no hope. I felt resigned to a worthless fate. Sometimes death seemed an acceptable alternative; I wouldn't have to deal with the pain of the past or the hopelessness of the present. Looking back, I see that death just wasn't in the plan for me. I had a bigger purpose—a purpose that was revealed to me around the fourth or fifth day of isolation.

I stood atop a hill in what seemed to be a dream, yet I didn't think I was asleep. What I saw before me was a long, winding road through a dense jungle with many animals. Each group of animals was at various stages of doing things I couldn't understand. I remember feeling somewhat confused at the sight, yet I knew that things were about to become clear.

I saw wolves, lions, jackals, and hyenas assembled in what seemed to be an uncommon gathering, and I remember thinking that at one point I too took my place among the assembly of hunters. I remembered adapting to the attributes the jungle had to offer because I only thought there were two options, either be a hunter or among the hunted.

Right before my eyes, all of a sudden—*enlightenment.* Where my vision had been bleary, I could see clearly now. Where my direction had been confusing, I now felt total understanding. I no longer traveled on the ground like a fox, wolverine, or a wolf. I flew high over the jungle in the form of an eagle.

I looked down from the sky, my vision keen, and I looked to see what once was. I looked back over the adversity I had faced—some battles fought and won, and some battles fought and lost. I looked back over my path to see fear conquered. At the very beginning of my journey, fear plagued me like lesions covering my skin.

I looked back to see a few trails walked more than once, wrong turns that I seemed to make again and again. I noticed a pit of blazing fire at the end of those wrong turns, waiting hungrily to swallow up any witless individual foolish enough to step over the edge. I had been one of those fools on more than one occasion, and now I saw many others surrounding the pit, their choices the only difference between life and death.

There are no wolves, hyenas, jackals, or lions. I see clearly now. I see misguided men trying to assume roles that are not authentic, roles that seem to fit a predator or a hunter, attributes adopted upon entering the prison jungle.

I flew faster and faster, escaping the darkness that once was, escaping the limitations that I restricted myself with, and escaping the confusion that clouded my thoughts with a giant storm cloud that emitted rain and hailstones repeatedly on my life. I bear the marks of those storms both externally and internally, yet in the deepest recess of my mind I understood that I needed those scars in order to grow, and the rain and hailstones only provided that which I needed to blossom into my full potential. Life will continue to offer its twists and turns, darkness and rain, but my lessons at the edge of the pit have taught me that it's my choices that will determine my future, whether I wilt or blossom.

I have to testify that even though the storms will rage as a result of terrible decisions, they too shall pass. Those storms will pass. No matter how strong the winds, no matter how large the hailstones, there will be a calm after the storm, there will be relief after the struggle.

People must know that, and I am to be a messenger.

THE PURSUIT OF DREAMS

I am now a new man with a new understanding. I now seek redemption through actions that are now not focused on me, but on how I can enrich the lives of others. I have taken so much that I am now determined to give back for the rest of the years I am blessed to live on this earth.

My dreams are not materialistic in nature. I only seek to give hope to the hopeless, help the ignorant learn the error of their ways, and to share my testimony on the need for accountability, responsibility, and change with those who are lost in the same false sense of reality that I once lived in.

I thought for many years that because of the terrible mistakes of my past I could not offer anything worth value to life, but it was through embracing change in my life that I began to understand that it's not about who I was and where I've been, it's about who I am now and where I intend to go. The past can't be changed, but the future is an empty canvas waiting to be colored.

I have debts to pay that can never be repaid, but God willing I will have a second opportunity to accept the responsibility of my past actions and show the remorse that I truly feel towards those that I have hurt. I've run from accountability for many years, but my days of running are over.

My travels haven't been easy, but they weren't meant to be easy. I am a product of the adversity I created for myself, but I will not allow all of the mistakes I've made to be in vain. My life will gain meaning by my actions today and tomorrow, and today I hope to have shared something that will have a positive impact on someone's life tomorrow.

SHELLEY MAC, *Michigan*

BEGINNINGS

I began my journey the day I was sentenced to one to ten years in prison. This was not my first prison sentence. When I was nineteen I was sentenced to prison and did a number of years. I went home when I was twenty-four and am now forty-three. It has been some years since I faced such an ominous situation. I was sure prison had changed in all that time, and not for the best.

While riding in the transportation van from county jail to prison, I notice the sense of shame that you try to fight as you pass vehicles filled with passengers that cannot help but stare. At the same time you must steel yourself against what is to come, because it is far greater than the simple shame caused by a passing gawker.

After about an hour ride, the prison comes into view. You try hard to memorize everything outside of the barbed wire, the free side. You know that this is a view you will not see for a while. As you enter the gates, a weight is in the air and tangible on every part of your body, mind, and soul.

Your first experiences in prison are of anger, frustration, and humiliation. It takes a special kind of officer to do prison intake, the kind that most likely kick their dogs. You are stripped of every last connection with the outside world: clothes, possessions, compassion, dignity; no mail and no phone calls. Then you are placed in a holding cell to await a long day of poking and prodding in order to determine your mental and physical state. You are also issued your new possessions: an ID, a duffel bag, some horrid underwear, two outfits, two pairs of pajamas, six pairs of socks, two towels, two washcloths, a tube of toothpaste, a toothbrush, a comb, deodorant, and some shampoo.

Approximately eight hours into this ordeal, you are led to quarantine. And, yes, along the way there are catcalls and comments. I chose to smile as if I were in a parade. Hey, why not have fun with it? Quarantine is about an eight-week process during which you are locked in a cell for twenty-three hours a day, even for meals, and must ask to use the restroom. Most often the answer to this question is, NO! You share this 9' x 12' cell with a person you may or may not get along with, two desks, two lockers, and a set of bunk beds.

During this quarantine experience, church comes to you. One Saturday morning I was awakened by loud singing. I was so angry that I couldn't see straight. As a means of escape, all I wanted to do was sleep. The following Saturday I figured I might as well go because there would be no sleeping through it anyways. The chaplain came with six women, inmates, to conduct service. Part of this service included these young women giving their testimony. A young woman got up and began talking about who she was prior to getting her case. She was driven by money, clothes-hungry, hateful, up for anything dangerous for the thrill of it, and basically moving at the speed of light, taking no prisoners (no pun intended). She in fact sounded like a version of me, though I have twenty years on her, in which time I have perfected my "crazy." Then, with a straight face, she dropped the bomb. She is serving a natural life sentence plus seven years! She said it devastated her to the point that she began praying for God to just kill her. She then began to cry. She said it was at that point that she began to look at everything in her life: an abusive childhood, toxic relationships, self-perceptions. She began to notice that she carried all these things like treasures and they led her to exactly where she was. She then explained how her prayer went from "Please kill me now" to "Please heal me and make me whole." At that moment she began to feel the weight being lifted off of her soul, her heart being mended. Then she wiped her tears and gave us a radiant smile and said, "I have never been so whole or had so much meaning in my life as I do now, in this place." WOW!

I found that I was crying. I was so profoundly touched by what she had said that I had to concentrate to breathe. I wanted what she had. I wanted it bad. I personally think that religious fanatics are annoying. That is not what I wanted. I wanted to be whole, to love myself. I realized that I had not loved myself in a long, long time, if ever. So began my real journey.

I decided, with all this "me time" on my hands, that it was time to do some work. Time to take a long, painful, and honest look at myself. I am telling you now that this endeavor is not for the faint of heart. Looking at yourself hard enough to be honest is something shattering. A counselor—yes, I sought out professional help because I was not prepared to go it alone—asked me one very simple yet very complex question: "Who are you?" After crying hard and praying about it and trying to avoid it, I made a list. My list would have been preposterous, laughable, and idiotic even for a twelve-year-old with good mental faculties.

What I found by writing it all out was astonishing. I had been nurturing the physical needs in my life, but leaving my spirit, my soul, deserted. I mean we think food, clothing, and shelter are basic. All of those are basic, but I was left with this aching need, a craving for something more. I filled this craving with booze, drugs, men, possessions, and experiences, relentlessly. Yet still I was left unsatisfied. I put myself in danger over and over, seeking out the next big thrill. Yet still I was left unsatisfied. I realized that I had no spiritual existence. I was trying to cram a square peg into a round hole. I could go no further without God in my life. I knew there was a higher power than me. I also knew the power of prayer and the grace of God could nurture a thirsty soul. I was not disappointed and have yet to be.

Now I pray about everything. I know that walking my own path, on my own, never was going to work. I know that going it alone, I would always be left with that empty feeling.

I have rediscovered my love for writing, which I had forgotten. I find so much joy in everyday things. Please don't get me wrong. I have had success in my life, but it never made me complete. With God in my life I start out, even with the smallest endeavors, already complete. I have found peace here in the midst of the constant chaos, malice, discontent, hate, spite, jealousy, and madness that is the prison system from the warden down to the inmates. I also see the world differently. I deal with people differently. I attract positive, like-minded people. I have also learned the power of forgiveness, even if the person you have to forgive is yourself.

I came to prison a broken and defeated individual. I will be leaving soon as a healed soul full of promise. I had to work hard, on my own, to find that here. Real help is not readily available. You have to want it bad.

I am involved now with all kinds of writing workshops and have submitted quite a bit of work for publication. I was also asked to be a journalist for the National Lifers Association, which was a great honor for me. I am not a lifer, but I was chosen to write, be published, and make a difference. Again, wow! God is good.

MICHAEL CRAWFORD, *New York*

THE THERAPEUTIC NATURE OF ART IN PRISON

My oldest memories of drawing start in grade school. I would mostly draw things I could not have or afford: the latest Jordan sneakers, a nice house, a new limousine. Mostly, the types of things an inner-city kid would see in advertisements, but never actually own. In this sense, drawing helped me cope with my inability to keep up with the Joneses; however, later in life, I would learn that drawing can serve a lot of functions. In prison, drawing helps me to escape my current circumstances, release built-up tension, and give back to society.

At twenty-nine years of age, after having served eleven years of a 22-years-to-life sentence for second-degree murder and robbery, I find the mundane aspects of prison life almost unbearable. I am like a horse with blinders on, trained to stop at yellow lines and respond to the sounds of buzzers and bells. Although the location of the prison complex may change, the many rules, small cells, and blue-for-officers and green-for-prisoners uniforms remain the same. I can look out of the window, past the bars, over the wall, and in the far distance see the clear blue sky merging with tree tops starting to brown as the seasons change. I cannot touch them. I cannot smell them. I am trapped in my cell. For me there is no vacation or possible release until 2020—or at least that is what I thought.

One day I sat down to draw a picture of a car coming out of a tunnel after a snowstorm. I started by blacking out an entire sheet of 18" x 22" drawing paper with a stick of compressed charcoal. Once the sheet was covered, I spread the charcoal out evenly by smudging it with my hands in a circular motion. I blew the excess onto the floor and started drawing. Because the sheet was coated with dark charcoal, I employed a drawing technique where one erases to draw the desired image. The method is called subtraction. I roughly sketched in the trees, the street, and the tunnel before I realized the prison's bell had rung. Buzz! Buzz! Buzz! It was time for chow. I had been drawing for over four hours, and I was nowhere near finished.

I went to chow because I had to eat, but I did not want to leave the drawing. Something was happening. I was not stressed or pressured to get the piece done on time as if I was under a contract. Nevertheless, I felt the need to keep on drawing. It felt as if the eraser had come alive and was calling me back into the land of the drawing. This was similar to the power of attraction that the magic ring had over Frodo in *The Lord of the Rings*. I was there inside the drawing; I could smell the exhaust from the car. The pine trees were freshly covered with snow weighing down their many branches. The scene was breathtaking.

The drawing became personal not because I made it, but because I was transported into its world. I was at peace in a wintry landscape for the hours I spent drawing. No bars, no counts, and no officers. I was in the zone; all that existed was me and the drawing. This was my vacation. I can now go anywhere, by giving myself completely to a drawing and becoming one with the piece. Through my art I have met John Coltrane, conducted an orchestra, and been to Africa. However, the only drawback is that eventually I have to return to the reality of my prison cell. One may ask, is such a temporary escape beneficial?

Some may say no, likening the escape to an addict's escape while high. When the trip is over, one is faced with the same problems that existed before the high. Although this may be true of both drawing and drugs, an added benefit of drawing is that it is therapeutic. More specifically, it leaves the artist feeling better instead of having harmful effects on the body like most illegal drugs. Some opponents of art programs in prison fail to realize that art can be used therapeutically to aid prisoners' rehabilitation.

For instance, because art is a form of expression, prisoners who have anger-management problems can use it as a vehicle to channel their anger. Instead of lashing out, prisoners can always pick up a pencil and draw! Just the time it takes to complete a drawing allows for the release of built-up tension. In the end, the prisoner will be in a better state of mind, and have a work of art as an added benefit.

In prison, it is easy to find men facing an array of different problems. Some struggle with the courts in legal battles, some struggle to keep family ties strong, and some struggle to remain sane in an unnatural environment. Stress, depression, loneliness, bitterness, anger, remorse, and anxiety are all commonplace in New York State prisons. Art can be used to address some of those issues. By having prisoners draw scenes and images expressing those feelings they wish to confront and conquer, they will begin to effectively manage their problems.

Over the years, I have experienced a multitude of these emotions; however, drawing has been like a medicine, as it changes my mood and uplifts my spirits. For example, if I start a drawing feeling lonely and depressed, I find company with myself as an artist and with the drawing as it develops. A completed drawing leaves me in good spirits because I have just created something beautiful that people will enjoy.

As an artist, I ask questions concerning the drawing and what I see. These questions turn into a full-scale conversation—sometimes out loud and other times in my head. The questions can be challenging: Is this angle correct, is that the right perspective? How can I make the piece more realistic, or capture the mood I want to convey? By actively answering these questions, I stimulate my mind and creative ability. I erase my loneliness. The answers to those questions also serve to intrigue art appreciators and evaluators alike. They are not the only ones, for I too am pleased with the outcome. The outcome is a work of art that leaves me depression-free.

Drawing allows me to give back to society. Whether I am drawing a poster, a custom greeting card, a design on a plaque or jewelry box, I am ultimately sharing my work with someone. A family member, a friend, or a prisoner's wife or girlfriend will find happiness and appreciate my creative ability. I am happy that in my current circumstances, I can use a gift that God has given me to touch the lives of others. After having caused my community much heartache and pain, I am pleased to finally be able to give back by sharing my artwork with others.

In short, drawing is a win-win for all involved. The artist builds upon his or her skills and shares them with the world; the recipient is allowed to admire and be inspired by the artist's creativity. Because drawing has helped me cope with prison life for the past eleven years, I recommend drawing to the world as a way to find a sense of peace in trying times.

INTELLIGENT ALLAH, *New York*

BREAD AND WATER VEGAN: STRUGGLING FOR HEALTH AND HUMANITY INSIDE PRISON

Milk and hamburgers are staples of the state prison diet, not almond milk and soy burgers. Processed, canned fruit soaked in high fructose corn syrup is a commissary privilege, but there is no fresh fruit. Suede boots are issued by the New York State Department of Correctional Services, yet animal-friendly boots are nonexistent. Absences like these have plagued my life for over fourteen years.

As a Black man with a family history of hypertension, heart disease, and diabetes, I developed a desire for optimal health. This desire prompted my first major dietary change, which led to perpetual alterations in my eating habits. After I stopped eating pork at age eighteen, I limited my meat consumption to fish at age nineteen. At twenty-one, I stopped consuming dairy, eggs, and sweets such as soda, cakes, sugar, and candy. I became a vegan after eliminating honey and animal-derived ingredients like whey from my diet at thirty-two. At thirty-three, I stopped eating potato chips and trans fats.

Becoming a vegan was inextricably linked to my maturing from the reckless seventeen-year-old teen that entered prison in 1994 into the responsible thirty-four-year-old man I am today. I discovered discipline through overcoming my appetite. I began applying this discipline to suppress my temper, resolve conflicts, and excel in other aspects of my life like education and exercise. Learning of the environmental and the moral implications of an animal-free diet helped foster my growing empathy for people I had hurt. I had rarely considered the feelings of people who were not my friends, because I had been desensitized to violence within the 5.5 square miles of the crime-infested streets of East New York, Brooklyn, where I was raised. But veganism helped me develop a worldview that entails my understanding and concern for how my actions—dietary choices and otherwise—affect our environment and other beings in our global community. I became a man determined to reclaim his humanity by embracing all life.

In prison, my inability to cease using all non-food items that contain animal byproducts has made a complete vegan lifestyle virtually impossible for me. The prison system does not provide animal-friendly toiletries, with the exception of Oraline toothpaste, which I appreciate immensely since toothpaste is the only cosmetic I ingest. The supplements sold in commissary—Vitamin C, protein powder, and amino acids—contain whey. The boots I am issued are suede. Because evading all animal-derived byproducts in all non-food items is impractical for me while incarcerated, I became a vegan only in diet.

Adhering to a healthy vegan diet in prison is a complex task. Mashed potatoes are whipped with milk, cornbread contains dairy and eggs, and the only meat alternatives are eggs and cheese, or texturized vegetable protein, often covered in a sauce laced with whey. I supplement my diet with commissary items like canned beans, tomato paste, pasta, and rice. My family and friends sporadically mail me care packages that contain hummus, eight-grain bread, rice- or soymilk, and fresh fruit and vegetables. I order soy products when my 8¢-an-hour "job" permits. Ultimately, the road to a vegan diet inside of prison is paved with bumps, but I still enjoy the ride.

Having compassion for animals is not a popular characteristic inside of violent institutions filled with some of the most dangerous men in New York State. I am frequently the brunt of wisecracks by my testosterone-fueled associates who brand herbivores "weak." My rebuttals lie in references to vegan bodybuilder Kenneth Williams, the strength of vegetarian animals like elephants and apes, plus the fact that I can outlast most men on the pull-up bar. A few men praise my discipline and diet, noting that they would like to embrace a vegetarian diet, but they could never do so under the rigors of incarceration. I have come to realize that many of the wisecracks hurled at me are rooted in the envy of muscular men who are physically strong but devoid of the mental strength and discipline required to maintain a vegan diet—especially in prison.

Although sustaining a vegan diet in prison comes with a cost, literally and figuratively, I am willing to pay the price. I have learned through observation and experience that adversity can build discipline, character, and strength. Had I developed these qualities in society, I might have avoided coming to prison. When I think of people like the late H. Jay Dinshah, who founded the American Vegan Society (AVS) in 1960, I am inspired by imagining what obstacles he overcame during his forty-plus-year mission to enlighten people about veganism. People like Ingra Newkirk, founder and president of the People for Ethical Treatment of Animals (PETA), who fight for the rights of animals worldwide, remind me of the global impact of my dietary and moral choices. When I envision Dr. Neal Bernard, founder and president of the Physicians Committee for Responsible Medicine (PCRM), his unyielding advocacy for healthy living through an animal-friendly diet reminds me that I have the resilience to rise above the hurdles in my path.

Though in prison I cannot abstain from using all items containing animal byproducts, I have found other ways to contribute to the promotion of a healthy lifestyle and the well-being of animals. I have pledged my support and become a paid member of PETA and AVS. I have also instructed classes on diet, nutrition, and veganism to a select few prisoners who were interested in broadening their perspectives on those topics. Knowing that there are groups like PETA and AVS in society, and that inside of prison there are so-called "hardened criminals" interested in my message of health and compassion, I am reminded that my struggle for health and humanity while inside of prison is worthwhile. As a published writer and reader of publications like *Vegetarian Times*, *VegNews*, PETA's *Animal Times*, and AVS's *American Vegan*, I am inspired to share my personal story through writing. Hopefully, my words will inspire others to live healthy lives for the sake of humanity and the animals we share our planet with. If a bread-and-water vegan can do it, so can a free person.

STEVEN F. LOMAS, *California*

MEDITATION

For me, meditation has evolved since day one. Prison is a noisy and crowded environment. During my first "sit," the relatively empty chapel and absence of noise appealed to me. These are what initially drew me to meditation. As I sat and listened to the talks, my budding practice began to take on a new dimension. I began to experience moments of peace and tranquility. I noticed that the frequency of those moments increased along with my practice. I then started to discover new things about myself and my situation.

Each new level of understanding spurred yet a different level of insight. During one of the talks, an outside sponsor/visitor/teacher, Heidi, shared with us the continuum of such things as infatuation, delusion, and aversion. Each one of these states operates on a scale from subtle and barely perceptible to overpowering, addictive, and compulsive. I have had some insight into forgiveness and anger as a direct result of my practice. Anger, for example, has its own subtleties. I discovered that in certain situations my anger really has been based on embarrassment or because I was uneasy in a situation. I realized that in those situations, it was my ego or idea of whom or what I thought I was that was angry and attempting to defend itself. It has been such self-discoveries, coupled with the weekly talks given by our community volunteers and the discussions that often follow, that have had a transformative effect. My self-discovery has been like my meditation practice; it has evolved over time. In fact, I would now be hard-pressed to separate the two. I am beginning to see and understand the process and the evolution, and the continuum that all of my experiences, understanding, and development stand on.

My meditation practice has been complemented and reinforced by other experiences. In a self-help program there has been mention of character and personal defects and the scales involved here. An example is procrastination, which is really a form of sloth. I think the understanding and insight gained with a meditation practice allows me to see these subtle issues, and that awareness itself is transformative.

Meditation has been a helpful instrument for daily living. Life in prison is one of limited personal control over day-to-day circumstances. That is especially true when the environment is violent. The environment is not always violent. Prisons, I think, are like other living things and have an ebb and flow to them. When tensions are high and the potential for violence is real, meditation has been an effective coping tool for me. The practice of being present in the moment is helpful in quieting my mind, which can be overactive in playing out scenarios. The ability to be in the moment, present where it is not currently violent, is calming. When the mind races, it can be gently guided back to the present—just like I practice during a sit, continually coming back to the breath with a gentle nudge.

My practice has allowed me to see my subtle defects. My practice has allowed me to be aware of detrimental mental loops. My meditation practice has led me to awareness and a lighter existence. As the things that prevent me from seeing the unity of all fall away, I become more at ease and more self-realized.

A self-help group that I participate in says that everyone has an internal light of goodness. This is covered with all sorts of muck in the form of pride, delusions, ego, and many other manifestations. Meditation has been a major part in uncovering this internal light and in helping me see it in others.

My meditation practice allows me the opportunity to regularly direct positive thoughts towards myself, those I love, the people around me every day, an individual I may have a difficult time with, and everyone I share this planet with. My meditation practice allows me to send thoughts of kindness, love, and general good will to everyone. Those thoughts are the positive seeds that can bud into positive actions. I think this is the greatest form of self-help. To be transformed into an individual who genuinely cares for others is the greatest type of self-help. Caring for others is, by extension, caring for yourself.

For my meditation practice to have started out of a desire to get away from the crowds and noise, and evolve into one where I understand that caring for others is the same as caring for myself—this tells me that there is more to sitting and being aware of the breath than meets the eye. If that is not evolution, I don't know what is.

Ticket In

JOHN H. SCHMIDT, *Delaware*

THE HISTORY OF MY GAMBLING ADDICTION

Going back as far as I can remember, my first encounters with gambling occurred when I was about seven or eight years old. I bet horses at Delaware Park with my dad. I also bet horses at Brandywine Raceway with my mom. But I remember playing the football tickets with my dad on the weekends the most. I'm not sure which one was first of these three activities, but I remember feeling pretty cool when I did any of them. When I was at Brandywine Raceway, my mom would just give me a couple of bucks, and I would go up to a certain window where my third-grade teacher, Mr. Groff, would put my two-dollar bets in. (Kind of unethical when you think about it, but I think he liked my mom.) He was my go-to guy for the next couple of years until the track closed down. He schooled me on exotic wagers as well as straight bets.

At the racetrack I also learned from my dad, and friends of my mom, how to read and understand the *Daily Racing Form*. I would get the money from my mom and go up to the stand where the man was selling programs. It just felt good to be admired by so many adults. I grew up with my mom and lived directly across the street from the track. Plus she was a bartender. All of her friends would be up at the track. Sometimes I was up until eleven or so on school nights. All of the neighborhood kids thought I was cool for being at the track late.

As a young boy, I felt my emotional needs were definitely getting met. I got plenty of attention, validation, and reinforcement that I was going to be a good handicapper of football and horse racing. It was my destiny. I was selling my dad's parlay cards at school. I got caught twice and was sent home by the principal in fourth and fifth grade. My mom was embarrassed. She hated my dad for that, and for not being in my life or paying child support. It's amazing that I wanted to be just like him. Another area of expertise was poker. I honed my skills playing poker with my stepbrothers and the kids in my neighborhood. But my strongest influence was my dad's side of the family. Every major family get-together included two tables for poker—one for the husbands and one for the wives, including my grandmom and grandpop.

Once I got to my mid-teens, I was sitting up at the table with my dad making strategic suggestions and helping play his hand. Then, when I turned eighteen, I finally had a crack at the table on my own. I was going head-up against the man who had taught me all I knew, my pop. Even if I played fifty hands and only won one or two, I was ecstatic any time I could outplay my uncles, dad, and my grandpop. In my mind, I was the man. Gambling became my validation. I would run to get all of the scratch-offs for the waitresses at Bob Evans when I worked there at the age of sixteen. I started running parlay tickets in high school and taking friends to River Downs. I got a fake ID when I was seventeen and started going to the track right after school. A few mothers voiced some displeasure because I was a bad influence on their sons.

I also started drinking late in my high school years. But it was the women that kind of catapulted me to a different level of behavior when it came to gambling, drinking, etc. My academics were pitiful. I barely passed any of my classes. I spent my time trying to impress the girls and my male peers with all of the gambling lingo, war stories about winning bets, and making up other crap, just to fit in. This was all a ploy to attract attention. I wanted to be popular for the wrong reasons. But at the time, my boys would jock me and give me mad props for doing my own thing when it came to gambling, staying out late, etc. There was constant reassurance that I was on the right track. So I kind of bought into the hype.

I called my dad on Saturdays and Sundays to play his ticket and also make some straight bets. It started out with ten or twenty. It then became fifty and a hundred. Then my line was "Hey, these bets are someone else's." My dad was poor at taking his own advice. He would always tell me that gambling was no good. He always said, "The best way to double your money when it comes to gambling is to fold it in half and put it back into your pocket." Sage advice from the ultimate addict.

After high school, I moved to Atlanta for a sales job. No supervision. I gambled profusely, unchecked. Scratch-offs and lottery started in Georgia the year I got down there. People were running around crazy. I was one of them. I found a couple of local bookies and started betting. I ran up a hefty debt and called my mom to Western Union me the loot. She did. Never did I pay her back. Meanwhile, I still gambled through my dad. One particular weekend, I won over $2,500 from my pop's bookie. I had big plans for that money. I called my dad on Sunday night and he told me the bookie got smashed and went belly-up., No money. The kicker was that my dad did not know it was my winnings. I was pissed! I made up people's names so I could bet big and not catch any flak from him. (I finally told him at a visit in Gander Hill Prison, six years ago.)

I met a girl where I worked and she left for college at Florida State. In 1995 I went down there to live with her. I frequented Biloxi casinos a lot with my coworkers. I found bookies down there, but ended up losing a lot of dough and had my eight-month-old car repossessed. I moved back to Atlanta with my roommate. I was working at Outback when I met a guy who turned me on to a bookie who took a lot of action. I got in over my head one particular week in late October 1996. I was also fielding bets for a few friends. We all had a bum week and tried for an all-or-nothing on the Monday Night Football game. Lost it all and found myself down over seventeen thousand. I ended up panicking and getting drunk to rob a bank. I guess that's where you could say things turned from bad to worse.

I was sentenced to forty months in federal prison. But I got to prison and really started gambling a lot. I also told everyone many stories about my life, my achievements, money, school, etc., that were not true. Even in prison I was seeking validation from my peers by continuing my self-destructive behaviors. I was convinced (and had this thought reinforced by others) that my gambling woes were just a streak of bad luck. So I operated off of that notion. I started running tickets in prison. I was gambling on my own skills at certain recreational activities like pool, bocce ball, softball, etc. I really felt appreciated by my fellow inmates. I formed close bonds with a few. But they never really knew me because of the lies I told to create this pseudo-image of myself.

Once I was released from prison, I went to the work-release center. I didn't really gamble too much there. Looking back, the opportunity didn't really present itself. But once I found employment, it opened up some doors. (Ironically, my dad never really lectured me or asked about my well-being regarding my gambling.) I started betting squares on football games and dabbled in the scratch-offs. Once I finished the work-release, I was put on probation. Even my parole officer minimized my situation by saying, "Don't go to D. Park or Atlantic City." Like that was going to stop me. From there I went all out. I started going to Atlantic City. I was promiscuous with several women and lied to them about my life. Again, I did not feel comfortable in my own skin. I would come to learn that so many of these actions were shame-based behaviors. Inadequacy and fear of abandonment were always front and center in my life.

I started bringing girlfriends, coworkers, and other associates with me to have a good time in Atlantic City. I only gambled big in front of people that I wanted to impress. I loved it when crowds of people would flock to the table. I would always up my bet to provoke reactions from the onlookers. A couple of my girlfriends did not like me betting large sums of money, so I would go off somewhere else for obscene amounts of time and go hard at roulette, blackjack, or the craps table. I would often ask these women to hold my money so I would not spend it. If I lost my money, I would get hostile and aggressive to the point where I scared the girls into giving the money back. This was not in my character at all. But I felt desperate to get my losses back. I always felt that way.

I made good money waiting tables and bartending. But the lifestyle I created was very tough to live up to. I told so many stories that I was stressed out trying to keep everything straight. My need for attention began to snowball into a constant need for fuel to gamble. Once my work money began to wane, I immediately knew that I could go to a financial institution and solve my problems. I began to feel a lot of pressure from my girlfriend because my lies and my actual living arrangement did not add up. More panic set in for fear of losing her. I had too many people that I was desperately trying to please and impress.

I slowly began to distance myself from my family because I knew I was doing wrong. I kept thinking that after I robbed a bank my problems would go away. I just did not understand what was going on. Right at the end, I was gambling at the casinos and with my bookie. It was like I was trying to punish myself. Right before I was planning to go with my girl to Atlantic City, I was arrested and incarcerated for several bank and hotel robberies. My life was officially over.

I was at Gander Hill Prison for about a week before I found the ticket runner on the tier and started going hard. I broke him and took over the operation in less than a month. (Not bragging, I just got lucky.) After filling out these diagnostic surveys and questionnaires, I realized how much of my life had been affected by gambling . . . all of it. I stopped gambling on January 10, 2002. I have not made a bet since. I sought spiritual guidance and I immediately went on to attend weekly Gamblers Anonymous meetings. It is now quite apparent to me how much I gambled, and the extent to which gambling preoccupied my life.

Family Life In and From Prison City

INTRODUCTION

We consistently fail to acknowledge that conviction and imprisonment, while perhaps bringing comfort to the direct and obvious victims of crime, sets off another series of victimizations—of the families and loved ones of the men and women sent to jail.[1] From the inside, no matter how well incarcerated people cope with life in prison, and no matter how many moments of peace they achieve for themselves, much of the pain that imprisonment creates is endured by those beyond incarcerated people's reach.

Prison City holds sisters and brothers, sons, daughters, aunts, uncles, and grandchildren. State and federal prisons exile the mothers and fathers of over two million American children, whose lives are thus profoundly destabilized.[2] Removing some individuals from their families and communities may be necessary, but we delude ourselves if we believe that this removal, especially when carried out on a mass scale, only reduces and does not also precipitate crime. Maintaining supportive connections with family on the outside is not only one of the surest indicators that incarcerated people will succeed when they return from Prison City;[3] such connections help break the generational cycle of incarceration. There are and should be consequences for the commission of crime. If we care about the common good, however, exile from family and the fracturing of communities should not be among them. Yet, in order to create prison jobs, states build and maintain facilities hundreds of miles away from the neighborhoods from which the police gather the men and women fed into the prison industry.[4] If we presume to claim that convicted criminals do not "deserve" to maintain such connections, we must also ask whether incarcerated people's sons and daughters, sisters, brothers, mothers, and grandmothers deserve this loss, or if families and neighborhoods deserve to be eviscerated by mass imprisonment. The essays here lead a multi-sided assault on all convenient presumptions about the family lives of imprisoned Americans. In each, we see another facet of the pain that Prison City spreads beyond its walls.

Perhaps the most painful fact about incarcerating parents is the damage meted out to children when their mothers go to jail.[5] This segment begins with three short essays from California, all by women whose motherhood the state has made into as much trial as blessing. In "Life Without Children," Linda Field describes a scene that takes place thousands of times every day: the joy in a child's visit to her incarcerated mother, and the pain of going away—a scene that the state has decided to make even less fulfilling than common visiting conditions allow. Author Running Water describes what she has faced as a victim of incest, of gang rape, and as a heroin addict, and the tall odds these experiences presented to any meaningful relationship with her son; her title "Prison or Kids: It's Not a Joke" poses the choice that's never offered to women in prison. The anonymous author of "Mother-Daughter in Prison" presents a case that is hard to imagine but all too real, when a mother and daughter meet in passing as they trade sides of the prison wall. These three essays together speak to the conditions endured by over half of all incarcerated women, and by their equally punished children.[6]

Andrew R. Sumahit, Jr.'s "The Incarcerated Father" offers a sketch of a man who never knew his father and was abused by his mother, but wants now to break this cycle and be a positive presence in his daughter's life. This essay describes the inadequacies of the prison and legal-custody systems in protecting children from real threats, which can include those presented by family members. Sumahit's essay offers evidence that the line between those in prison and those outside is not always the line between those that we should and should not trust with the care of the most vulnerable among us.

Marisol Garcia's "Choices/Consequences" depicts a moment rarely appreciated amid popular images of convicts as an unfeeling mass: the moment when she faces a loyal parent who is made to suffer through her child's incarceration. Garcia demonstrates, in a few clear strokes, that those prisoners fortunate enough to retain connections with family carry a second burden atop the shame and punishment decreed by law: the shame before one's loved ones for the punishment they must bear.

In "The Letter," Stephen Whetzel offers evidence of the value of retaining even a single connection to family. Whetzel also provides an example of a pattern made evident in essays throughout this collection: the road from an abusive childhood to Prison City is both short and straight. But Whetzel shows too the rewards of perseverance in working to make oneself the able recipient of even a brief encounter with family. Whetzel comes to see that it can sometimes be the incarcerated family member who alone achieves the perspective required to gain distance and recovery from the damage incurred in the home.

Jarvis Jay Masters's "The Inmate and the Prison Guard," documents a moment when the influence of family closed the institutionalized distance between an African American death-row prisoner and an African American guard. The occasion is Barack Obama's first election. These men discover they are men of one condition, like Obama: the products of the relationships they have enjoyed with family, with grandmothers who were supportive presences in their lives. Even in prison, we are composites of the circumstances we are born into, and of the relationships that are the most profound features of those circumstances.

For those with family inside Prison City, visits are a blessing, but prisons do not make them easy. The dark humor in Dean Faiello's "In Sanatorium" belies the stress that the prison environment and staff inject into attempts to make family visits into experiences that might revive a prisoner's sense of connection. The essay offers glimpses of how other men interact with their girlfriends, wives, and children; we see the dilemma of families offered no private space to interact, trying to care for each other amid other men and women in need of their own private space and time to reinforce the bonds that are the surest and most effective support for ex-convicts attempting to make constructive lives outside. We see here an institutional hostility to the moments that are most likely to give incarcerated people a reason not to return to prison.

If a social scientist wanted to study the effects of one man's incarceration on a family with no previous prison history, she could hardly find a more telling case than that of Peter Mehmel as he describes it in "A Hidden Cost." This is one among thousands of stories of how the prison twists the lives of the children of prisoners. It witnesses the damage that the mere fact of incarceration can have on families, and the tragic replication of this damage in subsequent generations. It is evidence, again, that when prison sentences are determined, they should take into account the welfare of *all* the innocent victims.

Turning from personal essay to critical analysis, Corey John Richardson's "Father Alert: How Prisons Destroy Families" takes a hard look at the wide-ranging damage of a men's prison system in which a majority of those held are fathers. Richardson looks at the backgrounds that imprisoned fathers come from, the harm their incarceration metes out to the families left behind, and the perpetuation of this cycle in the high rate of incarceration among the children and other young relatives of imprisoned fathers and mothers.

These essays make clear that prisons guarantee the destruction of families and communities that then feed the prison even more damaged lives, while politicians beat the drum for getting tough on the very crime that this cycle foments. Meanwhile, the media perpetuate images of prisoners as subhuman monsters, and businesses grow rich on the profits from building and supplying prisons. Family life in and from Prison City presents problems in which we are all—taxpayers, voters, media consumers, and investors—deeply implicated.

NOTES

1. See Sarah Schirmer, Ashley Nellis, and Marc Mauer, "Incarcerated Parents and Their Children: Trends 1991–2007," The Sentencing Project, February 2009, www.sentencingproject.org/doc /publications/publications/inc_incarceratedparents.pdf.

2. Ross D. Parke and K. Alison Clarke-Stewart, "From Prison to Home: The Effect of Incarceration and Reentry on Children, Families, and Communities," U.S. Department of Health and Human Services: The Urban Institute, January 2002, http://aspe.hhs.gov/hsp/prison2home02/parke%26stewart .pdf; Steve Christian, "Children of Incarcerated Parents," National Conference of State Legislatures, March 2009, www.ncsl.org/documents/cyf/childrenofincarceratedparents.pdf; see also Mary Patillo, David Weiman, and Bruce Western, eds., *Imprisoning America: The Social Effects of Mass Incarceration* (New York: Russell Sage, 2004).

3. "The Effects of Prison Visitation on Offender Recidivism," Minnesota Department of Corrections, November 2011, www.doc.state.mn.us/publications/documents/11–11MNPrisonVisitationStudy.pdf.

4. See Ruth Wilson Gilmore, *Golden Gulag: Prisons, Surplus, Crisis, and Opposition in Globalizing California* (Los Angeles: University of California Press, 2007).

5. See Barbara J. Myers, Tina M. Smarsh, Kristine Amlund-Hagen, and Suzanne Kennon, "Children of Incarcerated Mothers," *Journal of Child and Family Studies* 8, no. 1 (March 1999): 11–25.

6. See Lauren E. Glaze and Laura M. Maruschak, "Parents in Prison and Their Minor Children," Bureau of Justice Statistics Special Report, August 2008, revised March 30, 2010, http://bjs.ojp.usdoj .gov/content/pub/pdf/pptmc.pdf; and "Mothers in Prison: Children in Crisis," Arkansas Educational Television Network, www.aetn.org/programs/mothersinprison/facts.

LINDA FIELD, *California*

LIFE WITHOUT CHILDREN

I came to prison when Sara was seven. She was too young to understand 25-to-life meant she'd grow up without her mother. Her brother and sister, who were fifteen and twelve, didn't truly understand.

Sara's first visit was traumatic. She spent the day begging me to allow her to stay with me. She promised to be good, never leave my room, and never bother the guards. She couldn't understand why I didn't want her. She sobbed, clinging to me when it was time to leave. Her little arms reached out to me over her grandfather's shoulder; her hands rapidly opened and closed, begging me.

I kept telling her I loved her. When she was finally out of sight, the dam I had erected broke and I let the flood free. I cried for my children and myself.

I cried for every mother and child who went through this. Why didn't the courts understand? They passed a verdict not only on me, but my children. My children were abused by their father, orphaned by me, and abandoned by the court system.

After thirteen years of heartache, we now have a governor who doesn't want to hear any circumstances of why a murder was committed. He believes we should rot in prison. While I cannot justify my actions, no one is beating my children anymore.

The state decided family living unit visits were no longer acceptable for lifers, further punishing my children. No longer could we have visits in a little apartment in prison which allowed a pretense of normality. During those visits mothers could rock their children, cook for them, and talk for hours. No more can we maintain a thread of parenthood with children or grandchildren. Instead visits are conducted in a visiting room with cameras and guards who look at a mother-child relationship as abnormal. We cannot talk about important things because "Big Brother" is watching.

The playroom in Visiting has few toys, only foam-type blocks. There are no strollers, no high chairs, no outside toys or activities. The few board games are geared for older children and adults.

Our children deserve better. Punish us, but not our children. It is time for the state to reevaluate their treatment of our children.

RUNNING WATER, *California*

PRISON OR KIDS: IT'S NOT A JOKE

My name is Running Water. I want to tell the young women in here (Central California Women's Facility) about my life to help them with their own. I want you to know what drugs will do to you. I started sniffing when I was very young. My dad used to rape me since I was four years old. He would come loaded and drunk and beat up my mother and rape me. I think he used to hurt my brother, too. The first time I went to prison was in 1980. I did 4 years. I didn't care. I had no kids, just myself.

After I got out, I got hooked on heroin, running the streets, doing whatever. I didn't even know when I got pregnant. I went to a party, got jumped by three guys. I stuck one of the guys eight times in the heart. When I found out I was pregnant, I turned myself in.

I did three months in jail trying to kick heroin. I was really hooked. It was hard, very hard, and also sad, because I could feel my child inside me kicking. It was the most pain I've ever experienced. I was so weak and so scared—not for me, but for the unborn baby inside me. By the time my son was born, I was clean and sober. But I got in trouble again before he was a year old. I didn't get out till he was seven years old.

I really wanted to do some good and be with my baby. So I stayed clean for around five years. I was convicted of driving without the owner's permission (the owner did not want to press charges). The prosecutor wanted to make it a third strike with 25-to-life sentence. Boy, did my heart fall down. I cried like a baby. With some help I was sentenced to "only" 6 years with 85 percent time.

My son Timothy, who is everything to me, is now very hurt and angry with me. I promised him I would not mess up again. And here I am. So he has a right to be angry. I hurt him. I wasn't there to comfort him. You know, sometimes sorry is not enough to tell him. I have to show him.

Timothy was so hurt and angry he would not talk to me; he didn't answer any of my letters. It would be easy to slip back into drugs. It is the easy way out.

After three and a half years I am so happy because recently I got a letter from my son with pictures. My son is sixteen years old. Now I have something to look forward to in getting out of here. He told me I better be out there to see him graduate from high school. But how do I make up to him these last five years?

I don't think I can ever make it up. But I can be there for him now, and help myself and other girls like me that have kids and go through the same thing I've been through. I love my family for being there for my son and myself also.

So all you girls out there, prison is Not The Place To Be. Please don't do what I've done. Only we can help ourselves. So please put yourself and your kids first. Don't let drugs get the best of you.

My son wrote a school paper about heroin and what it can do to your baby's health. No matter what, your kids will come around and forgive you sooner or later. So please, try and think about it. Prison or kids. It's not a joke.

ANONYMOUS, *California*

MOTHER-DAUGHTER IN PRISON

I think about how different my life may have been if my mother would have never entered the system.

I wrote this a few hours before my mother went to heaven. For the first time, I finally had my mother in my life. Granted, we were sitting in the Pen, yet it was what I had dreamed of my whole life. It had finally happened; no one could keep her from me anymore.

It seemed that no matter how hard I tried when I was growing up, nothing was ever good enough to get my mother to stay out of prison. Each trip seemed longer than the last one, and each time I tried even harder to understand what I had done that time to make her "want" to go back. No one could tell me it wasn't my fault, though no one ever bothered to try. I just knew it had to be that test I took last week and only got a B+. It was the day she was arrested again. Or maybe it was because Dad said I didn't do the dishes right.

She didn't write because I don't spell good enough. Not because it's easier on her, or because Dad wouldn't let her write.

The worst part is now sitting here, doing life without parole. I was finally given my lifelong dream, a chance to see my mommy. The worst part was hearing her say she came here to be with me. The fact is, that was the benefit but not the cause. Yet the same guilt is alive and strong in me. It only sealed all those childhood beliefs.

I never thought I would hurt as bad as I did the day she walked out of those gates a little over a month ago. I knew I should be happy for her, yet feared I might never see her again. You see, for the first time, I actually saw her change and seem to want to stay out of prison. She will stay out of prison. On August 25th, less than a month after getting out of prison, she went to heaven to play with her grandson and the angels.

Looking back, I was very blessed for the time I had. As I watch women walk in and out of this prison, I wonder if they realize they are not building the children of tomorrow, but are destroying hopes and dreams.

Live each moment as if it was your last. You can change a child's tomorrow with a letter, a smile, or a hope for the future. Have you taken that time today? My mom did, and I will cherish that time. Can you say that?

ANDREW R. SUMAHIT, JR., *New York*

THE INCARCERATED FATHER

My name is Andrew R. Sumahit, Jr., but for the past two years I have been inmate #08A6102. In the past two years, I have only seen my daughter three times, but I have seen at least five people stabbed or cut. I am sharing the story of my life, one man's struggle to break the cycle, the story of the incarcerated father.

I never met my own father, and I've only seen a picture of him once. Just last year, I finally began to learn some details about him. So, needless to say, I was raised in a single-parent home. My mother abused me throughout my childhood to the point where I would pray every night that I wouldn't wake up the next day. But every day I woke up, and every day I had to suffer again. In 1996, when I was ten, someone finally came to help me. Social services came to our apartment building to take me away. My mother took me and ran out the back door. Later that week, we moved to Richmond, Virginia, and she started using a different name. On August 11, 2002, she finally lost her custody and I returned to New York to live with my grandmother.

When I turned eighteen, my grandmother kicked me out because child support stopped coming. At eighteen years old, I was homeless. I slept in abandoned buildings until I got a job as an auto mechanic and began to support myself. On July 1, 2007, my life changed again. One minute, I was at a friend's barbecue playing cards. The next minute, I woke up on the ground and couldn't even remember my own name. I spent the next week in the hospital having multiple seizures. After a series of tests and observation, I was diagnosed with epilepsy. Doctors found a tumor in my brain, which causes my seizures. The tumor is the product of blunt head trauma from my childhood. In other words, my mother's abuse stopped in 2002, but I will suffer for the rest of my life. Due to my epilepsy, I lost my job as an auto mechanic and became homeless again.

A few months later, my girlfriend told me she was pregnant. I now had to support a family, so I began to lie about my medical condition on job applications. I ended up getting a job through a temp agency as a forklift operator. I worked in three different warehouses and was nominated for Associate of the Month in all three. At the Gap Warehouse, I broke the productivity record by over 1,300 boxes.

On May 3, 2008, my accomplishments went out the window. I saw a man attack my sixteen-year-old neighbor, Thomas. Because of my history of abuse, I couldn't just watch this. So, me and a friend assaulted this man. Me, my friend, and Thomas were all arrested, and I'm now serving a nine-year prison term. Ten days after my arrest, May 13, 2008, my daughter was born.

I always promised myself that I'd be the perfect father one day. Now, I feel as if I'm no father at all. Since my child's birth, I have only seen her three times; the most recent was October 2008. In March of 2009, I filed my first visitation petition, but was denied because I had not established paternity. After that, I began to research family law. I found the New York Putative Father Registry, and I filed with them. Then I learned that a putative father has less parental rights than a legal father, so I petitioned for paternity proceedings. After a long process, I proved my paternity and received the final paperwork two weeks ago. Now, I am preparing to re-petition for visitation.

In June 2009, however, my worst nightmare came true. I was contacted and notified that my daughter's mother was on trial for child abuse and neglect. I wrote the judge and was allowed to attend the court proceedings. I learned that my daughter's mother had been hitting my infant daughter. I also learned that this woman left her eight-year-old sister to care for my daughter. My daughter received a series of three surgeries to repair her arm after falling down the third-floor staircase. Her mother pled guilty and received a twelve-month ACD (Adjournment in Contemplation of Dismissal) with court-mandated programs. She still has custody of my daughter. Once again, the justice system fails.

As Dr. Carl Mazza said, "Incarceration doesn't excuse you from the role you play as a father." This has become my motto. So far, I have already completed two parenting programs: one with the Osborne Association and one with the Alternatives to Violence Project. Just this week, I gave a presentation on incarcerated fathers as my final project for my Inmate Program Associate class. Everywhere I go, I encourage men to step up and be men. Because there is a difference between a male and a Man, as there is a difference between a Father and a guy who has kids. I was twenty-three years old the first time I got answers to questions about my father. I refuse to let my daughter go through the same experience. Every day that passes is one more day my daughter is deprived of the love I have for her. So I spend every day trying to get involved in her life. I choose to be a man; I choose to be a father; I choose to break the cycle. My incarceration does not define who I am, but I am the Incarcerated Father.

MARISOL GARCIA, *Connecticut*

CHOICES/CONSEQUENCES

"Garcia, you have a visit. Sign out at the office downstairs," yells the officer through the door. My stomach drops. *It's time.* I had stalled for as long as I could: the stress of the arrest, adapting to prison, the actual trial, and finally, sentencing. The inevitable could no longer be postponed. My mother has finally come to see me. I check out of the building and head to the walk gate.

It's a beautiful fall day, the sun playing peek-a-boo through the clouds. A majestic oak stands in autumn Technicolor as chipmunks forage for the last nuts and berries before the first snowfall. Despite the beauty that surrounds me, I walk toward visits like I am walking the green mile: shoulders slumped and head down. *God, I don't know if I can stand to see the disappointment in her eyes. I'd rather die than break her heart. I don't know if I can do this.* With each step, my heart becomes heavier with both anticipation and dread. The officer buzzes me in.

I sit and wait for what feels like an eternity, my mind racing with jumbled thoughts. *How has she been? I hope her arthritis hasn't gotten any worse. I hope the kids have been good to her.* "Garcia, row 2, seat 3," bellows Officer S., interrupting my concentration. Proceeding to the table, I sit and wait for my mother to come through the door. How the hell had my life come to this? Being told what to do, how to do it, and when to do it. Unfortunately I know the answer. When I decided to break the law and take money that didn't belong to me, I chose to become a criminal and sit on the inmate side of the visiting table and wait to see my mother. Wrong choice.

The enormity of that choice hits me when my mother walks through the door. *God she's getting older. Her hair is turning gray and there are wrinkles around her mouth.* Memories flash in my mind's eye: her walking me to my first day of school, crying at my college graduation, helping me to dress for my wedding. As I hug my mother for the first time in over three years, my heart aches, experiencing both joy and self-loathing. *Why did I wait so long to see her? No argument was worth losing all that time. I don't care who was right. She never missed a court date, never refuses my phone calls, and never leaves my letters unanswered. What have I done?*

"I've missed you so much," my mother whispers in my ear as she clutches me tightly. Tears form in my eyes. "I've missed you too," I whisper back hoarsely. Looking into her eyes, I see nothing but her love for me shining out. That's it: simple acceptance, no recriminations. My mother humbles me.

STEPHEN WHETZEL, *Indiana*

THE LETTER

Last summer, I received a letter from Misty, my little sister—my first contact with anyone from home since coming to prison, my first letter ever from anyone in my family. For eleven lonely years, years when I felt forgotten, I had written and sent countless letters and cards to my parents, hoping to fan some imagined cinder of compassion. We were never close—never. In fact, the term *family* should be used loosely when referring to us collectively.

I never expected to receive a response to any of my letters. At first, I wrote of forgiveness, change, and family as if we had a chance of making amends and starting over, but as years passed, I wrote my letters more as reminders so they wouldn't forget that I was alive. For a few days after mailing each letter, I would approach mail call with shallow hope—no more than someone, numbed by disappointment, half-heartedly checking weekly lottery numbers. A "leave us the hell alone" letter would have been better than nothing.

While I was staring out at the top of a solitary birch tree, the only living thing not within the walls of this prison that I could clearly see from my window, something was slid under my door. It was about time for mail call. The sun was soon to set, and the sultry summer heat would slowly dissipate. I wanted only to drink in the cool air and relax, my only reprieve from doing hard time locked in a steel and concrete sauna. The letter was no more than four feet away from me, but I would check it later. It wouldn't be anything important.

Then I saw my sister's name above the return address on the envelope; the calloused skin that I wore like armor against the horrible reality of prison was suddenly ripped from me, leaving me defenseless against genuine emotion. I was more afraid than I have ever been during any conflict or fight. A multitude of questions flooded my mind. Why write now? Did someone die? Was I going to be accepted? Was I going to be asked to stop writing? I felt weak and confused and agonizingly excited. I may even have bargained with God to wheedle him into blessing me for once in my miserable existence.

Despite my anticipation, I opened the envelope carefully, as if it were from the notorious Ted Kaczynski. A bomb was about to go off. I counted four typed pages, single-spaced, and like a seasoned pessimist, I started reading the last two paragraphs on the last page. If the letter ended on a good note, I would read it immediately. Otherwise, I could read it later, after my hope had ebbed and my shielding was back in place.

To my relief, the letter ended with Misty's hope that we could develop a relationship. She had offered to help me, her big brother. She apologized for not being there with support all those years. Her words touched me deeply. Even when I was out there, my family had never helped me. At that moment, I felt wanted, needed, welcomed as if I were being invited into her home, as if I had pulled up to the curb of the upper-middle-class suburban estate she shared with my mom to find her excitedly waving to me from behind an upstairs window.

Turning to the beginning of the letter, I began my first of many emotionally charged readings. I scrutinized every word, searching for subtle clues that would reveal the author behind the crisply typed words. Elation flooded me when I read that Misty remembered me as her favorite brother, the brother who taught her to play chess and who took her for motorcycle rides. Sorrow gnawed at me because my brother Mike was homeless, living day to day on the discards of a society unmoved by his plight. I felt indifferent to my sister Tina's problems with men and money, a condition she appears destined to live with for the rest of her life. I was proud of Misty, the youngest of us, eleven years younger than I am, for earning a college degree and pursuing a career in medical diagnostics. I felt some emotion when I read of my mother's regrets concerning the abuses I had suffered as a child by her hand (and anything else she could wield). But that part of the letter seemed unconvincing, lacking heartfelt genuineness. I never knew the Devil, the scourge of my childhood, to have any regrets. I found it unbelievable.

If you don't talk about it, it doesn't exist—that may be the first and foremost rule of my family. My parents *never* beat me or forced me to beat my brother and sister. They *never* locked me in a small closet or starved me for days. They *never* threatened my life, told me, "Just die already," or otherwise degraded me. That is what they choose to believe in order to live free of guilt for their crimes.

Misty was the privileged child, a spoiled brat compared to the rest of us. That's the way Mike and Tina saw it, and they resented her for the special treatment she received. In my opinion that just meant that Misty wasn't receiving a regular beating. As the eldest, I understood that the abuse I suffered wasn't Misty's fault. Our cold and calculating overseers drove wedges of hate and mistrust into our young hearts and minds with their wrathful words, their flailing fists, and when they had tired or wanted entertainment, with their grim games of torture, where we were forced to hurt and humiliate each other. They had done a good job of programming us into versions of them, lacking sympathy and emotion.

"The Game of Liars," as my parents called it, was a long, grueling event. It usually began with a simple question like "Who left the light on in the bathroom?" followed by three replies of "I don't know." Then, in turn, Mike, Tina, and I would be hit, usually with a belt. The question would be repeated. Should a confession not emerge, another round of painful wallops would follow. The interrogation would last for hours while we stood at attention with our noses pressed up against a wall. My parents claimed that they couldn't stand to look into our *lying faces.* There would be no bathroom breaks or time-outs to eat. In my parents' eyes, it was better to torture the innocent than to let a liar go unpunished. In a particularly memorable instance, after my parents had beaten and tortured us for hours in order to find out who had adjusted a setting on the sewing machine, my mother burst into laughter. "I remember," she said, "I think *I* changed the setting." My dad joined her in laughing at us before dismissing us to our rooms.

Sometimes, when my mom or dad tired from swinging a belt, we were forced to hit each other. There comes a point when an area of a person's body has been hit so many times that even the movement of clothing over the skin feels like the skin is immersed in flame, and after the underlying nerves, exhausted from extreme sensation, stop sending pain signals to the brain, a person simply feels nothing. For me, no torture hurt as much as it hurt to beat my own brother and sister or to receive a beating from them. It was games like that that destroyed any chance we might have had to form any real bonds of attachment, trust, or love.

I learned early that there are worse tortures than being hit. Those are the ones that stay with you, that bring the nightmares.

I wrote my first reply to my first letter from Misty with the utmost attention to detail. This young woman had mustered the strength and bravery to write a letter to a convict, a person my parents could create but would not accept or support. She had to have broken free of the cruel bondage of our parents. The letter was proof of that. But after thorough consideration of what she had written, I realized that she was also the product of the people who had raised me. I recognized the problems that plagued me when I was her age: low self-esteem, inability to trust, melancholy—traits I shared with Mike and Tina. On the other hand, Misty could not possibly know who I had become, the product of more than five years of substance-abuse treatment, anger-management treatment, stress-management classes, and one-on-one counseling, followed by four years of college studying psychology. I had become strong. I understood myself better. I knew to choose my words wisely or risk losing her.

After 11 P.M., when prisoners are locked in their cells for the night and the lights are dimmed to a faint glow, a calming silence settles throughout the dorm. Free from the usual yammer, I can hear myself think. My diligent work continued deep into the night, until my vision blurred and my fingertips numbed, until my will to continue writing was dashed by the realization that I was crossing out more sentences than I was keeping.

Sleep was impossible, but I was content lying in my bunk and thinking how lucky I was to have such a wonderful sister who had written such a wonderful letter. I hoped that she was real, genuine in her desire to have a relationship with me, free from the heart-rending legacy of our parents. I took pride in my persistence, which had allowed me to endure eleven years of emotion-draining rejection in order to maintain contact with my family. I had earned this letter, and I believed that my family was salvageable. If we worked together, we would heal together as a family. For the first time in my life, I felt real joy.

Although a few more letters followed during that summer, it is that first letter that I will always treasure as one of the rare good memories of my life. That letter healed many of the emotional wounds inflicted by my family. An ability to feel happiness, free from guilt, shame, or fear, was reawakened. Despite being locked away like an animal, in conditions not fit for an animal, I felt freer than at any other time. I had been reminded that there is more to life than merely reaching the other side of the wall that locks me in this prison.

But now, months have passed since I last heard from my sister, and once again, I find myself sending letters and cards to a black hole. At first, I thought something terrible had happened: a car accident, a robbery, Mike acting out his frustrations upon her to get back at our parents. Then I feared that I had written something inappropriate about her personal relationships, her issues of self-esteem, her issues of trust, her issues of conflict resolution and interpersonal relationships. Finally, I accepted the fact that my family is dysfunctional. My parents have never apologized for their crimes. Any words of wisdom that I could give to Misty, when filtered through her skewed perceptual lens, ran the risk of being misinterpreted as harsh criticism or personal attacks. She is a prisoner of the bitter upbringing that once fettered my heart and mind. I realized that I am free from the past, free to embrace life. Often, when I am deep in thought, I will look out my window through the dark, rusted screen, around a thick iron bar, past a tall chain-link fence, to the top of the implacable concrete wall that marks my horizon, to the uppermost branches of that lone birch tree. And I am reminded of life outside prison. The thin branches move with the wind, long slender arms stretched to the sky.

JARVIS JAY MASTERS, *California*

THE INMATE AND THE PRISON GUARD

I had known this particular correctional officer for close to twenty-five years. The conversation we struck up the evening after the 2008 presidential election had us idly looking at each other's perspectives as African Americans—mine as an inmate on death row, and his as a prison guard.

On any other evening, this particular guard might stop to say hello, just to pay a visit, due to the many years we had known each other. But on this night he passed the other cells and, with a wide grin, he waved to me in front of mine.

"Man, man! Could you've ever in all your life?" said the guard. "In your whole lifetime believe something like this could happen?"

"Not in ten lifetimes!" I said.

On both sides of the cell bars, we stood surprised. Unlike a prisoner face to face with a guard or vice versa, it was as if we had lost our way of seeing anything concrete, or being part of any prison way of thinking. Indeed, it was a rare moment to share in a once-in-a-lifetime experience.

"Man, check this out!" said the guard after he stepped up closer to my cell. "Here's a serious true story! I get this phone call last night. And man, it must have been 'bout four in the morning! I was tired, had crashed out on the couch, asleep! But come to find out it's my grandmother on the other end. So I go ahead and sit up and hand-wipe my face and clear my eyes."

"Where she's calling from?" I asked.

"She's way down in Mississippi," said the guard. "A country woman, ninety-six years old!"

"Is she?" I asked.

" . . . had raised me for a time," said the guard. "Even today, man, she's still something else!"

"So she's still doing well," I said. "That's good, man! Real good!"

"Oh, yeah she is!" said the guard. "She's one of those ol' deep southern women, wanna feed you all the time, you know the kind, everybody's her grandchild! And when not cookin', or hunched over the stove—"

"Yeah, I know. She's out dem doors, eh?" I asked.

"Man! Sitting there on her ol' porch!" said the guard.

"In her . . . in dat grandmamma ol' chair, too?" I asked.

"Oh! Yeah, right der, inside dat chair!"

"And wit' she Bible?" I asked. She was so much like someone who had once been very special in my life but had long passed.

"Man, you got it! That's my grandmamma!" said the guard. "And hey, you know as well as I do having someone special like this raising you for a time, you hear their voice."

"Yeah, yeah. I know I would!" I said.

"So . . . when I put my ear to that phone," said the guard, "I hear, 'Baby, Baby, can you hear grandmamma?' and even before my mouth could even come open, she says, 'Oh praise God. Oh praise you holy Jesus. Please! Please get my grandchild on this phone.' I said, 'Grandmamma anything wrong? You alright?' All I can hear is this crying. She's cryin' so bad. To just hear the sound of my grandmamma like that, you know? Ahh, man, it's like, it's goin' straight into me 'cause I can't do a damn thing, you know? I ain't goin' to lie, it was hurtin'. All I was able to do was listen. Grandmamma said, 'Baby, you still there?' I said, 'Yeah, What's going on?' 'Now you listen,' says my grandmamma. I hear this sniffling and she's trying to catch herself to blow her nose. 'Do you know I'm alive? I'm alive, is alive to see this day!' I said, 'You are alive?' 'I sure am!' she said. 'I sure am! To see we get us a Black President of dis here country! To see one us get that far, be answered prayer for dis, our peoples! I'm jus' so happy I'm 'bout to die . . . Baby, I'm just a sitt'n here crying my eyes out. My mama, you granddaddy, I'm jus' cryin' for dem, too! You don't mind if Grandmamma sit here, do you? Cause now, you all I have left.'

"'I know I am, Grandmamma, I am so, so glad that of everybody,' I says to her into the phone, 'that of all our family who can sit there, right there and still be to this day alive and to truly witness this night, it's you Grandmamma! Because,' I says, 'I still remember stories. Those ones, you know which ones? You use to go outside to tell?'"

"That she had to go outside and tell? They that painful?" I asked the guard. "Just hearing how you're describing this, your grandmamma voice and what I see you hearing, it's really tearing me up, man! So I know it had to for you!"

"That's just it," said the guard. "My grandmother's heart talks. She say, 'Yeah, um-huh! Dem der was bad times, child, some real bad times, child,' she spilling over in tears."

In front of my cell, the prison guard silently started to cry. Wiping his tears on the green arm sleeves of his uniform.

"Man, I swear," he said, with both hands latched to the bars. "I'd never forget it. It was like my grandmamma had once more gone outside. 'Boy, don't you see how our peoples done so much for you? Don't you see?' She kept sayin', 'Don't you see? Don't you see, child?' which really broke me up inside! I ain't goin' to lie, it did! The way I heard it, man, you know? You can just feel everything, seeing in my mind, that old couch she sits in . . . And, and just it being past her bedtime, alone!"

"I never thought," I said. "Not ever! That I'd be standing like this at these cell bars. Dude, we are literally looking and staring at each other, having seen each other's real tears about all this, you know?"

"Man, let me just tell you something about this madness," said the guard. "Let me run it down to you like this, OK? All the being 'a guard' or a 'correctional officer' stuff that a lot of us talk about around here, that is supposed to mean, especially around inmates, 'No, we don't cry!' Well, hey, you and I have been here long enough to know where that comes from."

"Yeah, we know," I said, "what a place like this prison needs to make for its own image. But, man, I also know just what this death row thing suppose to mean, what that suppose to say to you about me, and me to go on thinking about you . . ."

"Still, man!" said the guard. "We both know that's not what it's about. It was about me staying here and telling you this, about my ninety-six-year-old grandmother. It was about being men and showing just how blessed I was to celebrate with her probably the best thing, if not the one miracle, she's been praying and asking to be alive to see for all her life!"

"What I keep thinking about," I said, "is how she's lived almost a whole century in this country and has seen things we can't even begin to imagine, you know?"

"So, yeah, man," said the guard. "I did. I cried with this woman whose faith has guided her through so many things. Man, she's taught me to grow, both as a man, a father, and still today made me realize more about these past elections, you know? Brother, that's who was on the other end of that phone line. And since the time I can remember, my grandmamma use to always say, 'It's not what you are, it's who you are and what you have to live with inside yourself.'"

"It' not easy to see," I said, "how your grandmother, as have many others, been carrying so much. They have both the pains and hopes, and all the prayers nobody else has, to have believed in something as possible as seeing Barack Obama with his beautiful family on television become the President. Can you imagine this? Ninety-six years old?"

"I ain't never," said the guard. "Never! Never heard my grandmamma like that. We cried. Man, we did until she says 'Uh-huh! God, the Lord has been so, so good to me,' her voice feeling really tired and needing to lay down. It had been way past her bedtime. I couldn't believe she had stayed awake so late, you know?"

It was this moment that the guard and I just happened to glance over at my small television on the shelf in my cell.

"Take a look, a look at that," said the guard, pointing over at the screen. A picture of the late white grandmother of Barack Obama was shown hugging her grandson, the now new President- Elect.

Seconds passed.

"Man, that's being it," I said.

"Huh, what's that?" said the guard.

"That picture there," I said, "you see it? It's everything we've been talking about, you know? It's your grandmother, Barack Obama's grandmother, an image of the Deep South, slavery, an African American now being elected President! Their faces are everything that's been reflecting and bouncing off where you and I have been, you know? It's both of us, too! A prison guard, an inmate, and right here on death row!"

"Hey, just being here and looking," said the guard, "at myself, who could have easily been in your cell, this cell, or it being you out here on the tier. I'm thinking it's really about a lot more. It's sort of like what I told you my grandmamma had kept saying: 'Boy, don't you see how our peoples done so much for you? Don't you see?' I guess being here now is seeing more in that, you know?"

"There's no doubt," I said, "because anyone who's looking, that can see this across their own

TV screen will almost unavoidably come face to face with some sense of history. Hell, man. No wonder your grandmother cries! It's overcoming so much, this kind of love? Who's hugging this man Barack Obama like that? That there, look at it," I said, having known this kind of nurturing. "It's unconditional! The same I got as a little boy."

"Nah, you?" asked the guard.

"Man, I'm not jiving!"

"Really? You wait till now to tell me?"

"Can still remember as if it was yesterday, five or six years old, my very first foster parents. And I tell you . . ." I said, "I will never ever forget what it had opened in me, that I could feel special to at least someone, you know?" For seconds, I thought back to my once being the only child of two loving, elderly foster parents, and the memories of wanting to become an astronaut, and the way they had thought the world of me, that I could.

There was some light laughter that had come from down the tier, as we became aware that others were listening to our conversation.

"How much have they heard?"

"Who cares, you?"

"Not me," said the guard. "You see, you see this other picture?"—quickly pointing into my cell at the television.

"What? Obama? His grandmother?"

"Yeah, you see 'em? That's her, my grandmamma! That's her up and down! With that same big smile," said the guard, pointing to a much younger Barack Obama being wrapped in his grandmother's arms. No one could ever have convinced us that this proud, loving face of Barack's grandmother had not been our own. She had.

"You see that? Man, you just don't know the way my grandmamma touched and affected me in what she said."

"Brother!" I said smiling. "Yeah, I do, too! Man, just look at Barack Obama! The way he has touched and affected the whole world over this night!"

As the guard went on sharing his grandmother's story, I realized there was another story taking place. It became a story about a prison guard and an inmate learning that, despite the hardened world around us, an almost dehumanized culture of separation, a wall that had stood between the two of us for more than twenty years had in fact, for a few minutes, come down.

What the two of us, the prison guard and the inmate, saw that night, and spoke of, and felt . . . all of it brought tears to our eyes. As men we learned to experience our lives, in those few moments, without shame or fear, in longing more than anything else to be better human beings.

Together we had stepped beyond the prison walls and had become part of the hundreds of thousands of people who came before us, knowing it was because of them, and all of their courage to love and to hope, that the rest of us found the strength to see past our limitations, even those of a wounded prison culture. Their determination brought us to this moment in time, an African American being elected President of the United States.

DEAN FAIELLO, *New York*

IN SANATORIUM

Dawn breaks over a snow-covered prison yard. Dots of light gradually appear from cells as ice-coated razor wire sparkles. A seagull circles the yard, bleating a plaintive cry.

My steel cot, thoughtfully welded to the cell wall, is covered with several handsome shirts I am considering for my ex-wife's surprise visit. After twenty-two years of our roller-coaster relationship, I have learned to read between the lines of Patty's letters. When she writes, "What is the date of the Catholic Christmas event which you will *not* be attending?" she actually means, "You better be shaved and ready when I get there, or there's gonna be a scene."

In an effort to further erode the fragile bond between inmate and family, the Department of Corrections no longer allows families to visit during Christmas festivals. Their sensitivity is touching. I am boycotting the Catholic event this holiday season.

In preparation for shaving, I heat a small cup of water with a Bic lighter. Hot water is considered a luxury, along with a mirror. But thanks to Patty's thoughtfulness, I angle a four-inch plastic mirror so that I can remove my two-day-old beard.

In further preparation for Patty's surprise visit, I lie on my cot and study my Spanish/English dictionary. Patty, a South American, wisely encouraged me to become bilingual in jail. While I'm still in the "A's," my cell door opens with a heart-stopping bang.

"3814, report to the desk."

I walk the 240 feet from my cell to the desk. Ninety-six cells line the sides of the sepulchral corridor. Inmate faces, framed by cell portals, pass my peripheral vision like telephone poles on a highway.

"I done wrote to my baby's momma last mont'. I says to ha, 'Bitch, where's ma package?'"

"Yo, yo, Dean, lemme get that sweata."

"Dese PO-lice be mad stupid."

Corrections officers sit at the head of the corridor, surrounded by bullet-proof glass. (As if we're a threat to *them*.) The company officer looks up from his Masonite clipboard. Biding his time until retirement, he leans back in his swivel chair and exhales.

"I got a call from the visitin' room. A Latino woman down there's talkin' Spanish a mile a minute and throwin' your name 'round like salt inna ice storm. Go see if you can calm 'er down. Emergency Response Team's on coffee break."

"Yes, sir."

The officer signs a blue pass and I commence negotiating my way past six officer-manned checkpoints. A clammy perspiration develops under my sweater.

I arrive at the gate called Traffic Control: another bullet-proof bubble. One officer mans the electric gate controls. The other stares menacingly at approaching inmates.

"Where you goin'?"

"Visiting room, sir."

"Lemme see ya pass . . . What kinda name is that?"

"Orecchio, t's Italian, sir."

"'Talian, huh? Some kinda mafioso? We don't like no troublemakers. You got me? Keep it movin'."

The next few checkpoints go more smoothly, mostly grunts and stares. I arrive at the visiting room. The officer pulls out his nightstick and points it at the entrance. "Walk through the metal detector. If the alarm goes off, I'm gonna club you like a baby seal."

I pass through the metal detector without incident. I approach the visiting-room desk and four seated officers, middle-aged, prematurely balding, and paunchy; puffy, bloodshot eyes hint at hangovers. One leans way back in his swivel chair, eyes closed, mouth agape. Two are reading newspapers. The other is dunking his glazed donut in a Tim Horton's coffee cup.

"You 3814? You the one visitin' with that crazy Porto Rican? Tell 'er she ain't in New Yak City no more and stop with the *puta* this and the *puta* that."

"Yes, sir."

Patty is delicately perched on a plastic cafeteria chair. The table in front of her is covered with bags of M&M's, turkey sandwiches, salads, and a clear plastic purse bulging with coins. Her brown hair perches high, defiantly, reflecting her outlook on life. Her eyes, black as olives, sparkle within her Ecuadorian complexion.

"Ah, my prince has arrived. You look wonderful. Is that the sweater I sent you?"

"Lands' End. Nice, huh?"

We embrace and kiss. "It's nice to squeeze your bubble butt. You gained a little weight."

"Patty, cut it out, people are looking."

"Oh please. That guy's had his tongue down that girl's throat for fifteen minutes."

I glance over. At a black Formica table, the guy has pinned the girl to the table with his steel and diamond-encrusted teeth. She's reading *Ebony*. A five-year-old girl in a pink sweater and pink hair beads sits under the table with a coloring book and Crayolas. Behind her, heavy-gauge steel mesh forms cages for inmates in "the box," separating them from their visitors. Welcome to family time in prison.

We sit. I keep my hands visible to the guards. My mother's Art Deco pin glints on Patty's breast. Before passing away, she asked that the pin go to Patty.

I choose a breakfast of peanut M&M's to go with the French vanilla cappuccino Patty brings me from the vending machines. I've shed my finicky eating habits. Due to chronic hunger, I now eat anything.

"So, were you surprised by my visit?"

"Shocked. I was dressed and shaved before you even got here."

Patty frowns, hands on her hips. "How did you know?"

"Well, you wrote asking the date of the festival you know I'm not going to. I knew you were busy planning something, *mi bruja.*"

"Give me another kiss. I've missed you so much." We stand, hug, and kiss. I squeeze her buttocks. Just as plump as ever. We sit.

"So, did you fly in last night?"

"Yep, I'm staying at the Antioch. They got new carpet. Now I can take my shoes off." Patty wets her thumb and removes lipstick from my cheek.

"How was your flight?"

"*Ay, la puta de su madre* Jet Blue. *Qué cabrones!*" I hear about air traffic delays, Homeland Security, and rude ticket agents. At a nearby table, a woman in a leopard-print blouse squeezes the zits on her boyfriend's forehead. He smirks in delight.

"So while I was waiting for the flight, I did shots of tequila with Corona chasers, fresh lime, and salt. I went back to the waiting area. Empty. They changed the gate. I had to run past sixteen gates. *Hijo de la puta madre! Malditos cabrones! Que se vayan al infierno.*"

Two guards look up from their donuts. "There she goes again. Where's immigration? What happened to tightening our borders?"

I try to distract her: "So, how's your mother?"

"Fine. Dropped Corky off and flew to California. *La puta floja! Yo no tengo una vida? Al infierno con la vieja!*"

Wrong subject.

"*Mi cielo*, could I have another cappuccino? That was excellent."

"Anything for my sweetheart. Oh, it's so good to see you."

She squeezes my M&M-filled cheeks.

In spite of my excitement seeing Patty, an air of melancholy pervades. I am embarrassed. I cannot get up from my seat, not even to peek into the vending machines. A fellow Catholic sits at a table nearby, yet I'm not allowed to speak to him. Officers stand with arms folded, glaring at inmates. Above the vending machines, opaque windowpanes spill gray light into the room. I wonder what the weather is like.

When Patty returns, I talk about changes at the Transition Center. I'm lucky to have a prison job. Nine hundred inmates are idle—no job, no program, nothing to do except go to the yard and get into fights. I orient newly arrived inmates and prep those going home. It's frustrating at times, trying to maintain order in a small room with fifteen restless, sometimes angry prisoners. But occasionally, I see a smile of comprehension, a moment of epiphany. When change actually happens in prison, it's magical. When an ex-con actually makes it on the outside, reconnecting with family and settling into a sustainable life supported by others, it's a miracle. But there's also the burnout factor. Many guys in prison simply don't want to learn. They reject knowledge instinctively. As a neophyte, I enjoy the teaching challenge.

Patty and I also talk about the new director, Mr. O. Besides being in favor of programs, he is bilingual, married to a South American. (I can see why he works so much, to avoid the wrath of his Hispanic wife.) Still, many of the prison's classrooms sit empty. They are a testament to the administration's intransigence. Many of the civilians are opposed to changes too, just like any employee used to a routine.

Patty looks at me somberly. "Sweetheart, you can't force change on people." She raises one eyebrow. "You should know that. I finally learned that when I wanted you to go right, I said go left." She places her *café au lait* hand over mine. "Honey, can I heat up this turkey sandwich for you? I'm not leaving until every scrap of food is eaten from this table."

Patty starts opening packets of condiments. I begin piling lettuce, cheese, and mayonnaise on my turkey sandwich. I overhear conversations from neighboring tables.

"I don't give a shit about the rent. Just send me ma package."

"Dese niggas be stupid."

"Where's ma child?"

A corrections officer patrols the visiting room. "Put ya hands on the table . . . slide ya chair forward . . . no crosstalkin'."

Patty and I discuss the prison's AA meetings. I had never felt comfortable speaking in front of groups. That silence kept me from working on my issues and finding the reasons I drank and drugged. Now that I chair meetings, I share secrets and open up. Compared to the stories of those around me, I've little to be ashamed of. We've all done heinous things.

A gluttony of food and conversation have zapped my stamina. My brain is like a muscle: lack of use causes atrophy. Demanding conversation, like heavy weight-lifting, leaves me lethargic and dazed.

"Patty, could I have another cappuccino? Make it a double."

While Patty fights the mob at the vending machines, I look around the room. A couple stares intently at one another. She is removing blackheads from his nose with her fuchsia-painted fingernails. Bare cinderblock walls and fluorescent lighting provide a backdrop.

Patty returns. "Hey," I ask, "how come you never do that for me?"

I glance at the couple, now removing ear and eyebrow hairs from each other.

Patty wrinkles her nose. "This is like the Discovery Channel. Primates grooming each other, lions pulling meat from bones, silverbacks beating their chests. Who needs Tivo?"

"It's my inspiration for writing, you feel me?"

"Sure honey. Slide your chair a little closer." Patty scoots her chair closer to the table.

"It's an expression, sweetheart. It means do you identify with my feelings?"

"Oh. I see." She pauses. "You sure I can't feel you anyway?"

"I don't think the COs would go for it."

"*Al infierno con los malditos cabrones.* Listen, I gotta get to the supermarket and buy you goodies before they close. Got any special requests?"

"Yeah. Chateaubriand, beluga caviar, and live Maine lobsters."

"Right. You're gettin' tuna in a can and better like it. Now give your shorty a big kiss before I go so I can squeeze your buns again."

"How 'bout squeezing my zits, too?"

"If you don't get up right now, I'm gonna squeeze your nuts."

"Thanks for the offer, but the COs are gonna do that on my way out."

"These two hands and these two lips better be the only action you get till I see you tomorrow. You got me?"

We embrace, kiss, and fondle. The COs look up.

"Thank you, baby Jesus. Thought she'd never leave."

Patty joins the queue waiting to leave. Some continue conversations with their loved ones, shouting, gesticulating. Others air-kiss. Patty looks at me. Sadness pervades her smile.

The moment the visitors leave, the atmosphere leadens. The officers adopt menacing stares and bark orders.

"Don't get up till I tell ya!"

I sit at my table, staring at the black surface. I try to retain the mood that existed only moments ago—the sound of Patty's voice, her animated eyes, the aroma of her perfume.

One block at a time is called from the visiting room to undergo searches. A line of officers wearing latex gloves awaits us. We are stripped naked.

"Lift up your arms."

"Open your mouth."

"Lift up your nuts. Separate the shaft."

"Turn around."

"Lift up your feet."

"Bend over and spread your cheeks."

"Get dressed."

I emerge into the airless corridors. I force myself to remember I am no longer a human being. I am a number in green. I keep my mouth shut until asked a question.

"Where ya goin'?"

"C-3."

The electric gate rattles open. The officer brusquely hands back my blue pass and ID card without a word. As I continue to my cell, he ignores me. I am already forgotten.

I close the steel gate to my cell with a bang that never ceases to unnerve. I lie on my back on my steel cot. I try to let the good feeling of the day's visit persist. Patty's love still exists, despite my lies, insanity, and the drug abuse that precipitated our divorce. Her devotion amazes me. I doubt that I am capable of having such compassion for another person.

A blue blur passes—the officer taking the chow list. Thankfully, I'm still sated. The mess hall is a depressing experience. Officers stand near the tables, batons gripped with both hands, ready for use in a millisecond. The noise is deafening, and the conversation a litany of gripes about the nameless "they," the food, and "niggers." I hear that word hundreds of times a day, yet I still find it offensive. I'm tired of hearing it. At this moment, I'm just plain tired.

The following day, Sunday, Patty returns for part two of our weekend visit. She's calmer, having avoided Jet Blue, and there are no warnings from the COs in the visiting room. But they seat us in the back of the visiting room, out of their earshot.

When I arrive at Patty's table, we hug, kiss, and she squeezes my butt again. I squeeze her nipples. The COs tell us to cool it and sit down. Patty decides that we're going to speak Spanish all day to help me master the language.

I soon regret not having my Spanish/English dictionary. Patty becomes animated, speaking faster, with lots of hand gestures. I struggle to keep up. Talking about her job and the attorneys with whom she works, "*hijueputas*" and "*cabrones*" fill the air. I tell her she talks like a Mexican drug dealer. She says something about cooking and eating "*huevos,*" which are scrambled eggs, or deviled eggs—something with eggs. I forgot which.

We're more relaxed the second day. We laugh a lot. Memories of my drunken, drugged exploits provide much fodder.

We switch to English. Patty tells me she's proud of me. The events that brought me to prison were very painful for her, like watching a train wreck. As the smoke cleared, she realized that she too was a victim, bloodied and hurt. But she is now recovering. She has come to accept that this part of my journey is necessary for me to realize my calling—"To teach, just like your mother, Karen." I'm here to allow others to see the cliff before the plunge to the rocky shore. Many men will plow straight ahead, cocksure of their direction. But a few of the willing can be turned around, just in time.

"Patty, my ego was so huge, I couldn't even see my feet."

"I know, sweetheart. But you've changed. I'm so happy. The Deany I fell in love with has returned."

My eyes water. Patty smiles and gently cups one hand against my cheek. I'm glad the COs put us in the back of the room.

After the visit, I return to my cell with a massive Spanish hangover. I lay on my cot and pull out my Spanish/English dictionary. *Huevos, huevos . . . huevo*—n.m., egg; *huevos*—pl., slang for testicles.

La puta madre!

Then I fall into a blissful, dreamless sleep.

PETER MEHMEL, *New York*

A HIDDEN COST

The eve of my son's fifth birthday seemed especially cruel. I'm sure he woke up excited and happy to celebrate his special day, only to find that his father was gone. I can't imagine how my wife, six months pregnant with our daughter, managed to find the words to tell him.

The party arrangements were done, the cake safely stashed; we'd confirmed who would attend and even had a few bucks left over. That evening, friends were playing in a band at a local bar. Maybe everything was just too right not to go wrong. Most bar fights don't end in death. Mine did. And suddenly everything changed. My loved ones had to live in the wreckage I left behind. This was clear in the eyes of my son.

When my family brought him to our first visit a month later, he had dark rings around his eyes as though he'd been crying the whole time. His haunted, frightened look ground salt into my pain. He lunged to meet me, hugging tight. His skin was hot, feverish, and he didn't let go after the initial greeting. I searched for an answer to his unspoken plea for an explanation. The small, unadorned visiting room was crowded and seemed to close in upon us. I found no answer in the water-stained ceiling, the pale yellow cinder-block walls, the speckled concrete floor. I just held him, fighting back my own emotions. Maintaining a front grew harder as the visit continued. My voice threatened to break. I managed to ask about his He-Man Castle Grayskull birthday present—fun to assemble but tricky to wrap. I'd imagined watching him play out each character's role. We didn't get the chance to share that birthday, or any since. Some things cling and won't let go—like his hug, and how I had to pry his tiny hands apart when the visit ended.

Prison has extracted pieces of all of us. Happy childhoods. Bonds between brother and sister. My son went to live with an uncle in another state. My daughter, who I've held only a few times as an infant, stayed with her mother. The logic may have been sound, but it wasn't mine. My children were split up to grow under others' guidance without my nurturing. I didn't appreciate it then, but they were fortunate to have family looking after them. They would be loved, have a home, and were spared being thrust into foster care.

None of us saw the stigma they'd endure. Schoolchildren can be mean. As a convict's kid, there is no acceptable answer to "What does your daddy do?" Sporting events, musicals, any public outing where parents normally appear, scarred my children, who had to hide the truth from their peers. They learned shame and how to lie. They grew thick skins to shield them from the abuse. Laughter isn't joyful when it's aimed at you. It shaped their views of the world, and determined who they associated with and ultimately who they became. They saw the pecking order from the bottom and had to fight to fit in where they could. They migrated to the misfit groups.

Drug use became abuse. Maybe it dulled the pain, maybe it enabled them to socialize. In either case, it brought more trouble than they could handle. Through no fault of their own, they grew up experiencing prison secondhand. As if that wasn't bad enough—what weighs upon me now—both went to prison themselves. "Visiting the iniquity of the fathers on the children, on the third and fourth generations . . ." So the pattern is set for the third generation: they too suffer a parent in prison and bear the marks. It's said that people are responsible to carry their own cross. I bear the weight of how my children turned out.

When the judge's gavel slammed like a lightning bolt from above, my family was sentenced too, the consequences piling on with each passing year. As I've learned, so my children have learned to question everyone's motives. It's a knee-jerk reflex with every relationship. People abandon convicts. There are so many hardships, few survive the distance a long bid demands. These facts twist a convict's psyche, making us less likely to reach out, trust, or even begin new relationships. My children will learn to keep others at a distance. All that I've experienced will be passed on.

For over a decade, my son believed that I did not love him. My daughter had her first child at fifteen. Neither finished high school. Treasured moments in their childhoods never became memories of mine. My triumphs were never theirs. They didn't share their first bike rides with their father, or fishing trips, or Easter egg hunts, Sunday morning pancakes shaped like elephants, or even the mumps. Decorating the Christmas tree, who lifted them to place the star? Did they miss me at tea parties? Who patched up their skinned knees or built their tree forts? Was the very thought of me so painful that they built a wall to keep it hidden? Was I a traveling companion on adventures into lost worlds, or was I the enemy they rallied the troops against? I never met the people they loved. My grandchildren, all born out of wedlock, never met their grandfather.

Both my children went to prison when their own children were young—so repeats the cycle that I started. No doubt they too have learned the anguish of restricted space, resources, and actions. They will have no careers, no pension plans, and college is out of the equation.

My brother wrote a while back. He told me to sit down because he had really terrible news. Two of my daughter's three children had been killed in a house fire. I sat stunned. I wondered how my daughter received the news in her cell. Did her hands shake like mine? Did she utter prayers to reverse time? No doubt, her distress is much greater than mine. I'm sure it's killing her to be caged while her remaining child is in such need.

I had no way to contact her before the funeral. Maybe she tried to reach me . . . maybe not. I would not have been allowed to attend anyway. I wonder whether I would have been welcome. I'd never met them. I fear she didn't consider me worthy to grieve with her.

I still don't know the details of the fire. I only hope I can learn where they were buried, to pay my respects, and place a few flowers.

COREY JOHN RICHARDSON, *Kentucky*

FATHER ALERT: HOW PRISONS DESTROY FAMILIES

One of the most effective systems we have today to locate missing or abducted children is the Amber Alert. Though this national system rose out of tragedy, its current use has facilitated the return of countless children. In a way, we are facing a similar problem: missing fathers. And maybe it is time to create a Father Alert system. I know where we can begin to implement such a system—U.S. prisons.

The U.S. prison system houses millions of men; millions more are caught up in the system through probation, parole, halfway houses, etc. One of the few studies on incarcerated fathers found that over 60 percent of men in prison are parents. Let me say that again: over 60 percent. While much effort has been placed on maintaining a bond during imprisonment for women with their children, next to nothing has been done for incarcerated fathers.

When a father is sent to prison, all parental responsibilities, economic or social, are left unfulfilled, thus straining or destroying familial bonds. Experts agree that these men lack the insight to view their world and their place in it clearly. Only after the fact do most begin to feel the full weight of their actions. By that time it is far too late, and fatherhood consists of short, monitored visits and collect calls home. And that is in the very best of circumstances. For many, their fatherhood will cease to exist outside a distant memory or fantasy.

When a prison sentence is handed down, we rightly consider the victims directly affected and their respective families. But, for a moment, let's do something unseemly. Let us consider the other victims indirectly affected: (1) the children of the convict, who have now lost access to a father; (2) a spouse or partner, who must raise the children on her own without the much-needed assistance and participation of the father; and (3) the incarcerated father, who statistically is not only likely to be a product of abuse, poverty, violence, and addiction, but will now be thrown into prison, where years of violence, abuse, disease, and isolation will take their toll—not to mention a diminution of an already scant list of legal employment opportunities, few of which offer a living wage. When we discuss true recovery and healing, we must include all pertinent points of view. In doing so we can heal not only victims, but also the "other" victims, and possibly begin to address the larger problem: mass imprisonment and its effects.

The number one indicator for future imprisonment is having an incarcerated parent or familial role model. In this way, prison is a self-perpetuating reality, like a gene passed on generation after generation. The idea of a parent in prison is often painful, confusing, and frightening for children. Removal of the father creates an increased burden on these affected families, which by and large exist in impoverished communities. These children often find themselves caught in the criminal-justice system during adolescence.

Though their crimes are always before them, convicts do not see themselves in purely criminal terms. Incarcerated fathers self-identify as parents, though removed from the family unit, and rank the value of relationships at an extremely high level. This identity is extremely important for these men, particularly for those with no wealth, no property, no education, and no viable employment opportunities waiting for them upon release. Right or wrong, having children validates incarcerated fathers as few other attributes can.

Difficulties maintaining these relationships are obvious. Far-flung and costly travel weigh on already constrained family budgets and limited transportation options; brief visits in tightly controlled conditions, cards and letters with their intrinsic limitations, and expensive collect calls, all added together do little to keep the family together. They in fact have quite the opposite effect. The inclusion of another male role model, usually supplanting the father for brief periods of time, often adds to the confusion and overall difficulties. The rates of anxiety and depression for the incarcerated fathers and their children are high.

On visits to prison, incarcerated fathers devour the attention of their children, as if they could absorb the lost years of ball games, family outings, and other shared moments in a one- or two-hour visit. The children cling to their fathers, the younger children attempting to drag their dads home from the visiting area once and for all. I have seen their pained, flustered expressions as they are carried away, reaching out one last time until the next visit, months or years away.

Aggressive, hardcore convicts morph into extremely paternal and loving men during phone calls home to their kids. One can hear in their voices a sincere desire to connect on some deeper level with their sons and daughters. They spend hours decorating cards and building crafts to send home, as if these things could substitute for the real closeness and intimacy they desire. But there is little else to do, and something, anything, is better than nothing.

Sadly, these limited means are often extinguished for men who have acrimonious relationships with the mother or guardian of their children. Many men do not realize they and their children have a legal right to this relationship as long as maintaining it does not pose a risk to the children. Being in prison does not bar the relationship; it only creates obstacles.

As stated, men entering prison statistically are undereducated or functionally illiterate, come from impoverished communities, and have few marketable skills. The fact that they will often leave prison with five, ten, twenty, or more years of back child support owed, and they can expect little more than a minimum-wage job, does more than complicate the problem. Prison exacerbates disease and dysfunction that often began well before prison, then adds a criminal record. Where are these men to work when they could hardly find work before? If they had a livable wage, would they have spent half the night on the street corner to sell only ten or twenty dollars' worth of dope, or robbed the local convenience store? Now, if they try to go "straight," they can expect the state to take up to half of their take-home wages. If the minimum wage is not a livable wage, then what is half of it? The result is clear: men trying to make it—filled with anger, frustration, and hopelessness—often returning to prison for non-support or for simply returning to the activities which got them locked up in the first place.

None of this is meant to diminish the incarcerated father's responsibility for his actions. Quite the opposite. But let us not only understand what he did, who is generally affected, or even how we might help him and his family heal. In addressing these needs, let us understand the problem in its totality, which means its historical, economic, political, and social origins as well. We must also ask ourselves if we have bought into the idea that the prisons are filled with sub-human monsters hell-bent on violence or destruction. Are they moral degenerates? Or are these people who have made decisions based on limited choices and inadequate information and societal forces much greater than they could appreciate? The prisons do house persons overwhelmingly from impoverished communities, made up of ethnic minorities, but research demonstrates conclusively that addiction and crime occur in all social strata. Yet it is the poor who go to prison.

This is not a pleasant realization. Nor is it palatable to most to consider that the media, politicians, and business all have an interest in presenting the criminal in an ugly light. Today, due to the continuing criminalization of addiction and the use of habitual-offender laws, we can find men and women serving 25-to-life for simple drug possession. The middle class and wealthy do not usually get arrested or prosecuted for these crimes, and almost never go to prison. The upper classes go to treatment, while the poor can expect to endure long, traumatic years behind razor wire. While the crime rate drops year by year, politicians and the media have sold us on the idea of a worsening crime problem in this country, and private companies with a vested interest in prison expansion have raked in the profits funded by taxes, and rural communities desperate for jobs have sought more and more prison construction.

I often imagine how much health care, education, housing, transportation, research, and so on we could have bought with all the money it took to expand our prison population from 200,000 to 2.3 million. It only took one generation, and the bulk of this growth was for nonviolent drug offenses. How much treatment could we have bought? Instead, we took those from our poorest communities with the least amount of quality health care and education, and made their situation even worse through enforcement of laws that lack proportionality and focus on the most marginalized of our society. "Tough on Crime" laws have been repeatedly referred to as "Tough on the Poor," with families suffering. I truly believe that when we begin to promote laws and programs that take into consideration all of these factors, and appreciate the many and varied ill effects, only then can we begin to seek recovery, healing, and prevention.

This may all sound very academic as one reads in the comfort of a living room or a subway ride to work, but for millions of fathers and mothers and children it is desperately real. Either one mistake or a series of them, usually due to a lack of insight, and larger societal challenges, have destroyed these families. On Father's Day 2008, President Obama, then on the campaign trail, gave a stern remonstration against the absent father, particularly African Americans. White, middle-class voters rallied around these words, but I was left with this: There's much pain, grief, anger, and remorse tied up in the realization that your one chance to be a father to your children has been wiped away. I have seen men try to stuff their emotions and live off of hate just to get through the day. Most are left embittered, hostile, and maladjusted. The Black Community has been hit worst. It is hard not to be an absent father when you are in prison. It is shocking to hear that over 50 percent of the prison population is Black when Black people make up only 12 percent of the U.S. population. That means that about one out of three African American males can expect to serve time in prison. The numbers for Hispanics are little better, at one out of six, while white males are looking at one out of every seventeen. All groups commit crimes, and the "white collar" crimes of the upper classes, such as tax evasion, price fixing, employee theft, etc., create a much greater overall societal burden. And yet it is through inadequate legal representation, police targeting, the ease with which "street" crimes are detected, differing outcomes due to judicial discretion, etc., that the poor, predominantly ethnic minorities are incarcerated. The families of these communities are left in pieces.

The walls that hold incarcerated fathers are much higher and broader than the mere concrete and metal that you see. Many of these fathers are not much more than children themselves. They have little education and disturbing childhoods, and it is often much easier to vilify them than try to understand and help them. Maybe we need a "Father Alert" program for these men and their families. The Amber Alert works due to the fact that (1) specific information about the lost child is known and made available, and (2) people work in concert to find and bring the child home. This is exactly how we need to approach our Father Alert system. Information and delivery.

Most men enter prison undereducated, underemployed, addicted, abused, and unhealthy, and they leave even worse as a consequence of many years of violence, abuse, isolation, and difficult living conditions. Their families suffer, and often a cycle of imprisonment is continued in the next generation. Many young men have only spent time with their fathers on visits or as cellmates. Though this knowledge does not excuse criminal action, it does give therapists, social workers, psychologists, etc., insight and the direction necessary to treat and develop programs to meet the needs of incarcerated fathers and their families.

Beyond this, we must become socially active and promote common-sense laws that include proportionality and allow for diversion to treatment where applicable. We must also demand effective, quality rehabilitation within prisons, offering much of what these fathers never had prior to imprisonment: safe housing, medical education, vocational training, addiction treatment, family planning, and a variety of psychotherapeutic programs that offer more than the rote nonsense proffered by former guards promoted to administer "treatment." We should demand a livable wage for all citizens and do more than just tell ex-cons, "Good luck going straight." We should make prison aftercare a priority. We should begin to shrink the U.S. prison population and begin to spend adequately with respect to the social programs needed in impoverished communities. That's true crime prevention. And we should reevaluate how we target, arrest, and prosecute in this country.

I know most would rather blame incarcerated fathers. It would certainly be much easier than understanding the problems and seeking solutions. But we are in an age when all of this is truly possible. I believe that we must do more than merely claim to be a just society. We must act. Those of us who truly believe in recovery and healing have special insight and can do more. We have to help fathers out of prison, keep them out, change this venal system, improve our communities, and prevent the next generation of fathers from going missing due to incarceration. It is far from easy, but it is a task that we are uniquely able to address. And the very foundation of our Father Alert program should be those various therapies, programs, and interventions—be they legal, social, or psychotherapeutic—that reconnect incarcerated fathers with their children, their families, and their true potentials.

Ticket In

RAHASHEEM BROWN, *New York*

THE MENTALITY OF AN INCARCERATED CRIMINAL

PART ONE: YOUTH

The mentality of the criminal is acquired at a very young age, in most cases. This is why a pre-sentencing investigation (PSI) report goes back to your parents' history, the history of your siblings (especially if any of them were incarcerated or in trouble with the law), and so on.

There were role models in the 'hood (neighborhood) from which I hail, very few of whom had never been incarcerated. Even fewer had never committed a crime in my presence. When I was young (and looking up to them), they did not know—and probably could not have known—that they, indirectly, planted seeds in my young mind.

I eventually learned to think in an "every man for himself" sort of way, and when my young age denied me the opportunity to seek legal employment, I sought other means of obtaining capital. Crime in the inner city will always offer a means to those who are willing to break the law to earn a dollar. These dollars were fast and easy to make, without any hard labor.

I remember walking past the Schenectady County Jail once (where several people I knew had been), thinking, "I wonder what it looks like in there." I knew I need not contemplate that for too long, because I would eventually find out. So I began contemplating what I would be doing to get my name up (become known and respected, or better, feared) while I was there.

By this time, I had already been to DFY (Department of Correctional Services, Division for Youth) for four years in total. This was a combination of two stays, less than ten days apart. I had also been on probation for two and a half years. I was taken off of the streets before completing my third year. I was eventually sent to DFY from the group home that the Department of Social Services had placed me in.

The first DFY facility I was in was Pius XII, in Westchester County. While there, I became a better and more organized criminal. Prior thereto, I would steal from establishments (sometimes I'd get caught and have to be picked up by adult family members, or by the youth division of the police department), hold drugs and/or guns for the older hustlers, or I would steal drugs from the dealers who allowed me into their homes; I would sell the drugs for less than their street value.

In Pius XII I started a team (a group) called the Inch-Mob. I was the youngest in the group at the age of ten. The other members were eleven, twelve, and fourteen. We would jump older or bigger kids, rob people for their money and property, etc.

The facility circulated a phony money called "Dinosaur Dollars," in denominations of $1, $5, $10, or $20, with different dinosaurs on them. For every Dinosaur Dollar, you would be given a real dollar when you left the facility and went on home visits or on off-grounds trips.

At different levels you were allowed greater freedoms. I never advanced to the level to go on home visits, because I was always in trouble; but I did reach the level for off-grounds once. So I would spend most of the money I'd take at the facility's store.

For every member of the Inch-Mob, there was a seventeen- or eighteen-year-old who would "hold him down" (protect him); so these older dudes would get a cut of the money we would come up with. These seventeen- and eighteen-year-olds would also school us. This is where I learned about getting a drug connection, and the cost to purchase drugs for sale.

Originally, I was only supposed to be there for a six-month evaluation, but I spent ten months there due to my behavior. When I left, it was to a more secure facility, called Oatca, in Monroe County, just outside of Rochester.

Oatca had a three-level system at the main facility: *Yellow*—these individuals would receive the most freedoms (e.g., they were allowed to watch TV and communicate with one another); *Level*—most of the same privileges as those who were Yellow, but to a lesser degree; *Frozen*—all of your privileges were restricted or frozen (e.g., an individual who was frozen would have to face his chair away from the TV, in the TV area). There was also an "all privilege" dorm called 79, which was on the Industry Facility's compound. Industry was another youth facility down the hill from Oatca.

At the main facility, I was always Frozen, with the exception of one week. That week, I made it to Level, and was even sent to the "all privilege" dorm. I never made it to Yellow, though I do not remember doing anything to get into trouble there. I was always frozen for an accumulation of small infractions, I guess. When I was sent to dorm 79, I avoided getting into any trouble because I didn't want to be sent back to the main facility.

I eventually went home from Oatca, to an aftercare program called HBIS (Home-Based, Intensive-Care Supervision). This lasted a little more than a week, until I drew a weapon on my HBIS supervisor for making a statement directed toward my mother. When I went back in, I went through Highland Falls Youth Facility, Tryon Youth Facility, Buffalo Residential Center, and ended up in Great Valley Youth Facility in Salamanca, New York.

During my second incarceration as a youth, I was away for nearly two years. Most of that time was spent at Great Valley Youth Facility. I eventually made it to the facility's highest level, but it took me a long time. It was a very "short-lived" stay at the top. When I went home, my mother sent me to live with my brother Keith and his wife in Columbia, Maryland.

The state of Maryland wanted to put me in youth detention because I was getting into a little trouble out there. I wasn't involved in any criminal activity, but as a nonresident of the state, my general behavior warranted this action. For this reason, my brother sent me back to Schenectady. But it was there, in the state of Maryland, that I held my first legal, under-the-table job: landscaping and passing out the company's fliers.

My brother Keith has been to prison once, back in the '70s or '80s, but has never returned. Aside from myself and him, three of my mother's other children have been to prison (my brother George, my brothers Charles and Andrew—who went to prison for nothing more than falling asleep at George's house). My mother bore ten children. I am the youngest. My father, who himself passed away in prison, had six children. Of that six, three of us have been to prison (myself, my only younger brother, Jahmal, and my sister Vanessa, who is serving a 25-years-to-life sentence).

Once back in Schenectady, I was back with those I started out in the streets with, but with new additions from New York City. I also had a new mindset that sat well with my circle. They were selling drugs, having sex, carrying guns (this was nothing new to me; I had been arrested with a gun before I was ten years old), robbing, shooting, etc.

To all of this I adapted quickly. I had been schooled at Pius XII in stealing Dinosaur Dollars and how to put up and save money. There were also my dealings with drug dealers and older hustlers and gunmen prior to my initial youth incarceration. Coupled with my "hands-on experience," this gave me a complete understanding of the lifestyle I was living.

Back from out of state, same people, same places, same results! Only my next stay in DFY was on a nineteen-count robbery and assault indictment. Despite the seriousness of these offenses, this was my shortest incarceration. After four short months, I fell very ill while at Rochester Residential Center. I was diagnosed with Crohn's disease/ulcerative colitis. While it is very treatable now, back in 1994 the medical field knew little about my condition or its causes. I was taken from Rochester General Hospital to St. Clair's Hospital in Schenectady so the probation and child-placement department would be able to monitor me.

Upon discharge from the hospital, I was placed under house arrest, to avoid going back to DFY. I assume the court believed such a blow might slow me down. Fat chance of that! Bracelet on my ankle and all, I was back on the streets.

I was later on house arrest for stealing a motorbike. I was, again, taken to the youth division of the Schenectady police department. When I was asked if there was someone who could pick me up, I told the detective, "No."

The detective researched my juvenile record to see if there was a number he could call. He discovered that I had lied about my age, and that I was actually sixteen years old. I was transferred to the adult side of the police department, and the house-arrest bracelet was removed.

PART TWO: ADULTHOOD

I was sent to the Schenectady County Jail the next morning. I was sentenced to thirty days jail-time, of which I served twenty days; this was where I used up my YO (youthful offender) status. While I was there, I went to the "box" (SHU, or Special Housing Unit) twice, once for a physical altercation with two county officers. I went home from SHU and went right back to the streets, but not until after my brother's funeral.

Just two days before I was set to be released from Schenectady County Jail, my brother Charles suffered a massive heart attack and passed away at just twenty-six years old. Just one week prior to his passing, my brothers George (who was Charles's only full brother) and Andrew were arrested in a drug raid at one of my brother George's apartments.

Our brother's passing left us heartbroken; but the street was our medicine. My brother Charles's funeral was important to us all, but especially to my brother George, who was his closest ally. So he was bailed out of jail (on a bond) with the help of our mother, who put a lien against her home as collateral.

After the funeral, me and my brother George were back to the streets and the lifestyle full-time. Eventually, George went to prison, which left me to control his areas as well as those I already controlled or co-controlled. This went well for a time, but I fell out with my original constituents, who were jealous of my situation. Guns were involved, so we parted ways to avoid killing one another.

I set up shop, full-time, in a different area of town. A fallout with a man from New York City over that territory led to me shooting him. The man I shot told officers, and I was arrested. That led to my first state prison sentence of thirty to sixty months.

After a six-month stay in county jail, I was moved to Downstate Correctional Facility, in Fishkill, New York. From Downstate I was sent to Greene Correctional Facility, in Coxsackie, New York. Greene was the streets behind a fence. Weapons and more weapons, drugs and more drugs, robberies, extortion, stabbings, fights, etc. At some point, my younger brother, Jahmal, came to Greene. Instead of being a good role model, I corrupted him even worse.

From Greene, I was moved to Mt. McGregor Correctional Facility, where I completed the ASAT (Alcohol & Substance Abuse Treatment) program. While there, I was charged with obstruction for refusing to admit that I was assaulted (or by whom) while at the facility. The charge was eventually dropped because I held fast to my assertion that I accidentally cut myself while opening a can. To explain how it had gotten sewn with sewing thread, I told them, "I passed out, and woke up in my bunk, stitched up already."

After receiving several tickets for refusing to cut off my "locks" (despite the fact that I was registered Rastafarian), I went to SHU and was moved to Great Meadow Correctional Facility. All told, I received forty-eight days of keep-lock time while at Mt. McGregor.

I spent twelve of my forty-eight days on D-1, keep-lock reception, at Great Meadow. From there, I was moved to B-2, which is long-term keep-lock, for eighteen days. Over there, it was nothing to wake up to a rat hanging out on your chest or in your locker across from you.

When I was down to my last fifteen days in keep-lock, I went back through Downstate Correctional and eventually landed in Bare Hill Correctional. There, I vowed that I would never allow myself to be incarcerated ever again. In truth, I did a lot of work on myself there.

I began to view my incarceration as an opportunity for higher learning. I would go to the facility library and take out books: business and small-business management books, accounting books, marketing, trade, international trade, and trade law. Aside from that, I would study history and science, which are both fields that I have always had some interest in.

What I hadn't changed were my behavior issues, in regard to my impulsiveness and my need for instant gratification. One incident I vividly remember involved taking it upon myself to harm another man—for a cause that I thought justified the action, though I know now that there is no lesser of two evils. In hindsight, it shows nothing more than that I was still impulsive and had a propensity to commit crime.

What took place: A man came to the facility claiming to be a member of the Nation of Gods and Earths (an advocate of peace), as am I. It was later learned that he came to prison for the rape of a seven-year-old child, which is a crime frowned upon even by other criminals, and people who commit such crimes (according to an unwritten rule) are to be mistreated. I was told by other members of the Nation of Gods and Earths to "leave the man alone, because we advocate peace, and let those who do not care about peace handle him if they choose to." Instead, just seven days before I was to be released, I assaulted this man, hitting him in the head with a large, sharp stone.

Seven days later, I went home. Just as I had planned, I got a job and went back to school. What was not in my plan was selling marijuana, which I began doing just days after being released from prison. I chose to sell marijuana because to sell cocaine, crack cocaine, or dope meant going back to prison if I were arrested. In my foolish mind, I was willing to accept frequent stays in a county jail rather than go back to prison. But if nothing changes, nothing changes. So frequent stays in a county jail was what I got.

What I didn't know is, if the state chooses to set a person up (as they have done to me in this case), being in the streets, selling marijuana makes whatever they want to do possible. My current incarceration came about in this way:

The district attorney and the homicide detectives (Schenectady) were investigating a murder. It was believed that I had information about the crime, due to my prior association with a particular suspect. So on several occasions I was arrested (and charged) for petty crimes, solely to justify searching me for more incriminating paraphernalia. None was ever found.

The leverage the DA and detectives needed to get me to offer information was a felony complaint. Thus I was framed for possessing and selling crack cocaine. The only problem was, I had no information to offer. I was no longer associating with their suspect, and hadn't been for quite some time.

My lack of knowledge eventually led to an 11-year prison term, with 3 years of post-release supervision. At times, I point my finger at the justice system for my current situation. Only every time I do, I look at the three fingers bent back at me and say:

1. you were still in the streets, committing crime, which made it possible for you to be framed;
2. you previously associated with an individual who you knew the judicial system would stop at nothing to pin up (because he had been given a 52-to-111-year prison term, of which he did only a fraction due to a technicality); and
3. you still needed to work on your impulsiveness and your need for instant gratification.

Some people, knowingly or unknowingly, glorify their criminal behavior. I do not. I know that it is this mentality that has gotten me incarcerated again and again. Because of my new accountability, I'm looking forward to a bright and promising future. I have both skill and knowledge, as well as a support group: my brother Keith, who never came back to prison; my mother, who worked hard for everything she has; my sister Eileen, who is moving on the right path, and my niece Shawanda (Eileen's daughter), who is following in her mother's footsteps.

So now that I have focused my attention upon rehabilitating myself in the areas of impulsiveness, instant gratification, selfishness, etc. (problems that have cost me so many years of my life), I can finally live a productive life and become successful.

THE RULES OF LAW, POLICY, AND PRACTICE IN PRISON CITY

Inside Justice and Injustice

INTRODUCTION

Assuming a grasp of the lifestyle, culture, and psychological challenges of life in Prison City as documented in part 1, part 2 deals with institutional policy and practice: in the administration of prison justice, basic civic functions, mental and physical health care, and prison and reentry programs. A fifth section offers a venue in which prison community activists describe their efforts to improve these and other dimensions of life in American prisons. We begin with a problem that emerges as a regular motif throughout this collection: the absence of oversight of those who patrol prisons.

An administrator at a maximum-security prison has the following statement tacked up behind her desk: "Criminals come to prison *as* punishment, not *for* punishment." The implication is clear: if it is the job of corrections officers to control imprisoned people, it is the task of prison administrators to control corrections officers.

Imagine a city where the police have less training than in any other city in the United States; a city where the police bear virtually no oversight by the public; a city where the police enjoy the protection of some of the most powerful unions in the nation;[1] a city in which any legal action taken against the police in federal court must overcome obstacles set in place by Congress (in the 1996 Prison Litigation Reform Act); and a city wherein the police, under constant threat of assault, suffer the effects of life-threatening stress (hypertension, alcoholism, depression, suicide, etc.) that is built into their jobs.[2] And all of this on a population scale larger than Houston. Now try to recall a case of police brutality inside Prison City that made national or even local headlines.

In theory, Prison City is not beyond the pale of criminal justice, but is a place where free-world criminal-justice procedures and protections, within reasonable limits, continue to apply.[3] Convicted people are regularly convicted of crimes against each other and against prison staff. In turn, the police here should conduct themselves professionally, without committing crimes against their wards or striking out from personal resentments and frustration. But what incarcerated people see too often are uniformed men and women whose professional standards have been compromised by the strain of working inside.[4] As its inhabitants see them, justice and injustice inside Prison City are reflections in a funhouse mirror: meanings, roles, policy, and practice morph into shapes that mock any public hope that prison staff might act as examples of professional behavior, let alone instill in convicted people respect for official rhetoric about proper behavior.

Chastity C. West's "Left Behind" tells the story of a cellmate who dared to speak out against sexual abuse by staff, and whose passing the author finds herself envying. West's essay suggests that the situations of women living under the rule and desires of male guards can make suicide look like a reasonable choice.

In "The Special Prosecutor," author Richard Lyon shows us how cavalierly courtroom cases are treated when suspicion falls upon an already imprisoned man or woman. But for Lyon, the stakes are high. Though the charge is minor, if added to his life sentence, a conviction would mean life without parole. Here we see judicial protections successfully extended to a previously convicted suspect. Yet the essay reveals the prosecutorial culture in which such cases are tried, and thus helps us to understand the rule of law in Prison City.

Implicit throughout this collection is a prison that has normalized the humiliation and degradation of incarcerated Americans. A. Whitfield's essay, "JCF Welcome," gives us a painful example of what such moments feel like, and the effects they have on those forced to witness them. This essay makes us wonder whether the institution described does more damage to the bodies and souls of those stripped of power, or to the minds and souls of those whose power over others is virtually absolute.

Jane Dorotik's "Doris" presents an elderly victim of the culture described by Whitfield and West. The essay shows how every phase of abuse of prisoners can be couched in the language and procedures for charging *prisoners* with crimes against staff. This is not only the Orwellian world of the California Department of Corrections, from which Dorotik writes. It is the situation of justice and injustice wherever they are arbitrated by officials suffering the effects of working inside Prison City, while protected by its walls from legal oversight.

Throughout this collection, we see writers like Dorotik, West, and Whitfield who expose the victimization of other incarcerated people; we also see those, like Richard Lyon, who describe their own cases in order to help us understand how justice operates inside Prison City. In "An Ordeal," the prisoner who writes as "Sandy" places his life at risk of retaliation by other incarcerated men in order to do what he believes is right by victims on the outside. The author clearly does the right thing; but he does it in a place where the right is rarely the safe course of action.

In "My Voice through the Prison Wall," Ricky Vincent Pendleton II offers his experience of a prison where the rule of law seems arbitrary at best, and all Black men are assumed to represent a threat. His frustration remains hot at every piece of evidence that prisons are simply parts of a multibillion-dollar for-profit punishment industry. Here we see again what Richard Lyon's essay describes: a place where, even when justice is served, the process prisoners must endure in order to achieve such (rare) ends reveals just how steeply prisons are pitched against the few rights to which their wards are entitled.

Valjean Royal's "Survivor Testimony" offers a harrowing story of her repeated rape inside state and federal institutions. As a male-to-female transgendered person living in all-male prisons, Royal comes at one point to accept rape by prisoners and staff as her fate. Finally, as in so many cases in Prison City, Royal must do what she can to negotiate for her own protection, since she can't trust the prison to help.

Corey John Richardson's "Back to Attica" is a plea to remember the conditions that led to the prisoner uprising at Attica Correctional Facility in 1971. Richardson's essay is not about any one injustice perpetrated inside prison walls. It is about the widespread neglect of prisoners' rights, and mass-scale abuse that have overwhelmed even the organizations traditionally committed to the interests of incarcerated people.

This segment above all others makes us pause again to consider the consequences of locking men and women in cages, of hiring others to keep them there, and the tragedy that ensues for all behind walls and razor wire.

NOTES

1. See Joshua Page, *The Toughest Beat: Politics, Punishment, and the Prison Officers Union in California* (New York: Oxford University Press, 2011).

2. E. A. Paoline III, E. G. Lambert, and N. L. Hogan, "A Calm and Happy Keeper of the Keys," *Prison Journal* 86, no. 2 (June 2006): 182–205.

3. DeShaney v. Winnebago County Department of Social Services, No. 87-154 489 U.S. 189 (1989). Wolff v. McDonnell, 418 U.S. 539, 555–556 (1974): "But though his [the prisoner's] rights may be diminished by the needs and exigencies of the institutional environment, a prisoner is not wholly stripped of constitutional protections when he is imprisoned for crime. There is no iron curtain drawn between the Constitution and the prisons of this country."

4. See John J. Gibbons and Nicholas de B. Katzenbach, "Confronting Confinement: A Report of the Commission on Safety and Abuse in America's Prisons," The Vera Institute of Justice, June 8, 2006, http://www.vera.org/content/confronting-confinement (esp. parts 2 and 3).

CHASTITY C. WEST, *Connecticut*

LEFT BEHIND

"Everybody lock up!" the guard barked over the intercom. "Get in your cells, now!"

"Oh God, what now?" one of the girls asked, picking up her plastic bowl and gathering her belongings beneath her arm.

"There's a code purple," someone announced as she stepped through the door that had been electronically unlocked by the fumbling guard at the control panel. "Somebody hung up in Building 2." Building 2 hosts the youthful offenders and a mental health program. This wasn't good. Either a child or someone emotionally fragile had attempted suicide.

I took one last glance downstairs as I stepped into my cell. Just below, I could see a guard with his foot on the chair, standing two feet from the television designated for inmate use, flipping through channels with the remote control. The other guard pushed a few buttons on the panel and then joined his partner at the TV. I shook my head and let the heavy cell door shut behind me. My roommate was out of the unit so I stood alone in the dark cell. *A code purple?* Whoever she was, whatever her story, I knew that it wouldn't end well whether she lived or died. If she lived, they'd cart her off to the hospital and then ship her back to York in a couple of days, strip her naked, and lock her up in an observation cell in the prison's mental health unit. She'd surely regret having survived once she found herself locked in that barren and frigid cell, deprived of even the most basic comforts and human dignities.

The cell door opened with a click and my roommate came puffing into the room. Her hand groped for the light switch and flicked it on.

"Did you hear?" Mimi asked. "There was a code purple in Building 2. They said it was Rosa."

"Rosa? Really? That doesn't sound like something she'd do."

My roommate shrugged her shoulders and plopped down onto her cluttered bed.

"Everybody has a breaking point," she said. "Staff kept fuckin' with her once she went off on that red-headed rookie who was messing around with Cammie. Once she let it rip, the staff targeted her. Kept harassing her, ticketing her. When she came out of the hole, she just wasn't the same."

"Yeah," I replied, "LaRay was telling me about it while we were waiting for our appointments."

In the medical unit, LaRay sat beside me in the waiting area, her fist sunk into her substantial hip; the other hand wagged a pointed finger as she spoke: "That officer ain't have no business being in no inmate's room. Plain and simple. Hmph, you know somethin's afoul when you can't even get in you own cell 'cause staff in there with your bunkie. You gotta sit outside the room, wait 'til they done doin' whatever they in there doin'." LaRay shook her head in disgust. "Rosa ain't make no mess like that up. He got Cammie to suck his nasty little pecker and can't nobody tell me otherwise." Her finger waved emphatically as if she were shaking something off the end of it. "He show up for work every day and go home after eight hours of doin' nothin' while Rosa sittin' in that pissy little cell in solitary confinement. They need to walk his ass off. Terminate 'im, relieve 'im of his duties. But nooo. Yet they got the nerve to stick her in 2-North with the loonies to make everybody think she ain't got good sense. Rosa got a lotta shit wit' her, but she ain't no liar and she damn sure ain't crazy." LaRay swatted at a fly that was circling her helmet of neat finger-weaves. "Uh-uh, she ain't just pull an accusation like that out her ass. No, ma'am, somethin' ain't right here." She leaned toward me and lowered her voice: "Chas, you mean to tell me that you ain't never wondered why Cammie the only one prancin' around here in full face, poppin' bubblegum and sportin' penny-blonde hair when commissary don't sell none of that shit?"

Back in my room, I wadded up a bunch of damp paper towels and wiped down the countertop. "I wish Rosa would've just kept her mouth shut," I thought. "No matter what you say around here, an inmate's word means nothing. Because we wear maroon shirts, we have no credibility." My anger surged. How many times had I witnessed a staff member, arms crossed, scowling at a teary-eyed prisoner, dismissing her with these words: "You're an inmate, so you're a liar," or, "If staff said it happened, then it happened." As if an iron-on badge and a walkie-talkie makes one exempt from any form of dishonesty or corruption.

"Well, something must have set her off." Lowering myself to my knees, I began scrubbing the floor with a sponge. "Rosita isn't the type to set it off for no reason."

"I guess that officer wouldn't let her get a drink of water from the fountain and she went off. You know she's always thirsty because of the diabetes, so when he denied her that drink, she said she wasn't gonna suck his dick for water, right in the common area in front of everybody. There were a couple of nurses and two other guards there, too, so you know he had to cover his ass. He wrote her up for it and threw her in solitary. Staff's been riding her ass ever since. I passed her on the walkway a couple of weeks ago and heard one of the guards threatening her. He said that her days were numbered. She was on her way to the medical unit, minding her own business. She just kinda looked at me and shrugged her shoulders."

Disgusted, I stood on a chair and began organizing books: "So, what about the accusation? He's still struttin' around here. Isn't anybody going to look into *that*?" I dropped my coffee mug and cursed underneath my breath. "Yeah that sounds about right for this place." Stepping off the chair, I retrieved my mug, slammed it onto the countertop. "Come to York CI, unzip, and take your pick. That's what their 'help wanted' ad should say." Mimi nodded in agreement. "Hey, that rhymes," she added thoughtfully, shoving her fist into an open bag of potato chips and stuffing her mouth. "You should make a jingle for their hiring slogan."

I hadn't seen Rosa in weeks, but I was all too familiar with this classic DOC technique: punish and silence the inmate who knows too much and dares to make a public accusation; and the most effective way to break her spirit is to throw her into solitary confinement for a few weeks. Put her on "investigation," teach her a lesson, and let it serve as a warning to anyone else stupid enough to think that they have a choice. I climbed up onto my bunk and snatched my sheet over my head. "I hate this place. I hate the way they talk to us. I hate the way they treat us," I said. "I bet 'prison guard' is the only occupation in this country where someone can do just about anything and never have to answer for it."

"We're prisoners, a bunch of nobodies," my roommate said in between her chews. "We don't matter. All we are to them is a steady paycheck and an early pension."

I didn't respond. What she said was true. Even though most of the staff here are decent human beings, there's still the *other* ones: those drawn to this work by the allure of dominating the weak and crushing the already broken. Even with those who perform their duties with dignity and compassion, still, there will never be enough decent and humane people working in corrections to completely shield us from those who seek out this line of work for all the wrong reasons. We remain targets for any power-thirsty asshole with a score to settle with his overbearing mother, his unavailable father, the playground bully, the girl who rejected him in high school, or the police exam that he just couldn't pass. Who better than female prisoners to ejaculate one's anger onto, and to act on one's own feelings of frustration, inadequacy, and lack of control when naked of the blue uniform? I lay on my back and swallowed the painful lump in my throat. I closed my eyes tightly and felt hot tears stream toward my pillow.

Rumors quickly circulated throughout the prison. "She's a vegetable," a girl seated beside me in the cafeteria stated. "It sucks, because her mind is fully functioning but she can't move a muscle."

"No," her lunch partner corrected. "I heard that she woke up and took a breath on her own. They said she even had a cup of ginger ale and a few saltines last night."

Who's they? I wanted to ask, but I didn't. I'd heard enough. The rumors were only upsetting me more. I stood from the table and went to dump my tray. At the tray receptacle, I heard another group of girls talking about it.

"As soon as the swelling goes down in her brain, they're going to ship her back here. But she'll be housed in the hospice unit because she won't be able to feed or bathe herself."

"She coded in the hospital," a passerby chimed in.

"No, that's not true," a blonde-haired girl with her mouth full of sandwich yelled after her. "She's in stable condition."

"Nuh-uh, critical."

"No, no. She's being discharged by the end of the week."

"How can that be?" A thin voice cut in. "I heard she's dead."

I walked out of the chow hall and pulled cold air into my lungs. Rounding the corner, I stared at Building 2. Which tier was she on; which cell was she in? What was going through her mind when she looped that noose? I reflected on my own suicidal impulses, but quickly shook those desperate moments out of my head. I could relate to Rosa's feeling of anguish and desolation all too well. Somehow, I'd survived those weak, vulnerable periods, and surely there'd be many more that I'd have to brace myself against. But Rosa, she was a fighter. Never someone that I would think would ever carry out her suicide, even though I knew that she didn't have it easy. She's lost her trial and had been sentenced to almost twenty years. Still she kept her head above water. Her two girls, Jasmine and Destiny, were what she had to live for; she told me this a few weeks after she'd survived the shock of her mother's death.

"Can you help me fill out these papers?" she had asked, unfolding some life insurance documents. "I want to be sure that my babies are taken care of in case anything ever happens to me. You know my health ain't too good. I'm a real fragile diabetic and I have epilepsy. Anything could happen. Not to mention the shit that goes on in here. One of these dick-heads could kill me," she said, referring to the staff.

I took the papers and heard her ruffling through her things. She produced a picture. "You see these two little girls, Chas?" Rosa handed me a photograph. "They're all I have left. This is what I live for."

I looked at the picture and saw two smiling children that resembled their mother.

"These two girls are the light that will lead me out of this place. Do you have a light, Chas?" she asked. The question took me off-guard. "Everybody needs a light. If you don't have one out there, you need one in here." She put her fist to her chest and then to mine. "Everybody needs to find their own light."

A couple of weeks later, Rosa stood waving at the threshold of her door the moment I came into view. "Hey, *amiga*, guess what I did this morning." She had a big smile on her face. "I smudged! I've been fighting for that for seven long years."

"That's great, Rosita," I answered and hugged her tightly. I had learned a little about this sacred Native American ritual, of the mixture of herbs that were set aflame in a ceremonial abalone shell. I was told of the prayers to The Creator, and of the circle representing all humankind as one race. I knew of the scattering of white and desert sage, sweet grass, juniper, and tobacco ash onto Mother Earth, the ever-fertile provider.

"I didn't want to sue for my rights to practice my religion, but I would've. The men prisoners who follow Native American beliefs been smudgin' a long time ago. They have sweat huts too, but I'm just happy that I had the chance to smudge today. All my bitchin' finally paid off." She shook her head but still had the same look of contentment on her face. "What you gotta do around here just to make these people understand that we have something that we believe in too?" She turned her forearms out to me, exposing columns of ugly scars of shed blood, something that she told me that she did in the name of her belief. "In my religion," she explained, "we shed our blood in sacrifice. Nothing in this world or the next can be gained if you're not willing to give something precious in return." I guess that made sense. Christianity required sacrifice for both earthly and heavenly treasures. Why would her God not have a like request?

After I gained a small degree of understanding of Rosa's beliefs, I'd bring her feathers and stones whenever I'd find one that was particularly beautiful, and she'd thank me with the sincerity of a child and carry them around her neck in her medicine bag. I'd never known anyone who so appreciated a gift that most of us would view as valueless. Her love of the earth was a rarity in an environment where some inmates didn't think twice about throwing candy wrappers in the grass, and where staff thought nothing of spewing globs of brown-tinged tobacco spit onto our walkways.

Sometimes, it was easy to forget that Rosa was around; she was a recluse who spent most of her free time locked in her cell. But one trait she possessed would remind us all that she was definitely present. She had a hair-trigger temper. Like an angry wasp, she'd emerge from her hive in a rage if she was awakened from sleep, or jolted by someone calling to a guard, or the slam of a door, or if she was disturbed by the volume of the tier television, or just by laughter.

"Shut the fuck up, you dumb bitches!" She'd jump up from the bed and snatch her cell door open: "I'm trying to sleep!" After she'd administered her sting, she'd retreat back into her cell.

Rosa had classic symptoms of post-traumatic stress disorder, the most obvious one being noise sensitivity: the slightest sound would set her off something fierce. I felt bad for her and always wondered what had happened in life to make her so volatile, so fragile. One day I decided to ask. Rosa, sitting Indian-style on her tightly made bed, stood and leaned against the bedpost; she said, "When you were little I bet you fell asleep huggin' your little teddy bear after Mommy and Daddy read you a bedtime story and tucked you in. Well, where I come from, we slept with one eye open, clutchin' the handle of a gat, not knowin' when somebody was gon' try to rob us or shoot us up. And if that ain't bad enough, how can you sleep when you never know if the narcs gon' show up, kickin' the door in for a raid? When you ain't never had no peace, you try to find sleep whenever you can get it. You crave silence." In fact, most of the arguments that Rosa got into were over noise and her inability to sleep. She wasn't easy to live with, and some of her roommates would be in tears, begging to be moved out. They would check themselves into mental health, or Rosa would take it upon herself and have the unwanted cellmate evicted. She went through more roommates than anyone I know. Rosa was a tiny, ninety-pound firecracker, feisty and explosive, but she was also lovable and true. Strangely, that was her: earth lover and earth disturber. But Rosa was always willing to apologize whenever she was wrong, or even if she were a little too hard on one of us. I'd been on the receiving end of her tirades many times, and each time had received a warm apology and a hug the very next day.

I sat in the dayroom, in front of the television that might as well have been watching me.

"Chas"—Dee-Dee's voice broke through my train of thought—"are you thinking about Rosa?"

I nodded my head.

"She's good people."

I nodded again, unable to speak for fear that I might start crying. I was doing an awful lot of that lately, and my inability to control my emotions was becoming a bit embarrassing. I was broken-up about Rosa, but I think, in a small way, I was also crying for myself. Crying for my loss, my loneliness, for having traveled there in my mind and knowing much too much about a beat-down and desperate woman's capacity for self-harm.

"She remembered my birthday," Dee said almost in a whisper. "Actually, I didn't even know that Rosa *knew* when my birthday was. Remember, the morning of my birthday? She'd put a card and a Hershey's bar on my pillow. I found it when I came in from school that afternoon."

I couldn't hold it in, and when I glanced at Dee's reddened face, neither could she. I rested my head against the curve of her neck as she put her arm around my shoulder and held me there.

"Try not to think about anything negative," Dee-Dee encouraged, taking a deep composing breath. With the sleeve of her sweatshirt, she wiped her own tears and then mine. "Think about all the fun we had. Remember how you always use to go to her door and ask her to show you her titties, and she would crack up laughing?" I smiled at the memory. "That was always you guys' running joke," Dee said. "You'd ask to see her titties and she'd laugh and fold her arms across her chest and say, 'No, you're my *amiga*!'"

"I know," I sniffled. "Rosita was a lot of fun. I remember when she told me how one sexual experience made her "un-gay." She said Fuzzy was so bad at it that she gave up trying to be a lesbian. That was a funny story. Did she ever tell you about it?"

"You started telling me about it in front of her, and then she took over and finished the story," Dee-Dee answered.

"I'll never forget that," I said with a smile. "I've never heard no mess like that in my life. I've heard of women saying that a *man* turned them gay, but never a woman turning another woman un-gay!"

Rosita had a comical side, but more times than not she was all about business. We talked a lot about the injustices within the Department of Corrections, and the injustices of the judiciary system. Rosa and I talked about our sentences, and how we were going to get out of the system one day. We brainstormed about court appeals, sentence modifications, applying to the board of pardons. We talked about finding loopholes, never about looping nooses.

"I'll write the goddamn President if I have to. Obama's in the house now," Rosita said, half-joking—but I knew she meant it. Our judges had sentenced us to a long time, but we were determined to get out someway, somehow.

Gabrielle, one of the facility social workers, came by a few days after Rosa's suicide attempt. I knew that it couldn't be good. Of all the social workers, Gabbi has the best rapport with the long-term prisoners. Even though she had been transferred out of the Zero Building months earlier, she had enough decency and compassion to personally break any emotional news to us. So anytime Gabbi showed up to the "lifers" building, we knew to expect bad news.

"Whatever you believe in," Gabbi said as she took a seat at one of our tables, "now may be a good time to offer some good thoughts for Rosa. It doesn't look very good for her right now."

Gabbi's pretty face was masked with a somber expression. Some of the girls began asking questions, looking to dispel some of the rumors that were still traveling around the prison. The only thing Gabbi was able to confirm was that Rosa was in a bad way, and that her life was hanging in the balance. At the moment it could go either way.

When Gabbi left, I stood with my back facing the door and felt the inside of my nose stinging. Finally, I just allowed myself to cry. I imagined Rosa's small body draped in a pale blue johnny, lying still in a white hospital bed, her ankle shackled to the bedrail though she posed no threat to anyone. I could hear the rhythmic gush of air made by the respirator, the beep of strange machines. I could see each of the plastic tubes that were connecting her to life. I saw small bruises atop her pale hand and in the crease of her arm, the small strips of medical tape holding needles in place. I wondered if there was some form of consciousness beyond her unconscious body. Would she have frightening, fragmented thoughts, or experience a complete and euphoric clarity? What did it feel like to slip into a perfect peace, to have a day outside of these walls? I wanted to speak to Rosa, to hug her, to hold her hand. I found myself feeling guilty that I was not able to be there for her in her most vulnerable moment. How many times had she been there for me? How many occasions had passed when Rosa had just taken one glimpse of my face and known I was in distress?

"I'm here for you, Chas," she'd say. "Don't let them get you down. They can't keep us here forever. We'll get out of the system someday. You and me, we'll do it together, Chas. You and me."

It was on a Saturday night when Gabrielle and Naomi, another social worker, showed up at the building. Immediately, everyone began to murmur. I came out of the room and faced the news head-on.

"Rosa has been taken off life support," Gabbi announced as gently as possible. "I know this must be hard for you girls. It's hard for me. I just didn't want you to hear it from anyone else. I wanted to tell you so that you won't have to sift through gossip and rumors."

The day room was silent but for the sound of sniffling and soft weeping. Mimi took a strong hold of my hand, and my friend Liza took hold of the other one. I put my chin to my chest and cried for Rosa.

On Monday morning the administration called for a full facility lockdown so that the guards could search each cell for contraband. As if what grieving women needed was for reckless and overzealous staff to barge into our cells and vandalize our meager belongings and confiscate our precious mementos, leaving us in the wreckage to bemoan our lost property. This, of course, would be followed by a period of complete isolation lasting up to five days. Didn't we already have enough to mourn without facing the despair that comes with a twenty-four-hour-a-day lockdown? I guess the administration wanted to make sure that we had ample time and opportunity to stew in our grief, to make absolutely certain that women like me, who have contemplated suicide but were just too damn afraid to do it, had sufficient time to envy Rosa's courage. Perhaps my anger and grief may have caused me to project this motive onto the department, because, truthfully, I don't know if this was their intent. But certainly, our despair wasn't one of their concerns.

On Friday, when we came off lockdown status, we had yet to hear anything about Rosa from the administration. The following Tuesday, a group of girls gathered around a memo that was posted in the dayroom window. I assumed that it must have been a memo generated by the administration about memorial services for Rosa, or maybe a way that we could access grief counseling. I stepped through the crowd and read the memo for myself. As my eyes went from line to line, I became incensed, almost faint with anger. It was a memo signed by the deputy warden, the deputy warden of *Support* Services. The memo mentioned nothing about Rosa, but rather issued a threat of disciplinary action in the event that graffiti was found in a prisoner's cell: "*All* offenders will be held accountable via the code of Penal Discipline should they deface their cells," the memo read. "This will include restitution for cleaning materials and/or paint if necessary." *Graffiti? Penal Discipline?* What about Rosa? What about *her* restitution? I asked myself this question first, and then I found my voice and asked it aloud. "What about Rosa?" I demanded. "We just lost Rosa and all they care about is graffiti?" This was too much. I stormed into my room, slammed the cell door behind me, and gave it one good hard kick. And then another. And then another. My roommate's words resonated in my throbbing head. *We're a bunch of nobodies. We don't matter. We're just a paycheck and an early pension . . .*

In my ten years of incarceration, I have seen a lot of insensitivity by staff—either by their actions or inactions. But even I was shocked that the administration didn't feign the slightest bit of interest or compassion, or even acknowledge that someone had just lost her life a few days earlier. Cell graffiti had trumped Rosa's worth.

I think back to my conversations with Rosa. I remember peeking into her room to check on her and seeing her furiously writing letters to the court by the light of her television. I could hear her voice and see her looking at me with those big owl eyes. "We'll get out of the system one day, Chas. We'll do it together. They can't keep us in here forever, *amiga*." Panic clutched my heart. Thoughts of my own desperation and mortality ricocheted through my skull. Rosa was half-right. She had found her way out of the system, but she'd left me behind.

On the night of Rosa's death, when I went to bed I lay on my bunk and gazed out at the stars that speckled the black sky. *Do you have a light, Chas?* Rosa's words resounded over and over again in the silence, and I could almost feel the flickering of a struggling little flame inside my heart. And as deserted and dismayed as I felt at that moment, I knew that I could not allow myself to be shaken off course. I would have to follow the words that my dear friend had imparted to me. My heart was wrenched, for I knew that we had reached our crossroads, that our journeys had drifted in separate directions, and that I, alone, would have to press on and find that very light that Rosa once told me to hold onto. As my eyes began to blur with tears, they caught hold of the brightest, most distant star in the surrounding blackness. *Go, go towards the light, Rosita,* mi querida amiga. *Find peace, find sleep, find silence . . .*

RICHARD ALAN ABOOD LYON, *Texas*

THE SPECIAL PROSECUTOR

When I finally had the courage to recount my showdown with the Special Prosecutor, over a decade had passed. Neither of us will forget. At this moment, in my mind, I see him leaning back in his oak chair, catching my eye. He knows something that I don't.

It is sometimes best to start at the beginning, but I'll skip the trial that got me a life sentence, concentrating instead on this trial in Walker County, the seat of the Texas Department of Criminal Justice. From this courtroom, death warrants are issued for youngsters, women, and the mentally compromised. I was not facing the needle; no, my charge was much more mundane. I was charged with possession of a controlled substance, namely, marijuana, in a penal institution. If I was found guilty, this sentence would be added, "stacked," onto the end of my life sentence. I would never get out on parole.

Prior to meeting the Special Prosecutor, I worked as a prison unit artist, creating, for free, oil paintings, as well as the endless painted stainless-steel milk jugs for prison officials. Texas proudly holds the title of the most primitive penal system in America. Prisoners are not paid for their labor, nor do the decades of work count against their sentences. If you are not going to be compensated for labor, you might as well have a comfortable job, and I stumbled upon one.

As a result of a surprise shakedown of the craft shop, I was charged with possession of an

eighth-ounce of marijuana. A prison shakedown is typically the result of a snitch note informing an officer that contraband exists. Officers encircle the shakedown area wearing latex gloves,
stripping prisoners, searching clothing and then their lockers. I was not present when an officer
found a baggie of marijuana. The guards had me handcuffed in the building major's office.

Prison officials are allowed to stack more prison time onto a prior sentence for certain offenses; this was one of them. So, I am sitting in a gray-tiled room with a stainless steel toilet/
sink combination. In this tiny, humid, pine-oil-scented room there are eleven prisoners. We have
been indicted; now the machinery of justice will grind us down. The smell of sour chili fills the
room as the fluorescent fixture flickers in the corner. A gray steel door separates us from an outer
dressing room. At eye level glows an index-card-sized plexiglass window. We sit glumly on the
wall-mounted wood bench, facing more time in prison.

Each of us arrives in separate white vans originating from one of the many prisons in the
Huntsville area. We are all dressed in white cotton. Seven administrative segregation (Ad-Seg)
prisoners are wearing white jumpers with no sleeves, snaps up the front, with soft rubber-soled
black canvas shoes. In here we call these shoes "winos" after the shuffling feet of the drunk tank.
One guy paces and mutters about a shank. He grumbles about the stacked 25-years-to-life.
One Ad-Seg prisoner is indicted for possession of a photo of a postage stamp he clipped from a
postal catalog. Indicted for altering a government document. Two of us in general population
are charged with possession of marijuana. All of us await the arrival of our state counsel lawyers.
This meeting with the State Counsel for Offenders reveals the plea-agreement offers from the
Special Prosecutor. The Special Prosecutor is never special in my book, just a mean guy with
unlimited power. He and his team prosecute inmates for crimes committed while incarcerated.
Typically the prisoner is advised to take the plea offer, as trials against the Special Prosecutor
always result in conviction.

The key clicks in the lock. The mutters stop as the guards signal for us to come out. Our hands
cuffed in front, we jangle to chairs in the large, sunny, hard room. Sitting across from me is a
fifty-year-old woman with gray and brown shoulder-length hair and black plastic glasses, wearing
a dark blue jacket over a floral print dress covering her calves. She shakes my cuffed hand while
holding my four-year plea agreement offered from the Special Prosecutor.

"That's their offer," she whispers.

"Can you handle a jury trial?"

"I'm what they call a 'baby lawyer,' which means I just got my bar number and am beginning
to practice. This will be my first trial."

"Well," I respond, "it will be my second, so I get first chair."

While Cindy holds the plea agreement, I sign the "not guilty" section, moving both hands in
tandem, creating a mark on the sheet.

Our legal visit ends as quickly as it began, and we return to the gray room. Nine have signed
the guilty section of the plea agreement, accepting the additional sentence from the Special
Prosecutor. Stampboy also pled not guilty and he will be scheduled for trial with me next month.
The gray room was quiet and musky. Everyone else knew that by signing the plea there will be
no trial, just a new time sheet arriving in the mail.

We shuffle and slink across the terrazzo floor in the spacious third-floor courtroom. Along
three sides are floor-to-ceiling windows, which open onto the branches of the white plane trees
framing Courthouse Square. Surrounding the courthouse are commercial buildings, housing the
Prison Museum and the Texas Cafe.

The guards hold our elbows as they lead us down the hall to a back stairwell. We jangle on each riser, careful not to snag leg chains. We hold the railing, sliding our hands down to the landing and then down again. These are the same prison guards who make a sport of pushing cuffed prisoners down stairwells. We are the only two who refused the plea agreement from the Special Prosecutor. I tighten my grip.

The jangling chains' echo ceases once we reach the ground floor and the door opens. Silently our elbows are pinched as we hustle past glass-walled offices. We are watched. The white van's back door opens and we kneel on the chrome bumper, crawl to the bench seat along the sidewall. No seat belts. The doors slam shut, locked, then a brass lock slips into an exterior hasp. As we race off to the prison, I picture a flaming van and a lost key.

The driver keys the microphone: "86 times two, 95 times two." The other adjusts the radio to Country Gold.

Since Stampboy is an Ad-Seg prisoner, the van slides through two sliding chain-link gates while guards in the towers cradle shotguns. They release my shackles and allow me to walk back to my cell. They have me trained.

Three weeks later we go through this ordeal in reverse, arriving at 7:30 A.M. and waiting for Stampboy's jury pool to arrive for his trial at nine. As I look out the watery plastic window, I see Cindy and her boss talking. A guard opens the door, calls Stampboy out. I can see him smile; he signs some papers and returns to tell me that the Special Prosecutor has dropped his charge. Consequently, his jury pool is now mine.

Cindy asks the guards to let me out of the gray room. We sit in the dressing room's molded blue plastic chairs.

"Well, here we go. We'll pick the jury and then present opening arguments today."

"What can I do?"

Her elbows rest on her knees when she looks up and sighs: "Well, you could write down any ideas about your argument of not having care, custody, or control." She stands, touches my shoulder, and says, "I have a jury to select." (Her first.)

Stampboy looks at me when I return to the gray room. "What happened?"

"It appears that your jury pool is now mine, not that it matters."

He smirks. We know that of the eighty potential jurors, most will either work for, are related to, or will be suppliers to the Texas Department of Corrections (TDC); the remainder will be in law enforcement. The potential jurors, when asked, will swear that they could render an unbiased verdict. After the twelve jurors are selected, Cindy and her boss convince the judge to allow me to wear street clothes at my trial tomorrow.

The following morning, just before 9:00 A.M., Cindy huffs into the changing room, hands me a suit and a shopping bag, and says, "Hurry and put this on; the trial begins at 9:00." She has purchased a suit coat, Docker-style slacks, brown suede shoes, and a club tie. The door slams shut. I have worn white pullover shirts and elastic pants for over a decade, and belted pants feel great. The Windsor knot takes two attempts, then the door opens. Cindy smiles and off we go to face the Special Prosecutor.

As we walk out of the dressing room, I feel the knot at my throat; I glance down at the colorful clothes and catch the look in the eyes of the guard. Yeah, I look like a normal human now. We walk across the open room. The shoes are tight, but a nice tight. I glance at the twelve jurors as Cindy parts the bat-wing gates. She points to the first chair, nearest the prosecution table, which is nearest the jury box, and I sit down.

The bailiff stands and bellows, "All rise."

We do. In long strides, the Judge climbs to his perch on the bench. Cindy tells me in a whisper that he's a legend; he certainly is old enough. If Ichabod Crane ever wore a coal-black cowboy-cut suit, white shirt, string tie, and boots, I see him this morning. This character noisily adjusts his skinny butt in the high-backed leather chair; his black eyeballs, surrounded by thin white hair and sunken cheeks, stare at me. He sits. We sit. He fidgets with papers beneath a wall-sized image of the Texas state seal, flanked by the state and national flags. Rumor has it that he installed a holster for a six-shooter under the bench. I imagine from the look on his face that he was itching to pop a cap in my drug-dealing ass. Then the black-suited skeleton speaks.

"Mr. R, please begin."

The Special Prosecutor pushes his chair back while turning to the jury. The Special Prosecutor works directly for the attorney general, prosecuting prisoners and finalizing death warrants. He always wins. Opening his jacket to reveal a badge clipped to his silver and black ranger-style belt, he turns his back to the defense table. He begins his opening statement, harping on about how outrageous it is that prisoners commit crimes while in prison. He has a slam-dunk case.

Cindy focuses on the lack of evidence and the requirement of the law to show care, custody, and control in order to meet the burden of establishing possession. She closes her opening statement by reciting the current definition of reasonable doubt. The Judge excuses the jury for the day.

When the room clears he asks, "Mrs. T, I do not recall you in my court before today."

"No, your honor, this is my first trial."

"You mean your very first trial?"

"Yes, your honor."

"Well, welcome. I can assure you that we all work together to get them through in a professional manner."

"Thank you, your honor."

"Now"—he looks down at me—"Mr. Lyon." Cindy touches my elbow; I stand with her. "Your motions are denied. Your lawyer will handle your motions from now on. I will not have hybrid representation in my courtroom, is that clear?"

"Yes, your honor," we reply in chorus.

"You may be seated."

I lean close, smelling old-lady perfume. "Did you file any discovery motions?" Indignantly she answers, "Yes."

When the judge finishes his discussion with the Special Prosecutor, they decide that they can finish in a day. Cindy stands. "Your honor, I filed several motions yesterday; did you have a chance to rule on them?" The Judge smiles; it's more like a liver-colored line extending across the lower third of his face.

"Mrs. T"—lifting papers—"your motion for suppression is denied, your motion for change of venue denied, your motion for an investigator is denied in part."

Looking down at Cindy, he says, "The prosecutor tells me TDC has provided your discovery documents. Your jury charge will be ruled on later. Anything else?"

"No, your honor."

"The trial will continue tomorrow." He swings his gavel. We rise in unison as he strides off.

Moments later I remove the club tie and shoes. Cindy taps on the door. "Come out when you're dressed."

We sit again in the blue plastic chairs, huddled close so that the transportation guards cannot hear us. Our strategy is what? I didn't have a clue. There is a cardboard box of files at her feet.

"What's in there?" I ask.

"These are the discovery items from the TDC."

"What are you going to learn from that?" I ask.

"I'll go through them tonight. Tomorrow the state will present its case. I expect you'll have to take the stand after that," she says.

"That's our strategy, me on the stand?"

She looks up. "Richard, they see this trial as a slam-dunk. They want to show us how the Special Prosecutor operates, but you never know what a jury will do." She continues in a softer tone, "I assume you would elect to have the jury assess punishment; they'll be able to enhance it to a second-degree felony, so it'll be 2-to-20 stacked." Not much of a choice. The Judge would sentence me to death.

They came for me early the next morning. I am suited up when Cindy shows me some of the papers she spent the night reviewing.

"Cindy, these are the count sheets for Administrative Segregation, not the craft shop."

They were trying to place me at the scene. I reel away from a vision of hell, life with little chance of parole, before I can look at her again. While we realize they are playing for keeps, the Special Prosecutor is thirty feet away, yucking it up with the guards and the judge.

Cindy tosses the papers into the box, kicks it into the corner. "I want you to write down everything that happened on that morning."

"Cindy, I can remember every second, but I was not there when they found the weed." We stand.

"Let's go," she sighs.

We step out of the dressing room in the back corner of the court. We slide past the eyes of several armed guards and take our seats. While we wait for the judge, the Special Prosecutor leans back in his chair, catches my eye; a subliminal message is passed: "Are you really so stupid to think you could win in my world?"

Since it is his world, our table is the furthest from the jury and the witness stand. Of the twelve jurors, only four can see me. We all rise on orders from the bailiff as the Judge enters, wearing his all-black suit—no robes for him. He says hello to the jury, the Special Prosecutor and his team, and to Cindy, but not a glance at me. He invokes the rule to all the sworn witnesses.

"Mr. R, please begin the state's case," he rasps into the microphone.

"The state calls Jeffery S."

The Special Prosecutor guides him through the standard witness questions: name, age, residence, and then his involvement in the drug bust at Wynne Unit. The Special Prosecutor walks him through the search, concluding with his shaking a wrapped painting. He testifies that a baggie fell out of the wrapper and it contained a green powdery substance. He says he gave the baggie to his supervisor, Sgt. S.

Cindy stands: "Your honor, may I approach the witness?"

"Certainly, hon . . . Mrs. T, we are not formal in my courtroom, you just go right ahead."

"Thank you, your honor."

"Mr. S, you've been a correctional officer for how many years?"

"One year."

"You testified that the green powdery substance in a baggie fell out of a wrapped painting?"

"Yes ma'am."

"How did you determine the baggie belonged to Mr. Lyon?"

"It had his name and number on it."

"You're telling the jury that the marijuana was in a painting with his name and number on it?"

"Yes ma'am."

"Officer S, could you show the jury exactly how you found the painting wrapped?"

She hands the brown wrapping paper and the oil painting to the officer.

This may be her first trial, but her ruse is the same used in the O. J. Simpson trial. If the brown paper don't fit, you must acquit.

Officer S is a new boot, and a rookie at gift-wrapping as well. He cannot get the paper to fit the painting in any manner.

Cindy moves on: "Where was Mr. Lyon when you found this wrapped painting?"

"He was in the hallway."

"Pass the witness," Cindy says, glancing at the jurors and the wrapping paper.

The Special Prosecutor stands, removes his jacket, places it on the back of his chair. "A moment, your honor."

"Yes, of course."

He leans in close to his assistants, stands straight, revealing his belt badge ensemble to the jury, and asks, "Is it your testimony that the painting with the baggie inside had Mr. Lyon's name on it?"

"Yes sir, it is."

"Pass the witness."

Cindy stands. "No further questions at this time, but I reserve the right to recall him."

The Special Prosecutor calls Officer Latisha F to the stand and asks her about the shakedown and the baggie of weed.

Cindy stands, asking Officer F, "Do you know what marijuana looks like and smells like?"

Flowers turns to the judge and asks, "Would I be getting anyone into trouble if I answer this?"

I am awake now. Maybe she and the warden are blowing doobies in the front office.

She stammers, while still looking at the Judge, "Well my sister smokes marijuana, so I know what it smells like."

"Pass the witness."

"No further questions," says Cindy.

The next witness is Sgt. S, the supervisor of the shakedown. He waddles to the stand with his geek-squad outfit containing every known attachment to his utility belt, including an empty gun holster.

After the Special Prosecutor finishes his questions, Cindy approaches the witness.

"Good afternoon, Sgt. S. Do you know what marijuana smells like?"

"No," he says.

Cindy is already on to her next thought when his answer registers. "You don't know what it smells like?"

The Special Prosecutor jumps up: "Asked and answered."

"Please move on, Mrs. T."

"Did you find any other contraband in the art shop?"

"Yes, we found tobacco products."

"Did you charge Mr. Lyon with those?"

"No ma'am."

"Did you give Mr. Lyon a THC urine test?"

"No, ma'am."

"Pass the witness."

Standing with his fingertips on the table, the Special Prosecutor says, "No further questions. The State rests."

"We will break for lunch," says the Judge.

After spending two and one-half hours in the gray room munching on my hotlink sandwich, the trial commences again.

Cindy stands and says, "The defense calls Richard Lyon to the stand."

I move to the witness box.

Cindy adjusts her glasses. "What was your job when you were arrested?"

"I was the unit artist. There are three of us in the sign shop. We paint signs and paintings for TDC. Much of what we paint is used for fundraising, like at the Shriner's Burn Center here in Huntsville."

I put a plug in for good will's sake; fear has me thinking clearly.

Cindy hands me the painting in question and asks, "Did you paint this?"

"No, ma'am," I reply.

"Where were you when they found the baggie of marijuana?"

"I was in jail."

"What do you mean by jail?"

"I was in prehearing detention, lockup."

"Were you given a prison disciplinary case?"

"Yes, ma'am. I was."

I know Cindy is trying to have me connect with the jury in a sympathetic manner. She wants to ask how I saved Bambi from the forest fire, but passes me to the Prosecutor instead.

The Judge delays my encounter with the Special Prosecutor by talking over my head to the jury. He says, "I have to attend the funeral this afternoon of Judge E, who passed away on Saturday. You all know him. He sat on this bench for forty years." The jury nods in unison and so do I. Sad day, sad day.

The morning is cool and the gray room smells strongly of pine oil. In the dim light I think that this could be judgment day. Listening to the machinery of the courthouse hum, I sense that this trial is an extension of the Special Prosecutor. The entire building, the van, the gray room are his element, including Cindy. Paranoid? Likely, but I am facing life without parole. A guilty verdict and even a two-year sentence stacked is essentially life without parole. Shadows pass the door's window and it opens.

"Showtime," says an officer. I am dressed, having mastered the half-Windsor, ready to face the Special Prosecutor on his home field. As I sit in the witness box, the Special Prosecutor stands, adjusting his badge again; if he could check the bullets on his revolver, he would spin them in front of the jury to be sure they know he's the only good guy. He walks towards me.

"How do you pronounce your last name?"

"Lyon," I say.

"You're lying?" he smirks.

"Yes, sir."

The judge laughs, the jury laughs. I've heard it before, start with a joke, the sign of a good public speaker.

"Mr. Lyon, you testified under oath in your 1991 Dallas murder trial, and the jury found you guilty, is that correct?"

"Yes, sir."

"Why should these good people of Walker County believe you today?"

"Objection, your honor." Cindy is standing, holding her half-glasses.

The Judge slowly says, "Sustained. Please move on."

The Special Prosecutor hooks his thumb in his belt, swiveling at the waist, surveys the jury and then back again, and says, "Pass the witness."

Cindy stands at the defense table and asks, "Mr. Lyon did you ever have care, custody, and control of the baggie of marijuana?"

"No, ma'am, I did not."

"Pass the witness."

"No questions."

"Step down, Mr. Lyon," says the Judge.

Billy P was a delicate, pale punk who was hired by the old man in the craft shop. The old man had been on death row for possession of the reproductive organs of his victims, but his sentence had been commuted to life. Billy was as close as the old man would get to a Cub Scout in here. Billy and I never got along. Since we had so few attorney-client visits prior to the trial, I was not able to lace Cindy up on this situation.

Leaning close to Cindy's down-covered ear, I whisper, "Why do you want him?"

She bends forward, seeming to adjust some folders on the table, and says, "He said he made the frame." I feel the awful mist of sweat that covers your body as fear rumbles inside.

Billy takes the stand, glancing around the room, looking at all the guards and the jury, blinking away uncertainty.

I pray.

Cindy goes through his job and skills in making frames, where he works, and how he moves the completed frames from workshop to sign shop. He tells the jury he recalls making this frame.

"Pass the witness," says Cindy.

"A minute, please, your honor," says the Special Prosecutor.

He leans towards his assistants, dressed like Young Republicans, in navy with white shirts, one with a club tie, the other a print scarf. They listen and nod in unison. The Special Prosecutor stands, puts on his jacket while walking towards Billy.

He stands at an angle that blocks us from the jury and points to the painting and asks, "Did you make this frame?"

Billy, proudly, "Yes sir, I did."

"Did you make this stash box?"

"Yes sir, I did."

The invincible Special Prosecutor knows he has heard the click of the land mine arming itself to explode. Now he gracefully has to muffle the explosion.

From his position in front of the twelve, he asks, "So is this your marijuana too?"

"No, sir." Billy smiles and with a smirk turns towards the jury.

The Special Prosecutor says, "Pass the witness."

Billy leaves the courtroom without ever looking back. Cindy says, "The Defense rests, your honor."

"Mr. Prosecutor?"

"The State rests."

After ten minutes of closing arguments, Cindy returns to the table and slaps down a stack of papers. "They won't budge on the jury instruction. It is slanted towards guilt; it has every charge from growing pot to marijuana oil sales. I did the best I could, but this is his court."

I am in the gray room. The guards toss me a johnny-bag lunch that lands with a damp thud on the wood bench. It is eleven fifteen. I slip the rosary from my pocket as a comfort while I wait. Pacing back and forth in this gray cave consumes three hours before I see shadows in the tiny windows. The door opens.

"It's showtime," smiles one of the guards.

I adjust my tie again, slip on my jacket, run my fingers through my hair, and walk out.

As we move out into the bright sunlight, I blink and see the room is now filled with deputies, several suits I have not seen before, and many more TDC guards. When we reach the gate, Cindy grabs my elbow and leads me to the table. Once we are seated, she turns to face me; her hand touches the edge of my finger as it rests on the table. Her eyes are tired and frantic. "Well, they reached their verdict."

Iced tea and cheeseburgers for twelve and a verdict in three hours.

"That was quick. Is that good?" Knowing the answer, I still have to ask.

"We'll find out soon."

We all stand. I glance to the jury box as it fills, trying to read their faces. All I see are the clear colors outside the windows behind them, the blues and greens broken by the flashes of the white and gray bark. In stalks the Judge, trailing black.

"Mrs. T, is the Defense ready for the verdict and sentencing phase?"

"Yes, your honor."

"Mr. Prosecutor, is the State ready?"

"Yes, sir."

"Ms. P, is she here?"

A twenty-year-old bottle blond stands. "Yes your honor, I am here."

"Do you have the pen packet on Mr. Lyon?"

"Yes, your honor."

The Judge looks around the room, spying the quiet audience, and says, "This reminds me of a joke I heard recently: 'Give a man a fish and he'll eat for a day; teach a Texan to fish and he'll sit in a boat and drink beer all day.'"

Real laughter breaks out.

I smile. I sure hope that the blade on the guillotine is sharp, as I'd hate to hear his follow-up. I try not to think as the bailiff walks to the jury foreman for the verdict. Does Cindy already know the verdict? Is she standing close to comfort me, or did the bailiff give her the throat-slash signal that I missed? Perhaps everyone in the room knows but me. Why would the *Huntsville Item* newspaper be here if they weren't going to convict? There are a few situations when fear has to be restrained to the movement of your fingers; this is one of them.

"Be seated," says the Judge.

Cindy and I remain standing.

"Please hand your verdict to the bailiff."

The bailiff takes the packet of papers to the judge, who then flips to the final page and hands it back. The bailiff hands it back to the foreman.

"Please read the verdict."

The foreman, a thirty-year-old architect in a tweed sports coat, speaks clearly but simply, "For the charge as stated in the indictment, possession of a controlled substance in a penal institution, we find the defendant Richard Abood Lyon, not guilty."

All I hear is a rushing sound, which I assume is blood in my brain. I turn towards the jurors and silently thank them as each looks at me. When I turn back to Cindy, her eyes are filling with tears. I shake her hand; tears spill down her cheeks. She has made history. This is the first acquittal of a prisoner in Walker County. Ever. In her first case with State counsel, she has beaten the Special Prosecutor. He walks over to Cindy, turns his back to me, and says, "I made your case for you; good luck in the future," and walks away.

When I turn around, only two guards stand with their hands on the railing. I ask Cindy, "Please let me get a copy of the verdict before I leave."

She nods her head. I am led quietly back to the gray room to change back into whites and shackles.

Cindy waits while I clink towards the back staircase again. She places a roll of papers in my hands. She smiles. My encounter with the Special Prosecutor ends suddenly and quietly. On the way back to my life sentence, the van is quiet as well—no Golden Country sing-along this time. The Connecticut Yankee survived a Texas Court.

A. WHITFIELD, *New York*

JCF WELCOME

From the outside, JCF, with its thirty-foot gray walls and spired towers, resembles a medieval fortress, an idea no doubt clear in the minds of the penologists who directed its design. The inside is crossed by expansive corridors of beige cinderblock. Here the sun never seems to shine, shrinking the passages into dark and ominous tunnels. Twice a day for more than ten years, I've trod down one of these corridors, usually to and from my job in the mess hall. The incident I'm recounting occurred a while after I arrived at JCF. It wasn't the first to which I had been a witness, nor was it the last.

I was with a group of eight inmates walking to program in silent formation, as required through these corridors, when the group was ordered to halt just outside the lobby of C-Block. I read again the Old English script on the ledge above the steps: "Watch Your Step When Entering C-Block." Along the walls of the lobby stood a group of new arrivals—new jacks—like a display at the army surplus store: seven mannequins dressed in dark green, not quite at attention but certainly not at ease.

Any halt in inmate traffic spells trouble. Something was going to happen. The con directly behind me whispered, "This ain't good." One of the new jacks was summoned forward by a crooked finger, and one of five surly correctional officers stationed in the lobby gave a loud, guttural bark: "You. Yeah, you, with the slanted eyes and sloping head."

Pointing to the floor directly at his feet, he continued, "Well get your ass here, and the rest of you dirtbags stand where you are with your fuckin' mouths shut and your hands out of your pockets."

Another guard took a couple of steps our way, glared, and said, "No talking in formation. Face the front." He turned on his heel and rejoined the others, having arranged their audience. The con standing beside me sighed and whispered through clenched teeth, "I hate this shit."

This is a situation so common, one comes to ignore (or tries to ignore) it. Ritual humiliation leaves nothing out of bounds: race, sexual orientation, physical stature, parentage. They'll say and do anything to get the reaction they want from us. Someone behind me whispered, "That guy looks like a little kid."

I looked again. He was young—a young Asian kid with a childlike face, set with a strained grin and the sad eyes of a boy who hadn't known much happiness. I thought he looked too small and soft for this life.

He stood there silently, in clothes two sizes too large for his thin frame, delicate hands at his sides and legs spread as though expecting to receive a blow. I began to squirm, as did a couple others in my group—fidgeting with our pants, checking shirt buttons, making sure our clothes didn't reveal any infractions that would draw unwanted attention. My mouth turned dry and my breath quickened. It wasn't hot, but I could feel the sweat forming rivulets on my brow.

In my experience, the Asian is the rarest of all prisoners. And it became painfully clear that this particular inmate had been selected because of his race. It felt wrong, on many levels.

My group could easily have been ordered to continue through the lobby to our program. New arrivals are marched in almost every day, and small groups like mine traverse the corridors with regularity. But we provided an opportunity for these COs to impress upon us once again what they were willing to do. A bearish-looking brute, wearing yesterday's beard and that morning's coffee, issued forth from an office doorway and rose up behind the Asian kid. With a paw-like hand he grabbed him by the shoulder and spun him around with no more effort than it would take to flip a coin. The CO bent his huge frame, and with less than six inches separating his toothy maw from the inmate's face, spat, "Roo no spreek Enrish?"

The boy's frozen grin showed no signs of thawing. No attempt at an answer—none wanted. Yet another of the five blue-clad welcomers quipped: "We got no fish heads and rice here." They all laughed, with one adding, "Mmm, fish heads are good eatin'."

Maybe the kid was less than fluent in English, or smarter than I would have been, and chose to pretend he didn't understand. He just stood there, transfixed, looking into the face of each CO as they took their turns at him. His expression didn't change as the milling group guffawed and slapped one another on the back.

"Why the fuck do they let them into the country if they can't speak English?" grumbled one. Apparently the kid didn't understand this any better than any of the other invectives hurled at him, because no sign of comprehension appeared on his face. He remained motionless and silent, like a bird comprehends that the cats are stalking.

The scene must have continued for ten minutes, but it seemed endless. I shuffled my feet, checked my bootlaces, and occasionally stole glances through the grimy windows, wishing between sighs to be anywhere else. I don't know if it was the growling and cursing or the spitting laughter, but I saw those placid, sad eyes moisten and the grin dissolve into a fearful grimace. As the cats continued to circle and yowl at their prey, my head began to pound, my blood pressure rising. As I grew increasingly angry, I realized that it was not so much the actions of these jackboots, but that I had no power to remove myself from witnessing this inhumanity. And I hated it. But there was nothing I could do without jeopardizing my safety. We all stood there, silent. Then I began to feel like a coward, and that brought the bile into my throat, and I was sure I was going to vomit. In a fantasy, I grabbed the big ugly guard by the collar, pulled him close and held him tight in my grasp, and asked if he'd like to try to feed *me* some fish heads and rice.

A harsh voice barked, "Get where you're goin'," and jarred me back into step. Their unwilling audience, having served its purpose, made its way through the lobby. As we passed, I glimpsed the kid carrying his bedroll up the company stairs. Another of the new arrivals had taken his place. All but two of the COs had moved on. Exhausted? Satisfied? Proud of themselves?

We arrived at our program, "Action for Personal Choice," designed to make us aware of how our actions affect our rehabilitation. I was curious to know how many of the other cons in our group felt as I did. I don't know who brought up the incident we had witnessed, but discussing it filled the whole meeting. Very few weren't affected. Many felt anger, even rage. Nearly all of us expressed feelings of helplessness and frustration and fear. I asked the counselor how that type of treatment prepares us for release or contributes to our improvement or rehabilitation. She closed her eyes, shook her head, and softly shrugged her shoulders. She didn't have the answer. No one ever seems to have the answer.

JANE DOROTIK, *California*

DORIS

A lot has been written about the prison system lately—why we as a nation incarcerate so many, why the bureaucratic and unwieldy California system is only expected to make minimal cuts to its eleven-billion-dollar budget while education and social supports are slashed to the very core, why California's prison system has the highest recidivism rate of any state in the nation.

But little is written of the individual suffering that occurs in devastating ways inside prison walls. That's because the system does not *want* you to know. It's easier for all of us to compartmentalize our thinking and believe all of those behind bars are monsters of one kind or another—undeserving of kindness or consideration.

I'm going to tell you one story of suffering, so you can know, really know, what it is like to be incarcerated. And also know how your eleven billion in tax dollars are being spent.

Doris has been locked away now for more than twenty-eight years. She is seventy years old, stands 5'1½" (that ½" is important to Doris), and weighs less than one hundred pounds. She's a very gregarious little lady, talks with her hands a lot, and always has a smile for anyone, guards and prisoners alike.

I don't know what sent Doris to prison; whatever happened twenty-eight years ago doesn't matter to this story. I only know Doris is a lifer, and as a lifer her hope of ever being released from prison is kept alive by a very tenuous thread. I know her demeanor and interactions now, today in this prison. I know she has never had a serious disciplinary write-up . . . until now.

You'll probably find it hard to believe these events occurred, but I assure you it is all 100 percent documented. You can look it up on the court's PACER website in the writ Doris has filed to try and clear herself. The really unbelievable part, beyond the personal pain and grief Doris suffered, is the cost to society that incidents like this inflict. As taxpayers and members of a so-called civilized society, we *all* pay in ways greater than the tax dollars.

Doris is very expressive, effusive in her speech, with her ready smile, and her silver blunt-cut hair falling over her eyes in a youthful style. She reminds me a little of Yenta from *Fiddler on the Roof*, only more petite. On this particular day, she was sitting in her cell chatting with a friend. The housing CO (guard) was conducting a cell-to-cell search for "excessive toilet paper."

Searching cells for these personal hygiene "excesses" is a phenomenon peculiar to the prison system. Why any woman would hoard toilet paper, in the tiny cell space available, is a question that is never asked. It is a prison rule, and that makes it inviolate.

So the CO asked how many rolls of toilet paper were in Doris's cell. Doris answered, "I see three." Well it turns out there were more than three rolls stacked beside the toilet and this angered the CO. The CO began yelling at Doris.

"DO YOU KNOW WHY I AM CONFISCATING YOUR TOILET PAPER? BECAUSE YOU LIED AND THAT MAKES YOU A LIAR."

As the CO pulled out the toilet paper rolls and confiscated them in the plastic bag she carried, Doris got up from her bunk and went to look. From the anger emanating from the guard, Doris thought something must be terribly wrong.

"I'm so sorry, I didn't know," Doris said as she leaned over to look at the stack of toilet paper. In leaning over, she *may* have inadvertently touched or brushed against the CO's uniform. After all, Doris is seventy and balance can be a problem.

Now the CO was angrier than ever.

"YOU COULD BE CHARGED WITH ASSAULT!"

Doris was stunned and asked, "What?"—unclear about what the CO was intimating. Every prisoner knows when faced with an angry cop, the safest demeanor is to shut up, and grovel if necessary.

Finally, after the requisite tongue-lashing, the CO left and continued on down the hall, collecting and confiscating more and more "excessive toilet paper" from another fifteen cells . . . and this should have been the end of the unpleasant interaction.

Thirty minutes later, Doris was summoned to the program office and handcuffed by toilet paper cop and her partner. The sergeant was notified, comes in, takes one look at the frightened Doris, and asks toilet paper cop if she feels threatened by Doris. The CO answered "no," and so the sergeant orders Doris unhandcuffed and tells her to go back to her cell. Sergeant also tells toilet paper cop that "There is no need for a 115" (disciplinary write-up) as "it will not fly."

Now this *really* should have been the end of the issue. But it wasn't.

Enter new, more aggressive sergeant spoiling for a show of dominance. He was overheard to say: "I'll make sure she gets arrested." "I'll body-slam that old bitch."

The previous, more humane sergeant was not to be seen for the rest of the night, and the new sergeant sent the goon squad to escort Doris back up to the program office. There she was spread-eagled against a wall, feet kicked out to a wider and wider stance by aggressive sergeant, pat-searched, handcuffed, and escorted for a medical evaluation. She was then sent to Ad-Seg ("the hole") for 60+ days. She was charged with "Assault on a Peace Officer." The toilet paper cop substantiated the charge by her own trip to the medical evaluation clinic (more than two hours *after* the alleged incident, according to the time on the form). The evaluation form stated, "Slightly reddened forearm."

(This same CO had a habit of taking her pepper-spray gun out of its holster and twirling it or shaking it. . . . Perhaps she bumped her own arm with pepper spray and that's how the "redness" occurred. . . . It wouldn't be the first time!)

The prisoner-witnesses who saw the whole exchange in the cell wrote statements that no assault occurred, but they were not allowed to testify at Doris's hearing. And so, of course, Doris was found guilty.

Doris spent 60+ days in Ad-Seg, had a serious disciplinary on her record (her first serious in over twenty-eight years of incarceration)—all over the presumption of what constitutes "excessive toilet paper."

Does this sequence of events make anyone wonder how the California prison system's eleven-billion-dollar budget is being utilized?

Does anyone wonder how Doris may fare with the parole board (*if* she is ever even allowed in front of them) with this kind of charge on her record?

Does anyone even care about what goes on behind prison walls?

The sequel to all of this—now six months after it all happened—is Doris's seriously deteriorating health. She has now suffered a perforated bowel, requiring emergency surgery, secondary to debilitating ulcerative colitis (a disease closely related to psychological stressors). She's lost more weight than she can afford to lose and looks more waif-like than ever.

As Dostoyevsky writes, "The degree of civilization a society exhibits is best determined by how it treats its prisoners."

SANDY, *Pacific Northwest*

AN ORDEAL

I'm a prisoner serving consecutive life terms. I'm also a Christian. In the late 1980s, another inmate, who was serving Life without the Possibility of Parole, told me about two rape/murders that he'd committed that he'd never been caught for. This inmate's name was Michael. I asked him if anyone had been charged or convicted for the crimes. He told me, not that he knew of. I thought about what Michael had shared with me. He professed to be a Christian, too. He'd told me that he'd confessed his crimes to God and didn't think it needed to go any further than God.

As time passed, I'd kept wondering if someone innocent might have been convicted for the crimes. If someone was in prison or on death row for the crimes, it would be a terrible injustice. I also thought about the relatives of the victims and their need for closure. I thought about how painful it must be to live with the loss of a family member, relative, or friend to murder. How they must long for justice to be served. For a couple of years I struggled with the information that he'd given me. I prayed many times and was prompted by God to step forward. I'd promised Michael that I'd never tell anyone his secret. I couldn't keep his confidence in good conscience.

In the early 1990s I finally contacted the authorities in California where the rape/murders had occurred. I immediately got a reply, and they asked for more information and for Michael's name. They knew Michael and quickly connected him to one of the rape/murders. They charged him after matching his DNA to the victim and took him from the Department of Corrections to California to face his actions.

The victim's name was Lisa. She was seventeen years old when she was raped and murdered. She had overcome obstacles in her life and was planning to join the Navy after high school. She was very active in her school drama club, too. She was also the niece of a police officer. She was sick and on her way home from the doctor's office when Michal viciously raped and strangled her to death. He left her buried under a bunch of garbage. She was later found, and the case went unsolved until I came forward. Lisa was a very beautiful teenager with her whole life ahead of her. It's so very sad that she was taken before her time and in such an evil way.

California authorities came to interview me. They asked me if I'd be willing to go to California and testify in the preliminary proceedings. I agreed. Michael had several friends who were also serving life. They lived in the same unit that I was in. Once they found out via Michael that I'd informed on him, it became very difficult for me to live around them. The prison administration placed me in the Intensive Management Unit on protective custody status. I remained in that unit until the trial was over.

After testifying in the preliminary hearing, I was sent back to my home state and told that the trial would be in a year or longer. I knew what I was doing was right, but I also knew that there would be struggles to overcome. I'd made enemies in the prison system by my stance. I was branded a "rat" by some. Others could care less, because rape is a bad crime. In the mid-1990s I was returned to California to testify as a state's witness. A few of Michael's friends, "lifers," were also sent to testify on his behalf and against me. Before returning to California, Michael's attorney illegally gained access to my psychological records, and these, despite my protest, were revealed during the trial. I was subjected to a fierce cross-examination by Michael's defense attorney.

During the trial, I had to be transferred to a different jail for my safety. Authorities had uncovered a plot laid against me by other prisoners. I was moved and the trial continued. During my stay in the California jail I was in isolation, so I read a lot and prayed. I was under a lot of stress and used exercise and prayer to cope. My grandparents, aunt, and a cousin came to the jail to visit me, too. It was a wonderful treat to be able to visit with them. I hadn't seen them for almost twenty-five years. After testifying, I was sent back to my home state.

Michael was convicted and the penalty phase of the trial would determine his fate. I'm opposed to the death penalty. I prayed and asked God not to allow them to kill Michael. I also wrote the judge asking him to have mercy on Michael.

He was sentenced to death. The case had mainly been made on DNA evidence. The prosecutor, after the trial, went on the circuit lecturing on DNA evidence, and he later became a superior court judge. Michael died of lung cancer on death row about four years after his conviction. My grandparents have since died, and I continue serving my sentence.

In retrospect, what helped me get through the situation was my Christian faith and dependence upon God. I couldn't have done it otherwise. I'm almost fifty-three years old now. I was twenty-one when I came to prison. I may not see the free world again. I live each day by faith in God. I'm just a pilgrim passing through on this earth. Life is brief. I live with the future in mind. The future that's after death.

"All things work together for good to those who love God . . ."

RICKY VINCENT PENDLETON II, *West Virginia*

MY VOICE THROUGH THE PRISON WALL

How am I supposed to cope in here while seeing the corrupt acts of staff? I have to control the things in my life. Rehabilitation is on the individual prisoner. He/she has to dig deep within to correct the errors of their ways.

How do I cope in a place like this, warehoused in a prison like produce with an item number? Well, I first have to atone for the errors that I might have committed against myself, my family, and others. Knowledge of self is the key for growth and development, and expressing it with words and one's actions brings forth understanding, which is the combination of knowledge and wisdom. I strive to better myself to move forward into my next chapter.

Now I am in here, a prison, a first-timer—though there was no actual evidence, only circumstantial. The real perpetrator cannot be prosecuted, being six-feet-deep underground. It is hard in here just like out there in society; the protocol is that the Black man is a threat to any community. This is what the media projects. Each time one of us in here gets a disciplinary rule violation, we are tossed in segregation, but non-ethnic inmates get probation or community service. I can say that because I see it all the time. In my situation, I once kept a journal of my days in prison. I recorded each important episode throughout the day. I tend to be opinionated, also sarcastic, and then I would be writing in a hypothetical manner to put my points across. I wanted the reader to see what I was going through in here. In a routine shakedown, a guard found my journal and confiscated it. The administration misinterpreted my writings and then considered it a "threat." I was immediately put in segregation. I was given a disciplinary rule violation report and later found guilty. I was sentenced to sixty days in segregation, and then the prison committee recommended that I be placed in the eighteen-month administrative segregation program, and the warden later signed for approval. I wanted to someday write a book about my life in prison. I was using the journal to help put the events and experiences together. Well, I appealed the decision through all of the necessary levels and ultimately appealed it to the court. This court ruled in my favor. The court said that there was insufficient evidence to justify the prison administration's guilty verdict. Finally, the court ordered me out of administrative segregation, back to general population, and for my original journal to be given back to me.

My vision of a better way to operate in this place is to stay away from stupid people who get you into trouble. I call them "crash dummies" and we can learn a lot from them. They are self-hating inmates who find themselves in trouble all the time. They are inmates that don't have a positive way about them. I was told by a conscientious inmate that to stay out of trouble, stay away from homosexuality, gambling, and drinking homemade wine, and to just research my case if I wanted to get freed from this place. I utilize the law library most of my time because the place is our laboratory for change, to get out of this hellish place. I strive to research my case to find errors made by the court. Education and fighting their case is the best thing a prisoner can do while incarcerated. The other work I do for dealing with time inside? I just build my temple. I work out, read books, and study myself to get to know more about me. Most people are too afraid to learn about themselves because they are afraid of what they might uncover.

So I manage psychological survival by having discipline and patience when there are guards who don't have respect and yell at you. Sometime they talk down to the inmates, and I have to speak to them in a way that I don't get into trouble. Most prison guards don't have very good communication skills; they're programmed to react in a tactical way when dealing with inmates. I survive by being respectful and I hope to get respect back. This works for me because I make it work. I stay away from trouble. What doesn't work is when a person is saying he wants to change but still finds himself gambling, etc. If you say one thing but do another, you're faking. Life is what one makes of it.

Prison is nothing to glorify; it is the most inhumane place to be in. I am just angry at the fact that a poor county in this country needs the prison industry to boost up the economy. They have no other means to generate revenue. Crime is the way to make money. Does crime really pay? People live their lives on the backs of inmates who are now corporate fictions (moveable properties), as wards of a state. Each indictment is a bill of exchange. The employees program themselves with comments about prisoners, such as "They're the scum of the earth," "They are bad people trying to cheat society," to justify working in prison employment. Now, there are even prison reality shows where cameras go inside a prison to capture the moment. One thing I notice about those programs is that they exploit inmates, but give the society who watches the program a false and negative projection of how prisoners are, throughout the country. They project fear by giving the society the notion that "The society needs to build more prisons because if these criminals were to ever get out, chances are that they would harm someone." The media never focus on the positive part of a prisoner's life, such as how a prisoner's case has gotten overturned, or won on appeal. The media doesn't want society to see that the judicial system and the courts can get a case wrong.

The media go to one of the roughest prisons, and then go straight to the administrative seg-regation units and turn on the camera, then watch the out-of-control inmates act up, giving the world the impression that *all* inmates act like this. Then there's a team of guards who take the situation under control—what an illusion they are feeding the masses. Don't get me wrong, I respect law and order because every society needs it, but don't make law and order a "for profit" business. In this prison, there are inmates who are mentally ill. Most are depressed, on some type of medication. I have to choose who to share a cell with because many inmates are so damned depressed that they don't want to do anything, including showering. They just stink, like they're slowly rotting away. There are a few who keep talking about committing suicide. I talk with other inmates who say that they would consider this. The prison environment has a strong, tense atmosphere. One could cut it with a knife, it is so thick. At any time, a negative element can trigger a raw explosion. There are a lot of personalities in this prison; some cannot control their emotions, and others are so damn feeble-minded it is so damn terrible. The prison is also divided into groups, such as the religious groups, the hate groups, the homosexual groups, etc. It is like where everyone belongs, they will go, if they cannot stand alone. Well, I stand by myself in any situation. I am on my square at all times. I am not a follower but a leader. I strive for freedom, justice, and equality. Although I am in this prison environment, I am not of this prison environment. This is my voice through the prison wall.

VALJEAN ROYAL, *Indiana*

SURVIVOR TESTIMONY

I was just seventeen when I was arrested for female impersonation and prostitution. I was placed in the county jail for adults and gang-raped. As a male-to-female transgender (pre-op), the juvenile detention center would not allow me entry there, stating their concern for the effect of exposure to my alternative lifestyle on the other boys I would have to be housed with.

As I entered the cellblock at the county jail in all female attire, the men became silent. For a moment you could hear a pin drop. This was 1970; transgender wasn't even a word yet. We were just considered half-male, half-female. Freaks of nature. As I lay in bed that night with the man that promised to protect me from all the others, I felt hands gripping my ankles and pulling me out of bed toward them. I started to kick, scream, and struggle. My protector was outnumbered and there was nothing he could do. I was taken to another cell where I was placed on the floor and raped by twenty or more men.

I was eventually able to throw a note at the feet of the turnkey making rounds on the catwalk with just my name and "HELP ME" written on a piece of paper. I was moved into another cellblock, a smaller one. I only had to service one man, who was the cell boss. He sexually abused me whenever he felt like it. In return, I was protected. I felt like I deserved no less than the treatment I received. I was confused and ashamed. I didn't know or understand why I was born so different. The sexual assaults in my life started occurring long before the county jail incident. I was first raped at age nine, and then again at twelve.

In 1975, 1976, and 1977, I was raped by inmates and a staff correctional officer. Again, I experienced an ongoing sexually abusive arrangement for protection. I became dependent on marijuana use every day in order to rise above my circumstances. I had to numb my emotions to survive. In 1982 I was removed from the Indiana State Prison and placed in federal prison for protection.

In 1991, at a federal correctional institution in Memphis, Tennessee, while in segregation, an officer let an inmate into my cell to rape me. I was placed in the hospital after reporting the rape. The investigation conducted by Internal Affairs concluded that I was raped, and videotape showed the officer letting the inmate in and out of my cell. The dismissal of the officer was recommended. I was transferred to another facility. It seemed by then that rape had become a normal part of my life. I continued to experience feelings of worthlessness and shame.

In 1997, my marijuana usage landed me in the web of another predator. A prison drug dealer. I accepted his gifts of free joints, knowing better, but allowing my weakness for the weed to influence me to act against my better judgment. When he came to me for sex and I refused, he threw me on the floor and raped me. After this sexual assault I started to really look at the choices I had been making. Wondering, if my choices had been different at times, would the outcome have been different? I began to seek help with my dependence on marijuana through substance-abuse counseling. Today I have been drug-free since 1998.

The last time I was raped was in 2006 at the Pendleton Correctional Facility, Pendleton, Indiana. After the 1997 rape at the federal correctional institution in Jessup, Georgia, I was later returned to the state facility. I have continued to be celibate since 1998. When I returned to Indiana, I met a man at the prison who I became inmate-friends with. I explained to him that I was no longer sexually active while we dated and courted each other. We eventually became roommates.

On the night we moved in together, we were lying in bed together and relaxing. He forced himself on me and raped me. Afterwards, he begged my forgiveness. I cried and told him I hated him and would never forgive him. I kept telling him that I had trusted him and I had grown to even love him.

He continued to beg for me to forgive him, and not to move. He promised he would never touch me again. I forgave him, and he kept his word and never touched me again. We became best friends.

The memory of that night was always coming back when I least expected it, so the forgiveness process was always starting over again. I remain celibate to this day. I never want to even think about prison and sex together. I would much rather share in a loving marriage in a real relationship in a home, sweet home that is really ours.

As a pre-op transgender Christian, in here my faith is tested sometimes. I, however, continue to have faith and hope for a better future.

My life as a surviving rape victim, in and out of prison on multiple occasions, has been a powerful testimony that has touched the lives of some inmates that were like me in a way—mad at life and at living. I've gained a light of wisdom from the pain of abuse. A light I want to share with others so that they can see the better choices they can make, even in the dark places.

COREY JOHN RICHARDSON, *Kentucky*

BACK TO ATTICA

"Attica! Attica! Attica!"

The Attica riot of 1971 was a prisoners' response to the inhumane conditions and abuses suffered at the hands of "corrections." The response to injustice is, though, only part of the equation. The transformative process began in the 1950s out of the struggle by African Americans for civil rights. The year 1972 alone saw twenty-five serious riots, which threatened the foundation of the U.S. prison system. But prisoners had suffered for decades in these deplorable conditions. What changed? The true change came from a change in perception.

Those in the prisons saw the demonstrations on the streets of Birmingham and on college campuses like Kent State, and perceived their own struggle. These men, poor and predominantly from ethnic minorities, had been sentenced, rightly or wrongly, to "Time in Prison." Not to starvation, abuse, medical neglect, disease, and violence. The political activism throughout America, often mixed with violence, resulted in an awakening of the social conscience. Prison rioting resulted in class action suits and various other actions where judges ordered prison administrators to make specific changes regarding crowding, nutrition, medical care, prisoner abuse, and so on to protect the prisoner's Eighth Amendment right to freedom from cruel and unusual punishment.

Interestingly enough, while judges were addressing the extreme depredations experienced by prisoners, legislatures were enacting some of the most extreme sentencing laws conceivable, the results of which are still being felt today. In the early 1970s, U.S. prisons held fewer than 200,000 men and women; today, the number is 2.3 million. With only about 5 percent of the world's population, we hold 25 percent of the world's prisoners and can brag of the world's longest sentences for offenses. The War on Crime/War on Drugs (aka War on the Poor) has in effect rounded up those from our most destitute communities, predominantly ethnic minorities, and created what has been called the Prison Industrial Complex.

But when the reduced budgets of economically depressed states meet the ever-expanding numbers held within prisons, the result is clear: a multitude of abuses have begun to raise their vile heads once again. A smattering of news reports by various journalists have covered the story, and a few small riots have made the national news, but not once did we hear a serious discussion during the '08 presidential campaign of the most massive imprisonment phenomenon in the history of the world, and what a sharp economic slowdown will mean to these several million men and women behind concrete and razor wire.

Point of fact, each and every recession in this country is met with increasing rates of crime. It is a simple survival mechanism for those already struggling within impoverished communities and for those falling into poverty. But when low-level property offenses and simple drug possession will bring decades of imprisonment, where will these newly or re-convicted go? Our jails are packed with the convicted awaiting bed spaces in prisons at or above double capacity already. One out of every fifty-five Louisiana residents is in prison, and one death per week occurs in California's system due to neglect; yet such statistics barely provoke a nod from the general public. Meanwhile, the electorate is mesmerized by middle-class tax breaks, the ethnicity of its president, and the latest techno-fad.

Lives are ruined from years on the inside, and the families of the poor are decimated. So, while the voting public buys T-shirts about Hope and commemorative plates about Change, we in prison must fend for ourselves. I have fought a few of these legal battles. They are long, uphill processes. They are costly by prisoner standards, where filing fees or copying charges mean that you may have to go without something else. Learning procedure, statutory law, case law, etc., can be a daunting task, particularly for a prisoner who has just earned his GED. It will take years to reach a verdict, and a win against the state or federal system's attorneys is rare and the rewards seem nominal.

While researching a possible claim, I thought to inquire with at least twenty or so civil-liberties, special-interest, and human-rights organizations. I found a policy that overtly discriminates against a whole class of people, those within the prison system, and I wanted to pursue an action addressing this policy. There are many obstacles to filing and arguing such an action, and judges are eager to dismiss your case for procedural error, or on a weak legal theory concocted to thwart a prisoner's efforts for change. (Anyone who believes that "Fighting the System" is a glorious act has never attempted it.)

So, for weeks and weeks I waited for some response from any of the organizations that I just knew would be interested. Nothing came. Then finally I received a response from Human Rights Watch. I was thrilled as I ever so gingerly opened the envelope. The form letter read as follows:

Dear Sir,

Thank you for your recent letter . . . unfortunately, staffing constraints have forced us to cease reading and responding to correspondence from persons in state or federal custody. We understand that the information you have shared with us is important and that your grievance deserves serious consideration and attention, but . . . we are no longer able to be of assistance . . . We ask that you do not write to us . . . and we hope that you will pursue other avenues in seeking assistance with your situation.

The ACLU and its various branches did not even send a form letter.

It confirmed my belief: no one will fight our battles for us. Few publications will even touch on our issues, no matter how extreme and pervasive the problems are. The new left-leaning political vision stops abruptly at the prison gates; the myriad of progressive organizations turn their backs on us as they try to garner members. I see that the Spirit of Attica must rise again as we take the fight for true justice and fairness to those who benefit from our appalling treatment, or to those who simply refuse to be concerned.

Some are fighting. A federal judge in San Francisco ruled that Gov. Schwarzenegger must reduce the state's prison population by an astounding 55,000 within three years. And as I scan news reports from around the country, I hungrily seek other evidence that we have had enough. I also check for my own name on the daily legal mail list. On March 27, the Kentucky Court of Appeals rendered a ruling in my abuse-of-power case against the state (*Richardson v. Rees, et al.*, No. 2008-CA-000721-MR).

It was a while before I could even open the letter because I knew I had lost. I had long since exhausted the necessary administrative remedies and had had my case thrown out of the lower court. I thought, I may lose again and again, but if these people want to treat us any way they like, regardless of their own policies and state or federal laws, well, I'll make them work for it. Then I opened the letter, and there it was. The appellate court's decision: "Thus we believe that there was no substantial evidence to support [the Kentucky Dept. of Corrections'] decision." I had to read it twice. I had won. All of the judges concurred in the published ruling that the KDOC had abused its discretion.

Before the day was out, prison legal aides were scribbling down the citation for their own cases and mailing it on to other prisons to use as well. We simply are unused to wins, and this win has application in a multitude of cases where the prisons abuse their power. Yes, personally, the gain may be nominal, but to all of us inside, the gain was much more important. I may even suffer from petty retaliations from the prison (a common tactic is to lock a man away in segregation on a trumped-up "investigation," or to ransack his cell looking for a minor infraction which can be turned into a write-up), but nothing can remove this case from the law books now, and no one can take away this win.

Maybe I was wrong after all. Every now and then, fighting the system can be a glorious thing. Maybe I have latched onto some of the change and hope going on in the "free" world. Maybe I can help change people's perceptions from this side of the concrete and steel.

Enter: Attica 2.0

Kite Out

BRANDON MARTINEZ, *California*

FIFTEEN YEARS SINCE INCEPTION

It's been fifteen years since inception, locked down here in the department of correction. I must say it's been a horrific ordeal indeed. Started out just a young buck in my teens. Had no idea what tragedy I had imposed upon myself, and family would ultimately suffer right along with me, from my absence. Looking back on my former days, I wish I could turn back the hand of time. Wave a magic wand, erase that day, that fateful day that changed the course of time, the events that occurred and ruined my whole life. Although I was quite young, lacked the maturity to make the proper decisions, I won't sit back and attempt to make excuses, at this age and in this age. It's time, son—time to come clean. For the sake of closure—closure for all parties involved. The victim's family has endured enough grief. Oh, what I would do to mend the wounds. If I could only massage the heart. We all could lay our heads down at night and sleep in peace.

How many days, weeks, and years have we been carrying this, this heavy load? I just want to serve notice on you, we can find the strength to let go, and let go to muster up the courage to heal ourselves. We can't alter what happened on that day. But what we can do is put the pieces back together; slowly but surely we shall survive, we will make it—not only survive, but thrive. Thrive in the midst of utter darkness. You see, my friend, I too have suffered. I too am familiar with heartache and pain. I know what it's like, my friend. Is it okay to call you that? I hope so. I too have had my share of sleepless nights. I've tossed and turned. Late in the midnight hour, I've had death come visit me. All I can say, Here by the grace of God go I . . . The Lord made death behave when I walked the floor at night. Didn't think I would make it. Pulled out my hair—sit back, listen up. Because I am coming for you today.

I know you looking all fly, you got your hair all slicked back, all flossed out with the flyest gear. But behind all that, behind all the pretty makeup—you too, ladies—when that door closes at night, you all alone, so alone, the li'l tears trickle on down. I don't know what thorn in your flesh exists. Don't know who let you down. Who did you wrong. I can't answer why it had to pop off. But none of that matters. It's all irrelevant. What matters, what's most important, is to focus on the road ahead. If we're ever going to get steppin' on this journey of life, we got to bury it all in the tomb of time. Leave it there, so it can't hurt us no more. No more, I say. This stops right here, right now. No more, son, no, no, no; I declare right now, "You will live and not die." You hear me, you will live and not die. Although you don't understand, the future appears to be bleak, as so much uncertainty abounds. Although we may be lost, we shall be found. In the gutter of despair. You can, you will rise on up out of that. That foul spirit of depression that comes to wreak havoc on our minds. We've wasted too much time. Let dwindle away opportunities. All because we couldn't catch a glimpse beyond the clouds. If we had only taken a moment to look, we would see. Behind the darkest cloud often follows a bright sunny day. Enough is enough. Get busy living. You will make a way, you will find a way. Inside of you. That's how. Inside of you is all you need to know, to discover the gifts and talents that reside. Reside all inside of you.

Come on, don't let all the doom and gloom destroy your life. There is a future. Can I letcha know something? There's good news, there's still time, you can overcome, get past, and beyond, what has brought you almost to the verge of giving up. In the nick of time you kept on steppin'. If you hadn't took another step, you would have died in your misery. I applaud you for your efforts on moving forward. Keep moving, keep on keeping on. You're like the Energizer Bunny. You literally take a lickin' and keep on tickin'. That is what you must realize, the tenacity. The strength. You got what it takes, you got heart. Even when you stumbled all over the place, you still moved forward. But you're running out of time. We ain't getting no younger. It's now or never. Get up out of that mess you're in. It shall, it will, it certainly will come to pass. Take the measures, take the steps. Do what you got to do to get to your destiny. The reason you didn't die, the reason you're still here, didn't slit your arm, cut your wrist up and down and all around. The reason you didn't die when you took all them pills (that should have took you out, by the way, that potent amount), when they pumped your stomach, emptying the poison, my God, Lord have mercy. What? Been there, done all that, got a T-shirt. Don't look at me crazy. Like you some saint who got it all together. Don't even try to explain to me how all your i's are dotted and your t's are crossed. I know your screws are all on tight. Funny, you're quite a character, but I ain't got time for the games. Save all that for whoever you choose to project an image or perception with, portray all the greatness to them. I ain't the one. I know the real you, the lonely you, the broken-hearted you. The one with issues—so many, too many problems in abundance. They say when it rains, it pours. When will it ever let up? Hold up, stop the whining. Let us pause for "I Pray," sung by Amanda Perez . . . See, as difficult as it is for you to accept, grasp it all, it's not profound. It ain't no big fancy concept. All I ask is you begin to become aware of the power you hold. That willpower to make a difference, alter the course of your life for the better. You, all by yourself, got what it takes; that's the reason you're still alive. Because there's a purpose for you. You were put here for a reason—don't ask me, you going to have to define that purpose, carve out your own niche, dawg, you know. I won't give you a heads-up; trust me, you'll know when you have arrived. But I must caution you. The path, my friend, won't be paved with gold. I can't promise you that along your journey there won't be turbulence in the atmosphere. You may have to find some steppin' stones. And often more times than not, you'll have to battle with them demons. It's OK. It's alright. As long as you strive daily to stay positive, stay focused, sow the seeds by your actions, them demons can't touch you—see, they can only run amok, 'cause so much grief only when you're depressed, when you hold them pity parties, you invite them in. They prey on the weak; that's when you're most vulnerable. There's too much at stake. Your life. Your future. Please promise me, you won't give in, you won't give up, that you'll keep hope alive. There's so much worth, too much value left in you; you're precious to so many folks; there's only one of you. We can't replace you, we can't afford to lose you. If you never hear my voice again, because I'm almost on the by-and-by, it's getting late in the evening for me, it's almost time to roll into my grave. Sometimes I get scared that blue walls of death will begin to settle in my eyes. But I shake it off. I've come today with one purpose—to save you, your life. Your future. That's all that matters to me now. I want you to have a life I never had; I want you to laugh; I want to see you smile again, to lay, to play, to dance. I hope you dance, kid—oh, I hope you dance. The people are depending on you. Don't you dare let them down. They stood by your side with that uncon-ditional love. Please do it for their sake, all the ones you love and care about in this ole world. Your life ain't just about you. You have the potential to impact a generation. Do the right thang, as your sole success will pull so many others out of their misery. They'll be inspired, knowing all the pure hell you went through and made it. I'm doing my best to school you down. You hold the ticket out of poverty, to get out of the ghetto. They need to see someone familiar—without a face, they won't be able to relate. Who's going to reach them? I'm sorry to put all this on you. Forgive me. I mean you no harm. It's just so critical that you succeed. Only you can save them now. *Are you sure, me, I'm the one?* Yeah, I'm sure. *But you know I'm the chiefest of sinners, you know I act a fool.* Sure. *And you're aware, I ain't got it all together.* Hush, hush now. *Someone else. I'm cool.* No, you're the one for the job, that's the reason you been chosen. Because you didn't have it all together, you represent the least of these. *That's deep.* Let that sink in, son. You've been ostracized, ridiculed, never did fit in. It was all for the glory—no grit, no glory. In order to testify, you had to be dragged through the mud of affliction, for your good. All by your lonesome . . .

Why? We couldn't risk contamination. Although you were in the crowd, you were never of the crowd. My, my, my, so we separated you from the pack. The rest of your life is all on you. Don't let the blood remain on your hands. It can be made right. We can redeem ourselves.

Many years ago, as a teen, I was involved in a murder. I didn't commit the actual offense. My codefendant, on his own volition, decided to blow it out of proportion in a fit of spontaneous, drastic rage. Oh, how I wish I could of prevented it from occurring. But there was nothing in my arsenal to stop a madman. I was fortunate enough to escape with my own life, but how I feared him. I was physically outmatched in strength; there was nothing I could do to stop the actions of this individual. Which brings us to the question, what murderer leaves behind a witness? My life was spared, and I'm thankful, grateful for that. Perhaps if I had a gun or weapon I could have pointed it at him and said, "That's enough." Many may differ, but it is my opinion that my life was spared to be used as an instrument of change. I know my heart; I know what I've accomplished. To reach the sin-sick soul has brought my life much meaning. To inspire, motivate, bring hope to the table is to know my life hasn't been lived in vain. Someone somewhere will walk away from the street life, or someone, at the right place, in the right time, will hear just what he needed to hear. If he had not heard, he would have fallen victim to the grave. If I had not stood in the gap in prayer, we would have had another young buck walking into a life sentence. All I can say is that many are sent but few are chosen. This is the direction; my life had to be this way—for my family, friends, loved ones. You must not feel sad for me. Sure, there certainly was a price to pay, as I've been beat, raped, traumatized significantly over the years. I too have lost family. I too have seen folks close to me pass away. Am I not a human being? Are the only positive eyes on me the man who sits on high? Is that divine hand the only one who believes in forgiveness? I'm so glad that the Lord is much more forgiving than man, otherwise we all could be in jeopardy.

I must take my seat now. Before I take my seat: to the victim's family, I send you my deepest, sympathetic apology. I'm sorry your loved one perished that night. I'm sorry for all the pain you've had to endure, for the holidays he couldn't be in your presence. Birthdays, New Years, Christmas . . . I'm sorry for that void in your heart, the lonely nights and unsettling days. You got to find peace. Closure. Go ahead. Usher it on in. Don't be afraid. There's life—can I letcha know that there's life after the worst, no matter how tragic, how horrific the turmoil? It can, it will, it shall, somehow, someway, the pain, the hurt will ease on up. Time will, if you let it, it will heal that broken heart. I'll stand in the gap in prayer, in which I have stood all these years. Don't let it destroy your life any longer. Find, seek the courage to slowly but surely live, live, live life to the fullest. In the good, the bad, the indifferent, live life to the fullest, I say. No matter what, always keep on walking . . .

Civic Dysfunction and Its Critics

INTRODUCTION

From their perspectives inside different state-sponsored neighborhoods of Prison City, the writers in this section offer critical assessments of the civil dysfunction of a city that, after thirty-five years of expansion, housed one out of every one hundred Americans.[1] These writers present practical evidence of how well imprisoned people understand the obstacles to turning American prisons in the direction of serving the public good.

Kenneth E. Hartman's "The Trouble with Prison" is a passionate condemnation of the prison complex as it operates today. After thirty years as a California Department of Corrections prisoner, Hartman knows just how deeply this institution is invested in its own failure. Real reform will require the political will to counter a multibillion-dollar industry that is dependent on large prison populations.[2] Hartman's essay makes clear what is implied by each of the pieces in this section: if we want to transform Prison City into one that works for its citizens, and thus for the citizens of the other American cities where all but 5 percent of prisoners will return,[3] we would be well advised to start by listening to what prisoners themselves have to teach us.

Charles Hammer's "Why Are We a Nation of Prisons?" offers a rapid-fire explanation of how the judicial and penal systems work to overcrowd prisons. Hammer limits his claims to practices in Oregon. But he confirms what social scientists and legal activists have recognized for years: the United States incarcerates more of its own citizens than any nation on earth for identifiable reasons—reasons we could address and change; reasons that result in no more real public safety, at massive cost to taxpayers.[4] Sound social science and legal analysis will be needed to ground any changes in this system. But Hammer brings home, once again, that the conclusions penal science and the law will reach are already apparent to observant men and women on the receiving end of these practices.

In "Real Life in Prison," Royal Gene Domingo Jones, Sr., presents himself not simply as critic of the prison but as one of its exemplary products. Without disclaiming responsibility for his actions, he speaks out against the system's crimes and failures, and chief among these, he concludes, are the crimes of neglect. His offenses are his own. But the failure to offer the tools for men and women like himself to live differently rests with the prison.

Shaka Senghor's "23 and 1" is included in this section because of its close descriptions of the conditions endured in administrative segregation, "the hole," and the effects of solitary confinement—which many consider torture[5]—on men's minds and spirits. This essay serves as a critique of a disciplinary procedure imposed on recalcitrant prisoners—a procedure carried out without any inquiry as to why prisoners resist prison practice. Further, if we want to congratulate ourselves for living in a "post-racial" era, Senghor makes us think again. From where he sits in confinement, among other Black men under the rule of white state employees, the frontlines of state-sponsored racism have simply been shuttered up inside prison walls, where Black men who resist affronts to their personal integrity suffer and die. Yet, in the end, despite these conditions, Senghor uses his time in isolation to dig deeper into himself, to transform anger and bitterness into more constructive emotions.

However we might admire Shaka Senghor's defense of his personal dignity, most men and women in prison serve their time quietly, absorb the abuse of the prison, and serve fewer than the maximum number of years to which they are sentenced.[6] In "A More Perfect Union," Ronald (Rashawn) Hughes presents his view of the responsibility borne by conscientious parole-board members, who are charged with deciding who can be safely released and who cannot. Hughes's central message is about the responsibilities of those applying for parole: to take in earnest the need for real change, and to bring an equitable attitude to the process. If parole-board members can resist the public-relations politics surrounding their decisions, these decisions will be based on the behavior and attitude of the potential parolee.

Curtis L. Downing's "Reflection on the Work of Dealing with Time" represents a large number of essays submitted to *Fourth City*: brief as messages among a flotilla of bottles, all hoping to make us understand just how toxic the atmosphere is inside prisons that call themselves correctional facilities. Succinct, focused, and anxious to be heard from a place where no one does much listening, Downing's essay is one among many, and the many representative of the toll that Prison City exacts on its inhabitants.

The implications of Jane Dorotik's "Calif Lifers Search for Parole" are clear: Prison City is the most overcrowded in America not only because too many people enter and too few get the help they need, but because too little practical sense is used in deciding who leaves. Dorotik looks at two cases of the latter problem, and at the burden it lays upon the backs of taxpayers. Dorotik's solutions to this problem are so strikingly clear and simple, they make us reconsider where the real threats to our collective welfare actually lie.

In Jon Marc Taylor's "Bolshayazona (Big Prison Zone)," the author examines and critiques a troubling possibility: the erosion of prisoners' legal, civil, and human rights may be a harbinger of a creeping prisonization of all of American life and culture. As civil liberties inside and out narrow down, free citizens may unconsciously be readying themselves to live in a Big Prison Zone. Taylor suggests that Prison City may be a preview of the Prison Nation where we may all soon be living.

Writing from first-hand experience, Dostoevsky (among others) has famously claimed that to understand the state of civilization of any nation, one should look at how that nation treats its prisoners. These essays suggest that such assessment may reveal as much about causes as about symptoms: to become a more civilized nation, free people might begin by civilizing the places where prisoners live, and the first step may be to heed the warnings of the most viable frontline agents of such change.

NOTES

1. Adam Liptak, "1 in 100 U.S. Adults behind Bars, New Study Says," *New York Times*, February 28, 2008.

2. John Schmitt, Kris Warner, and Sarika Gupta, "The High Budgetary Cost of Incarceration," The Center for Economic and Policy Research, June 2010, http://www.cepr.net/documents/publications /incarceration-2010–06.pdf.

3. Timothy Hughes and Doris James Wilson, "Reentry Trends in the United States," Bureau of Justice Statistics, http://bjs.ojp.usdoj.gov/content/pub/pdf/reentry.pdf.

4. See, for example, Jonathan Simon, *Governing through Crime: How the War on Crime Transformed*

American Democracy and Created a Culture of Fear (New York: Oxford University Press, 2009); Christian Parenti, *Lockdown America: Police and Prisons in the Age of Crisis* (New York: Verso, 2000); Ruth Wilson Gilmore, *Golden Gulag: Prisons, Surplus, Crisis, and Opposition in Globalizing California* (Berkeley: University of California Press, 2007).

5. Atul Gawande, "Hellhole: The United States Holds Tens of Thousands of Inmates in Long-Term Solitary Confinement. Is it Torture?" *The New Yorker*, March 30, 2009.

6. "Community Supervision," Reentry Policy Council: A Project of the Council of State Governments Justice Center, http://www.reentrypolicy.org/Report/PartII/ChapterII-E /PolicyStatement26/ResearchHighlight26–1.

KENNETH E. HARTMAN, *California*

THE TROUBLE WITH PRISON

Plato's "Allegory of the Cave" describes how the limited perceptions of men leave them measuring the world with only the distorted *reflections* of reality. The trouble with prison, as it is perceived from outside, is that the shadows are further distended by a variety of prisms that bend reality to suit a host of preconceptions and special interests, resulting in self-fulfilling prophecies. The end result of this shape-shifting is a system that produces failure as a matter of course, that pretends to protect the mass of society, and that destroys whole communities in its voracious appetite. The trouble with prison is prison.

I serve the other death penalty—life without the possibility of parole—for killing a man in a fistfight when I was nineteen years old. In that I will never get out, I am freed to speak a more direct and unfiltered truth than those who must convince a panel of unsympathetic officials they should be returned to the real world. My twenty-nine years of direct experience, coupled with a powerful thirst to come to grips with my own personal truth and gain an intellectually sure grasp of this world, have taught me a series of lessons. While I do not claim to have unchained myself completely from the bonds of ignorance, I believe I can read and interpret accurately the tortured shapes on the dull concrete walls of this particular cave.

People are put in prison because nothing else works to control their behavior. This is the foundational misperception that supports the prison edifice. The truth is far less simple. There are prisoners whose lifetimes of dangerous behavior leave prison as the only choice for society. But these are a tiny minority in the sea of pathetic misfits and perennial losers walking the yards.

Most prisoners are uneducated, riddled with unresolved traumas and ill-treated mental health problems, drug and alcohol addictions, and self-esteem issues that are profound, far too often bordering on the pathological. The vast majority have never received competent health care, mental health care, drug treatment, education, or even an opportunity to look at themselves as humans. Had any of these far less draconian interventions been tried before the descent into this wretched cave, no doubt many of my peers would be leading productive lives. *Nothing else works* is not a statement of fact; it is the declaration of an ideology. This ideology holds that punishment, for the sake of the infliction of pain, is the logical response to all misbehavior. It is also a convenient cover story behind which powerful special interest groups hide.

Prison employees benefit by our failure. These well-organized government workers created the victims' rights movement, a sad shill for the prison-industrial complex. Using the handful of politically active victims of crime to obscure their actual agenda, propositions are passed, laws are changed, and policies that really could prevent victimization in the first place are suppressed. Both of these groups, working in tandem with the corporations that construct and supply prisons, pour millions of dollars into the political process to achieve a system guaranteed to fail. But this failure by any other measure—high rates of recidivism, high rates of internal disorder, growing prison populations serving longer sentences—results in greater profits to the corporations, increased membership in the prison-staff unions, and ever-growing piles of dollars to buy still more influence.

After reading a small library of books and studies on the subject, along with my direct experience, it is clear only three rehabilitative programs have proof of success. This golden triad includes increased and enhanced visiting to build and maintain family ties, higher education, and quality drug and alcohol treatment. It is not a closely held secret that these work to lower recidivism and, thus, to prevent victimization. This is obvious to anyone who really studies the issues. Nevertheless, the special interest groups lobby incessantly against all three. In my twenty-nine years, visiting has deteriorated from a slightly unpleasant experience to a hostile and traumatic acid bath that quite effectively destroys family ties. Higher education is virtually nonexistent but for those few with the substantial resources needed to purchase it. In those rare cases where innovative ways have been found to bring education back into the prisons, the special interest groups have mounted vicious campaigns to terminate the programs. The opposition to drug and alcohol treatment, much more widely supported in the body politic, is subtler. Using the proven method of compulsory participation by the least amenable, those programs that are instituted are crippled in the normal chaos of prison. All of this opposition stands behind the banner of protecting victims' rights, as if only the desire for revenge by past victims of crime matters, taking precedence even over the potential losses of future victims.

With recidivism rates well beyond two-thirds, the assumption for all prisoners is that of failure. It is written into the prison policies that force parolees back to failed situations, that site prisons far from the urban areas most prisoners come from, and provide no after-parole assistance. When I first came into the California state system in the late '70s, a parolee received a decent set of clothes, a bus ticket, and $200 in cash. Today's parolee receives a sweatsuit unsuitable for a job interview and $200, out of which is deducted the cost of his bus ticket and decades of devaluation. The parolee, having received no real substance-abuse treatment, no serious education or training, no useful mental health counseling, and holding barely enough money for a short stay in a flophouse, is cast back out into the free world to swim or, more likely, sink. The aid that might make the transition successful is denied—ostensibly to save money. The pennies it would take to reestablish the parolee vanish next to the fifty thousand a year it costs to re-incarcerate a parole violator.

Yet again, sadly, it becomes clear on close inspection that without our mass failure the gears of the prison-industrial complex would stop. Jobs would be lost, rural communities devastated, and the flow of political contributions would dry up. From the perspective of those who depend on our failure to sustain themselves, our success would be a disaster. In my state, an admittedly extreme example, on any given day about half the prison population are parole violators, a majority of whom have broken no law, but rather violated one of the vast web of confusing and devious tripwire rules they must navigate on the other side of the fences.

Failure is expected—a bad enough thing, to be sure. Worse, failure is celebrated and lauded. The primary rationale of parole provisions is to lock as many ex-cons as possible back into the prisons. There are gang task forces, drug task forces, absconder recovery units, and high control teams, all of which operate on a presumption of failure. These black-clad, helmeted law enforcement platoons prowl the alleys and back streets of the inner cities hunting down parolees. They justify the overapplication of picayune rules as preventing the assumed major crimes the parolee is bound to commit eventually. After the high-fives and backslapping are over, parole officers content themselves with their sense of exacting a frightening prospective form of justice. The ex-convict heads back to another year or two of dehumanization for forgetting to report that he moved, or for talking to a cousin who was also on parole.

The prison system dresses itself in a cloak of respectability by claiming to protect society from the "worst of the worst." At a certain level, this is true. There are some irredeemables, those who should not be allowed to prey on society ever again. The trouble with this assertion, and the direction it has taken, is there just aren't enough worst of the worst to justify the concrete and razor-wire empire that exists today. The definition of who fits into this excluded class has expanded dramatically over the years, along with the borders of the system. Now, along with the serial predator is housed the serial drug addict and the serial shoplifter and the serial loser, all serving extraordinarily long sentences on prison yards devoid of even a semblance of rehabilitation. This in the name of protecting society.

Policies are enacted that are purposely, brutally enforced by staff who have been trained to view prisoners as less than human, to believe that their official role is to exact revenge, who see us in all ways as the enemy, the dangerous other. This message, that we are not fully human, is pressed into us every moment of every day in a multitude of ways, from the mundane (being forced to wear pants with "PRISONER" stamped on the leg in neon orange lettering), to the profound (being prevented from conducting a business or owning property). This results in a diminishing of our consciousness to that of the unwelcome alien. From inside this dark recess, it is near impossible to imagine rejoining humanity. As one state senator in California observed, "If you were to set out to design a system to produce failure, this would be it." It is not surprising that this elected official represents an area that has disproportionately suffered due to these policies, and was a professor of psychology before assuming office.

Whole communities have been decimated, literally, by this system. People of color, the poor, and the dispossessed are represented in numbers far exceeding their share of society. It starts on streets patrolled by an occupying force of police who view these people as less than, as suspects first and foremost. Arrests are made for the most trivial offenses, for the little acts of rebellion and frustration not uncommon to young people everywhere. But down on the occupied bottom of society there is no call made to mommy and daddy. No well-dressed lawyer will show up in court with a privately contracted psychologist to explain junior's learning disability. A bored, too often hostile public defender will convince the youth to take a plea bargain that twenty years later becomes the first strike in a life sentence for boosting a ham. Once a name has a criminal-justice system number affixed to it, the move from possible suspect to probable offender is complete. In some of the worst-off communities, every third or fourth man, and a growing number of women, carry numbers on their shoulders.

As the mass of people in this country who carry a number grows, so too does the harm caused and exacerbated by the prison system. No longer a tiny fringe of malcontents and unrepentant thugs, we who have sprung from the electrified fences and gun towers, from inside the racially polarized and ganged-up yards, who have spent a significant portion of our lives locked into tiny concrete boxes bending over and spreading our cheeks, are a growing segment of the real world. We have spouses and children, parents and siblings, and our influence on the collective consciousness is solidifying. It is seen in the glorification of violence and the fascination with acts of irrational and pointless rage that fill the media and dominate the lives of prisoners. It is heard in the adoption of jailhouse terms applied to schools put on "lockdown" and street cops "kickin' it with the homies." It is felt in the tighter ring of controls that encircle the lives of free people in the real world, a disturbing reflection of the world of prisoners.

Prison is insatiable. It devours everything in its path and swallows whole anything that attempts to deter it. All these years I have spent inside, I have observed just how effectively the system crushes its opposition. The well-meaning and good-hearted eventually surrender to overwhelming force and terrible despair. I see that despair in prisoners beating their heads against the walls of our internal exile with a maniacal ferocity. We internalize the separation and removal, the assumed less-than status, and hold up the idiotic and vainglorious pride we pretend to, like clown's makeup, to hide our shame. Some of us profess to be immune to the battering we endure; many of us deny it's happening, in spite of the obvious bruises. In the end, the vast majority of us become exactly who we are told we are: violent, irrational, and incapable of conducting ourselves like conscientious adults. It is a tragic opera with an obvious outcome.

The talk lately making the rounds in political circles, among the power brokers and well-heeled, is of reviving the idea of rehabilitation. The past decades of exploding costs and terrible outcomes, particularly as schools and old-folks homes are closed to bridge budget shortfalls, have allowed the concept of using prison to correct, to heal and restore, to be taken seriously again. This is a good thing. It is long overdue. But it is an idea that will have to battle powerful forces determined to dim it into a shadow without substance. It will face the added complexity of implementations managed by guards and administrators, teachers and counselors who fundamentally reject the notion that prisoners are capable of being restored. Along with this uphill climb—dragging along the recalcitrant—will be the added obstacle of the special-interest groups defending their world of failure. The simple truth is: the fewer of us, the fewer of them. If we stop coming back, their world will collapse.

Still, the greatest struggle in effecting change will be convincing the mass of prisoners, the millions of men and women who have been brainwashed into believing they simply cannot become better. At the head of this mass will be the seeming leadership from our own ranks, those who have used the status quo to achieve a perverse success. They are the drug dealers and negative leaders, the phony writ writers, the whole group of profiteers and self-servers who will seek to undermine positive change because in it they glimpse the end of their own domination of dysfunction. That they aid and assist the special-interest groups, the organized-revenge groups, and the corporations profiting off of our collective misery is obvious. Yet they will seek to maintain the failed system through acts of violence and jackass resistance. They might succeed in stifling change, and not for the first time. This is the modern world of prison, constructed after twenty-five years of surrendering to fearmongers and manipulators. It is a fearsome mess.

The trouble with prison is, indeed, prison itself—the way prison is managed and envisioned. The idea that by humiliating and brutalizing damaged people some possible good could result is simply absurd, a lie perpetrated by interests who benefit from failure. It has never worked. It is not working now. It will never work. No amount of money poured down society's communal drain will buy success. No minimum number of broken bodies and tortured spirits will purchase rehabilitation. No pyre of burnt offerings, no matter how large and hot, will somehow result in better people walking out the front gate in their gray sweatsuits. The problems are systemic and resilient. Nothing short of radical and sustained reform will be enough to overcome the resistance of a system built to fail. It may not be possible, but to not try is to condemn thousands upon thousands of our fellow human beings to a witches' brew of victimizations, in here and out there. To not try would be an act of cowardly capitulation to bullies and thugs. To not try is to become like those who have erected this system, who keep it going, who must somehow sleep with what they do.

CHARLES HAMMER, *Oregon*

WHY ARE WE A NATION OF PRISONS?

Is our prison system a mystery to the average citizen? An uncomfortable mystery best not examined too closely? So it was to me until I became intimately involved in its workings. No doubt the greatest part of the mystery is: why does it cost so much? Why are our prisons so full, and why do we need more?

Unlike what many Americans may think, the justice and correctional systems of this country are built on retribution, not rehabilitation. And, retribution is expensive—very expensive.

Our government (past and present), supported by the media, controls the masses through fear. Remember the War on Drugs, War on Crime, War on Terrorism? We have been convinced that if we can just lock up *enough* people, we'll all be safe—all will be well. This despite recent Rand studies indicating that we are not significantly changing the crime rate through these policies. In fact, we may well be fostering an environment that produces more violence and, certainly, ever-increasing fiscal costs.

Let's start with the dollar cost: In the year 2001 the State of Oregon said that it cost $60 per day to lock up one inmate. (I'm sure it's higher now.) The facility I was in housed 3,000 inmates, so—$180,000 per day or $5,400,000 per month! That was just daily operations, forget the cost of building the facility and other maintenance, and that was just one of sixteen facilities!

Bear in mind, a great many of those inmates were once taxpayers, and some were even employers. That contribution to the tax base is now gone; they went from a plus to a minus in the state's economy—a double whammy! And then, there are the families who were supported by an inmate and who must now seek public assistance. And, don't forget the cost of prosecution and putting people in prison.

Are there not, then, people who are dangerous and should be locked up? Of course there are—but they are a surprisingly small percentage of the total prison population. But since we are operating in a system of retribution, all must pay, dearly. Of course, Joe Citizen does not realize that the more he makes the inmates pay, the more *he* pays—often at the cost of public education and other social services.

Now we come to mandatory sentencing and prison packing. Under mandatory sentencing, at least in this state, the prosecutor actually runs the court. The judge will almost entirely defer to the prosecutor except when it comes time to check the sentencing chart and sign off (as in my case). Until recently, the judge could upward depart a sentence (above the sentencing chart) without a jury, and in rare cases might lower depart a sentence.

The public defender (or pretender) is almost always the creature of the prosecution, picked for his ability to *not* defend his client, never challenge false information, never object to *suppression* of evidence that might exonerate his client. In fact, I am aware of two cases where the public defender pretty much slept through the trial. Truly, this is not *Perry Mason*!

We must understand that the district attorney or prosecutor is elected on the numbers (to some degree, this is true of judges as well). Out of so many cases, what was his or her percentage of convictions? In most cases, it's nearly 100 percent. One might ask, "Were they really all guilty?" Probably not, but who cares? This is how prison-packing occurs.

While a stated principle of law is supposed to be "Innocent until proven guilty," the opposite is true in practice. To be accused (and there need be no complainant in this state) is to be found guilty. How is this done? The accused is always offered a plea bargain. One crime is spun out into innumerable counts. Here's a for-instance: a fistfight. Besides the usual assault charges, there is also a kidnapping charge (worth 20 years) by virtue of one person causing another person's body to move. It's done all the time in this state . . . Innocent or guilty, you don't dare to roll the dice or you could be doing *a lot* more time than is offered in a plea bargain.

Bear in mind that in this state, hearsay or second-hand testimony is perfectly acceptable, and one may not even face their accuser in court (they only need say "I'm afraid for my life"). The opportunities for manufacturing evidence (I am familiar with several such cases) abound. Secret grand juries are the norm here as well. And, yes, there really *are* a lot of innocent people locked up—the system simply does not care.

Nowhere is this more easily seen than in sex crimes. All it takes is an estranged wife who is going through a divorce and (a) wants to get back at her soon-to-be ex-husband, (b) wants to be sure to gain custody of the kids, and (c) wants all the property. It's simple: accuse him of a sex crime, coach a daughter to say the magic words, and it's all hers. This also happens with ex-girlfriends.

Some people may be unaware that sex crimes encompass everything from a high school student sending a picture of a partially clad classmate to a friend, to a person arrested for urinating in a public park behind a bush, to actual rapist/murderers. They are heaped under the same heading, "Sex Offender," expected to fulfill the same requirements and equally ostracized by the "solid" prisoners who do not have "skin beefs."

So, why do so many come back to prison? There are several good reasons: there are more than a few who have been locked up since their teen years, often early teens, who have no life experience outside of prison. Usually, they will get out without any job skills or high school diploma, not even knowing how to balance a checkbook—if they know what one is. If they are lucky, they will at least start off in some kind of transitional housing or at a mission.

Repeat offenders are seldom given any reason or motivation to change their ways, especially since work is nearly impossible to find. Prison has trained them only to be better criminals. Picture this: a young first-time offender in a large prison being mentored in all the ways to cook, grow, or sell dope. Yes, a fine education! By the way, most college programs have disappeared, at least in this state.

The kind of genuine one-on-one counseling that would do the most good is simply not available. People with the title "counselor" in our system are simply bureaucrats paid to keep inmate records in order; any attempt at genuine counseling can result in disciplinary action against said counselor for "inappropriate inmate/staff relations." (It has happened.)

Also, consider this: the longer people are incarcerated (think mandatory minimums), the less chance that there will be any support system in place when they get out. Spouses will divorce them, other family and friends disappear or lose interest, old employers go away or lose interest in rehiring them. Often, whatever savings they had will be magically gone by the time they get out. Also, they can become institutionalized.

Prisons cannot simply be looked at by themselves; they are part of a much larger system that includes law enforcement, the judicial system, and the parole system.

First, we need to recognize that not *everything* needs to be criminalized. (How's the War on Drugs going? Are we winning? How about prostitution?)

Up front, there must be a concerted effort to find out if someone is *actually* guilty—that would help. First-time offenders, in many cases, should be put on probation with real community service (maybe something that fits the crime?) rather than being immediately hauled off to prison.

There are many cases where convicted persons do not pose a threat to a community and might better serve the community through fines, community service, and counseling. It has often impressed me, while in prison, that there is a huge waste of smart, creative, *gentle* people who are serving time, wasting the taxpayers' money simply because they shouldn't be here.

Last I heard, some years ago, Denmark had a recidivism rate of 23 percent! Yes, and a number of other countries had similarly low numbers. Is it possible we could learn something from them? Of course, they are *serious* about dealing with recidivism and know that longer sentences are not the answer. Here, people are so concerned about the up-front cost of rehabilitation, they forget about the background cost of *not* doing it: the cost of new crimes against property or people, the cost of new prosecution and imprisonment, and the cost of another lost life. Post-prison reentry should be about helping people succeed, rather than looking for reasons to send them back to jail.

If we will look at countries that are succeeding at this game, we will realize that there *is* a better way.

ROYAL GENE DOMINGO JONES, SR., *Wisconsin*

REAL LIFE IN PRISON

I remember it as if it were yesterday. I was seven years old, it was 1975, and we had just moved from San Francisco, California. Mom was a single white mother with three mixed-race children—my two older sisters and me. I recall this being the only normal part of my life. I was just a little boy: I played in the dirt with my toy trucks, I even had a G.I. Joe doll—like I said, just a little boy.

Some days I'd walk to the store with a note to get smokes for my mother—it was a common practice back in those days. Some days I'd just be a little kid out and about with no real purpose other than being a kid who was out and about. The first time the police were ever called on me was when I climbed the fence in our backyard and went into the next yard and stole apples off the tree. I know, it doesn't sound like it'd turn to a life of crime. The next time, though, was the serious stuff. I went into the Albertson's and stole a candy bar. It wasn't no big deal, considering I'd done it dozens of times before, only this time when I walked out of the supermarket a huge man approached me and asked to see what I had in my pockets. I was busted, and I guess he must've been obligated to call the police. I remember it like it was yesterday, and the ass whippin' was old-school. You know, the one where the more you move during the beating the more you get it?

I don't know how I picked up stealing, I mean, I wasn't raised up around it at that point, and I hadn't been exposed to it. I guess I was just sneaky and felt if I could outsmart you then you were just outsmarted. For the next thirty-five years I never took a break. I started off going to the Contra Costa County Juvenile Hall at age seven. I knew all the counselors, the judges, and probation officers. By the time I was thirteen years old, I'd done more time than the average person would do in a lifetime. My criminal history went from theft to assaults, to weapons, to drugs, and to murder, and everything in between. Over those thirty-five years I have spent nights or days in over two hundred different cells, two state prison systems and the federal prison system (BOP), and in over seventeen different prisons. Since 1975 I have had two birthdays on the street: the first one was in 1991, and the second one was in 1993 after serving a parole violation.

When I was seventeen, I managed to find myself being tried as an adult and sentenced to six years in state prison, and because of my criminal history up to that point I was sent to Folsom State Prison, which at the time was the worst of the worst of the California prison system. While I was in the Sacramento County Jail in Sacramento, California, my oldest daughter was born. Her mother brought her to see me when she was just a few days old. I didn't see her again until she was seventeen months, and by then I was in Folsom. When I finally did get out, I met the woman I would later marry. Our first daughter was born in 1989 while I was back in prison serving a parole violation. When I got out after the year violation, I caught another violation, and it was at that time our second daughter was born. After I got out we had our first son. I was there for his birth, though as I recall I had a warrant out by that time for failure to appear in court. I had taken my wife to Mexico to Christmas-shop and had managed to get a speeding ticket as we were flying through Southern California on our return to Sacramento. I failed to go to court because my son was due around that time, and I just didn't feel like traveling back to Southern California just for a speeding ticket, and I really wasn't concerned about a warrant. In 1993 I decided that it was time to leave California, and so we packed up and moved to Montana. It was there in 1993 that my youngest son was born, and then, too, I was already in jail. However, the sheriff there in Lewiston, Montana, came to my jail cell and said, "Royal, the Mrs. has had the baby and so I'm gonna take you to the hospital to see your son." When we were getting all ready, the sheriff made certain to tell me that he didn't want no problems from me. When we got to the hospital, I got to see my baby boy. Though when my wife asked could the sheriff take off the handcuffs so I could hold him, the sheriff was very direct. No!

Over the years, I've watched the entire system change. I've seen the lawyers get worse, the judges get worse, and the prosecutors get worse. I've watched the law-enforcement officers lie on the witness stand even though they didn't have to. I've seen the guards beat prisoners, I've been on the end of those beatings a time or two, and I've seen the guards set the prisoner(s) up too, and again I've been on the receiving end of that as well.

There was a time once while in Folsom State Prison I had protected an associate from being stabbed. I knocked the knife out of the hand of the would-be attacker moments before it was to sink into my associate's back. It was agreed, however, that the matter was over. Yet two months later while I was sweeping the tier, I felt this hard blow to the left side of my lower back. When I turned around, I noticed this man trying to get his knife unwrapped from within his coat sleeve. It appeared that it got tangled, or caught in his sleeve when he drew back prior to his strike. His knife slid down his palm, causing me to receive a hard blow from his fist with no penetration from his blade. I knew the situation required immediate attention and I immediately went to work assaulting him. I knew it would only be seconds until the gunmen started shooting. But strangely I never spoke, didn't shout, just turned toward my attacker and became the attacker. Seconds later there were gunshots ringing out into the building. Once I was shot at three times. It was September 27, 1987, in New Folsom State Prison. These two guys were walking and they kinda got too close to me, and so I struck to the left, and then to the right, attacking both men. They fought back as though they were being attacked by a crazy person—which I am not, but after the first attempt one never knows when the next one is coming.

The things I have learned about doing time have really given me a different outlook on life, as well as on this entire prison life. I see the things they don't talk about in the news, or put in the movies. In fact I have never seen a single movie that really gives a true account as to what prison life is like. Sure, there have been those movies that might touch base to some degree on points here and there, but for the most part no movie I have ever seen really portrays prison life the way prison life really is.

Many people have no clue as to all the politics that go on every single day, whether amongst prisoners, within the administration, or between the administration and the prison. I know the truth about the system, how it works and the true hidden demons. I know the public only sees the Rodney King events as being a rare case of law-enforcement misconduct, when I know it to be a very common thing, both by law-enforcement officers and prison personnel. Anyone that has been arrested knows that law-enforcement officers and/or agents can be very controlling and disrespectful. They tend to have this attitude that they are "above" the law simply because they have the gold stars on their chests. Yes, it is fair to say that an officer has to have some form of control in any given situation to ensure they can maintain order during their investigations or get a particular situation under control. However, many times when guards or police are on the scene of a situation, they become rude and disrespectful as if you don't have any rights at all. If the police are telling you to "shut up" and you don't for some reason, they will believe that this gives them the authority to slam you on the ground headfirst, to shut you up.

We often hear about how dangerous these prisons and jails are. We automatically associate the dangers with the prisoners. After all, there are gangs, drug dealers, murderers, rapists, and just plain criminals. With such a group of individuals, one would have to think the environment is going to be dangerous. However, you hardly hear about the dangers of staff misconduct. With all the jails, prisons, camps, ranches, and juvenile centers, there are hundreds of thousands of complaints filed each year. These complaints range from rape to murder. Many complaints against prison personnel are "inconclusive." This is mostly because there are no witnesses, or those witnesses are other staff members. Thus the Office of Inspector General, which is responsible for overseeing prison personnel, often concludes that there is not enough evidence to support the allegation of staff misconduct. However, one can find a lot of cases where staff members have been tried and convicted over the years in the *Prison Legal News*, a monthly legal newspaper that specifically deals with these issues. Guards might simply not like a prisoner, and out of this dislike tell other prisoners false things about an individual, and these false statements could very easily get other prisoners to respond toward that prisoner in a very serious and violent manner. Last year a guard told some prisoners that a particular individual was a child molester. That person was killed by other prisoners, though he was not a child molester.

The truth about prison is in many cases so disturbing that the public really doesn't want to know about it. For the most part the prisoner has free food, no bills, free rent, cable TV, microwaves, workout tools, free education, and so much more; so some individuals are able to do five and ten years as if it were a walk in the park. Many times the prosecution already knows what type of deal it can offer an individual simply from understanding what that individual has already experienced. For example, an individual who has done his entire life in and out of prison and lockup isn't going to be concerned about a five-year sentence, so if the prosecutor wants to end the case and just secure the conviction, he simply tells the lawyer for the defense, "Tell your client I'll give him five." Depending what the charge is, ten may even sound good. The system is so broken that today the United States houses over 2.2 million people in jails and prisons. Complaints about (not) care taking, abuse, and/or other violations often fall upon deaf ears. As stated by a warden once, "Society has real problems out there; they have children they're trying to feed, tuition they are trying to pay, bills they are trying to pay, and jobs they are trying to keep or find." (This came after some stabbings on the yard, which led the warden to hold a town hall meeting to tell the prisoners that he would lock the prison down for the next three months, and that anyone having a problem with it could write their judges, lawyers, congressmen, or the President, because in his view the "real world" was going through real problems.)

Society doesn't want to believe that the very people maintaining "order" in the prison system are doing wrong, and even if there is a case from time to time that is exposed, no one wants the prison guard to take the blame on his/her own. After all, they will proclaim, "If you didn't go to prison in the first place it would have never happened."

The reality is that prison is a completely different world from anything one could envision. It is not like the movies, where you stab me and that is the end of it. A stabbing could ignite an entire war between different groups of people. To end a war could take years. In the meantime, people can be stabbed every single day. In Folsom State Prison, just in 1985–86 there were close to one hundred stabbings. The aftermath of the war was almost worse, as individuals stabbed people in their organizations that didn't do enough stabbing in the war. People can point fingers at whomever they want to: the cause for the majority of prison violence is not simply who is in the prisons, though that does play some role; rather it is how these environments are run and overseen. Some prisons have just as many violent offenders as the next but have less violence. This is evidence that something is in fact working, while something else is not working. A lot of this can be attributed to the lack of programming, or how those programs are run. When I was in Folsom State Prison back in the '80s the government still offered prisoners the Pell grant. Back then I took English Lit, believing for some reason that being able to write a paper on Ben Franklin was in some way going to place me back into society with some type of meaningful goal. That was not the case. However, there were those individuals that did in fact take advantage of the education and turned those grants into degrees. It was these successful individuals that caused the government to rethink the grant for prisoners and pull it out of the prison system. It could be argued that it was unfair to give the prisoners free college educations while individuals in the free world were struggling to get one. However, the taxpayers may have saved a million over the years in college tuitions, but I'm certain they have spent billions over the years on re-offenders. There fails to be a balance between what the goal is and how to achieve it.

Sure, as a free society we want safe communities for ourselves and our families. We want to know that our persons and property are safe from foul play and unjust treatment. But when the very foundation on which criminal-justice employees stand becomes corrupt, vile, and criminal, then we as a society have a bigger problem. Where there is corruption, it is never seen as a system problem, just a local one, merely the acts of individuals. However, if you look objectively, you see that it is in fact a system breakdown and not merely a local problem. Thousands upon thousands of prisoners each day file complaints with courts, administration, civil organizations, congressmen and congresswomen, senators, commissioners, etc. etc., all alleging some form of mistreatment, abuse, neglect, or other violations.

Prisons benefit society, and they also harm a society. Individuals that violate the rights of others have to be held accountable for such violations. But our society has left it up to officials who for the most part have their own hidden agendas. We simply lock an individual away for an appointed amount of time, only to release him back into a society where he/she has already had problems, with no new skills or trade. The public for the most part is misled to believe that every time they see someone get arrested again that "He's just a mess-up." True, we are accountable for our own actions, and I am the last to suggest otherwise. However, we also have to expect that the individuals hired to help inmates will in fact do all they can to help the individuals that may pose a threat.

There is a common question prisoners hear: "Why did you return to a life of crime when you got out?" Criminals, and I identify myself as one, do not look at the "criminal" aspect of their lifestyle as a means to harm others. Rather they see it as a means of survival. In fact, there are few criminals that commit crimes that are "senseless." The individual trying to eat who steals, well he's trying to eat. The intention behind the action wasn't to wrong someone, rather it was to fulfill a need.

Though I do not point the finger entirely at the system for me breaking the law, I do present a question to all those over the past thirty-five years that have dealt with me: "What did you do to help me better myself?" I don't suggest that I am in prison because *they* didn't do enough. I am asking because I believe that somewhere in the answer lies part of the problem we face in trying to fix the system. When your hired guards hit me, do you think that pretending that it didn't happen will resolve the matter? When I seek to gain a higher education and you tell me that the taxpayers don't care if I get an education or not on their dime, is it going to help me?

For thirty-five years I have seen your doctors and talked to your psychologists who hope to probe the mind and find the hidden secrets as to what makes a criminal tick. Well I'll tell you, being told your prosecutors didn't lie in court, or didn't set me up with a weapon; that your state employees didn't assault me unjustly, that they didn't damage my property, and didn't subject me to injustice . . . What makes me tick is knowing that the system tries to suppress the truth because this truth exposes its own criminality. The system doesn't work as it is today, and the evidence is in the 2.2 million people incarcerated and the 65 percent returning to prison each year. Sure, it is easy to think and say that we are the problem; after all, we are the ones returning. But if I just spent thirty-five years of my life in and out of a system, doesn't anyone want to know what is wrong with it? If I went to the University of California, L.A., for thirty-five years and still couldn't get a degree, would anyone simply pin the entire blame on me? What if 65 percent of us didn't get degrees?

The taxpayers are spending billions of dollars to make sure not only that the individuals are held accountable for their misconduct, but that when they come out of prison they will be productive individuals. A man serves ten years in prison, he gets out with no family or support. He has no skills in a job market where even the highly skilled are having trouble finding work. What does he do? I will tell you what he will do: he will survive the best way he knows how. His goal or desire isn't necessarily to wrong anyone, it's simply to have a place to sleep, food to eat, and clothes on his back. Does that in and by itself make him a criminal, because he desires to live? After all, we live in a world so selfish that we walk right by the poor and hungry without shame. There is a country song I love called "Don't Laugh at Me." The singer talks about that individual standing there on the corner holding the "Need Food" sign, and explains that you don't know how he got there. You don't know how that man lost his wife and son and what state that left him in. What about the hundreds of thousands of prisoners that started life in broken homes, being abused by parents, had parents on drugs, didn't have food to eat so they stole to eat, that were raped by their own fathers, brothers, and other family members? What about that child who started off using drugs because no one was around to tell him not to, because no one cared? What about the individual who started life taking care of her siblings because the father was gone and the mother was on crack? It is so easy to say that prisoners are grown men and women, and they knew what they were doing when they broke the law. For the most part you are right. But your reasoning and theirs are different. You think that if someone doesn't sit down and study what they need to know to get that job, that individual has no one to blame but himself. What you fail to consider is that maybe that individual doesn't have discipline, a characteristic that requires patience. Discipline isn't just something you wake up one morning and find under your pillow left by the Discipline Fairy, it is something that takes years of sound teaching. But how does the child that was never taught discipline learn to be disciplined? The reality is that prisoners don't just pop up in prison, or return to prison because they are simply stupid individuals with no sense of direction. They may not *understand* how to get from point "A" to point "B" because no one ever properly explained it. Sure you can say to me, "Get a job"—but what if I just don't understand how to get one, let alone keep one?

I sit here today after doing time for everything from petty theft to murder, and I ask myself, "What have I done to succeed, and what have I done to fail?" I believe that this prison system needs to do more, and I also believe the prisoners themselves need to do more to help themselves; I understand the system and I know what it offers and what it does not offer. I understand that if the prison system and prisoners work together with the community, then there is a better chance of success. Until then, this is real prison life, in here and out there. There are millions of great men and women behind these walls, millions of stories. We are not all *failures*, we've just *failed* a time or two.

SHAKA SENGHOR, *Michigan*

23 AND 1

I stared through the barred windows at the heavy gray clouds that hung above the maximum-security prison I was housed in, listening to the sounds of rapper Beanie Sigel's acidic voice pour through my headphones. As Beanie angrily spit the verse "What you know about 23 and 1 lock down / all day underground / never seeing your son," his words carved a fresh wound in my battle-scarred soul. I knew all too well the 23-hour-a-day lockdown he was talking about. At the time, I was deeply entrenched in what turned out to be a 4½ year stretch in the "hole."

It was not the first time I had done a stretch in the "soul-breaker," as we called it. In my first year in prison, I found myself serving a one-year stint in solitary confinement for "assault on an inmate," "assault on staff," and "dangerous contraband." I split that year in the hole between the Michigan Reformatory and Standish Maximum Security Prison. It was my first foray into the abysmal subculture that was the subject of whispered conversations on prison yards and behind the closed doors of the administration's office. It was a place where a twisted game of tug of war played itself out between the humane and inhumane. It was in this cold, dark, heartless place that I came face to face with a gruesome reality: the isolation and inhumane conditions of solitary confinement were responsible for distorting the psyches of countless men and women.

My first stint in the hole was the first time I had witnessed the tearing asunder of the human soul. At nineteen years old, I was thrown head-first into a subculture of despair, loneliness, and deep-seated anger. I remember when the officer placed the burning cold handcuffs on my wrists and told me I was being taken to the hole. I literally thought they were going to throw me in a dirt-covered hole in the ground until they were convinced I had changed my behavior. I twisted and jerked around in the handcuffs as everything inside me told me to fight to get free; it was a deeply entrenched defense mechanism encoded in my DNA. I was a descendant of a slave people, and I was sure that my ancestors had rebelled against their captors. It felt natural for me to resist as much as I could, even though I knew deep inside that I couldn't burst out of the handcuffs. But resist I did.

After being subdued by several officers, I was carted off to the hole and thrown into the shower, where I was strip-searched. The officer conducting the strip search nearly broke my arm as he pulled it out of the slot in the cage to remove the cuffs. I had assaulted one of his coworkers, and he was letting me know that he didn't appreciate it. Once the cuffs were off, I was forced to strip out of my clothes. As I stood naked in the middle of the shower room, I felt like a slave on an auction block. When the officer returned, he threw an oversized brown jumpsuit through the slot. I dressed hastily and was then escorted to a segregation cell. When I realized the "hole" was nothing more than another cellblock, I calmed down a little. At the time, I was at a new regional facility called Carson City, so the cell was modern and clean. A smirk crossed my face as I looked around. I thought to myself, if this was all they had to control me, they would be in for a surprise when I was released. It wasn't until a couple days later that I realized I was the one in for a shock.

One evening after chow, I was told to pack up all of my property; I was getting transferred in the morning back to the Michigan Reformatory in Ionia, where I would be placed on long-term segregation status. In prison vernacular, we called it "lay down." When I first came to the hole, I asked one of the inmates who had been in prison for a while why they had given it that name. He responded with a laugh before saying, "Because down here, all you can do is lay your ass down and read, lay your ass down and write, or lay your ass down and talk shit all day. So it's up to you, young blood, how you do it, but all I can tell you is, don't take this shit laying down." The administration, on the other hand, chose to use the much more lofty euphemism "administrative segregation." It sounded politically correct, and oh so professional, but when they weren't on record, they called it the "hole" like the rest of us.

During the forty-minute ride back to Ionia, thoughts of what the "hole" would be like tumbled through my head like a gymnast. Horror stories of how inmates in the hole had been found hung in their cells, or mysteriously suffocated with their own socks, or how the officers would come into your cell with the goon squad and beat you two breaths short of death, all ran tirelessly through my mind. What about all of the resistance I had put up? What if the officers at the other prison called their buddies to give me a nice work over?

After being processed, I was escorted to the hole in a cellblock known as the "Graves." It had earned the moniker from the captives there because once you were thrown in the "Graves," it was like being entombed in a place where you lost sight of time. It was as though you were dead to everyone in general population, and the cells were so small that you felt like you had been squeezed into a coffin.

Being sentenced to "lay down" was to be sentenced to an indeterminate amount of time in hell. The first thing I noticed when I entered the cellblock was the gloomy ambiance. The windows were painted gray, and the only natural light present was the few streams that snuck through when the officers were nice enough to leave one of the windows cracked, which was very rare. Being stripped of all personal belongings, with the exception of the bare necessities, made it impossible to tell if it was morning or night unless you asked the officers or the windows were open. Other than that, I had to guess the time based on when my meals were passed out.

As I was escorted down to my cell, I had to navigate my way around spoiled food, empty milk cartons, fecal-stained towels, and piles of shredded and soiled paper. I kept my head straight forward as I walked toward my cell, but out of the corner of my eye, I could see several captives standing at their bars looking out curiously. I had learned from day one inside of the Reformatory not to look into another captive's cell. It was an old code of respect. Since we were already being deprived of so much by the system, we didn't want to deny each other the last semblance of privacy, so we didn't look into each other's cells. Not everyone stayed true to this code, and it was often the cause of conflict, leading the Peeping Tom to be stabbed on the yard, or flashed with genitalia. I had no desire to see another man shaking his private parts in anger, nor did I have a desire to stab anyone or get stabbed for looking in someone's cell, so I always kept my head forward.

When I reached my cell, the bars squeaked open and the officer ordered me to step inside. Once the bars closed shut, he removed the handcuffs and left. I looked around at the dingy cell in disgust. The bed was six inches off the floor and the toilet was stuffed behind a small footlocker. In order to sit down and take a dump, I had to remove my whole jumpsuit so that I could fold my legs behind the locker.

After my initial observations, I stood at my cell bars for the next hour waiting on the officer to make his round so that I could get some cleaning supplies to sanitize my cell. To my surprise, it was relatively quiet, but as I would soon learn, this was the calm before the storm. Most of the captives in the hole slept the bulk of their days away, only waking up to get their food trays. Once the final meal of the day was passed out, the cellblock would come alive with activity.

When the officer returned, I asked him for some cleaning supplies and was informed that the porters would pass them out after lunch, so I continued to stand at the bars until lunch. There was no way I was going to sit or lay down on a mattress that someone else had sweated and farted on without it being sanitized. When the porters arrived with our food trays, I took mine and stood at the bars eating the hastily thrown-together meal. The portions were nearly a half-size smaller than what I was used to receiving in general population. I devoured the small meal in all of five minutes, like a ravenous wolf, and placed my tray on the bars. I didn't really like drinking milk all that much, so I left the carton sitting on the locker. When they came around to pick up trays, one of the porters whispered that I had better hide the milk in my locker unless I wanted to be placed on food loaf. I placed the milk back on the tray as I looked at him curiously. I had never heard of food loaf, but from the way he conveyed the message, I could tell it was something very bad. I also realized his "Man, you crazy" look was letting me know that in the hole, no food was to be wasted. That milk I threw back on the tray could have bought me a bag of cereal, a juice, or an extra piece of toast. In the hole, everything pertaining to eating and smoking was to be bartered, and nothing was to be wasted. Once they banned smoking, a cigarette smuggled in could net you three dollars in store items. It was in the hole that I learned to start eating Brussels sprouts and a few other things I would have never eaten if I were in general population. Every time I ate green beans or Brussels sprouts, I thought about all of the times my parents had tried to get me to eat them when I was a child, and I felt some shame.

After the trays were picked up, a porter came back and handed me some cleaning supplies. I swept beneath the small bunk and was surprised at how much dirt and dust came from under the bed. I washed the mattress, toilet and sink down before making my bed. After I cleaned up and laid back on the bunk, I drifted off into a fitful sleep. My mind was full of thoughts that I had stuffed deep down inside where they were safe. All of the things I had hidden from while in general population by watching television or playing basketball to exhaustion now came rushing back to the forefront of my mind. I dreamt of how soft my son's mother's lips used to feel against mine. I dreamt of how good it used to feel to guzzle down an ice-cold forty-ounce on a hot summer day. I dreamt of the late-night laughter that echoed through the 'hood as we sat on the porch at two in the morning playing the dozens. My dreams were a kaleidoscope of all that my life had been, and all that it could have been.

I was awakened by the sound of the chow cart squeaking down the tier. I retrieved my tray and sucked down the bland slop that they called dinner, and this time I drank the milk. Despite my aversion to plain milk, it sure beat the brownish water that drizzled out of the old porcelain sink in my cell. I set the tray on the bars, laid back on my bunk, and forced myself back to sleep in an attempt to retrieve those lost and stolen dreams, but to no avail. After the officers picked up the food trays, they passed out mail, and the cellblock was pretty quiet for the next few hours. The hum of a few conversations could be heard as inmates discussed religion, politics, and stories of their lives on the streets. Stories shared between inmates were our way of staying connected to the neighborhoods we came from. It was one of the few means we had of touching, tasting, and smelling our former lives, if only for a few minutes. It didn't matter if you were part of the conversation or not, you could relate, because when it was all said and done, most Black communities were pretty much the same. So when I sat back on my bunk listening to guys from Flint,

Saginaw, or Lansing talking about their neighborhoods and what they had been through, it was like reliving my own memories of life before prison.

One of the things about prison is that you have some very amusing storytellers with expansive imaginations, capable of creating the kind of vivid imagery that would put Hollywood screenwriters to shame. I have always marveled at how a person could remember the exact color of their socks, how much money they had in their pocket to the nearest dime, and all the ingredients that were used to make the meal on the day they got shot, had sex for the first time, or made their first thousand. When retelling a story, everyone has a tendency to embellish things a little, but in the hole, there were a few captives who were infamous for their ability to tell a lie-filled story that was so entertaining that each night everyone would grow quiet as they recounted their neighborhood exploits.

As the voices hummed about from cell to cell, I found myself thinking about how I had arrived at this point in my life. Growing up, I never imagined that I would be living my life out caged in a cell like a wild animal. I was too smart for this shit, I thought angrily as I stared up at the paint-chipped ceiling. But no matter how many times I closed and opened my eyes, my nightmarish existence was still there. After speaking with several captives at length, I realized that most of us go through this extreme feeling of disbelief. At some point, we all think this is a nightmare, and that at any moment we will awaken and be back home in the warm comfort of our own bed. But we all learn after years of incarceration that prison is all too real. And for me, things were about to get more real than I could have ever imagined.

After getting bored listening to the conversations going on around me, I decided to get up and write a few letters. The first I wrote to my son's mother, and then to my ex-girlfriend in Ohio. Before I knew it, I was writing to everyone I knew. The hours spun past quickly as I scratched out letter after letter with a dull two-inch pencil. When the third shift came on at ten o'clock, I was still immersed in writing letters.

It was through writing letters home that I realized writing was my escape. With a pen and piece of paper, I could get away whenever I wanted to. I could go stand on the corner in my neighborhood and no one could stop me. I could drive down the freeway and go see my ex-girlfriend in Ohio if that was what I wanted to do, and the bars and wired fences couldn't hold me back. Writing was freedom! So I wrote until midnight when they cut the power off and my fingers became sore to the bone.

When the lights went out, the cellblock had an eerie feel to it. I was on the bottom tier toward the end, and there were no lights in the hall near my cell, so I couldn't stand at the bars and read or write like guys who had lights in front of their cells. I climbed into my bunk and prayed that I could drift off into a deep sleep before the dreams of my life before prison came back to haunt me. I had to get away from them; otherwise I knew I would go insane. There was nothing I could do to change my reality, and I didn't need to be constantly reminded by the dreams. As I lay there trying to capture sleep, the world around me exploded into chaos.

"Get y'all bitch ass up. Ain't no sleep around here," a loud voice called, followed by a sound as loud and startling as a shotgun blast in a small church. Boom! Boom! Boom! The sound came relentlessly as the voice banged the lid down on his footlocker over and over, which set into motion a chain of events that was unlike anything I had ever imagined. For the next four hours, the hole became an anarchist stronghold as inmates banged lockers and hurled racial epithets and disparaging homosexual remarks through the air like hand grenades. Some stuffed their toilets with sheets and flushed until water cascaded over the tier like Victoria Falls.

I stared out of my cell in disbelief as the floor quickly became a small wading pool. Trash and sheets that had been set on fire flew out of countless cells. After their initial attempts to restore order by turning off the water supply to all of the cells, the officers gave up. As dawn slowly crept upon us, everyone settled down and the cellblock grew quiet again.

The only thing that seemed to be stirring was a giant rat the size of a possum, who the captives had named "Food Loaf," after the loaf-of-bread-sized brick of mashed-up food that was fed to recalcitrant captives. I watched as Food Loaf sludged through the murky water to retrieve the soggy bread and rotted apple cores that had been thrown out onto the cellblock floors. He moved with a quiet confidence about him that came as a result of being around hundreds of people every day. The rest of the vermin that darted in and out of the cells were more cautious. I often wondered why no one had killed Food Loaf, but then it dawned on me. In a lot of ways, he was a lot like us. He was an outcast, and for the most part, he was despised by everyone and we could all identify with that. Though the term "rat" had been used over the years to describe someone who told on others to protect his own ass, Food Loaf had won our respect and was therefore allowed to coexist with us. His mousy cousins weren't as fortunate. Every opportunity we had, we killed them because they were invasive of our territory. It is hard to get along with vermin when they get in your bed at night or nibble on the food you had stored away to get through another day.

My days in the Graves were pretty much the same, night in and night out. After a few days, I too learned how to sleep through the mornings and afternoons. After nearly six months in the Graves, I was transferred to Standish Maximum Security Facility, where a whole new level of hell awaited me. Upon my arrival at the newly designed facility, I was brought into the control center where several officers stood around glaring at me. I maintained a stoic expression as they talked their tough correctional-officer talk. I was no longer new to the psychological warfare that was waged between officers and captives. It was a protracted war of attrition that had been ongoing from the time the first prison was built. As I glanced around at the technologically advanced prison, the officer began removing the black box that was wrapped around my handcuffs to prevent an escape. Once he removed the black box, another officer approached with a pair of handcuffs that were attached to what looked like a dog leash. It was the first time I had seen anything like it, and my immediate thoughts were that it had to be in violation of the Universal Declaration of Human Rights. But I guess, in the prisoncrat's mind, being leashed like a dog didn't violate Article 5, which states, "No one shall be subjected to torture or to cruel, inhuman or degrading treatment or punishment."

Despite what they thought, I definitely felt degraded. I mean, how could I not feel degraded when I was being treated like a common house pet? One officer placed the handcuffs on as the other officer removed the first pair. They did this in a synchronized way to minimize the time in which either of my hands was free from the other. After removing one pair of shackles and replacing them with another, the officers chatted with each other before the transfer officers left. I was then taken to the hole in Cellblock 1. I shuffled along in the shackles as two officers held on tightly to the leash that was attached to my handcuffs, until I reached the unit. All was relatively quiet when I first stepped into the block.

The design of the prison was totally different from the Reformatory, which was over one hundred years old. Inside the unit, there were four wings—two upper wings and two lower wings. I was taken to the lower wing on one side of the unit. The first thing I noticed was that the hallways were free of debris, and instead of bars there were large steel doors with window covers on them.

Once I reached what would be my cell, the officer in the control bubble hit a button, the cell door slid open, and I was ordered to step inside. Once inside, the door slid shut behind me with a finality that resonates inside of me to this day. As the officer removed the handcuffs and shackles and prepared to leave, I asked him if my window shutter could remain open, and he said no, before banging it shut.

For the first time in my short incarceration, I felt alone as I looked around the spartan cell. A flat green mattress lay folded on top of a thick slab of concrete that protruded from the wall. Another shorter slab of concrete protruded from the back wall over the concrete bed, and I soon discovered this to be the writing surface or television stand for those who had a TV. A steel toilet/sink combination sat in the corner up by the door, and a large steel locker was bolted to the floor adjacent to the concrete bed. I rolled the mattress out, placed the sheets on it along with the blankets, and then sat back. A few minutes later, a piece of thick paper attached to a string came sliding beneath my door. I didn't know what it was, so I just sat on my bunk staring down at it until someone called out my cell number and told me to pull on the line. I didn't know what was going on, so I came to the door and asked who it was. I was informed that it was my neighbor across the hall. I climbed down on the floor, peeked under the door, and saw the string coming from his cell. As I began to pull, I noticed a few magazines slide from beneath his door. I pulled them in and took them off the line. Inside was a short note introducing himself and letting me know if I needed something else to read to just holler over at him. His name was Lowrider, and he turned out to be a cool older guy. He understood the old convict code that said when someone first arrives, you do what you can to make their time a little bit easier, and that was something I could relate to.

Within a couple of days, I found out some of the guys I had been at the Reformatory with were there; they, along with Lowrider, filled me in on the running of the prison, and I soon got into a nice routine. I had always loved to read and Standish had a very nice library, so I started sending over there for books whenever I could. I also read every magazine that someone was willing to slide under my door. I quickly learned to make a fish line like the one Lowrider had slid beneath my door, and I used it to drive up and down the wing to retrieve whatever reading materials people had for me.

My stay on that wing was short, as I was going back and forth down to the county jail on a writ regarding the case for which I was serving time in the hole. When I returned a few months later, they moved me to a different wing, and it was then that I was introduced to a form of madness that would characterize the rest of my stay in the hole at Standish Maximum.

When I first got arrested in 1991, my father and stepmother were working at Lafayette Clinic, which was a psychiatric hospital close to downtown Detroit. While I was in the county jail, my father was on the local news speaking out against the budget cuts, which caused the state to close a lot of its mental institutions. This trend continued throughout the nineties, and it wasn't until a few years into my incarceration that I was able to make the connection between what I witnessed in prison in general, and the hole in particular. Instead of keeping the psychiatric hospitals open throughout the state, they closed them down and herded all of the patients into various state prisons, with most landing in maximum security. Because most of the patients with psychiatric needs are hard to manage in general population, they end up being housed in the hole, where their psychiatric problems are exacerbated by the hostile environment. In addition to the hostile treatment they receive from the officers, they also have to face hostility from other captives who don't understand psychiatric disorders like schizophrenia, bipolar disorder, and the like.

I was like many of the captives who didn't understand what was going on when I returned to the prison from the county jail. My first day back on the cellblock, they moved an inmate across from me named Reed. As they were putting him in the cell, he and the officers were having a heated exchange. I jumped down on my floor and peeked beneath the door to see what was going on as they forced him into his cell. Once inside, I heard them giving him an order to turn around so that they could remove the mask from his face. I stood back up, listening and peeking out the crack of my door so I could see what they were talking about as they left. I noticed them carrying a black mesh mask that looked like something out of a fetish magazine. I would later learn that they placed masks on the heads of captives who they considered to be spitters or biters.

When lunchtime came along and the officers arrived at Reed's cell door, they asked him if he wanted his food loaf, and he told them to get the hell away from his door. He said he would rather starve to death than eat food loaf. As I sat there listening, I looked down at the small rations on my tray, and despite how hungry I was, I knew I couldn't eat my rations without offering to share them with the brother. I liked the fact that he wasn't willing to bow down and accept inferior treatment. I slid my "car" over to him with a small note attached, asking him if he wanted half of my food. He wrote back that he did, so I took half of my food and placed it in a few envelopes, attached them to the line, and slid them across to him. He pulled in quickly so as not to be detected by the officers. For the next two weeks, I shared every meal with him until he finally got off food loaf. I was happy to see him get off meal restriction, because that meant I could go back to my full rations and he could go back to his. When they passed out trays and he got his, he called me to the door. Sometimes on first shift, when one of the cool officers was working, they would leave our window shutters open until they picked up trays or until they got ready to change shifts. So I stepped up to the window. It was the first time they had left his window open, and it was the first time I got a chance to see him face to face. He was a tall, corpulent brother with a full beard that made him look like a brown-skinned version of the Ayatollah Khomeini.

"What's going on, Reed?" I asked as I approached the door.

"You know what?" he began.

"Naw, what?" I asked.

"Man, you a bitch-ass dick sucker. Now get your hoe ass on your bunk and lay down," he said as he broke up into maniacal laughter.

I stood there with my mouth agape for a few minutes as my temper burned red hot. It was the first time I had been blatantly disrespected since I had entered prison, and I was completely thrown off. Add to this the fact that I had shared half of my meal with him for two weeks, not only starving myself, but also risking being placed on food loaf along with him. Of course, I was pissed, and I knew the first chance I got once I was out of the hole, I was going to stab Reed in his neck. I had to, otherwise the rest of the captives would feel like they could get away with disrespecting me, and I would rather die than live without my dignity and respect. He continued to hurl insult after insult as I sat on my bunk steaming. I even had to go back and ask myself if I had done something unintentionally to make him feel slighted in any way, and decided that wasn't the case. Maybe it was just a case of him taking my kindness for something other than what it was; whatever the case, I had made up my mind, and I was content with my decision to take care of Reed the first chance I got.

A few weeks later, I was released from the hole, and I patiently waited for the day when Reed would be released, but it never came. As I would learn over the years, there were some inmates who did their entire sentence in the hole to prevent anyone from getting to them. Any time they were scheduled for release, they would catch another misconduct so the Security Classification Committee would keep them in administrative segregation longer.

It wasn't until seven years later that I really began to understand the hole for what it was. On a crisp fall day in October 1999, my chances of ever getting out of prison were within two minutes of being stripped away forever, and I was once again returned to the hellish existence of the hole for nearly five years. It started on a cold Friday morning. The day started off normal enough, or at least as normal as a day in prison could be. I went to breakfast, and then to school. I had been at Muskegon Correctional Facility for two months, and I was really feeling good about where I was at that stage of my incarceration. It was the first time I had been placed in a lower security level, and I knew this was a step in the right direction as far as going home. When I initially arrived there, I decided to sign up for the automotive technology class. It was one of the better vocational classes in the system, and upon completion, the job prospects were good. The class was interesting, and I was learning a few things about cars that I knew would be beneficial if I stuck it out. But I have to admit, I always looked forward to Fridays, because I really hated having to get up early in the morning during the weekdays. So when the emergency-count siren began blaring, I was a happy camper; it meant I would be out of school early and we had the whole weekend ahead of us. The teacher dismissed us and we all walked back to our respective units. As I entered my unit, my bladder was on the verge of exploding, and I knew I had to make it to the bathroom before being locked down for count.

The sound of the siren pulsated through my brain; it was a sound that I had grown familiar with over the years. At some point each month, it was blown to signify emergency count, and we all had to drop whatever it was we were doing and return to our units. The only other time the siren was blown was when there was a serious assault, murder, rape, or an escape attempt. The frequency of the siren often depended on what joint you were at. In prisons like the Michigan Reformatory and the State Prison of Southern Michigan in Jackson, it could be heard more frequently.

When I reached the top of the steps in my unit, headed for the bathroom, I noticed several captives scurrying in and out of the bathroom. It was their last-ditch effort to relieve themselves before being locked down for the next hour and a half. As I approached the bathroom door, I knew there was going to be a problem. The officer standing at the door disliked me because of an incident that had occurred a few days before. It all started when I had been released from class early because our teacher was absent. It was during our morning yard period, and when I returned, I approached the desk and asked the officer to write me a pass to yard. At the time, he was engaged in a conversation with a new female officer. He looked up at me contemptuously and refused to write me a pass. I was not moved by his refusal, because I knew according to policy that I was entitled to go to yard. My citing of the policy compelled him to write me a pass, but deep inside, I knew that it would not come without a price. I figured he would, at a minimum, go and shake my cell down and throw my meager belongings around. However, I had desensitized myself to the value of property, so I wasn't really concerned about the shakedown. I had grown to understand that in order to survive in prison, I could not afford to grow attached to anything or anyone.

I knew that in his eyes, I didn't fit the criteria of the complacent, subservient captives he was accustomed to dealing with. I wasn't supposed to challenge his authority or quote policy, even though he was clearly in the wrong. As he saw it, I was supposed to walk away with my head lowered, mumbling to myself. But I refuse to accept a lesser status just because I am being held captive, and my refusal was the equivalent of a recalcitrant slave defying the authority of the plantation overseer.

It was not the first time I had witnessed the deeply entrenched white superiority complex common among white officers rear its ugly head. It was deeply embedded in the psyches of those white officers whose first contacts with people of other races came when they were hired, and could be activated by what appeared to be a shallow victory by a captive; there was just no way he could let a "nigga" get away with outsmarting him. Even the officers who professed not to have any racial prejudices were prone to exact revenge on a Black captive if they thought he had gotten over on them.

This dynamic is an indictment of the racial reality of America. Most white people cannot come to grips with the fact that Black people deserve to be treated with the dignity and respect that's due to all human beings whether we are incarcerated or not. When I started my incarceration, I vowed to never be one of those who bowed down, and I intended to do my time with as much of my humanity intact as my circumstances would allow. I was working every day to better myself and to learn all I could to deal with my anger and bitterness, and I realized that this rubbed a lot of officers the wrong way. As long as I refused to joke with the officers, waste my time playing cards and sports all day, and spent my time cultivating my mind, body, and spirit, I would be perceived as a threat. It was a reality that I refused to run from, and a reality that nearly cost me the rest of my life in prison, and this officer his life.

As I approached the bathroom, the officer asked me where I was going in a sarcastic way, indicating that I would not be allowed to use the facilities. I told him that I was going to use the bathroom, and he responded, "I don't think so," as he let other inmates go in and out of the bathroom. My choices had been narrowed down in a matter of seconds, as the officer wasn't wavering. I could either accept a "disobeying a direct order" misconduct, or I could urinate on myself or out my cell window, neither of which appealed to my humanity. To this day, I always choose my dignity over the prospect of a misconduct. So I brushed past the officer and entered the bathroom. The few captives who were in there hurried out; they all knew about me and my previous confrontations. I had recently spoken at the Million Man March Anniversary Celebration in the prison auditorium, and I had used words and names that conjured up images of resistance. Words like Revolution, Self-Defense, Black Panthers, Nat Turner, George Jackson, Assata Shakur, and Malcolm X. I used those words not to incite, but to inform brothers of our historical legacy. I wanted them to know that not all of our people sat around twiddling their thumbs and tap dancing; that there were strong African men and women who took a stand for justice. But these were the kinds of words that the prison administration held secret meetings about. Unfortunately, there were a lot of captives who talked the talk, but very few who were willing to take a stand for anything. It was those others who ran off to the comfort of their cells when they saw me push past the officer in order to use the bathroom.

"That is an assault on staff," the officer said as I used the urinal. As his words echoed in my ears, a brief view of the situation flashed through my mind. I knew I had a "disobeying a direct order" coming, but I had not assaulted him, and if I had, he would have immediately pushed his PPD (Personal Protection Device). I was vexed at the thought of a trumped-up charge. As I washed my hands, the officer and I exchanged glances. There were still a few captives in the hallway standing around to see what was going on. A few of them pleaded with him to let me out of the bathroom. He responded by ordering them to lock up.

"Give me your ID," he stated, blocking my exit from the bathroom. I informed him that I didn't have it on me and asked him if I could leave. He smiled sardonically, which made me realize that this was a sick game he was enjoying immensely. It was like a schoolyard bully shaking the life out of a kid who had told him over and over that he didn't have any lunch money. The officer continued to egg me on by saying, "You will produce an ID or you won't leave out of here," as he stepped so close to me that I could feel his hot breath. It felt like the whole world was closing in on me.

I attempted to slide past him, and that's when I heard the word "nigger." The officer hadn't moved his lips, only his hands, as he pushed me in the chest demanding that I produce an ID that I didn't have. All I could hear and see was the harshness of the word "nigger" over and over again, telling me that I was less-than, and that my personal space could be violated at any time. It made me think of all the Black men who had been dragged from their beds kicking and screaming only to have their cries silenced by the thick rope that was wrapped tightly around their necks as they were hoisted into the air and dangled from trees—strange fruit. It made me think of all the Black women who had been raped in the slave quarters while their husbands stood by, holding in all of their rage in order to prevent them all from being brutally murdered.

A sense of calm overcame me before I attacked with the fluid motion of a panther. It was the instinct of survival that had been honed in the alleys and streets of Detroit. With each blow I landed, I felt free of all the years of oppression that I had felt since being imprisoned. I now understood what Frederick Douglass felt like when he whooped the overseer who sought to break him. I was no one's slave, and I would rather die or live the rest of my life out in prison before I allowed anyone to trample over my dignity.

As I stood over him, choking away the racism, the superiority complex, and the four hundred years of oppression that African people had endured, I felt liberated, even as my hands were being twisted behind my back by another officer. Several officers dragged the unconscious officer into the bathroom, where they fought to save his life. Two officers escorted me to the hole, but before I left the building, I looked around at the captives who had stood by watching, and what I saw in their eyes caused my spirit to buckle. The hurt I felt when I looked into their eyes was worse than anything the State would ever be able to do to me. In their eyes, I saw contempt and anger, all directed at me, and it was then that it clicked in my head. I had exposed the talkers for what they were, a bunch of "kneegrow" slaves who would kill each other at the drop of a hat, but who refused to stand up for their own humanity. It was a sad and costly day for me, but it was also a moment of epiphany that I couldn't ignore. I now knew what it felt like to be condemned by the brothers who I loved and wanted more for.

As I sat that first day in the hole, I had to ask myself some very serious questions. I stared out the window at the captives who were walking by, and wondered if Nat Turner felt like I felt when he was turned in to the slave master by two slaves. I wondered if Malcolm X felt the way I did as he took his last breath, slowly dying from gunshot wounds inflicted on him by the very people whose lives he was trying to save. As I thought about all of my ancestors who had taken a stand for justice only to have their own people turn their backs on them, I couldn't do anything but shake my head.

Within two hours, several officers came and told me to back up to the door so that they could handcuff and shackle me; I was being transferred. I was then hustled out to a waiting van, which shuttled me to Oaks Maximum Security Prison. It was my second time being at the prison, but the first time I would be spending time in the hole there. I would soon learn that it was by far one of the worst places that a human being could find himself in.

When I arrived in the control center, several officers stood around in a small circle holding handcuffs and shackles. The officers who brought me in had to get their cuffs back, so they were forced to switch without freeing my hands and feet in the process. The switch with the handcuffs went smoothly. When they got down to my shackles, it was discovered that in their haste to get me out of the other facility, the officer had placed them on upside down, which made it difficult for him to get his key in the lock. He attempted to twist the shackles around so that he could see better, which caused the shackles to bite into the tender flesh on the back of my ankles.

After a few frustrating minutes, another officer took it upon himself to come and kick the shackles, causing them to sink deeper into my flesh. We exchanged glares, and I warned him if he put his feet on me again that he would find himself lying in a hospital bed alongside his coworker. He glared at me without saying anything, but he didn't kick the shackles again. Once they made the switch, I was escorted down to 5 Block and introduced to Michigan's version of hell on earth. I was placed in a shower cage, where I was strip-searched, and then taken to a temporary segregation cell. As the officers opened the cage, they threatened to slam me to the ground if I made any sudden moves. I laughed inside as I knew they were cowards who didn't want any problems. It was quite amusing that people who were supposed to be responsible for our rehabilitation could be more criminal than those who they were supposed to be helping. Over the next couple days, I felt like an animal in a zoo exhibit as officer after officer came to my cell to see what I looked like. They were all curious about the "monster" they had heard so much about, and they all needed to see for themselves.

Over the next four and a half years, a lot would change in how I was perceived by my captors and how I perceived them. It would also mark the beginning of a very powerful transformation inside of me. Prior to going to the hole this last time, I was a very bitter and angry young man. Like all of the rest who felt like they were dealt a bad hand in life, I was vexed with the world, and it dictated how I responded to situations. During the first couple of years of my incarceration, my anger and bitterness had intensified to a dangerous level, but the power of redemption is capable of conquering all internal foes.

One of the first and most prominent things I remember, when I was finally escorted to the cell I would occupy while at Oaks, was the unbearable smell of human despair. It is a smell that will forever be burned into the memory of my olfactory system. The smell of defecation, unwashed armpits, soggy toes, and spoiled booties mingled in the air with the pepper spray that the officers used to extract captives from their cells. Within a few weeks of being in the hole, I was introduced to a whole new language and culture of madness. Being caged inside of a cell for twenty-three hours a day breeds an animalistic mindset in the captives as well as the captors.

In an attempt to gain some semblance of control over their environment, captives waged battle after battle with each other and the officers, and the officers waged war against the captives. For captives, the weapon of choice was what we called "Weapons of Ass Destruction." These feces-filled bottles were smuggled to the showers or yard cages like pistols. Captives took deadly aim on anyone they considered an enemy, and once they squirted their shit pistols, the smell clung in the air for days. If they couldn't get you with a pistol, they would make "shit patties" and slide them underneath your door. Every day I had to wage a war inside myself to ensure that I did not fall into the abysmal mindset of those who had allowed this environment to reduce them to savages.

I refused to sit up and play in my own feces, or to subject myself to the feces of another captive. The unfortunate reality, however, was that no one was immune to a misdirected attack. There were a few unsuspecting captives who were drenched with someone else's bodily waste because they weren't paying attention when they walked to the shower or the yard.

Captives devised every way imaginable to get to their enemies, and for every measure of prevention that the officers came up with, the captives devised a way around it. After one incident, the officers placed bolts on all of our food slots. It happened one day while two captives were arguing. After shift change, one of the captives was being escorted to the shower. The other one manipulated his food slot open and calmly waited for the officers to bring his enemy past his cell. When they got in front of his cell, he kicked the food slot open and squirted a thick stream of feces on the inmate and the officer from his colostomy bag. Both the inmate and the officer screamed as they rushed past. No matter how many showers they took, the thought and feeling of being drenched in another person's defecation was not easily forgotten. The smell hung in the air like a miasmic cloud for the next couple of days, and stood as a reminder to everyone else to be careful.

Once the bolts were drilled into the food slots, several inmates went into MacGyver mode as they figured out a way to jimmy the locks open. First you had to slide a comb attached to a piece of string out of the top of the door while your neighbor across the hall guided your movements. Once it was lined up with the bolt, you pulled the comb up until the lock came undone. After that, all that was left to do was slide a cable cord beneath the door, twist it around the knob and continue twisting until the slot popped open and it was business as usual.

Another weapon of war was sleep deprivation. Usually when people were in conflict with each other, they would beat on the steel toilets or walls all night with a brush or some other hard item, which usually impacted the whole wing. Sometimes these wars lasted for weeks, or until one of them was moved to a different cell. There was never any regard for innocent bystanders, and this often led to others being drawn into their wars. Another method of getting even was to blow the power, which meant the other three inmates who shared the same breaker would be unable to watch the three TV channels we had.

Every day, there was something going on that chipped away at my soul. After the first two years, I was growing tired of seeing grown men act like children. But instead of complaining, I sought to gain an understanding of my environment and why captives reacted to it the way they did. First, however, I had to gain an in-depth understanding of myself. Though my reaction to the environment wasn't expressed externally, it didn't mean that I wasn't being as psychologically scarred as the rest. And to a degree, the internal scars I bore were far worse. If I had allowed them to remain beneath the surface until I was released, the consequences could have been catastrophic. I knew that a complete change was needed, and I set out to transform my thinking.

The Honorable Elijah Muhammad said, "In order for a man to completely change his conditions, he must be completely dissatisfied with them." There was no doubt that I was completely dissatisfied with where my thought process had led me. The first thing I began to do was keep a journal, and it was within the thin pages of my note pads that I found some peace of mind. It was within those pages that I was able to be me for the first time in a long time. I got down to the roots of who I am as a person, and I realized that I wasn't much different than those who used "Weapons of Ass Destruction," because inside of me burned that same rage, the kind of rage that nearly cost an officer his life and earned me the rest of my life in prison. It was the same kind of anger that clung to my back while I was on the streets, leading me to take another person's life. I was tired of living in a ball of anger and bitterness. I was tired of hurting people, and I was tired of hurting myself, but I didn't know what to do or where to turn.

As I sat back and listened to the chaos on the wing, I knew that I could never leave prison the same way I came in. I had to change. Prison had nothing to offer me other than more anger and violence. The officers had no interest in seeing me turn my life around; to most of them, I represented job security. Foremost, the State had long ago given up on rehabilitation. In order to be the man and father I was destined to be, I had to take a long and painful look at myself, so I began to chart my anger, and my reaction to my anger.

One day my neighbor blew my power while trying to get a light for his cigarette. When I asked him about it, he lied, and my immediate reaction was that I wanted to kill him. To me, his life was worthless and he deserved a swift and painful death. A few days later, after I had calmed down, I returned to my journal and read what I had written in response to my neighbor. I found it quite disturbing. Despite his inconsideration and blatant disrespect, I knew that what he had done wasn't worth me killing him or inflicting any physical harm on him.

Throughout the rest of my journey through the iron inferno known as the "hole," I would chart my anger and my response to it. Through this process, I slowly began to realize that I had some deeper issues that I had never addressed. I began to write about how I felt about the lack of a relationship I had with my mother, and how my parents' divorce had impacted me. I started writing about how I used to feel as a child when my mother beat me for minor infractions. There were many things that came to the surface as I wrote in my journal, and it felt like a great weight was being lifted off my shoulders. No longer did I feel the old familiar bitterness that I had carried around inside of me in a tight little ball, keeping me one provocation away from exploding. I wrote about all of the physical violence I had suffered in my life and how it made me feel towards people. There were layers upon layers of scars, and I realized that I was like a whole lot of young, urban males who walked around suffering from the effects of post-traumatic stress syndrome.

I had been forced to suppress my feelings for years. There was no one I could share my pain and fears with, and it began to manifest in anger and violence toward others. I felt like no one ever felt anything for me, so didn't feel like I should care for anyone else. As I went back and read page after page of my journal, I could feel myself growing stronger and stronger with the passing of each day. As the pain from years of abuse and neglect began to dissipate, my feelings toward my fellow captives began to soften, and I started to become compassionate toward them. I had already understood to a certain degree how the hole was supposed to impact me, and that helped me to avoid falling into the abyss of despair and insanity that claimed so many. I knew I would leave with some indelible scars to my psyche, but I had to do all I could to minimize them if I wanted to be the father I needed to be to my children.

Every day was a test of my will to survive as I watched the insanity taking shape all around me. Yet I continued to write about the things I saw and experienced. By writing about them, it was as though I was taking the power away from them. In my journal, I wrote about the night a Latino captive set himself on fire. It was a moment of internal terror seeing someone so desperate for escape from the pain and misery of solitary confinement that he would rather end his life through immolation. His ordeal had begun weeks before when the officers began harassing him constantly because of his sexual orientation. After days of harassment, he woke everyone up in the middle of the night with a loud and chilling rendition of the Lord's Prayer; the next day he set the cell on fire while he was in it. The officers rushed up on the wing and sprayed him with a fire extinguisher before taking him to a suicide-watch cell. Within two weeks, he attempted the same thing again, after which they removed him from the cell and never brought him back.

The depth of the psychosis I witnessed was terrifying, but the staff psychiatrist downplayed it by saying that these inmates were just "acting out." I know, however, from living in the hole around hundreds of captives for nearly five years, that being in isolation causes a disconnect in the deepest part of the psyche. There is nothing natural about being caged in a cell for twenty-three hours a day like an animal. In addition to all of the other stresses captives face day to day, including being neglected and abandoned by their family members, extended isolation was enough to cause a significant mental breakdown. There were guys who I had known for years as solid people who I witnessed having mental breakdowns after ninety days in the hole.

As the months passed by, I documented the wars that went on between the captives and the officers. Whenever the officers did something that we felt was unjust, we responded by flooding the wing with water from our toilets until they came and cut it off. I stood by my door watching the two-inch-deep pool of water ebb and flow outside my cell. This was the only way we had of voicing our grievances and getting an immediate response. The officers knew if they didn't pass out our mail in a timely fashion or served us our meals cold, they would have to wade through water until they got porters to clean it up. They knew if they played with the showers that we would beat on the doors relentlessly until they corrected their behavior. The way we saw it, if we didn't fight back, they would continue to run roughshod over us.

So with pen and pad, I clung to my sanity; between that, writing letters to my family, and reading the letters my family sent to me, I redeemed my soul. There were plenty of days when I felt like the hole would consume my spirit, but I fought tooth and nail to stay strong. There were days when I swore I couldn't take one more day of smelling another human being's bodily waste, or one more rejection from the Security Classification Committee regarding my release from administrative segregation, but then I would sit down and write out my thoughts or read an inspirational book, and I knew I had to keep on keeping on. My community and my family, including the brothers who had become my family in prison, were counting on me to be strong, so I fought for my sanity until the day of my release from the hole. It was then that the true test began.

RONALD (RASHAWN) HUGHES, *New York*

A MORE PERFECT UNION

When you make an observation, you have an obligation. These are words I try to live by. It's what encouraged this article, and hopefully what will inspire the commissioners on the parole board to open their hearts and minds, and to understand that people are capable of changing. In preparation for my parole interview, I found myself questioning whether or not an equitable hearing can be conducted when the commissioners are only reviewing an inmate's personal file on the morning of the hearing. An impartial discussion regarding my release should include several factors: the severity of my transgressions against society, risk assessment, and probability of success in returning to the community. Without this context, the victims, as well as society, would be left with answers that don't answer, explanations that don't explain, and conclusions that don't conclude. This ultimately opens the door for far-ranging criticism and controversial practices that many believe perpetuate a reign of error. The fundamental question therefore becomes whether or not the parole commissioners are able to determine which inmates serving indeterminate sentences of imprisonment should be released.

A parole board hearing may last somewhere between ten and twenty minutes. It is within this time frame that an inmate must state his or her case as to why he or she should be released. The pressure is immense, and the stakes are way too high for us to risk a flawed judgment.

Both supporters and skeptics of the state of parole must understand that the parole process should not be looked at in a vacuum. Inmates cannot afford to be narrow-minded about the process. They must find a way to move beyond the naive idea that the process of parole is simply about politics. If they are able to step out of that box and understand the difficulty involved in being a parole commissioner, they will enhance their chances of receiving a favorable decision. If just for a second, imagine having the responsibility of determining whether or not an individual is ready to return to society. It is both a complicated and convoluted task. Yet, if inmates are somehow able to shift their perception of the commissioners and empathize with them, they may be able to better understand how to prepare for the most important moment of their lives.

When preparing for parole, inmates stand at a moment of great challenge and great opportunity. In order to meet this moment successfully, they must shift their attitude, and understand that commissioners have the tremendous responsibility of protecting our families, our community, and society. In all walks of life, people are the instruments of their own destiny; for incarcerated individuals this rings even more true. Inmates must figure out how they can redefine the relationship that exists between parole commissioners and themselves. That dangerous "us against them" attitude will come across in your parole hearing no matter how hard you try to mask it. This attitude has caused many inmates to drift into the shallowest pool of expectation and anticipate a *hit*. If you truly want to stand on the side of responsibility, human dignity, and freedom, then you must do some dying. You must alter those old ideals and values that shape your current situation. If not, you will remain in the current crisis that you are in—a crisis in which you give parole commissioners total control of your future.

Yes, many inmates contain within themselves the contradictions of a troubled life—the good and bad of the community. *However, your goal, from the moment you were convicted, should have been about making shifts in your behaviors and attitudes.* Inmates must be determined to rise above their poor choices, and beyond the mentality that they will be hit just because of politics. That self-defeating attitude will only further normalize two-year hits—something we cannot afford.

If we are to put parole in its proper context, it requires us to understand the inextricable link between an individual who claims to have repositioned himself from the attitude that landed him in prison, and the principles and values of the commissioners who have been entrusted to make such crucial decisions. It must be remembered that parole commissioners are bound together within the same society; in many cases, they share the same beliefs and they depend on the same perceptions. They should be held to the same standards as a potential parolee.

A parole decision should be premised on the idea of impartiality. It should entail evidence of an inmate's remorse, things done to address the causes of their crime, the future plans of an inmate, and, most importantly, the likelihood of that person committing another criminal act. However, we should all be alarmed when Robert Dennison, a current New York State parole commissioner, states: "It is an easy job if you don't have the courage and you don't have the compassion, because then you don't really care. And then it is easy to make whatever decision you want without feeling guilty, without feeling, 'Gee, maybe I made the wrong decision.'"

Mr. Dennison pushes the bar even further when he states: "Many times, the parole commissioners feel differently from the judge and probably say to themselves or say to one another, 'I don't really care what the judge gave to the person, I don't feel comfortable letting this person out. And I am going to hold him for two more years.' And that can go on and on and on forever."[1]

This kind of practice, which some claim has been unfolding for years, is indeed problematic. As citizens, we would like to believe that the reason we have parole hearings is because the law, in its wisdom, knows that there are redeemable qualities in people who at one time committed unimaginable acts. It was Fyodor Dostoyevsky, the Russian novelist, who once said that if you want to know the true worth of a nation, all you have to do is look at how they treat the worst of their society—their prisoners. Hence, if the prisoner's fate represents or is symbolic of the nature of our society, we need to be more critical of those we entrust with making crucial decisions about the future of our incarcerated.

We need commissioners who are not only principled, but are willing to seize the opportunity to devise new methods of rendering parole decisions. Ralph Waldo Emerson speaks directly to the importance of this when he states, "As to methods there may be a million and then some, but principles are few. The man [commissioner] who grasps principles can successfully select his own methods. [But] the man [commissioner] who tries methods, ignoring principles, is sure to have trouble." By our nature as rational, conscious creatures, the one thing both parole commissioners and inmates can control is the mindset with which they respond to each other. For if we dare to see our society as a body politic, where all parts of our society are working together for the common good, then our ideas of an enlightened form of rehabilitation demand that we enforce a kind of parole process that restores rather than destroys. We cannot strengthen one segment of the population while ignoring another. The prisoner must be considered a potential citizen in order to strengthen the quality of our society as a whole, and to form a more perfect union.

NOTE

1. Trymaine Lee, "Convicted of Murder as Teenager and Paroled at 41," *New York Times*, June 4, 2010.

CURTIS L. DOWNING, *Nevada*

REFLECTION ON THE WORK OF DEALING WITH TIME

In the years that I've been incarcerated, I've experienced much that has been negative, and it seems to be getting worse. I am thankful to God that over these many years, I have been able to keep an attitude of gratitude.

Most disappointing is the attitude that is prevalent here at Southern Desert Correctional Center, exhibited by administration and correctional staff alike: Their attitude is to belittle, demean, and utilize vulgar language in communicating with an incarcerated person.

The situations and circumstances that occurred to Iraqi prisoners of war occur right here, at Southern Desert Correction Center, and it's not complained of more because the correctional officers are very quick to say, "Write a grievance, and be sure to spell my name right," because they know that nothing will ever come of the grievance.

What has not materialized in the field of corrections in the state of Nevada, since the departure of Director Jackie Crawford, is a director or warden that has a clear vision and ideas to lead the Nevada Department of Corrections firmly into the twenty-first century. The idea of corrections in Nevada is lockdown, and to restrict movement, cut programs, not provide jobs (in fact, should you not have a social security card on record at the prison, you cannot obtain employment that has a pay number), while our sentences are increased based upon the lack of a job. I currently have a case pending before the Nevada Supreme Court, case number 54687, that addresses this fact.

Being incarcerated is stressful enough: the environment is highly charged, with many already on edge, mostly due to racial tension and the lockdown environment. And there's no outlet, so all we do is turn on one another, for stupid reasons. What might make it easier is for those who are hired as correctional employees to be required to undergo psychological evaluations, to determine whether they are suitable for such employment. Will they provide what the job title supposes: "corrections," rather than subjecting incarcerated persons to their own ideas of corrections, e.g., "What the F—— are you doing on my tier? What the F—— are you doing on my yard?" "My this," "My that" . . . and our being continuously subjected to mental, verbal, and, yes, physical abuse?

There isn't anything that I've written that I cannot provide firsthand confirmation of.

JANE DOROTIK, *California*

CALIF LIFERS SEARCH FOR PAROLE

Most of us believe the parole board commissioners have a very serious job in determining who should stay in prison and who should be released. After all, the burden of public safety would seem to lie squarely on their shoulders. If a prisoner can't, after years of incarceration, prove to these commissioners that they are not a menace to public safety, then maybe they shouldn't be released.

My guess is this is what the public generally thinks . . . and who can blame them?

So, I want to offer you a different side of the story, based on actual cases, real women I see going before the board, hoping against hope to be granted their freedom after years and years of incarceration. And yes, I have an inherent bias—I am an insider, a prisoner who tells the story from this side of the fence (or razor wire in this case). Although I have not gone before the board myself—I am a relatively new lifer—I see and feel all the fear, the guilt, the remorse, and the tenuous hope each woman goes through in preparation for the hearings. The painful emotional roller coaster that a lifer, and his or her family, experiences each time they appear before the board is one part of it.

The incredible waste of taxpayer money to keep someone in prison who no longer belongs there is another part of it. Next come the court battles a lifer must fight to gain their rightful freedom—the filings, the legal fees, the hearings, the district attorneys, and public defenders— again, usually at taxpayer expense. These add up to incredible amounts of money, in hundreds of millions, all to accomplish what the parole board should have done in the first place.

The first thing to understand is that no lifer is even *eligible* to go before the board for their first hearing *until* they have served their minimum time.

The second thing to understand is how inept, arbitrary, and dysfunctional the board is in arriving at their truly important decision of who should go and who should stay. Well, basically they have a one-track mind—release no one! They are politicized to the extreme in that they, and the governor, are carefully mindful of the very vocal victims' rights groups (as well as of the generous contributors behind them). These groups are largely funded by the powerful guards union that obviously has a vested interest in keeping everyone in prison, *especially* lifers because lifers make prisons easier to manage. And let's not forget, one in five prisoners is a lifer in California's bloated, corrupt prison system, stuffed to almost 200 percent capacity with 170,000 prisoners.

The parole board commissioners' actual rate of suitability findings—deeming someone suitable for release—is around 5 percent. But even this miniscule release rate is misleading because the governor reverses about 75 percent of these suitability findings. So the actual release rate is closer to 1 percent of all those lifers who go before the board (even having already served their prescribed terms).

I'll leave alone the fact that the U.S. incarceration rate is greater than any other nation's. I'll not mention the fact that U.S. sentences are many times longer than other nations'.

Instead I'll give you a few examples of actual cases, women I've known.

Louise is seventy years old and has been locked away for thirty-two years, but she was originally sentenced to 7-years-to-life. She has recently been found suitable for parole *again* by the board. The governor has reversed her previous parole suitability findings by citing boilerplate rationale for the reversal: "the especially callous nature of the crime." Louise has always done her part, working in prison to overcome the addiction that led to her crime in the first place, gaining vocational certificates and laudatory reports. She participated in self-help groups to gain insight into herself and to learn how to become a benefit to her community. She steered clear of the darker side of prison life. She was what we would call a poster child for rehabilitation.

If the parole board had reviewed her fairly, putting politics aside and evaluating according to the written regulations, her earliest possible release date was in 1984. Yet here we are with Louise still fighting for her freedom, years later.

To gain her release she had to file a writ against the parole board in the courts; she had to obtain pro bono legal representation from the USC Post-Conviction Project; she had to wait for many years. But Louise's story finally did have a just and successful outcome—Louise left prison a few days ago and is now living at a transitional reentry house to help her reintegrate back into the world she was locked away from thirty-two years ago.

Let's see how much the taxpayers have spent to keep Louise in prison for twenty-six years beyond her minimum release date:

$$\$49,000/\text{year}^1 \quad \times \quad 11 \text{ years} \quad = \quad \$539,000$$
$$\$138,000/\text{year}^2 \quad \times \quad 15 \text{ years} \quad = \quad \$2,070,000$$

So, taxpayers have spent over 2.6 million dollars to keep Louise behind bars longer than necessary.

Or, let's look at Helen's story. Helen was eighty-six years old when she died alone and unnoticed last year. Helen was convicted of conspiracy to commit murder. Actually what she did was transport some money for her son without knowledge of what the money was intended for, but the prosecutor didn't see it that way. No one died; no one was even injured. In fact, no crime actually happened—it was all conspiracy theory. But Helen was shipped off to prison with a life sentence. Helen's kidneys were failing for the last several years of her life and she was taken out twice weekly, hands and feet shackled and a guard on each side of her, for dialysis treatment. So, the cost of keeping Helen in prison was close to a million dollars a year because of all the extra guards for the frequent medical trips out for dialysis.

When Helen had served her term, she too went before the board hoping for release, but the board found her to be a risk to public safety because she "didn't have firm employment plans." That's what the board actually cited in her hearing transcripts as the rationale for parole denial . . . at age eighty-five!

How could Helen be deemed a risk when she couldn't even walk thirty yards without stopping to catch her breath?? The *real* risk to public safety is the money siphoned away from education and social supports to fund this bloated and abusive prison system.

Can you imagine what Louise's $2.6 million could have funded? Or Helen's $6 million plus? Subsidized day care so mothers could work, after-school programs so kids can be diverted from gang involvement, medical clinics, the funding of colleges, aid to the underprivileged, and so much more!

But no, we as a society allow the prison system to suck up all of the state's resources under the guise of public safety. What safety have we achieved by keeping Louise or Helen incarcerated? As one journalist put it, Are they going to scale the razor wire and assault someone with their walkers?

Most lifers would give almost anything to be given a chance to become a *credit* to society, paying taxes instead of eating up those precious tax dollars.

At a time when California is raising tuition fees again and again and pricing most of our youth out of an education, at a time when California is slashing social supports for the poor and disadvantaged, shouldn't taxpayers demand that legislators fix the dysfunctional parole board?

A start would be to *follow* the codes that govern the appointment of parole board commissioners, making sure that the composition of the board represents a cross-section of the community (psychologists, retired judges, etc.) instead of the law-enforcement people Schwarzenegger continues to appoint. The current board is 100 percent law enforcement.

Another step would be to again *follow* the law: the Penal Code *requires* that a release date be set once the base term has been served. So it would seem reasonable to expect at least a 50 percent suitability-finding rate instead of the current 5 percent rate.

Finally, remove the governor's review process of the parole board findings (oversight that was instituted in 1988 for political reasons—"the Willie Horton effect"). This review has never really been a "review" anyway, in that it has *never* been used to review a denial, only to reverse a positive finding. You would think the governor would empower these commissioners with their six-figure incomes to do their job as the regulations direct and not second-guess them.

The rate of recidivism in California for older lifers released is negligible, less than 1 percent. Compare that with a 70 percent recidivism rate for all other prisoners.

We have a crisis here—a moral, ethical, fiscal, and societal crisis—and it can be corrected if enough people get involved, speak out, write legislators, and make their views known.

NOTES

1. For the years Louise spent past her release date *before* she turned 55, the *average* cost of incarceration in California is $49,000 per year per prisoner.

2. For the years Louise spent behind bars between the ages of 55 and 70, the *average* cost of incarceration for a woman over 55 is a staggering $138,000 per year per prisoner.

JON MARC TAYLOR, *Missouri*

BOLSHAYAZONA (BIG PRISON ZONE)

Over the last three decades, the political pendulum has been swinging towards culturally conservative political philosophy. With the election of Ronald Reagan in 1980, newly resurgent conservatives pushed two domestic-policy efforts, in welfare and criminal-justice reform.

The public was bombarded by stories of rampant abuse of its generosity by poor welfare mothers having babies just to qualify for an extra $54 a month in AFDC benefits, and of Cadillac-driving pimps drawing unemployment benefits. The nation was presented, as well, with a litany of horror stories of murderers receiving probationary sentences, and of activist judges making it all but impossible for law enforcement to "serve and protect" society, routinely dismissing evidence seized without properly acquired search warrants.

If any of these examples existed—and most did not beyond the "urban legends" we are all so prone to pass along—basing public policy on anecdotal occurrences is not a just or rational means by which to govern. To govern based on outright lies is even more morally suspect than the acts purportedly necessitating changes in the first place.

BAIT AND SWITCH

The nefarious sales tactic of bait and switch—of offering or demonstrating one thing, and then selling something else as the solution—has been effectively used by politicians to dismantle more and more of the New Deal and subsequent social welfare provisions, and to a frightening extent many of our fundamental constitutional protections.

An example from the 1990s is the Prison Litigation Reform Act, which severely limited prisoners' access to the federal courts for everything from criminal appeals to class-action challenges to prison conditions. As part of the "marketing" of the need for reform, a Top Ten list of outrageous prisoner lawsuits was trotted out by the state's attorney generals.

Perhaps the "frivolous" filing that received the most attention was that in which a prisoner sued the state for selling him smooth peanut butter, instead of the crunchy peanut butter he'd ordered. This seemingly ridiculous case ate up thousands of taxpayer dollars in associated adjudication costs; it was no wonder—even though less than 5 percent of the thousands of prisoner lawsuits have been dismissed by the courts as factually or legally frivolous—that politicians pontificated that reform was needed!

The AGs, however, omitted key facts of the case. The prisoner had ordered crunchy peanut butter from the prison commissary, and the day he picked up his order he was told they were out of crunchy, but he could have his list marked and wait till the next week and then receive the item he had ordered. He conceded to wait, and in the interim he was transferred to another prison. When he requested, with indisputable documentation, that his account should be re-credited with the cost of the peanut butter he had never received, he was denied. After a year of methodically exhausting the byzantine grievance procedures, resulting in the prison system telling him to sue the state for the $1.98, authorities admitted they collected money for but never provided the purchased item.

The man sued because he was denied effective due process to recover his property, which the state acknowledged they had deprived him of. In other words, the convict, instead of throwing a fit or shanking the store man, behaved like a rational and wronged citizen following the procedures of the law, standing up for his constitutional rights against the arbitrary power of the state to deprive him of his private property without due recompense. He filed a tort claim, a hallmark act of American civil jurisprudence.

These facts, though, were conveniently not outlined on the AG's widely touted list of Top Ten frivolous lawsuits, nor were they investigated or even questioned by the mainstream media that so readily and superficially reproduced the ludicrous cases. But what the hell, they were just prisoners, and what goes on behind prison walls should stay behind prison walls.

CREEPING INSTITUTIONALIZATION

What began with the easily vilified targets among the criminal class and welfare cheats, however, has progressed today to the average working Joe. Over the course of the past thirty years, adjusted for inflation, income for the top 0.01 percent of earners grew by 900 percent, while income for the bottom 90 percent of workers effectively stagnated, and today, fourteen years into the new millennium, nearly half of U.S. children (14 million in any given year) will be on food stamps at some point before they come of age. Meanwhile, the politicians played to the "cheap seats" with their inflammatory rhetoric, effectively banishing prisoner-rights and penal-condition law-suits from review by the federal courts. Since the passage of the Prison Litigation Reform Act (PLRA), not one major prison-condition case has been heard on the merits. Moreover, if re-stricted by these same rules three decades ago, Hurricane Carter would still be in prison (and Denzel Washington would have one fewer Academy Award nomination).

The criminalization of America has grown by leaps and bounds in the past few decades. Politicians' latest legislative fad is to criminalize bad to rude to merely stupid behavior. Spitting on a school bus or wearing pants too low can all lead to criminal prosecution. Millions are charged every year for criminal acts ranging from murder to failure to shovel snow from their walkways. As Jonathan Turley, the Shapiro Professor of Public Interest Law at George Washington University, comments, "In the end crime now means nothing if anyone can be a criminal." With over 64 million citizens having criminal records—approximately 30 percent of the adult popu-lation—perhaps the good professor's claim is not wholly unwarranted.

The title of this piece, "Bolshayazona," is a Russian colloquialism meaning "Big Prison Zone," and is what the inmates of the Soviet gulag system called the rest of the USSR. Ironically, there are more similarities to our Cold War nemesis than we care to accept. One of these is how the United States has developed its own capitalistic version of the gulag archipelago system, with the rise of the $60-billion-a-year prison-industrial complex. Creating the circumstances that exist today, with well over 2 million Americans behind bars—a sum that represents one-quarter of the world's penal population, from among only 5 percent of the planet's inhabitants—has taken the accumulation of the intentional and questionable changes of the past three decades: the War on Drugs, mandatory-minimum sentencing, abolition of parole, dilution of procedural legal safeguards, etc.

By 2007 the sweeping degeneration of civil-liberties safeguards, passed and renewed in the Patriot Act, have resulted in the revelation that the FBI has continually violated hundreds of thousands of citizens' privacy rights. In prison one expects to be subject to perpetual postal in-spection, random pat-searches of your person, and constant warrantless shakedowns of your liv-ing quarters. You just don't expect that in greater America, though. The prisonization of America has made a personal tour of our penal systems a "lifestyle" experience for a significant portion of African American males, who are more than twice as likely to go to prison as to graduate from college; more and more so for Hispanic hombres, who are locked up at twice the rate of Anglos; and increasingly for poor, undereducated white men. This prisonization of America has insidi-ously extended into the general culture as an accepted method for handling all sorts of failures in civil society, whether they be untreated addicts, poor criminals, or the fallout from dysfunctional family and social behavior. If incarceration rates remain essentially unchanged, one out of every nine American males will eventually serve time in prison.

The process has seeped into mainstream culture with the use of what was once purely penal terminology. Twenty years ago one never read headlines or heard news anchors using the terms "lockdown," "pat-searches," and "ionization scanning" as everyday reporting patois. A high school in Texas is now "dressing out" (another prison term) violators of its dress code in institutional jumpsuits, which are actually made by state prisoners. One parent protester of the policy cried, "They're not little prisoners!" More disturbing, though, is that the sartorially chastised, instead of viewing the jumpsuits with high dudgeon, have instead become cool fashionistas in the hallways, with some non-offenders buying their own jailbird suits to style about.

Consumer appliance tastes have been affected (or maybe the more accurate verb should be "infected") with the fashionability of institutionally mandated clear plastic (i.e., contraband-viewable) casings for electronic consumer items, the most "popular design" of the year. Jailhouse hostelry has now become the destination *de rigueur* among the B & B set, with hoosegow, $100-million conversions promising "plenty of luxury to go with the jailhouse vibe." This institutional glamorization, called "prison chic" by the avant-garde, extends to high-end architectural design, installing ten-thousand-dollar stainless-steel cellblockesque toilets in multimillion-dollar mansions. Now even the fat cats can crap like convicts.

THE HIT LIST EXPANDS

Americans have become conditioned to the Big Lie to rationalize choices and actions conducted in their names (e.g., phantom WMDs, Abu Ghraib, and torture of *suspected* terrorists). A recent petard in the national health-care debate has been that of tort reform. The changes called for are not to protect the average man, but are back-room lobbyist deals meant to further erode the citizens' abilities to receive justice. Sound familiar?

The imprisonization of America has now extended beyond the walls and wire with hip lingo and fashion chic to include tort (i.e., PLRA-like) reforms. For years the public has been barraged with the anecdotal "you-are-not-going-to-believe-this" stories of outrageous lawsuits, and how horribly inflated medical malpractice insurance rates are chasing doctors from practice. The problem with these politicized urban legends, however, is that collectively they simply aren't true. "Reformers" claim that the only way to stimulate job creation and provide enough doctors for everyone is to limit settlement compensation and restrict filing conditions in the first place.

Five years ago, Missouri served as the lobbying template for so-called tort reform that in turn had been perfected with the Prison Litigation Reform Act a decade earlier. The reality is that there never had been a flood of frivolous lawsuits as trumpeted by industry hacks and regurgitated ad infinitum by the mainstream media. Tort claims for workplace injury had actually been *declining*, and, moreover, only 2 percent of those injured by products or workplace conditions even filed lawsuits to begin with. Malpractice insurance rates may have been costly, but in Missouri the number of doctors had actually *increased* by nearly 10 percent the three years preceding the purported reform legislation. Not exactly the conditions meriting a "crisis" standard that required redress via the constriction of potential recompense and rightful access to the courts.

The Show-Me State, however, under Republican governor Matt Blunt—whose daddy was the then Republican majority whip in the Congress—passed a comprehensive reform package that limited the amount the injured could receive for pain and suffering in medical malpractice cases, capped punitive damages in all injury cases, restricted where cases could be filed, narrowed the definition of workplace injuries, and restricted the evidence of those injuries, producing what critics called "the most restrictive [legal] venue in the nation."

Turn the page, and five years later, the now-retired one-term politician heralded the august changes he brought to his state in a *Wall Street Journal* op-ed, exhorting Congress to include tort reform in the pending health-care bill. A little more shaving off the Bill of Rights. A few more restrictions on the protections we have assumed are every American's fundamental, inviolate safeguards. Just another step in the Imprisonization of America. Now everyone in the *bolshayazona* can feel a little bit of what it is like to be behind bars.

Kite Out

STEVEN G. AVALOY, *California*

VISIONS OF THE NIGHT

It is in the light of hope that I am reaching out to you through this true-life story.

> For God may speak in one way, or in another, yet man does not perceive it, In a dream, in vision of the night, when deep sleep falls upon men, While slumbering on their beds, Then He opens the ears of men, And seals their instruction, In order to turn man from his deed, and conceal pride from man. He does so to keep back his soul from the Pit, and his life from perishing by the sword. (Job 33:14–18)

Before something dreadful happens to us, we usually get some type of warning, which we never pay attention to. Most of the time our loved ones try to warn us that we are traveling down the wrong path. Sometimes that warning will come either to them, or to us, in a dream.

> God tries to warn His people before He does something horrible to them. Because I have called and you refused, I have stretched out my hand and no one regarded, Because you disdained all my counsel, and would have none of my rebuke, I also will laugh at your calamity; I will mock when your terror comes, When your terror comes like a storm, And your destruction comes like a whirlwind, When distress and anguish come upon you like a whirlwind, When distress and anguish come upon you. Because they hated knowledge, And did not choose the fear of the LORD. They would have none of My counsel and despised My every rebuke. (Proverbs 2:24–27, 29–30)

Before I was sentenced to 25 years in California State Prison for burglary and robbery, both my sister-in-law and my mother-in-law tried to warn me that something terrible was about to happen to me. They had been having the same bad dream about me.

My mother-in-law said to me, "I woke up in a cold sweat and my clothes were soaking. All I could see was your face. A lot of police were around you. Police helicopters and the news were there too, and a lot of people standing around watching. But I couldn't see what was happening to you. So please be careful out there." This was the dream, the night vision that she told me.

I didn't think anything of it. The next day my sister-in-law came and told me about the same dream. The exact same dream. "Then He said, 'Hear now my words: If there is a prophet among you, I the LORD, make Myself known to Him in a vision; I speak to him in a dream'" (Numbers 12:6).

I did not know that God showed people things through their dreams. However, when King Herod's men were sent out to kill Jesus, God spoke to Joseph in a night vision (Matthew 2:12–15). And Joseph listened to what was spoken to him in his dream and took Jesus where He was kept safe.

But what if Joseph hadn't listened to his dream? What if I had taken heed of my mother- and sister-in-laws' dreams? I probably wouldn't be here in prison right now.

My mother- and sister in-law were dreaming of me so much that they began to scare me. They believed in witchcraft and voodoo. That is what made me scared. I still failed to realize that God can speak through "anyone" to deliver a message He wants delivered.

They have forsaken the right way and gone astray, following the way of Balaam the son of Beor, who loved the wages of unrighteousness; but he was rebuked for his iniquity; a dumb donkey speaking with a man's mouth restrained the madness of the prophet. (II Peter 2:15–16)

That wasn't the only warning that God tried to show me. God tries to warn us in so many different ways. Oh why did I not take the warning? One night I had a little too much to drink and smoke, but I still wanted to get high and drunk. So I asked my father-in-law to let me use his car. He had a station wagon we called the "Honey Wagon."

He gave me the keys and didn't ask me a single question, but before I had a chance to walk through the door, my son's mother stopped me and asked me, "Where are you going?" "On 92nd," I replied. "For what?" she asked sharply. "To go hang out with the homies," I answered. "You don't need to be going anywhere!" she exclaimed in a dreadful voice. I kissed her on the cheek and walked out the door, got in the station wagon, and drove straight to the spot where they sold PCP.

From there, all I remember was driving through the projects. When I regained a glimpse of consciousness, I recalled driving around in a large, circular, left-looping motion, thinking that I was driving back home. Then, before I knew it, I found myself in LAX airport. When I looked up, I could see police cars coming towards me.

I don't know how I got out of there, or how I made it home that night. But the next morning my son's mother was screaming and yelling at me to get up. "You wrecked my father's car!" she yelled. "No I did not," I answered her. "Yes you did! If you didn't wreck his car, then who did you let drive it?" she demanded. "Once again, I didn't wreck his car or lend it to anyone," I responded, bewildered. She huffed, "Well, you need to come look at it then, and tell him that yourself."

When I went outside and saw the car, my chin dropped. The car was smashed. The engine was practically sitting in the driver's seat! I told him, "I don't know what happened." He said, "Were you that drunk that you don't know what happened?" I did not say a word. I was speechless. I just walked off.

Approximately two weeks later my father-in-law received a letter from the police department informing him that if he didn't come down to the police station they would put a warrant out for his arrest, his driver's license would be suspended, and his car would be impounded. He showed the letter to me and then somberly said, "Don't worry about it. I'll handle it." "No!" I said, "I'll go down there with you and tell them what happened and that I was responsible for your car that night." But he said, "No, you don't even remember what happened. You could have killed someone. You have my daughter to worry about, and your boys to think of."

Somehow another week went by before we got to the police station. We still didn't know what was going on. My sister-in-law and my son's mother took my father-in-law and me down to the police station. When we got down there, my son's mother said to me, "Don't go in there. Let my dad handle this." "I can't let your father go to jail for something I did," I said to her. "He's not tripping," she said. "Let him go in there to see what's happening first, before you go in." "No, I'll be alright," I said to her. Then my sister-in-law said, "Do you remember that dream I was telling you about? Well this might be it right here. You got your boys to think of." I didn't say a word back. I just got out of the car and walked into the police station with my father-in-law. My father-in-law walked straight to the desk and started talking with the officer, who told him to wait while he went to get the sergeant.

The sergeant took us to a room in the back of the building. Once we got in the room, the sergeant said: "You hit three cars in a head-on collision. One of the people whose car you hit followed you to the LAX airport and took down your license plate number. So what happened that night?" he asked. "I didn't know I hit three cars," I said. My father-in-law added, "He told me that he was at the gas station and some guy was trying to jack him for the car." "Is that true?" the sergeant asked me. "Yes, it is," I answered him. "Well, thank you for being honest with me. I'm not going to arrest you, because you came in and told me what happened." The sergeant then added, "As for me, I don't know whether you were drinking or not; we will let the court be the judge of that." The sergeant was then through talking with us. And my father-in-law and I got up and left the station. The meeting went better than we had expected.

> The LORD is not slack concerning His promises, as some count slackness, but is longsuffering toward us, not willing that any should perish but that all should come to repentance. (II Peter 3:9)

A month later I was at home, drinking and smoking with my son's mother and her best friend. My son's mother soon passed out, and her best friend left. Yet I still wanted someone to get high and drunk with. So I went by one of my homeboy's house to see if he wanted to party. But he had other plans—plans that I did not know about. He had noticed that I was loaded out of my mind, so he took me on a ride I will never be allowed to forget.

I can't forgive myself for what I did that night. I was so high on PCP and so drunk that I did not know what was going on until it was too late. When I became partly conscious again I found myself roaming around in someone's house. I remember thinking to myself, "What am I doing here? I don't need any of this stuff," just as I began walking out. As soon as I got out the door, the police were there, everywhere, with guns drawn and pointed at me.

The police had the house surrounded! Police and police cars everywhere. There were four or five helicopters circling over the house, and news reporters from every news station in the city. "*Freeze! You are under arrest!*"

My mother- and sister-in-laws' dreams came true. Now their dreams have become my living nightmare, all because I didn't take heed of the word and warning of God that had come to me in a Vision of the Night.

I leave behind two boys whom I love very deeply. I haven't seen them in over five years. I would love to see them, but their mother, my ex-wife now, has turned her back on me. And my family and hers have taken an "I told you so" attitude.

The only hope I have is in repentance of the heart, and the renewed trust that I have in the Living Word of God, Who has promised, and assures, that "All things work together for the good to those who love Him, to those who are called according to His purpose" (Romans 8:28). "Whom the LORD loves He chastens, and scourges every son whom He receives" (Hebrews 12:6). Because, "The goodness of God leads one to repentance" (Romans 2:4).

So though I now sit trapped in this night-vision-come-true, I know there is hope.

No one was hurt or killed by my crime. And to any and everyone whom I may have hurt or offended by my blind-eyed foolishness in the making of these truths, I repent. And I ask that you will please forgive me. And to anyone willing to extend a helping hand towards changing this situation from bad to good (or in helping me to keep ties with my boys, and to bring forth fruits befitting of repentance), please feel free to contact me—I could surely use an understanding friend.

Mental and Physical Health Care

INTRODUCTION

Health care is a problem—both practical and political—across the United States. Health care in Prison City is a serial tragedy. A federal judge has declared that the health care afforded to men and women incarcerated in California constitutes cruel and unusual punishment; it was these conditions that moved the Supreme Court to order the state to reduce its prison population by over thirty thousand.[1] California serves as the bellwether: Health care throughout American prisons is inadequate even when available, often exacerbates rather than ameliorating both temporary and long-term suffering, and costs taxpayers millions of dollars more than if responsible, basic care were available early and reliably.[2] Though one of the shortest sections in *Fourth City* (in both the number and lengths of essays) it deals with one of the most pervasive problems in American prisons.

Sundiata Acoli offers a succinct consideration of the enormous costs of keeping aging men and women locked up, when in fact they pose virtually no threat to the public. "Life, Health Care, Prisons, and Cutting Costs" presents a striking example of the unreasoning policy at the heart of many other prison problems: offering prisoners only what we believe (and those who profit by current prison practice insist) they "deserve," rather than looking at the established evidence of what kinds of policies might both maintain public safety, and spare punishing taxpayers with practices that make no public-safety sense.

The writer who appears under the name Topcat offers an example of what is common to health care in Prison City: only the most obvious problems are addressed (if they are addressed at all), in the cheapest and most cursory ways, while neglecting the complex set of needs within which any health problem is located. "HIV in the South Carolina Department of Corrections" suggests a system more concerned with appearing to care for prisoner health than with doing so.

As a former mental-health-care worker, dealing with her own mental and physical health issues, Colleen O'Brien is trained and situated to offer a broad perspective on the problems faced by incarcerated women, and on the conditions that exacerbate their problems. As represented in "Mental and Physical Health Care in Prison," many of the problems we hope that prisons will address can be remedied by providing incarcerated people treatment for the most easily identified problems that stand behind their criminal acts.

"Mass-Producing Mentally Ill Citizens in America's Prisons" is Andrew J. Smith's diagnosis of the ways in which prisons not only inadequately treat but also cause many of the mental-health problems suffered by prisoners. Smith's analysis takes us inside the wiring of the brain; he helps us see how inadequate sleep, excessive punishment, and other penal conditions manufacture the damaged personalities that emerge from and, predictably, return to prison. In the vocabulary of both a neurologist and of an incarcerated American, Smith confirms what George Jackson wrote over forty years ago: "To determine how men will behave once they enter the prison it is of first importance to know that prison. Men are brutalized by the environment—not the reverse."[3] The difference today is that the prison system has achieved mass scale by continuing that brutality.

Anthony Powers's "Medical Treatment" closes this section with a brief reiteration of many of the problems and issues noted by other writers here. Like Acoli, Powers offers suggestions about how prison health care might be improved by incorporating it into health-care coverage plans enjoyed by non-incarcerated people.

Courts have more than once determined that prisons and jails must provide their wards adequate food, shelter, clothing, and other necessities since the state has stripped them of their ability to provide these things for themselves.[4] The provision of adequate mental and physical health care, as writers here make clear, is not only a moral and constitutional necessity; it makes hard-headed, practical sense to anyone interested in lowering the costs while increasing the effectiveness of prisons that we hope might turn out men and women who will not return to Prison City and state tax rolls.

NOTES

1. Adam Liptak, "Justices, 5–4, Tell California to Cut Prisoner Population," *New York Times*, May 23, 2011; see also Chris Megerian, "Inmate Advocates Question State's Commitment to Prison Healthcare," *Los Angeles Times*, February 10, 2012; and Kimberly Leonard, "Privatized Prison Health Care Scrutinized," *Washington Post*, July 21, 2012.

2. See, for example, Tom Puleo and Lisa Chedekel, "Dollars and Lives: The Cost of Prison Health Care," New England Center for Investigative Reporting, March 27, 2011, http://necir-bu.org /investigations/taxpayer-watch-series/dollars-and-lives-the-cost-of-prison-health-care-2/.

3. Jackson to Fay Stender, April 1970, in *Soledad Brother: The Prison Letters of George Jackson*, forward by Jonathan Jackson, Jr. (Chicago: Lawrence Hill, 1994), 19.

4. DeShaney v. Winnebago County Department of Social Services, No. 87-154 489 U.S. 189 (1989) [HN6]: "When a state takes a person into its custody and holds him there against his will, the United States Constitution imposes upon it a corresponding duty to assume some responsibility for his safety and general well-being. The affirmative duty to protect arises not from the state's knowledge of the individual's predicament or from its expressions of intent to help him, but from the limitation which it has imposed on his freedom to act on his own behalf." See also Estelle, Correctional Director, *et al.*, v. Gamble, No. 75-929 (429–U.S. 1976); Plata *v.* Schwarzenegger, No. 09-15864 (US 9th Cir. 2010).

SUNDIATA ACOLI, *Maryland*

LIFE, HEALTH CARE, PRISONS, AND CUTTING COSTS

Health-care costs are soaring and have become unaffordable for many families. It is no different for the Prison Industrial Complex (PIC) except that the PIC is required by law to provide medical care to its wards.

Although much of prison health care is inadequate, many youthful captives can at least squeak by on what's presently provided. Not so for those over fifty years of age, most of whom are beset by the common old-age infirmities: high blood pressure and cholesterol, diabetes, clogged arteries, heart disease, cancer, and the need for body-part replacements. California has the largest prison population in the U.S. plus the highest health-care costs, and spends $98,000 to $138,000 per year for each prisoner over fifty.[1] An August 11, 2009, *New York Times* editorial noted that "just days before a Chino, California prison riot, a three-judge panel ordered the state to reduce its 150,000+ prison population by about 40,000 in the next two years as the only way to bring its prison health care system up to constitutional standards." The editorial concluded, "The riot at Chino and the federal court's ruling contain the same message for states everywhere: They must come up with a smart way to reduce prison populations and they must do it quickly."

More prisoners today are serving life sentences than ever before. Their numbers have quadrupled since 1984 to over 140,000, and they've become a driving force behind the explosion of health-care costs in prisons.[2] Many lifers are over fifty and most are parole eligible, while the remainder are doing life without parole (LWOP).

Reasons for the ballooning of life sentences include three-strikes-you're-out, mandatory minimums, the 100 to 1 ratio of crack- to powder-cocaine sentences, children sentenced to LWOP (in clear violation of international law), and other harsh edicts of the law-and-order climate of the last several decades. The other reason for the ballooning is the unrectified racial imbalance that has accompanied America's justice system since antebellum days. Two-thirds of prisoners serving life sentences are Latino or Black, and nearly half of those serving life are Black. In thirteen states, Blacks make up 60 percent of the lifers. In New York State, only 17 percent of prisoners serving life are white.[3] Many lifers over fifty have already done twenty, even thirty years or more, and some are sixty, even seventy years old and more. The crime rate has been decreasing for the last decade or two, and *all* indicators show that elderly prisoners, once released, rarely commit another crime and are the least likely to return to prison.

So it is self-evident that the smartest and quickest way to begin reducing health-care costs and prison overcrowding is to release aged and infirm lifers and LWOPs whose age plus years served equals a fixed number (say seventy years, for example)—a number that could be further reduced in light of the seriousness of the lifer's illness.

Such a release process would not only be smart but ethical; and prisoners' families, friends, and the public would be wise to urge their congresspersons to put such a prison cost-cutting bill into effect immediately.

NOTES

1. Solomon Moore, "Study Finds Record Numbers of Inmates Serving Life," *New York Times*, July 2009, sec. A.
2. Ibid.
3. Ibid.

TOPCAT, *South Carolina*

HIV IN THE SOUTH CAROLINA DEPARTMENT OF CORRECTIONS

The South Carolina Department of Corrections (SCDC) implemented an HIV program in 1998. This program was designed to help keep the spread of HIV in the prison system to zero new infections. It began with the Department giving mandatory HIV tests throughout the prison system. The prisoners who tested positive were transported to a facility dedicated to housing all HIV-infected inmates.

I will not disclose the name of the penitentiary because this will violate the privacy of the infected people housed there. However, I want the public to know, despite our misfortune in life and in the bad choices we have made, not one of us wants to be infected. Being infected doesn't make us less competent or less human.

The program would have been a very good program providing it achieved all it was designed to do—containing HIV that otherwise would be spread throughout the prison by neglectful, irresponsible people. The heart of the matter, though, is that SCDC does not live up to the image it presents to the public. To the public's knowledge, we have a program that cares for its HIV-infected inmates, in all areas: medication, proper diet, and proper health care.

The SCDC, I will grant, does provide our needed medications. Regarding proper diet and the actual health care, I have questions. The SCDC does not take into account the inmate's general health or how it is treated. HIV inmates are fed the same diet as noninfected inmates. As anyone with HIV can attest, diet is very important to anyone that is HIV positive. HIV medications are toxic and have to have something to feed on. The SCDC diet that HIV-infected inmates are fed is not nutritionally sufficient to deal with all the medications an inmate is given.

Additionally, the medications that the HIV prisoners take they have to pay for. By rights, medications are already funded by the government. If an inmate does *not* have money in his account, the inmate is given credit for the owed amount. When or if any money is received by the inmate, the costs of the unpaid medications are subtracted from the money the inmate has received. The inmate is made to pay $5.00 per prescription, up to $15.00 per month.

Another major flaw in this program has to do with custody level and work release. The prison in question is a maximum-security prison—a level-three camp. The majority of the HIV-infected prisoners have a custody level that warrants their prison time to be served under less restrictive conditions. However, they are not allowed to be a part of work release, but they do have to work on the compound without pay. Work release for an HIV-infected inmate would be a major help. Monies made would help in providing the proper amount of nutritional food for the infected inmate (via the inmate canteen), which would help maintain body fat and a healthier diet.

The HIV-infected inmates are also classified as "special needs" inmates. But what this classification was designed to provide to a HIV-infected inmate, the South Carolina Department of Corrections does not provide.

I should know; I am one of SCDC's HIV-infected inmates, and this is our story.

COLLEEN O'BRIEN, *Michigan*

MENTAL AND PHYSICAL HEALTH CARE IN PRISON

As I sit down to write this essay, I find it hard to believe that I am writing from a prisoner's perspective. Not in my most unrealistic worries did I see myself ending up in prison at forty-one years old. Nor did I ever think that I would be convicted of a Murder 2 charge, but here I am, a forty-six-year-old woman doing a 19-year bit.

I have decided not to write too much about the circumstances of my crime or my experience with the judicial system. I will make one comment and leave it at that. From experience I have learned that the judicial system is in great need of an ethical and moral cleanup. As a convicted criminal, my statement may not mean much; however, corruption is corruption no matter what side of the law you stand on.

Once upon a time I was on the right side of the law. I worked for the Native American Tribal Health Department for twelve years. I have a masters degree in counseling and a passion for helping others. I was good at my job and was loved by coworkers and my community as a whole. The love I had for myself was limited, and, as an old song goes, "I was looking for love in all the wrong places." The self-destructive path I was on ended up hurting others. I no longer was viewed as the woman who helped others. Now, I am a convicted criminal, one with a violent crime.

Coming to prison with a higher education in the mental-health field has been interesting because I see situations and behaviors with trained eyes. When I came to prison, I made the decision that I would use my education to benefit the prison community. At first I didn't know how I could be of help, but over the last five years opportunities have come my way.

Prior to coming to prison, I spent six months in Wayne County Jail. While in the county jail, I was treated for my chronic illnesses (diabetes, hypertension, asthma, and depression); when I came to prison, I was taken off all my medication. I had to fight (through the grievance process and my family's intervention) to get treated for chronic illnesses I was diagnosed with over fifteen years earlier.

I suffered with major depression off and on over the years, and untreated major depression played a role in my crime. Yet I was abruptly taken off my antidepressant after entering the prison system. I spent my first three months in prison in a zombie-like state. The antidepressant I took in the county jail and while I was a free woman eased the emotional suffering I experienced and helped me to think clearly. Without treatment for the depression, I needlessly suffered intensely while trying to adjust to my fate.

During the first four weeks of my prison stay, I was evaluated by mental-health and health professionals. The psychologist I saw for my evaluation had no interest in my depression. His main concern was to get his job done, which was to write a report about me and then move on to the next inmate. I read the report he wrote, and it reminded me of a poorly done cut-and-paste job. The report was a poor reflection of me, and it truly served no purpose other than for the psychologist to say he did his job.

My visit with the medical doctor was even less effective. I had to be reassessed for diabetes, and the health-care staff completely ignored the fact that I had hypertension and asthma. As I mentioned before, I had to fight for the health care I finally received, and if it weren't for my family providing outside support, I would be like a lot of the prisoners here who walk around with untreated chronic illnesses. It is the norm in prison to be sick (mentally and/or physically) and not get help.

I feel like I am one of the lucky ones because I now get treatment for my chronic illnesses. Since I take medication for my mental disorder, I qualify for other mental-health services such as individual and group therapy. There are so many women here who need help. Many women are continuously involved in destructive behaviors. Some of these women know better, but way too many of them don't and are suffering because of their ignorance.

Abusive relationships run rampant in prison. Three years ago I had put in a kite (a form of prison communication) to the psychologist who ran the domestic violence groups. I asked the group leader if I could be put in one of his domestic violence groups because I had a history of getting into abusive relationships, and being in an abusive relationship played a role in my crime. The response I received from him said I had been placed on a waiting list, which went according to my inmate Earliest Release Date (ERD). Since my ERD is 2024, that pretty much excluded me from receiving much-needed help. By the Grace of God I have managed to avoid abusive relationships, which has been a struggle because there are many aggressive women in here looking for a willing victim.

Along with mental health, substance abuse is a major problem in prison. Many women, including myself, end up in prison because of a drug and/or alcohol problem. There is some help, but the help is limited. I get most of my support from attending Alcoholics Anonymous.

There is also a problem with active substance abuse within the prison as well. Somehow street drugs get smuggled in (the rumor is that staff supply the illegal drugs). Some women get caught up in using street drugs, but the real problem is with prescription drugs. Psychotropic medication, seizure medication, and medication that treats urinary or bowel issues seem to be the drugs that get abused. Some of the women who receive these drugs sell them instead of taking them for their own illnesses. These women are letting their own illnesses go untreated, which causes further problems for them, and the women they sell these drugs to are taking medications which they have no reason to take.

Apparently, many of these medications cause drowsiness. The women feel high because they feel sleepy. The sad thing about this type of abuse is the damage these women do to their normally healthy bodies. I have seen (and heard of) women who abuse seizure medication actually developing seizure disorders. I have also heard of women who lose control of their bladders and/or bowels because they have abused medication that treated urinary or bowel problems.

In all fairness, the staff does try to make sure medications are taken by the people they are prescribed for. We have to go to medication line to take certain medications, and we take the pills in front of the nurse who administers the medication. However, the inmates are clever women, and the ones who sell their medications know how to not take the medication even though it looks like they have.

The living conditions in prison (this prison anyway) are the most challenging situation for me to deal with. I live in a twelve-by-twelve cell, which has a toilet and sink (a "wet cell") with a bunkie. The cell was designed for one person, but due to overcrowding it has become a two-person cell. U.S. inmates who live like this have to use the bathroom in front of their bunkies. As far as I know, there is nothing in prison policy that states that a bunkie has to leave the cell when the other bunkie is using the bathroom or dressing. Some bunkies show common courtesy, but the ones who do are a rarity.

Lack of privacy is the biggest mental-health issue I struggle with. There is no place to go to be alone, nor is there any place you can go to have some quiet time. Bright lights and loud noises take up at least two-thirds of an average prison day. My five senses are constantly overwhelmed with irritating stimulation that I have no control over.

Another prison issue that troubles me deeply is the sexual acting out that goes on. Many of the inmates are self-proclaimed bisexuals or "Gay for the Stay," as it is sometimes called. Having to bunk, undress, use the toilet, or shower with women who view other women sexually is difficult. To say that I feel uncomfortable in these situations is stating my feelings mildly.

Living in prison is extremely stressful and a waste of human resources. There is a saying, "Idle hands are the devil's playground." I find this to be true, especially in prison. Since the main focus of a prison stay isn't rehabilitation, many women come through the prison system only to leave in worse condition (psychologically) than they entered.

I am a long-termer, and I have managed to take the fragments of help available in the prison to facilitate my own healing (and rehabilitation). With a professional background in mental health and a lot of personal experience, I look at the women who for years, and unnecessarily, are in and out of the prison. I wonder what the prison system could do to keep women from coming back. I also wonder how long-termers and lifers could do their own rehabilitation, and then help in making the prison stay a healing venture.

As in any situation, accurate assessment and evaluation needs to be done in the beginning. The problem when I entered prison was that the mental and physical health assessments and evaluations weren't accurate. Many of my issues were overlooked. Not only is an inaccurate assessment useless, so is an assessment which identifies issues but offers no follow-up. Thus the time and energy spent on assessing and evaluating every incoming prisoner is often a waste of time.

In my experience with many inmates, I have met only a few real criminals who have a criminal mindset. The rest of the ladies I have come in contact with are women who have mental, emotional, and physical issues, and these issues (unaddressed) led them to their crimes. Thus with treatment for these issues, along with relapse-prevention training, we women with such issues can be rehabilitated and won't be a threat to society.

It takes willingness and time for wellness training and rehabilitation to take hold. Individuals heal at different rates, so any treatment program offered has to accommodate both the slow and fast healers. An environment that promotes healing needs to be created. Currently the prison environment is one of dominance and control. We prisoners are looked at as a threat. Conformity to an unnatural, hostile environment is expected of us. If some inmates fall into the expected stereotype of the criminal, they need treatment that specifically addresses their criminal mindsets. These women think and act like criminals, are usually a threat to other inmates and staff, and display behaviors such as stealing, exploitation, manipulating, bullying, physical violence, verbal abuse, and overall threatening behavior. These women generally see others as objects to use for their own satisfaction. Treatment of these women needs to be specialized according to the thinking and behaviors that make them a threat. Rehabilitation of these women will probably be harder to accomplish and will take time. Professional staff that know this from the beginning will be more effective. All of these conditions are made worse by overcrowding.

Even without the overcrowding, it would still be hard living here because of the random mixture of inmates in a living/housing unit. We are categorized by our security level. I would like to see further division of inmates based on their needs—such as now happens for seriously chronic-care inmates, who all live in the same housing unit, and women who are in Residential Substance Abuse Treatment (RSAT).

What I would like to see are women who are working on their mental/emotional/physical issues in the same housing unit. The housing unit could become a therapeutic environment where self-help support groups are offered in abundance as well as other types of groups. The goal for these women would be to learn to live their wellness and eventually carry these healthy behaviors back to their communities. Long-termers and lifers have unique needs, so their housing units would offer groups that address their specific needs.

Housing units that have the true criminals residing in them would offer a different type of environment as well as groups and education that are specific to these women. Staff are specifically trained to deal with criminal behaviors, but the goal should be assisting these women in changing these behaviors. Currently women who exhibit threatening behaviors are isolated in segregation for a period of time, then released back into general population.

Formal education such as GED preparation, vocational classes, and college classes is another service that could be of great benefit to prisoners. Educational classes are offered, but there are not enough spaces available to meet the demand. Waiting lists are long. In addition, lifers and indeterminates aren't eligible to take classes, so many of these women are left idle. As mentioned, idleness is trouble, and many of these new lifers get themselves involved in a lot of self-destructive behaviors. The behaviors exhibited by these ladies cause a lot of institutional strife and drain the time of the prison staff.

Education (academic or vocational) can give prisoners a purpose. It feels good to accomplish something, and educational goals can be helpful in providing women with a means to feel good about themselves. In addition, education programs in prison can be further developed to include educating women on how to be self-sufficient while living in a prison community. What I mean by that is, there is so much wasted labor in prison. Women can learn to provide for themselves, by growing their own food, making their own clothes, developing their own schools, fixing their own equipment, and so much more!

Currently, prison life in Michigan involves fragmented help that is probably only provided to prisoners because of the efforts of a few humanitarians. Many women are given long sentences and then simply warehoused. Women with shorter sentences are given some assistance and then sent out into society unrehabilitated and unready for the demands which living in society poses. These women come back repeatedly and end up doing long sentences in intervals. Meanwhile, the long-timers and lifers cease to be a threat to society, yet have to sit and wait for their Earliest Release Date or a rare pardon from the governor.

The prison system has become an expensive storage place for people society wants to punish. Obviously Michigan has no use for convicted felons, otherwise it would put forth the time, energy, and resources to rehabilitate prisoners prior to sending them out to the community.

Michigan prisons don't even give their inmates "good time." There is no incentive for an inmate to do good in prison. A model prisoner who grows and develops in prison isn't recognized at all, and I find that to be a shame. In society, incentives are offered all the time and incentives work, so why wouldn't they work on prisoners?

The prison system needs a total overhaul. The current system isn't working. The punitive approach to crime is barbarian. I am sure there are many people with vengeful spirits who would like to see us just fall off the face of the earth. Obviously that isn't going to happen. We prisoners have to be dealt with. The punitive approach isn't working. The "Lock the door and throw away the key" approach isn't working—so now what?

ANDREW JACKSON SMITH, *Alabama*

MASS-PRODUCING MENTALLY ILL CITIZENS IN AMERICA'S PRISONS

The purpose of this essay is to point out the dangerous trend that the United States has engaged in by conducting operations in state prisons as it does currently. The author acknowledges that Alabama's prisons are among the worst in the country, while drawing conclusions from general environmental factors common to all prisons.

Humans are highly adaptable to extremes of both negative and positive environments. This adaptability is first and foremost seated in the mind. The mind defines who the person is, and every thought of the mind is reducible to the neuronal cell unit. That is, the mind is the brain, and is made up of approximately one hundred billion neurons. The adaptability of the brain is referred to as "plasticity." Plasticity means the brain will change in structure (anatomy) and in function (physiology) in response to intrusions upon it. When the brain changes, the individual is changed, becoming fundamentally different to various degrees directly dependent upon the degree of brain change.

It is not a new observation that a disproportionate number of mentally deficient persons find themselves housed in America's prisons. A variety of deficiencies exist, from low IQ's to schizophrenia to cluster "B" type personality disorders such as sociopathy and borderline personality disorder. By any standard, these incarcerated mentally ill men and women are being treated inadequately. Likewise, it is not news to note that a population of mentally normal inmates, introduced to life in prison, will become mentally ill and after release remain so. These individuals will not adjust appropriately upon reentry into society. The APA (American Psychological Association) should develop a diagnostic criteria for this. It is important to note the direct correlation between length of incarceration and difficulty with adjustment to society.

The primary purpose of prison is to isolate a criminal segment of society from non-criminal citizens. Security takes precedence in a prison's operations, the security of inmates and staff alike. Some states sentence inmates to forced labor as well, such as in Alabama.

Initial incarceration is no less than a traumatic event for the well-adjusted, psychologically normal American citizen, and this by design. For example, when this author was arrested, he had left his apartment to help cooperate with police, who had fabricated a story. After some time at the police station, the author was told his fiancée was dead and he was under arrest for murder. He fainted and was propped up, and regained consciousness as a flash from a camera made his arrest photo. He was transported to county jail, stripped, placed in a paper gown, and put into a room so cold that the officers wore heavy coats, hats, gloves, and scarves in order to stay warm. This treatment was clearly designed to be torturous. Lights were never dimmed or turned off, a radio played continuously, food was scant and cold, no clothing was permitted, and inmates slept (when exhausted) upon cold concrete floors without any cover. This continued for months, while the author lost gross amounts of weight, hallucinated, and begged to be allowed a washcloth to cover his eyes. Instead he was frequently taunted.

When his lawyer came to visit, he was lied to and told his client had been transferred to another prison. His family would have to go eventually to the Mobile City Commission and complain before they were allowed to visit. The author was by then in such poor physical and mental health, he would have to be rolled in a wheelchair to visit, unable to stand or walk. The author was a totally and permanently disabled veteran who had worked hard, through years of treatment, to get back into educational and work endeavors. He would never fully recover from this new damage by the county jail system. He remained in county jail for approximately fifteen months, rarely seeing outdoors, and often the victim of daily violent assaults, typical of county jails. This is the beginning of the psychological damage experienced by inmates.

Once an individual is undergoing stress, a cascade of homeostatic events occur, one of which is the release of cortisol. Prolonged and increased cortisol release leads to the destruction of neurons in the brain. Situational depression alters the functioning of neurotransmitters such as serotonin, norepinephrine, and dopamine. The immunological system is weakened, and in an environment of increased pathogens (virus, bacteria, fungus) infections are commonplace. The inmate is deteriorating physically and mentally at a rapid rate while at the most crucial point of the judicial process and court appearances, where sharp and rapid cognitive functions are most needed. Health care in county and state prisons is substandard relative to U.S. standards and most world standards. While the Secretary of Defense Gates takes suggestions by Generals Petraeus and McChrystal to incarcerate enemy prisoners to international standards, incarcerated U.S. citizens are often clearly kept below those standards.

U.S. prisons are not simply "stressful" (which stress is bad enough to cause permanent neuronal loss in the brain), but would be considered often, at best, "soft torture." The public has been led to believe that this stress is no more than "discomfort" and warranted as part of punitive treatment. They do not understand that the man incarcerated due to criminal behavior will likely be released with mental illness that furthers criminal behavior. And then the public seems surprised at the high rate of recidivism.

The environment in the state prisons is likely to lead to mental illness and permanent brain change, reflected in destructive behavior and maladaptation to society.

It's not the neuron that makes our thoughts. Rather, it's our thoughts that make the neurons. When an individual experiences stimuli, either internal or external, perception is received by the neurons, and a cascade of events takes place which may ultimately lead to an action potential or firing of the neuron. Stimuli received by the neuron may be excitatory, but also inhibitory. As new stimuli are received by the brain, the brain acts to accommodate the stimuli. This may be thought of, in a sense, as learning. For example, if an English speaker learns Spanish, his brain has changed to facilitate his newly acquired skill. So, when the stimuli is received and the neuron fires from repetitive stimuli, gene expression in the nucleus makes possible protein synthesis of new substances, such as channels, receptors, and neurotransmitters; this essentially makes the neuron change and in effect then communicates with other neurons differently, and so then it is apt to change pathways of communications and thus change the neuronal networks of parallel and collateral connections. (I say "change" frequently because the change may be new and greater communication, but it may also be new and blocked or a lesser means of communication.)

The stimuli triggering or initiating these events are thoughts from internal etiology, or from perception of our external environment, or a combination of both. To understand how this works out in prisons, let's be clear about what the general state prison environment looks like.

Lights come on about two A.M. and stay on until eleven P.M. If a man wants to block these abundant fluorescent lights, he may put his head under the covers, restricting breathing, or tie a "blindfold" around the head. Intercom loudspeakers begin also at two A.M. and continue till eleven P.M. There is never an assured time of quiet or darkness. The environment clearly is never conducive to restful sleep. One sleeps on steel, on a thin mattress, upon a narrow bed, and in close (about two to three foot) proximity to others.

Smoking is continuous, twenty-four hours, seven days a week, even in nonsmoking dorms. Rules are mostly ignored by inmates, and little effort is made by officials to enforce them. Homosexual and perverse sexual acts among those consenting (and at times "not") are commonplace. The result is that sleep is poor and fragmented. Hygiene is limited by restricted (and often impractical) hours of "showers on." Soap may be issued once a week, in amounts sufficient usually for four to five days. Clothing is sent to be washed by inmates, who often steal clothing to barter for other items. There may be two TVs for two hundred inmates, and shows are voted upon, and so stay on Jerry Springer–type shows and movies that glorify crime and violence. Games consist of checkers, chess, and dominoes generally. Exercise is in about one-hour blocks, with one basketball court and a weight pile suited for about twenty-five, but available to over one thousand inmates. The overall atmosphere in prison is of "nothing to do"; much idle time is spent waiting on "court times," chow call, showers on, or yard calls. The therapeutic programs available are simply "eyewash" and would never be acceptable in any civilian setting.

Inmates who have access to money may attempt to pursue wholesome activities of study or reading, but these are met with great resistance by the officials, and then often made impractical. Rarely can an inmate pursue, for example, a college degree. Such programs are nearly unheard of in state prisons, and are highly discouraged by officials, who often note that they themselves have no degree and so why should an inmate?

To recap: Prisons are proud of environments that are oppressive and perverse, which do damage to inmates, and so reinforce the projected stereotype of inmates to the public. And public officials seem content with this destructive environment; it is part of the punitive process and loss of rights, and thus proper and just.

The social culture in prison would be considered "abnormal" by any reasonable social anthropologist or psychiatrist. And this abnormal environment then provides abnormal stimuli that shape the brain. It is this external (abnormal) stimuli and internal abnormal reaction or thought process (which is a necessary adaptive and survival mechanism) that triggers the neurons to change shape and function. The resultant abnormal behavioral signs and symptoms can be observed all around you. This, if allowed to continue for months or years, then "hardwires" the brain to function in an "abnormal" environment, and so the person is deemed "abnormal."

Once this person is released, you now have a programmed psychotic in society. It would be a stretch for any qualified, unbiased, and informed professional to find any improvement in one's cognitive neuropsychiatric functioning as a result of prison. The United States is creating an isolated, genetic island of sociopaths as a regular and revolving and ever-growing part of our culture.

If our government was to acquire data on this problem, a good starting point would be to insert an innocent, law-abiding citizen trained in various aspects of human behavior and medicine to observe and report on the conditions and resultant apparent abnormalities—a man such as this author. However, government officials, especially those of the judicial branch, seem to absolutely despise a convicted man who professes his innocence. And such a person is likewise despised by prison officials and inmates. And so an interesting question arises. Can a morally sound, physically fit, and psychologically normal individual sustain such a state in prison, and if so, how?

Although physical fitness, intellectually constructive pursuits, spirituality, and morality all play important roles in prison and aid in continuing the values and purpose in one's life, the single most important factor may be preservation of one's identity itself. This marks one's success in not succumbing to all the intrusions upon the mind in prison.

This author's habits are designed to avoid destruction of his own identity: spiritually, physically, and mentally. He prays daily, jogs daily, teaches classes weekly, studies daily, in leisure time seeks relationships with a few remaining friends and family, and finds relaxation (such as it is) in instrumental music. This is an odd pattern of behavior in prison and assures he remains mostly "isolated" in the close confines amid over a thousand inmates. This acquired practice, to maintain his identity in this foreign land, has surely been enhanced by a few key individuals (noted by affiliation and first names) who are familiar with and supportive of the author. Dr. C has encouraged the author and been a dear friend and also provided cognitively stimulating works. Dr. T has been a dear friend to share correspondence with. Brother David has furnished spiritual materials. Many (about a dozen) army friends have encouraged the author as well. One former inmate has continued to try to improve the work the author does for other inmates.

There is a tremendous amount of guilt that accompanies acceptance of help, knowing one is likely to not leave a prison before age seventy-three and thus possibly not ever be able to thank those so crucial to the author's well-being while enduring this hardship. The greater fact is not the enduring, productive author, but the loving and loyal friends who have not forsaken him, despite his unpopularity.

There are policies and designs that could be incorporated easily into state prisons, making them profitable to all, and these would likely require no greater economic or human capital. But that would entail another essay.

ANTHONY POWERS, *Washington*

MEDICAL TREATMENT

Medical treatment in prison is certainly some of the worst in the country. I can understand members of society not caring much for how somebody in prison is receiving health care when they may be struggling to receive it themselves, but in our country we treat animals found in the streets to humane standards as far as health care is concerned.

It would be one thing if inmates could afford to buy into their own medical plan, but they can't. Most prison jobs in the state that I am incarcerated in pay around thirty to forty dollars a month starting off. This is for a full-time job. We would never to able to pay for health care. Unfortunately the staff working in prison hospitals aren't the top of the line in the medical field. Most good doctors and nurses are working at real hospitals. That's just the truth of the matter.

What most taxpayers would probably be appalled at is that medical staff in prison repeatedly cost taxpayers money by trying to save money. This is done when they do not treat an individual for something in the manner that is really needed. The medical issue that the inmate is facing then worsens, to a point where the prison has to send him to an outside hospital and it costs the taxpayers many times over the expense to treat it in the beginning.

It would be like taking somebody who had been struck by metal from a bomb and just wrapping it up in a bandage and giving him some ibuprofen (prison's cure-all). Over time the person gets an infection, and they wait and wait until it becomes gangrenous. Eventually the problem gets far out of control, and the person has to go into emergency surgery and loses one of his limbs. All of this could have been prevented by just removing the scrap metal in the beginning, disinfecting the wound, and keeping it clean, but this was too much trouble to go through. Either way, staff get paid. The current medical system in prison is ineffective. Along with this there is the problem of individuals receiving the wrong medications when they do receive medical treatment. So, here are some suggestions:

- Enter all inmates into a collective medical plan, and let insurance companies compete for the contract.

- Hold medical staff accountable for their performance within the prison. Have yearly audits of their medical records at each facility. If it is found that they are overcharging the insurance company or are providing inadequate health care services, fire them.

- Aggressively attack, through treatment, infectious diseases in the prison system. I don't know the exact figure, but I have heard estimates that as many as 75 percent of the prison's inmate population are carriers of infectious diseases. The cost may be high to treat them, but the costs of spreading an infectious disease are even greater.

- Charge fraud fees to inmates who abuse the system. And make inmates aware that these fees exist. (Sometimes inmates will sign up for sick call or other medical services for fraudulent reasons.)

- Double and triple check the medications being issued to an inmate to ensure that he is being issued the proper medication for the problem that he is dealing with, and stop using ibuprofen as a cure-all.

There obviously would have to be a more thorough study of all the things wrong, as well as what is working, within the current prison health-care system. This is only a brief glimpse of some of the things that need to be addressed. An in-depth study should include interviews of inmates as well as staff. I don't know what types of challenges staff are facing in this area, and I don't want to be unfair to them.

Kite Out

SHAKKIR TALIB MUJAHID, *Maryland*

A MESSAGE TO THE INCARCERATED MUSLIM

Bismillahir Rahmanir Raheem
(In the Name of Allah, Most Gracious, Most Merciful)

I am sad today, for the Message I bring has been shouted through the halls and walls of these universities for years. "Say you believe in Allah and stand firm on it."

I don't know that many of you know what this actually means. It appears that you have let your life of anger, deceit, distrust, hatred, greed, and lust for power, control, and fame make you believe that you can change this life's game. The standard has been set by Allah (SWT, *Subhanahu wa ta'ala*) through His Speech (*The Qur'an*) and His human example of His Truth, the Prophet Muhammad Ibn Abdullah, the best example of a man. We need to cut the crap and stop making excuses and falling into the same satanic trap.

We have been told that Religion is based on "intentions" and that "every man shall receive what he intends." Then look around you, my brothers, at your life and the example we see in those who proclaim they possess the truth and the light! It is said that the truth shall set you free. But I walk through the crud of your misery every day, and so much insincerity.

I see the games you play with your brother's life—causing him all sorts of emotional strife while you sneak around fulfilling all of your lustful desires and vices. It's sad that you have chosen this road that will bring so much detriment to your soul.

You say you want to practice Islam, but you persist in demonstrating His-Lam. I see and feel your lust for control, power, and position, and your disdain for the truth when it is explained. You are walking around with these fake personas of toughness and roughness, but yet you whine, cry, complain, and lack the courage to stand up with justice and righteousness for that which you proclaim. Take off these masks, my brothers, and humble yourself to the Religion and the Lord you claim!

We can no longer continue to justify our weaknesses; we can no longer continue to directly and indirectly call Allah (SWT) a liar through the things we say, and by practicing deeds that go against what we teach. We tell the world Islam is the best way of life for all humanity, but we continue to allow the corruption of the *dunya* (world) to dominate our thoughts and actions, and we follow all of life's insanities. We continue to intoxicate our souls with the love of money, music, drugs, and illicit and sexual bonds while through manipulation, false promises, and outright lies we seek power, control, and the honor of men.

We have not humbled and completely submitted our egos, hearts, and minds to the one who we proclaim to have created "the Heavens and Earth and everything between them." We are playing games with our lives and souls like a person hanging over a fierce and blazing fire on a broken tree limb. I warn you, my brothers, from the deepest part of my heart: the only game being played is the one you're playing with yourself. The Lord, whom I serve, is the *Al-A'lim* (All-Knowing), *Al-Baseer* (All-Seeing), *As-Sami* (All-Hearing), *Al-Hakim* (Most Wise), and there is nothing that slips by Him. He definitely has an account of what you do. In truth, you are the enemy within!

It is my advice to you to make *Taubah* (seek Repentance) for your evil and deceptive intent, and change your ways before the Death Angel is sent. It is my advice that you stop hindering men from understanding beauty and truth, by your ugliness in speech, actions, and deeds. It is my advice, my brothers, that you get real with loving yourself and submit yourself wholeheartedly to this truth, so that you can experience the fullness of this truth and show your family and friends that this religion is the real deal. It is my advice to you to be thankful and grateful that you have been blessed to walk through Islam's door before it's too late for you, and death ends your opportunity with a severe punishment that I know you cannot endure.

It is my advice to stop being so ungrateful, rebellious, and foul in your behavior and speech, because one day the one you rejected you are going to meet. If you really love yourself and your family, then take advantage of the mercy and the love given to you and your family, by entering into Islam wholeheartedly. The promise is for those who live a life of obedience and sincerity; they can reap the benefits of this truth's reality. It is only Allah, The Most High, who can grant a blessed life in this life and eternity.

It is my advice to you that no matter what you think about this Religion, it is true, the Hellfire is true, the Paradise is true, and all of Allah's promises are true. The only thing that will save you is that you get rid of the corruption, deceit, lies, hate, insincerity, selfishness and rebellion, and bitterness in you.

Let us be the ones that set a better example of this Truth; don't you realize you are the mercy sent to your family to establish the Islamic roots? Stand firm on this Truth, firmly in your heart and soul, with everything. Stop miscommunicating through your actions that Islam is only a "jailhouse thing"; stand firm with courage, faith, and trust in Allah's (SWT) power and authority over creation to provide your wants and needs, standing firmly until death comes to you in this blessed and wonderful life's creed.

We have to stop making all these excuses and be Muslim Men. Knowing that the Truth molds the best of men who sacrifice, believe, and stand on the Truth to the end! So listen, O Believers; stop resisting this truth and believing the lies of Shaitan and his lying Jinns.

If this Truth is not your desire, my brothers, then get out of the way. This path is not for the weak and insincere; it's only for those who sincerely love Allah and are committed to die for Him and this Truth every day! But if you choose to be insincere, deceitful, rebellious, and disloyal while you stray, then know soon you will answer for the mischief in your heart and the mischief you perpetrated in the land, on Judgment Day!

I pray that you take heed of the warning and let us be brothers in Islam—unifying upon this Truth and standing firm as Muslim Men! May Allah continue to bestow His Mercy, Grace, Forgiveness, Love, Peace, and Guidance upon you and give all of us the Courage and Strength to establish Islam in ourselves and in the land.

I leave you with this from *The Qur'an*; *Surah An-Nur* (24); *ayats* 54–55:

Say: Obey Allah and obey the Messenger. But if you turn away, he [Muhammad] is only responsible for the duty placed on him and you for that placed on you. If you obey him, you shall be on the right guidance. The Messenger's duty is only to convey [the message] in a clear way. Allah has promised those among you who believe and do righteous goods, that He will certainly grant them succession to [the present rulers] in the land, as He granted it to those before them, and that He will grant them the authority to practice their religion, which he has chosen for them! [Islam] And He will surely give them in exchange a safe security after their fear [provided] they [believers] worship Me and do not associate anything [in worship] with Me. But whoever disbelieved after this, they are the Fasiqun [rebellious, disobedient to Allah].

This is my message to the Incarcerated Muslim Man!

If I have said anything good, this is from Allah (SWT), and if I have said anything wrong or evil, this is from myself and my own ignorance, and may Allah forgive me.

Community Activists

INTRODUCTION

No one feels the stakes of prison transformation more intimately than the prison's inhabitants. The essays that follow witness how well located they are to effect the change required. These are essays by men who dare to make improvements that would turn the American prison into a more functional, safe, and socially constructive institution—for staff, inmates, and the public at large. But even as the incarcerated enter the frontlines of community activism, we see them paying the price for their efforts.

Robert Saleem Holbrook represents a long tradition in American letters: from slave narrators like Moses Roper, Fredrick Douglass, and Harriet Jacobs, to imprisoned Black Power writers George Jackson, Nuh Washington, and Jalil Muntaqim. Holbrook is an African American man for whom legalized punishment has done less to wear down than to move his spirit into political awareness and action. Holbrook's "From Public Enemy to Enemy of the State" looks back at his youth, when he was the face of the enemy targeted by the War on Drugs. Today he is a man thinking and organizing for prison justice; although he is less violent and disruptive in his behavior, because he writes and speaks up for himself and his fellow prisoners, he is perceived by the Pennsylvania Department of Corrections as more dangerous than ever before.

Corey John Richardson's "The Convict Activist/The Convict Vote" lays an urgent charge upon other incarcerated people as well as those who have recently been freed. Richardson has learned to endure everything that's wrong within men's prisons. But what he cannot abide is the complaisance of his peers. In his exasperation, we get a glimpse of just how much political potential goes for naught,[1] unorganized and ineffective, both behind prison walls and among those who leave them. Richardson knows too much to expect changes in prison policies until pressure from higher, civilian authorities is brought to bear upon them. And no one has better reason to bring such pressure to bear than prisoners and former prisoners.

Larry G. "Rocky" Harris is a self-proclaimed jailhouse lawyer, using his skills to sue the state and the state employees who violate the law inside Illinois prisons. In "When Is It Enough?" Harris writes as a former taxpayer, angry about the costs incurred when the state covers the expenses of defending its employees. Like other writers in this volume, Harris bears witness to an institution that has eluded public accountability, becoming, to contractors and correctional officers' unions, an archipelago of fiefdoms; these interested parties profit from prisons that damage their wards and thus do little to aid, and much to chip away at, the public's physical and financial security.

There are few incarcerated men or women in the United States with more experience of, or who can point to more success in efforts at prison reform than Kenneth E. Hartman. His essay, "The Trouble with Prison Reformers," documents the formidable obstacles to reform presented by prison staff, their unions, politicians, and the images of prisoners entrenched in the minds of the public. Hartman presents a truth that would seem obvious were it not for decades of professional and popular complaisance with prisons that do no one any good: prisoners know what prisons need to do to help them quit the lives that brought them to prison. And no one can stand in the place of incarcerated people to provide this vital perspective.

This section of *Fourth City* represents a much larger number of men and women who might be empowered to make the changes that prisons need: the jailhouse lawyers, those who fight to create prisoner-grievance review boards (or make them effective), those pursuing the crooked path of legal redress for violations of basic rights, the program leaders trying to make existing structures work as well as they can, as well as those who have real organizing skills but have been stymied so often and so off-handedly by staff that they have returned to watching their own backs. The intellectual and organizational skills needed to transform Prison City exist today inside its walls. Once we see that they are not the monsters we like to believe they are, we might begin prison reform in conversation and collaboration with the incarcerated men and women who know best what to do and how to do it.

NOTE

1. See Christopher Uggen and Jeff Manza, "Lost Voices: The Civil and Political Views of Disenfranchised Felons," in *Imprisoning America: The Social Effects of Mass Incarceration*, ed. Mary Patillo, David Weiman, and Bruce Western (New York: Russell Sage, 2004).

ROBERT SALEEM HOLBROOK, *Pennsylvania*

FROM PUBLIC ENEMY TO ENEMY OF THE STATE

When I was a child, I used to walk past the old Eastern State Penitentiary on Fairmount Avenue in North Philadelphia and stare in awe at its high walls and ramparts seemingly towering into the sky, believing naively that the old prison was an ancient castle from the days of knights and kings. There were times when myself and other kids my age tried to scale the walls to get a glimpse of what was inside. How ironic it is that for the past eighteen years I've been trying to figure out how to scale out of the prisons I've been inside since the age of sixteen.

I've often sat in my cell in total isolation and solitude attempting to figure out what brought me to this point in my life where, at the age of thirty-four, I've been imprisoned for eighteen years, with the rest of my life destined for the same thing. During three years of confinement in the state's control unit (Special Management Unit) at SCI-Greene, I had the unique opportunity to actually backtrack practically every poor decision I made in my life that eventually culminated in my imprisonment. When you are locked down for twenty-three hours a day, seven days a week, you have the chance to engage in such personal adventures in discovery.

The decision that culminated in my imprisonment occurred when I was fourteen years old, hanging out with some friends on the corner, admiring a car an older guy from the neighborhood had.

He sold drugs and seemed to have it all, and that's what I wanted—i.e., the girls, the clothes, the respect, etc. It wasn't until years later, while in my early twenties, that I came to understand the distinction between my wants and needs, but at that moment I suffered from "reckless youth" and could only see the benefits that selling drugs provided. That admiration led me to compliment his car, and we struck up a conversation that culminated in my agreeing to sell drugs for him. It was that decision, combined with a series of other poor decisions and circumstances that resulted in a LWOP sentence two years later for being an "alleged" lookout for a drug-related murder. There was a time in this country when youth were allowed mistakes. However, that is not the case anymore, unless we're talking about President George W. Bush, who could blame his early cocaine addiction on "being young and a little irresponsible."

Little did I know, but that decision to become involved in gangs and the drug trade put me on a collision course with not only other gang members and law enforcement, but with the federal government's War on Drugs. Overnight I had unknowingly transformed from a "kid" to "public enemy" in the eyes and perception of the public and government. In order for the government to wage a "war" on drugs, it had to identify the enemy, or create "public enemies" the public can vilify and fear in order to justify its war and multibillion-dollar budgets. The enemies were identified. The government had declared war on a substantial segment of its citizenry—in particular, youth of color, i.e., "gangbangers."

With me identified as a "public enemy," it was therefore easy for the state to impose a life without parole sentence on myself and countless other juvenile offenders caught up in the street wars. Despite our age, we were the expendable casualties of the War on Drugs. From my arrest, conviction, and sentencing, I was a statistic on the policy charts of law-enforcement briefings to the media, politicians, government committees, etc., demonstrating law enforcement's "imminent victory" against street gangs and drug lords. Like the body-count tallies in Vietnam and Iraq, my imprisonment was a slogan or prop for public consumption, demonstrating that the war is being won and the bad guys are losing.

Initially content with the government-imposed *public enemy* label, I unwittingly played into the stereotype while imprisoned, accepting and conforming to the dog-eat-dog environment. I didn't care about anything and sought to adopt, hone, and sharpen the criminal and predatory traits that dominate the prison system and contribute to the criminality of its inhabitants. I saw no need to change or evolve. This was part of the game, and, on another level beyond my perception, part of the government's script for young public enemies.

In the controlled environment of prison the script is even more predictable. Act out, break the rules, be disciplined via the hole, be released, replay script . . . Like the script on the streets, both sides pretty much accept their roles. Imprisoned, we are society's public enemies, and in the eyes of the guards it is their patriotic duty to imprison us, having been conditioned to believe they are manning the walls in the nation's War on Drugs. The institution of criminal justice in this country, from the police, to the courts, to the Department of Corrections, is built on a war model, and its target is youth of color.

Somewhere in and around the tenth year of my imprisonment, at the age of twenty-six, I decided to stop playing out the script. No one single event or incident bought about this decision; rather, it was a culmination of events, maturity, and experience. For one, I started to question why the white kid received five to ten years for the same role in a murder that I received a life without parole sentence for. Why did the white man that murdered a childhood friend of mine in 1989, by penetrating his skull with a tire iron, receive only five years probation? There were a million other Whys that started to bombard my mind and subconscious. I could not escape by falling back into the script. I started to read to satisfy my questions. I had always read during my imprisonment, but now I started to take what I read seriously. I became angry as I became more aware of the injustice around me, and the feelings of anger and rage that at one time I directed at opposing neighborhoods and prisoners was now directed at the injustices of the state that imprisoned me.

It became impossible for me to play the script once aware of the injustice of my imprisonment and the criminal-justice system in general. I also could not just sit still and rage and condemn the system. I had to challenge and confront it as best I could from within the confines of the prison. I decided to become involved in activism against imprisonment and the government's War on Drugs. My politics and activism would spring forth from an oppositional perspective. The state and I were opponents, and the script was tossed out the window. This decision would give me a firsthand experience of the response of the institution of government when its legitimacy is challenged and questioned by those it attempts to marginalize, define, or ignore. I embarked on a transformation that led me on a collision course with a government campaign and policy. Overnight I went from "public enemy" to "Enemy of the State" in the eyes of the Department of Corrections.

The consequences of this shift in personal consciousness and institutional "classification" were substantial and a lesson in the art of institutional self-preservation. Since tossing the script that prisoners are expected to conform to, I have remained misconduct-free since 2001. In the eleven years preceding 2001, I had been kicked out of seven different prisons and done two tours in the state's Supermax Control Unit for incorrigible behavior, and had incurred dozens of misconducts.

Normally the DOC would reward or encourage such a turnaround in behavior, but in the eyes of the DOC the behavior I was engaging in was far more serious misconduct than if I was running wild in the system, breaking every rule on the books. What was this serious misconduct I was engaging in? Networking with activists on the outside who are challenging the injustice of the so-called criminal-justice system, writing articles and pamphlets exposing the injustices of prison, and, most serious in the eyes of the DOC, articulating a perspective on prisoners and prisons in opposition to the false perception of prisoners, and the need for prisons, that the DOC is articulating to the public. I have seized control of my image from the DOC and dared to define myself, fellow prisoners, and the DOC itself. No longer can the DOC at will define me as a gangbanger, murderer, public enemy, etc., without my response to the contrary.

The DOC's reaction has been a lesson in the fact that you cannot challenge or protest government injustice, repression, etc., without suffering the foot of the state wherever you are. In the past couple years, my custody level has been upgraded to a "High Risk Prisoner" despite years of misconduct-free behavior; all my mail is monitored and read due to "radical beliefs" and involvement with "questionable" publications—i.e., publications critical of the government's war on drugs and terror. In 2002 I was placed in the hole for fourteen months without charge because the prison thought I expressed sympathy with the terrorists the United States is at war with, because of my grievances and complaints challenging institutional racism.

How was a connection to the "War on Terror" made with prison activism? In response to a question I posed to a DOC security captain about the need to monitor my mail, I was candidly told, "We live in a new world since 2001, and the government and the DOC is concerned about this type activity." So, not content with being on the frontlines of the War on Drugs, the DOC has found a way to muscle into the War on Terror hustle by monitoring and containing prisoner activists and their supporters on the outside. The government has used the War on Terror to stifle anything outside of the "acceptable bounds of dissent"—e.g., writing or calling your congressman, writing a letter to the editor of your local newspaper, venting and getting over it. The DOC has manipulated the War on Terror to suit its own desire to stifle internal dissent and criticism of its policies and practices.

Despite the repression and personal difficulties imposed by the DOC, in the end the transition from public enemy to enemy of the state has been worth it, and I have no regrets other than I wish I had made the connection between the drug trade and the government's failed War on Drugs prior to coming to prison as a juvenile offender. Life is about transitions and transcending one's limitations, and sooner or later, for better or for worse, we all make or miss the transition that will define who we are and, most importantly, choose to be. No longer will the state define me. I will dare to define myself.

> In any place in the world, anytime, any man or woman rebels to the point of tearing off the clothes that resignation has woven for them and cynicism has dyed gray. Any man or woman, of whatever color, in whatever tongue, speaks and says to himself, to herself "Enough is enough!—*Ya Basta!*"

—SUBCOMANDANTE MARCOS

COREY JOHN RICHARDSON, *Kentucky*

THE CONVICT ACTIVIST/
THE CONVICT VOTE

I'm angry. No, I'm furious—and it's been stewing, brewing, and percolating for years. It's not because of deeper cuts in our already subpar education, health care, and other social services, due in large part to the continuous expansion of the U.S. prison system. Not because more and more evidence of rampant prosecutorial abuse surfaces all the time. Not because of the disproportionate application of the death penalty against minorities. Not because of the clear and unequivocal fact that we have two systems of "justice" in this country: one for the rich and one for the poor. Not because the majority of those funneled into our prisons are overwhelmingly from impoverished communities, and that they, in large portions, serve decades for predominantly nonviolent/non-sex crimes. Not because private industries which profit from incarceration affect sentencing laws due to their political contributions to lawmakers. Not even because prisoners survive decades of incarceration and its violence, humiliation, systemic institutional abuses, poor nutrition, counterproductive rehabilitation, isolation, dissolution of the family, lack of medical attention, and increased risk of disease—all sanctioned as "justice"—and then are released onto the streets unhealthy, traumatized, undereducated, and marked with the stigma of Convict . . . allegedly as "free" men and women. No—I'm mad at us. We, the prisoners, who get out and do absolutely nothing to change the egregious laws which have allowed for the prisonization of America. Nor do we do anything to improve the dehumanizing system of "corrections" that many of us have endured for much of our adult lives.

When I entered prison, I quickly realized what people meant when they said to me, "Stay out of the way." The way most of us prefer to do time is trouble-free, with the guards and administration far away from our cells. So, when asked, I always say, "Lay down," and I mean stay away from the prison drama and do something positive with the time that you have to serve. In this way, I found that I actually have more to accomplish in prison than I ever had as a free man, and I couldn't achieve the goals that I set for myself from a position of segregation. I stay out of their faces and I hope that they stay out of mine. I have had to pick my battles carefully with this policy. I know that I will aggravate the warden or the commissioner when they see their names at the top of a lawsuit; therefore I make certain that what I am fighting for (1) is justified, and (2) makes a real difference to those of us serving time.

Of course, not everyone sees it this way. They feel that they have to take advantage of the weak or perpetually scam those around them. As I see it, this is not the way to turn your life around. And I'm disappointed with those prisoners who limit themselves to chow, cable TV, basketball, and walking the loop, sharing the same old war stories for years when they could be taking back their lives. It's hard not to impart this without sounding fake or preachy. I try to just do my best through my own life as an example.

Quite separately, I've grown to resent immensely those prisoners who ingratiate themselves to the prison administration and staff by means of supporting this venal system, whether it's by snitching, voting against a grievance with merit while serving on a committee, obstructing in any way a prisoner's lawsuit or demand for a policy change, or simply being a "yes man" to the guards. But these "rats" mean very little in the scheme of things. Those that make me truly furious are those of us who make it home.

"What? Well, you piece of . . ." I hear what you are thinking already. I view the big picture like this: I'm always happy to see my friends, and even those I don't like, go home. I have photographs on my locker door of many of my friends that made it out there. The caption emblazoned above them reads, "Free at Last!!" It's sheer insanity how we've acquiesced to having entire communities of people locked up, and my greatest desire is to see that all of the prisons are emptied out, thus putting the guards, caseworkers, and wardens in the unemployment lines. (God knows that they are unfit for any real jobs.) But the sad truth is that we get out there and do nothing to change the system. Most just keep coming back to this place which they have hated for years; they were hardly out long enough to get acquainted with their own kids. When one of us fails, we all fail.

I believe we are called to do something more. Much more. I believe that we are called to be CONVICT ACTIVISTS. Before we step out into the light of freedom, we need to make a list of our experiences prior to our arrest, followed by what we went through during arrest and prosecution, then work over our years in prison. On your list you would probably find some of the following: a crumbling education system, lack of effective and free drug rehab, police corruption and racial profiling, criminalization of addiction, unnecessary physical violence against prisoners by guards, an arbitrary parole system, malicious parole officers, scarcity of diversion programs, the death penalty . . . the list goes on and on. And yet, when we leave prison behind, we seem to focus solely on getting back to our loved ones and finding a little creature comfort. After only a few weeks, it is as if we were never even in prison, and we've gone back in time to a life that looks exactly like the one that brought us to prison in the first place. When we do end up back on the prison yard, it is as if we are experiencing that same bad dream all over. "Damn, how did I end up back here again?"

When I help a buddy carry his property up front, I always hope that I never see him again on this side of the fence. I always want to believe that he has left this craziness behind. Unfortunately, it takes only a short time in prison to witness the revolving door. I'll admit it. It disheartens me. The same old faces return. The backslapping, all of the catching up, and the "Gotta get my TV money in." Back on the basketball court, as if the returnee only sat out one or two games. Then invariably comes the same old complaints: the disgusting slop they call food; the abusive guards; the ungodly cost of collect calls; how unjust the entire U.S. criminal-justice system is; missing your kids; and on and on.

Now, many states return one's voting rights upon discharge of parole/probation or serve-out. Some require some filing process and approval. With so many of us with felony records, it is undeniable that our vote could change this country for the better. We could easily affect the outcome of local, state, and national elections. With this power, politicians would have to listen to our demands, which don't just include equity in the courts and proportionality in sentencing, but include reform in prisons and sufficient programs in our underserved communities. It came to me as I watched this last election cycle, where I heard much explication about the Women's Vote, the Black Vote, the Gay Vote, the Pro-Life Vote, the Hispanic Vote, the White Male Vote, the Blue-Collar Vote, the . . . And I thought, "Where's the CONVICT VOTE?" Our sheer numbers would seem to necessitate some consideration. Aren't we a formidable political force? No. Even if we can, we do not vote. If as one body we chose to vote to address our beliefs, which come from our valuable life experiences, then we could effect change in this country to correct some of the most dire social ills that have led millions to prison and left them now victims of the most inhumane, abusive system in America today.

So, there you have it. Each of us must immediately register to vote as soon as it is legally possible and recruit all who share our ideals to do the same, be they convict or family and friends. We must check websites like "house.gov" and "senate.gov" to see who these so-called representatives are. We must find out what their voting records are and what their views are on the issues that matter most to us, our communities, and our friends still locked down behind concrete. Are they just a "Tough on Crime" advocate, or do they see the necessity of good public education, quality health care for all, diversion programs, free and effective community drug rehab, sentencing with proportionality, etc.? If they are willing to sacrifice so much good and progress to merely lock up those whom they perceive as "undesirable" in this growing cancer called the Prison Industrial Complex, then we must fight against them.

Our one vote is not enough either. We are called to an activism that involves us at every level. We show up at town-hall meetings and local political rallies. We write to the editors of our local papers about our concerns. We become fully active with organizations like National Death Row Assistance Network and the Innocence Project. These and many other organizations have been fighting for us, and now we must fight as well, politically. We can change our communities, our laws, and this travesty of prisonization. We can give our kids and grandkids a land that is truly free.

Is this all "pie in the sky" thinking? No, it is not. Just read your history. Ancient history. American history. Just look at who is in the White House today. If a determined people led by those with a clearness of purpose can effect earth-shaking changes time and time again in the course of history, then so can we, Convict Activists, as long as our will is fortified and our ideals are honorable. I for one crave change. Real change in our communities, in our courts, and in our prisons. I will leave these concrete walls in a few years and I won't be coming back, but I will never forget. I am going to do my damnedest to work with others to see that this country looks a little brighter without the blight of mass imprisonment. One day, social scientists will look back on what the Tough on Crime mania has done, and they will not look too differently than we look back with abhorrence on slavery or a woman unable to vote or own property. Prisonization is the social-justice issue of this era.

I am going to become a Convict Activist, and you can also. In prison, we must at times "lay low" and "stay out of the way" to get a little education or learn a trade when possible, or simply get home in one piece. But when prison is behind us, it is time to use the strength found while incarcerated to lift up your voice. Many believe that because you are now marked with the label Felon, you must put on sackcloth and ashes and lie in a ditch. They believe this is as true for a lesser offense as for a heinous crime. Do not believe the lie. It is never too late to make a positive difference. Upon your release, you do not have to stay out of the way ever again. Through your activism and your vote, you can make a way.

LARRY G. "ROCKY" HARRIS, *Illinois*

WHEN IS IT ENOUGH?

I have twenty-one years behind these walls. I never figured my life would spin out this way. When I was a young man I was buck-wild. I rode the iron horse and lived by no man's rules. Being a free spirit brought me into contact with the prison system at an early age. When push came to shove, I used whatever means was necessary to protect my family, myself. You can only beat "the man" for so long, then you got to pay the piper. At twenty-four I took the law into my own hands; I pulled a trigger. I did five years, on a dime sentence, for armed violence. Then I was paroled and wanted no more of life in a cage. My kids needed me. I went home on the straight and narrow. It did not matter what I did. Destiny had other plans.

I'd walked off the three years of parole. Bought my home contract for deed. Started my own business. Went to court on parole and got custody of my six-year-old daughter. It was the best of times in my life. In that little girl's eyes I saw the greatest praise a man can feel. In her eyes I was the world. I gave her safety, security, a home where she could be free to be a kid. She did not have to be afraid, to worry about not having a place to live. The peace that comes with a solid foundation showed in her eyes. She was my shadow and I loved it. Her need for security was what made me become a man, a father. Then the State stole my dream from me after only four years. Still, they were the best years of my life.

September 17th, 1993, was the last day I walked as a free man. The State convicted me of two counts of armed robbery. The sentence was sixty-five years.

Now you know my pedigree. What I speak now comes from my history in this closed society.

When I served time in the '80s it was a wild time. The prisons in Illinois had a lot of gang violence. Gangs ran a lot of the life behind bars. I did my five calendars in medium-security prisons. Those five years I worked as many jobs as I could. I literally worked those years away. The agony of my children growing up without me there to watch it happen ate at my soul. It was a big hole I could not fill up. I worked and slept the years away. My first stay with the State had taught me to get my head right. One thousand, six hundred, and ninety-nine days straight without my lady to hold, my kids to hug, good food to eat—it broke me of any ideas I had of life outside the rules of society. I went home to be the father I had so miserably failed to be as a young man.

Then I was convicted of two counts of armed robbery I did not do. I serve this sentence and time due to only one fact—the inept actions of my public defender. He took one look at me and decided I was guilty. He betrayed the contract of counsel, and sold me down the river. He destroyed my family with his arrogant attitude. I gave him all the evidence to investigate. To prepare to shred the State's case on the stand. He lied to me. At my trial he did not call one witness in my defense, or produce one document to rebut the State's false evidence. The circumstantial evidence used to convict me was false and manufactured. This happens in our criminal-court system every day. Public defenders (PDs) are overworked, underpaid, and jaded. After years of unappreciated work, some turn to cranking out the cases as fast as possible. More cases, more money. This causes the PD to start making judgments on guilt, then on the time they'll spend on each case . . . which allows the innocent to fall through the cracks in the system. The greatest betrayal happens when the PD turns his back on his client. Canon Rule Seven states, "A lawyer must defend his client to the best of his ability, to go to whatever lengths are necessary to produce the best defense possible." Our prisons are full of men who did not get a fair trial for this very reason: they were cast on America's reject pile by their public defender.

These are the cards I have been dealt to play. I am not the same man I was in 1993. I have become a "jailhouse lawyer." I fight to bring change to the prison system. As a reader you might ask yourself why you should continue to read this story. I think I can tell you why. Your tax dollars pay for a prison system that is a major failure. I was a taxpayer, and I would demand a whole lot more for the money taken from my check each week. The recidivism rate in Illinois is at 70 percent. That means that most prisoners released back into your neighborhood will be back within a year. That person will come back with a more violent crime. A longer sentence you will now pay for. You thought he was supposed to be rehabilitated when he served his first prison term. Sadly he was not; his body was warehoused, but his mind was not healed. The state title of Department of Corrections is a cruel joke on the taxpayer. There is no correction. There is no rehabilitation. There are only lazy state workers that have become complacent in their roles.

If you, the citizen, do not demand more from the prison staff, the system fails. There is no one to blame but yourselves. Every day I watch the security staff come to work, take a chair in the control booth, put their feet up, and earn a large salary for doing nothing. They do not sit on the wing and protect the prisoners. Instead they sit in the foyer, being lazy. The law requires the security officer to be seated at the desk placed at the head of the wing. Each building has four wings in an X shape. There are two tiers of cells on each wing. Two men per cell. Twenty-eight cells on the top deck, twenty-four cells on the bottom deck. A total of 104 prisoners on each wing. The security measures required by law are not followed. The guards have grown lazy with power from their union. They do not sit on the wings and protect the prisoners from assault. This is the very job you, the taxpayer, are charged for each week. Yes, the money taken out of your check pays these state employees' salaries. You also pay out the lawsuit settlements, from your check, when these prisoners are killed, beaten, raped, while the guards sit in the control booth playing cards and reading the papers. If you want more facts on this, pick up a copy of the *Prison Legal News* out of Seattle, Washington.

The pendulum swung from liberal treatment and rehabilitation to hard-core punishment while President Bush had his eight years in office. Little Bush let the right-wing watchdogs know that he had their backs, that they could do anything and he would protect them. Even earlier, the Prison Litigation Reform Act did great damage to the prison system. Only a well-educated jail-house lawyer can understand and navigate the federal court system now. The new grievance procedure created a loophole for the state prison administration. The prisoner is retaliated against for filing his grievance, if he even gets the grievance forms, and if the grievance is not thrown away by staff; he can never seek redress in a court of law. Therefore the prison administration and staff can never be held accountable for their illegal actions while acting under the color of the law. What is acting under the color of the law? Here is the definition from *Oran's Dictionary of the Law*: "Color, appearance or semblance; looking real or true on the surface, but actually false. For example, acting 'under color of law' is taking an action that looks official or appears to be backed by law, but which is not."

In Illinois the hard hand of the extreme right wing has created a system ripe for civil-rights violation. As a "jailhouse lawyer" I have become quite the civil-rights litigator. Why should you, the taxpayer, care about this? Well, let me explain it in real simple terms. I go to court, I win a cash settlement; it is paid out of your taxes, so I have a direct pipeline to your wallet. I am retaliated against by prison administrators and staff for exposing their illegal conduct. Then I sue for the retaliation and get paid again. I am getting rich off the taxpayer's wallet, and will continue to get richer until you demand change. One other thing: the guards and prison administrators are state employees. Therefore they are represented by the attorney general when they are sued for their illegal acts. When found guilty, the money does not come out of their pockets, nor do they have to pay for their representation by the attorney general's office. All these funds, millions a year, come from your paycheck, people. What a life they have. They can do whatever they want, get free legal representation, get found guilty, cost you millions, and keep their jobs while you pay the bill.

The prisoner is kept locked in a cell every day. The more the guards keep him locked in a cell the less they have to do. The prisoner is told he must follow the rules. The prisoner was placed in prison as punishment for breaking one of society's rules. Here he is to be rehabilitated and returned to society as a productive citizen. The constitution of the State of Illinois requires it. Article 1 of the Bill of Rights, Section 11 states: "All penalties shall be determined both according to the seriousness of the offense and with the objective of restoring the offender to useful citizenship."

Well, folks, that just ain't happening in Illinois. The guards are lazy and heavy-handed with retaliation. They lock the prisoner in his cell for as much time as they can get away with. They sit in the control booth, with their feet up. The prisoner is denied the yard time required by law. He is denied his dayroom time to shower and use the telephone, and general social interaction. He is talked to with shameful disrespect by the guards. What are you creating when this happens? I have been watching it happen since the take-back went into effect in 1996. The hypocrisy in place creates a meaner criminal to be released into society. Every day he spends in prison he is told he must follow the rules, and he is punished severely if he violates one. Oftentimes he is retaliated against by staff and punished harshly without justification. Every day he watches the guards screw him out of his yard, exercise, dayroom, commissary, and meals. They do this in blatant violation of the rules and the law while acting "under the color of law." How do you expect a prisoner to be rehabilitated when every day he is shown that the one with power does not have to follow the rules? It just makes him mad, meaner, as he sits in a cell all day, waiting to be released where he can put his lesson learned to work. Again he will seek power by weapon or force. Only then will he have power again. This is "the rule of law" pounded into his mental picture every day he spends in the Illinois prison system. This is why two out of every three who are released are back with a violent crime and longer sentence. The body was warehoused and the mind corrupted.

Now let's talk about money. The Illinois "pay to play" schemes are well and thriving in the prison system. As the taxpayer you may want to ask, why have the prison farms been shut down? Why is the meat to feed the prison population bought, instead of being raised relatively cost-free, on farms that are sitting empty? Why do we pay millions a year in electric bills for a system that could be self-sufficient? Why do we pay millions a year for canned vegetables when the men locked in cells all day could be working to plant and raise these same vegetables? Why, because then no money could be stolen from the budget in kickbacks. This will change only when you, the taxpayers, demand that it change. When you hold the staff accountable for their actions. Make them pay for their own lawyers to defend their illegal acts. Make them pay the settlements on civil-rights violations out of their pockets, not the state budget. Blagojevich's kickbacks started this monster, and it's still going. Why would you feed the men and women in prison a product that makes them sick, when you can raise cattle, pigs, and chicken at no cost to the taxpayer? Kickbacks.

The Department of Corrections is a joke. The "get tough on crime" rhetoric from the politicians scared the citizens into building a prison empire the state budget cannot support. The millions needed to keep these prisoners locked up, fed, clothed, and given medical care eats up money that could be used in our schools, building safer bridges and roads, and providing adequate health care. You are the ones who must demand change. You must demand that the farms are opened back up, and the beef, pork, chickens, eggs, and vegetables raised at no cost to the taxpayer. Use prison labor to build electric turbines, powered by wind and solar panels, that offset the millions spent in electric bills each year to maintain the prisons.

The prisoners could do all these jobs at low cost. It is a win-win situation. The men will learn a work skill. Most are the disenfranchised, uneducated masses from the inner city. Most hunger for a job to look forward to each day. They all want to learn a skill. To know they can be looked upon as equals in society, can get jobs and hold them, be treated equally upon their release. We must cure the mind, not just warehouse the body in a cell all day. The politicians have failed miserably with their "get tough on crime" rhetoric. The prisons are busting at the seams. Only when you, the taxpayer, demand better for your dollar will things change. When is it enough?

KENNETH E. HARTMAN, *California*

THE TROUBLE WITH PRISON REFORMERS

What appears to be virtually incomprehensible to non-prisoners, even those with the best of conscious intentions, is that our world is truly our world. It is not simply a warped version of the world on the other side of the fences, nor is it some kind of ephemeral, contingent existence. It is, most definitely, a separate and distinct world. Further, in this whole otherness, prisoners are not merely stick figures waiting to resume their full dimensionality on the other side of the fences. The vast majority of us are entire entities capable of rational decision-making and thinking participation.

It is difficult for me to recall exactly how many times I have watched a well-meaning rehabilitative program go down in a chorus of yawns. The hardest part for me is watching the inevitable disintegration of the program founder's or managers' resolve to continue prison-based work. I always feel sad for them, but the failure is entirely predictable and easily explained. The program was written for prisoners by non-prisoners.

Likewise, too many times to count, I have been compelled to debate with otherwise rational and well-meaning folks about why they are not helping. Usually, the struggle in these cases is one of control. And since there is only rarely any settlement reached, the result is the alienation of the prisoners involved in the program at issue, followed by the frustration of the staff member or volunteer.

Without our assent, nothing can succeed inside our world. While it is possible to bribe and even cajole some measure of interest, genuine participation in the complete sense is always a voluntary choice. Prisoners are masters at refusing participation in what we deem to be undesirable, regardless of the consequences.

The reason the most recent spate of efforts at reviving rehabilitation has met with spotty results, beyond the on-the-ground staff and other entrenched interests' resistance, is the tacit complicity of "reformers" in the dehumanization of prisoners.

If the unexpected opening in the punishment-for-the-sake-of-inflicting-pain wall is to be taken advantage of fully, prisoners must be involved in the conception, design, implementation, and operation of rehabilitative programs. Otherwise, we will continue to be reluctant participants, at best, in parachuted-in programs. And, yes, that is a sour statement, but it comes from watching scarce resources and scarcer opportunities squandered by people who are certain they know what is best for us regardless of what we think. More to the point, regardless of what we know.

In my more than thirty-one years of continuous imprisonment, I have participated in the conception of several worthwhile reform projects, all of which have taught me useful lessons. The biggest lesson, and the one with the most far-reaching and enduring consequences, is that prisoners must be allowed, encouraged really, to be a large part of the design of such programs. Back in 1998, at a point in the history of the corrections system in this state when the punishment movement had achieved complete dominance, I began work on the proposal for what would eventually become the Honor Program. I had to write it in such a way as to appear to be about rigid rules, but the heart of it was the idea of rewarding positive behavior. The acolytes of the "get tough" approach had settled on an all-negative reinforcement set of policies. As any marginally aware prisoners could have predicted, the result of this was mass chaos, off-the-charts violence, and the collapse of even the pretense of rehabilitation. Just as telling, the recidivism rate skyrocketed.

The Honor Program turned the system upside down by reviving a rewards system. It was not anything fancy: just more yard time, a little more property, and the promise of a respite from the lunacy that has overtaken the rest of the prisons. Luckily, the authorities saw the random drug testing and prerequisite disciplinary-free time, and overlooked the positive angle.

Within one year of full implementation, a facility that had been notorious for riots and drug trafficking went months without a single recorded disciplinary infraction. The program inspired bipartisan legislation and the ire of the old bulls running the prison-system hierarchy by exposing their failures. Prisoners did not do it all. Helpful and supportive staff played vital roles. Nevertheless, the program succeeded because prisoner experience and input informed the final product.

Years later, working with an extremely progressive nonprofit, I co-wrote the curriculum for a course called the Creating a Healing Society Program. The course has been taught now for more than six years to well over 250 prisoners. It continues to be among the most popular programs offered here, with a long waiting list. Again, non-prisoners played a vital role and continue to keep the program alive, but without the prisoner experience poured into the content up front, it would not have as powerful and resonant an impact, and not have such wide appeal.

With still other tremendously supportive and creative free people, I helped to create The Other Death Penalty Project, which is a true grassroots movement to end the use of life without the possibility of parole in the United States. There are now roughly ten thousand active prisoner participants across the country. We have issued national press releases, been contacted by media organizations for our input, and sent out thousands of organizing kits to help empower prisoners. Most recently, along with noted author Luis J. Rodriguez (*Always Running*), we sponsored a writing contest for prisoners serving "the other death penalty." A book of these collected stories has been published, titled *Too Cruel, Not Unusual Enough*. We hope to put it on the desks of one thousand decision-makers and persons of influence. I edited the book. All the decisions for the Project were made by prisoners.

To fully end our reliance on fiscal sponsors and other official intermediaries, we have now created the "Lifers' Education Fund," a stand-alone 501(c)(3) for the sole, authorized purpose of raising money to put life-sentence prisoners into upper-division, accredited college courses leading to a bachelor's degree. I am on the board of directors, and all the work of the organization will be done by prisoners, to whatever extent possible. Yes, free people will be involved in the operation—mailing, signing checks, doing the tasks that prison will not allow a prisoner to do—but the decisions will be made by prisoners for prisoners.

All of these are examples of the kinds of projects and programs that can happen with prisoner input and consultation. But even in this setting, where a powerful and forward-thinking group of prisoners came together and aggressively carved out a space to work within, the nature of the prison system can, and too often does, reassert itself. Under the guise of budget difficulties and labor unrest, programs have come under attack. There is an ongoing problem of kick-the-dog syndrome where line guards, angry at cuts in their pay, retaliate by making programming difficult to run in every possible way.

As the irresistible force of shrinking funds meets the unreasonable expectations of unionized prison employees, these acts of sabotage and unreasoned resistance will occur all over.

After years of study and countless hours of research and writing, a blue ribbon commission of the best and the brightest in the fields of criminology and penology came up with what is known in California as the "Road Map." I have read the Road Map, the supporting documents and studies, and many of the same seminal texts that inform the work produced. Much of it makes sense, in fact. The professionals who produced the Road Map are, obviously, sincere and committed to the idea of reforming the grossly dysfunctional, dystopian California Department of Corrections and Rehabilitation.

Nevertheless, the product of this massive effort was the so-called Solano Proof Project, which created a prison program laughably unsuited to an actual prison, filled with actual prisoners, guarded by actual guards. When I read the details of what was envisioned, I wondered if the idea was to turn the chosen facility into a suburban junior high school for "at-risk" youths. A common mistake of well-intentioned reformers is to assume that because many of us read at seventh-grade level we are thirteen years old. We are not, and being treated as if we are is both demoralizing and disrespectful.

There is a need for immersion criminologists. The life of a prisoner, being a truly total experience, is not something a non-prisoner can ever really comprehend. There are a handful of professionals who come pretty close to getting it, but they are few and far from the levers of power. It seems only rational that the practitioners of the "convict criminology" movement should be more involved in designing programs for prisoners. Likewise, and no less rationally, prisoners—meaning currently incarcerated men and women—need to be much more involved in the conception, design, implementation, and operation of programs aimed at other prisoners.

In California—an outlier only as regards the bloated size of the system—the past decade has seen concerned people trying to come to grips with what "get tough" policies have wrought; the idea of stakeholders' meetings became a vital part of the process. It makes perfect sense, of course, bringing together the various groups to try and balance out competing interests. But never was a prisoner invited to one of these convocations; apparently, we are not deemed worthy to hold a stake in our own lives.

Inside the prisons there is a dark force that works diligently and continuously against the kind of reforms that need to take place if any success is ever to happen. In contrast to the naive quality of the reformers, those who are part of this malevolent group consciously seek to disempower and dehumanize prisoners.

Over the past quarter of a century, there was an effective winnowing-out process that culled from the guard ranks anyone not on board with the new "get tough" mentality. Promotions were based on perceived harshness, and the best assignments went to guards with the most militant and hostile postures. Because most of the conduct of guards is rooted in fear, the result on the tiers and in the blocks is an increase in the level of violence bouncing back and forth between ever-angrier prisoners pushed around by ever more frightened guards.

After the mass sifting of staff to the new paradigm of punishment for the express and sole purpose of causing suffering, those left to run the prisons are virtually incapable of even conceiving of running a rehabilitation-oriented prison system. The language of rehabilitation, the concepts and precepts, the framework of creating a healing community, the very idea of treatment inside the antiseptic concrete and steel of the modern prison . . . all of this falls on ears unprepared to hear, on hearts hardened by a society brainwashed into believing the impossible notion that human beings can be made better by being brutalized.

The extension of this (un)thinking is possible only through guards who have been convinced that prisoners must be dehumanized. There is no other way human beings can be coaxed into treating their fellow human beings in such a manner as to deliberately cause suffering. The group doing the harm has to render the group being harmed less than human—dirty, dangerous, evil, worthy only of suffering—thus delegitimizing any claims to the protection of law. To accomplish this deconstruction of prisoners, a plethora of rules were enacted. Rules that run the gamut from how long your hair can grow to how you must divest yourself of all outside business interests. Rules that compel wearing clothing designed to demean and stigmatize. Rules that forbid adult prisoners from seeing an "R"-rated movie. Rules that, ultimately, prove the prisoner is not an adult, not a competent, thinking being, not fully human.

The logical conclusion of this systematic process of dehumanization is the denigrated status of the dangerous "other." It explains, to a large degree, the erection of all the seemingly redundant and unnecessary security measures. No prison system on earth goes to greater lengths to prevent escapes than those in this country; in California, the layers upon layers of razor wire and heavily armed gun towers ringing all of the prisons, even down to the lowest security levels, were not enough. To counter the remote possibility that a prisoner could theoretically escape, lethally electrified fences were installed. Powered up with enough amperage to kill a large man several times over, costing enormous sums, the electric fences proved inadequate to still the fear of the potential escape of the wildly dangerous contagion kept barely in check by the buzzing, impenetrable wall of wire. At least once a week (and more often in the summer) this prison is locked down by a local citizen calling in a sighting of a suspicious person wearing blue clothes.

The other expected outcome of so thorough and complete a job of dehumanizing prisoners is that the guards come to turn any programs, or whatever remains of them, into ways to serve guards' desires and interests, regardless of how their actions impact the lives of prisoners. Schedules are altered to provide men (and guards) with "down time," which is a euphemism for lockdowns. Programming is held hostage to what makes the guards less unhappy, hostage to the ludicrous expectation that programs need to meet arbitrarily fluid demands by job stewards, and show that sufficient obeisance has been offered to reified, all-powerful, all-consuming security.

The black heart beating underneath all the layers of unpleasantness, the diabolical engine of the system, and the actual prime motivator of all that happens in these places, is so simple and basic it hides easily in plain sight. The real purpose of the vast empire of concrete and steel, as it operates now, is the provision of well-paying jobs. And the deeper reason for the widespread resistance to the return of rehabilitation is the fear of losing those well-paying jobs.

The guards' unions latched early onto the panic that surged through the suburbs as crime became the lead story on the local news every night, as too many sons and daughters (lacking legitimate work futures in a globalized job market) adopted the wicked ways of the shadowy urban world, and as the mores and expectations of the past suddenly seemed endangered. The guards became uber-Republicans—giant-sized contributors to state-level politicians that toed their party line: more laws, more convictions, and more prisons to house the ever-growing number of human beings downsized out of the modern economy. It was a comprehensive strategy that went beyond just electing "law and order" politicians. In this state, the guards went so far as to create "victims' rights" groups and hire a lobbying army to write legislation codifying their dominance of the prisons.

As every prisoner knows who has been run through the gauntlet of life, prison, and frustrating parole-board hearings, crises tend to be the proximate cause of great changes in a life. In the life of an organization, crises tend to force reorganization of what matters most, often exposing the real raison d'être of the organization's existence. After all the years of championing victims' rights, of walking the toughest beats to defend society, of being on the frontline, Republicans realized that guards had simply become another avaricious public-employees' union. Overnight, the guards morphed into staunch Democrats fighting for sacred collective-bargaining rights.

The Democrats let them into the old discombobulated tent because the years of sophisticated messaging had convinced voters the guards were soldiers in the hundred-years war on crime. The ugly truth of it is that the monstrous prison system is nothing more or less than a place to get good, well-paying government jobs. Never mind the foundational damage to the social structure of the country. It is about jobs, the resistance to rehabilitative programming, and that is the heart of it. Any change of a positive nature would necessarily result in fewer prisoners, and fewer prisoners mean fewer well-paying government jobs. Anyone going into this struggle to bring about change must be cognizant of this truth, distasteful as it is.

That there is a desperate need for serious rehabilitative reform inside the prisons of this country is self-evident. The past generation of irrational, fear-based policies has purchased for society the worst-run, least effective, most expensive and inhumane prisons in the industrialized world, with the highest incarceration and recidivism rates of any nation, ever.

After the biggest (still unpunished) mugging of a body politic in the history of the world, the system is on its ass, as the saying goes. States are going broke supporting institutionalized dysfunction. The next couple of generations of Americans will be paying for the excesses of our times. Prisoners will be released back into society whether they are ready or not, whether society is ready or not.

Prisoners know what goes on in prisons better than anyone else. We know how this world of ours works. We know what needs to be done. We know how what needs to be done can be done. All the unmarked trails and switchbacks, the roadblocks, and the dead ends are on a map only we fully understand, and only we can well and truly interpret. At the very least, reformers should use the eyes and ears of prisoners to get an accurate sense of what's what in each prison community.

The bogus anti-ideology of "nothing works" is a fraud. Any successful programs must include the experience and talent of prisoners. Prisoners should and must lead the way to creating a prison system that turns out parolees ready to assume a productive place in free society. If, as in the past, prisoners are shut out of the process, then the same ignoble, ineffective cycle will resume. If, on the other hand, highly motivated prisoners are empowered to make a difference, there is a real chance that the failure of prisons and prisoners can be turned around.

The great lie that must be dismantled in the public mind is about prisoners themselves. The average prisoner is riddled with guilt and remorse for what he or she did to end up in prison. The drug addicts know how much they have let their families and friends down, how much they have let themselves down. The burglars are ashamed of breaking into someone's home, and the robbers are ashamed of the fear they brought into others' lives. And, most of all, prisoners who committed acts of violence, particularly those who took a life or left a life permanently scarred, are consumed with shame. No matter the image any specific prisoner may portray, under all the outrageous tattoos and ganged-up clothing, there is desperate longing to rebalance the scales, to repay the grievous debts incurred.

Prison, as it has been reconceived by the newly ascendant guard culture, denies to all but a very few prisoners opportunities to earn back self-respect and start making payments back to society. The new form of prison fears any rehumanization of prisoners. In the space of the three decades of my imprisonment, the purveyors of this regime of pain, backed by all the special interests who have gained, managed to transmogrify prisoners from human beings gone bad, to bad human beings, to inhuman monsters that must be contained at all costs. I am now so dangerous to the free world on the other side of the fences that the press, the "free press," is not allowed to interview me personally. My mere presence on a television screen or in a newspaper apparently traumatizes still more victims.

The actual reason I am held behind a screen of terrifying camouflage is because society might discover I look and act, think and feel, a lot like they do. Exactly like they do, actually. The worst thing that could happen to the current system would be for prisoners to lose their horns and fangs. Were we to become human again, much of what has been done inside these places would be found appalling and unacceptable.

Here and there, against the odds and often against the rules, prisoners have managed to carve out little spaces within which a patch of sunlight has been opened up in the gloom. If the putative reformers are serious about bringing rehabilitation back into the system, it is in these places that it can start.

Prisoners are an ingenious group of people. We are capable of crafting all manner of useful things out of the flotsam and jetsam of society. And we prisoners are fiercely loyal to our friends, to those who offer us a hand up, a chance to become better humans, a shot at redemption. It is in everyone's best interests for the reformers to come and sit down with us, to hear us out, to treat us with a little respect. If we all work together, the failures of the past decades can be turned around.

The alternative is too grim to contemplate.

The punishers will not be broke forever.

Kite Out

KARTER KANE REED, *Massachusetts*

LIFE ON THE INSIDE

I would like to start by telling you a bit about myself. Like any human being, I am a unique individual with my own eccentricities and idiosyncrasies while also sharing in common with you—and everyone else—many traits, characteristics, and quirks. I am very much different than you . . . and very much the same.

Growing up, I was a pretty smart kid and learned readily, something I carried with me into adulthood. I am an electrician by trade, or computer repair technician, depending on whether you go by my first or most recent trade. Along the way, I've been a mechanic, carpenter, welder, computer programmer, network administrator, electronics repair technician, laborer, furniture mover, chemical engineer, clerk, graphic designer, prep cook, poet, dishwasher, barber, janitor, personal trainer, writer, and public speaker. And today, of course, I'm the author of this essay.

I am far more than the things I've done or been. I am a reader—to call myself an *avid* reader would, at times, be an understatement: literature, history, science, mathematics, grammar, even commercial fiction. I have a fondness for the poetry of Rumi, Hafiz, and Rilke; share philosophical beliefs with Socrates, Nietzsche, and Voltaire; and am captivated by molecular biology and quantum physics. But I am more too than the things I have read. I am an athlete. I am a musician. A guitar player really, but I can play the bass, violin, piano, and drums. Still, though, I am more than my hobbies and recreation. I am all of these things and more: I am a prisoner, inmate, convict, felon, criminal . . . murderer. You probably didn't see that coming. I know I didn't. But life is complicated. As they say, "The truth is rarely pure, and never simple."

Today, I would like you to think about why: Why is it that you are sitting in a college classroom, or your living room, or on a bus, and I am sitting in a prison cell? What is it that allowed me, or pushed me, to cross the line from citizen to criminal? And what does it mean that I am not alone, that there are 2.3 million Americans incarcerated across the country, and millions more who've *been* incarcerated or *will* be incarcerated in the future? What does that say about our society? What does it say about me and you, about our differences and our similarities? These are questions that I have been asking myself for sixteen years, and I still have far more questions than answers.

Prison is not like anything you've seen on television or read in books, because on television and in those books, the prison population is comprised of two types: heroes, and anti-heroes. There's the stereotypical sociopathic, maniacal, predatory monsters bent on raping and pillaging without remorse—gladiators who live for the arena, who have never possessed, or otherwise been dispossessed of, any trait that might resemble human. They are something else, something foreign, something no "normal" person could ever relate to. Then there are pictures of the wrongly accused Atticus Finch–type paragons of virtue who've been framed or set up, who've never done a single wrong and in the end will narrowly escape total destruction at the hands of their nemesis. And that is the version of prison people are exposed to, a fairy tale full of *characters*—not fallible, empathetic, *normal* human beings like you and I, because people like us don't go to prison . . . or do we?

I wasn't always destined for prison. At one point, I was on the fast track to college, probably with a scholarship. And not just any college, but the kind of prestigious institution that would never *ever* produce a "criminal." I wasn't *born* a criminal. In fact, despite having now spent more than half of my life in prison for a crime that I clearly committed, and for which there are no mitigating factors that would absolve me of guilt, I don't consider myself a criminal. I do not commit crimes, do not have any intention or desire to commit crimes, and do not condone or support the commission of crimes. Therefore, I say emphatically that I am *not* a criminal. I am simply a human being; a person who has made a horrible, tragic choice to harm someone in retaliation for one of my friends being harmed. That's it, *one* terrible choice that turned on me and everyone else and became a word incomprehensible to nearly everyone, a word more red than any scarlet letter, more foul than any albatross, a word beyond explanation, and for far too many, a word beyond redemption: murder. A word that catches in my throat and reaches the world as a nearly inaudible whisper, choked with shame and self-loathing—a word I want to erase from my lips and tongue, scrub from my brain's synapses never to be recalled, but which will live as long as I do, in and around me, extracting from me infinitely the pound of flesh I owe.

In what some would say was a controversial decision, I was granted parole this year, which means I will be going home soon, returning to the society that I so long ago left. And perhaps I will stop my car to let you cross the street, help you put your groceries in your trunk at the local supermarket, hold the elevator door for you, or offer you my umbrella in the rain, and you will think, "What a nice young man," not suspecting for a moment that I'm one of *them*, one of the 2.3 million "others" you're certain are not like you. I will smile at the irony of this because I used to be you, used to be all of you, in as many ways as anyone who is not you *could* be. We are the same, you and I. Different, of course, but the same.

That we are alike in more ways than you can imagine—this is the most important lesson I would like you to learn, but there is another, just as simple and nearly as important. To succeed in life, you have to be yourself. This means pursuing your dreams, putting your best foot forward, leaving nothing to chance, and never giving up. It means trying and doing, not wishing and wanting. It means being honest, not just to others (after all, that's easy), but to yourself. Unfortunately, it took coming to prison for me to learn these things. It is my hope that it will not take the same, or some equally traumatic, experience for your eyes to be opened as mine have been.

Prison and Reentry Programs

INTRODUCTION

The bad news from Prison City is evident: this is a population in exceptional need of effective treatment, education, and training; but it faces exceptional negligence, indifference and often outright hostility toward the work of individuals trying to make something constructive of their years inside. The good news is less easily discerned and much less predictable: prison and reentry programming proven to reduce recidivism make up a tattered map of private charitable work and the exceptional instances of progressive, state-sponsored efforts. Once released, even those who have enjoyed effective prison programming face obstacles to employment, housing, and other basic needs that few of us could overcome.[1] The essays in this last section make three things clear: in-prison programming and community reentry efforts can make a real difference in the lives of people emerging from Prison City, such support for incarcerated people is irregular and precarious, and Americans both inside and out would benefit from making these programs and supports systematic and reliable.

Incarcerated people who earn college credits inside have recidivism rates as low as 13.7 percent.[2] Yet, in 1994, Bill Clinton signed legislation that made incarcerated people *in*eligible for the one-tenth of 1 percent of Pell tuition grants that had supported over 350 college-in-prison programs across the country. Overnight, thousands of American prisoners lost their best chance at beating the statistics that wall in Prison City.[3] Randall Louis Cole was among the last cohort of men and women afforded Pell-supported education, and he witnessed that program's demise. His essay, "The Power of Education," depicts the metamorphosis that occurred in many incarcerated people across the United States before 1994. Entering prison without the skills, knowledge, or motivation needed to change his thinking or behavior, Cole found discipline, a capacity for constructive action, even remorse, through higher education. His essay testifies to the good we can all do for ourselves—reducing the costs of a bloated system and sparing future victims—by restoring Pell eligibility to those inside Prison City.

Since 1994, the college programs that continue to operate in American prisons have been privately funded. DeShawn Cooper is fortunate to be inside a facility that still offers such programs. In "Notes from the Underground" he confirms the lesson delivered by Randall Cole, becoming the man he might have been had educational opportunities and motivation reached him sooner.

Edward C. Shelley is among the majority of convicted people who were under the influence of drugs or alcohol when they committed their crimes.[4] As other essays in this collection make clear, for a price, drugs and alcohol are available in prison. But many incarcerated people plagued by addiction choose to take this as an opportunity to clean up their lives. Shelley's essay, "Enduring Prison Inspires Hope and Change," represents a virtual genre of submissions to *Fourth City*: it offers the insights gained by former addicts as a result of the sobriety they have allowed the prison to force upon their lives. Once sober, they discover new people in themselves. Doing this work alone, however, is at least as hard inside as it is outside. Shelley is one of the few lucky people included in a program that allows men working seriously on their sobriety to live in a supportive community. He proves again that institutional commitment to rehabilitation is good for everyone, inside and out.

In his short essay, "My Greatest Fear," Jason A. Daugherty describes the work he's doing inside to beat the odds and prepare to make a successful transition out of Prison City. It's no wonder Daugherty is afraid. He details just a few of the obstacles that face former convicts who enter back into the very places and situations that led them to prison, but now carrying the added weight of a prison record. These are facts we all need to consider, since Daugherty's fears are shared by the hundreds of thousands of Americans released from prison every year.[5]

Unlike Jason Daugherty, Connie Gibbs writes from the rare position of an incarcerated American who will enjoy the benefits of family, home, and professional and emotional support when she returns to the world outside. None of these things have been provided by the prison. So her very advantages bring home to Gibbs what other convicted people need and will not receive. In "Recidivism: The Need for Transitioning Guidance" we get a unique insight into just how difficult such transition is. Gibbs is only in prison for one year. Yet she knows that all the resources she can muster will be needed to reenter her former life. This essay not only argues for more transitional services in and outside of Prison City; it suggests that the dehumanization that occurs there can make its inhabitants true aliens when they come out.

Facing the challenges outlined by Jason Daugherty and Connie Gibbs, the Americans released from Prison City every year are literally channeled into failure and return. Recognizing this situation and its destructive effects on individuals and neighborhoods, community groups, forward-looking prison administrators, academics, and others have begun to investigate and support the process of reentry that incarcerated Americans attempt to negotiate. "Smoothing the Road: The Formerly Incarcerated Get a Helping Hand" is Intelligent Allah's overview of the work of various groups who have been, and are now, working to make reentry to free society a one-time experience. In this essay, we not only see what is being done right; we see just how well incarcerated people can understand the odds against them, and understand the official practices and thinking that could help to even those odds.

If reentry programs are to become effective, they must treat each applicant as an individual with individual liabilities and vulnerabilities that can lead to recidivism. By documenting her own unsuccessful attempts to garner reentry support, Valjean Royal not only writes for gender-variant people in "Post-Release Programs and Gender Variant People"; she suggests that parole boards and the faith-based communities that support much of the reentry infrastructure (now with federal funding) cannot discriminate according to narrow doctrinal beliefs. All incarcerated Americans deserve a fair shot at release and reentry, not just those who fit within the mainstream.

In "Every Morning," James Castrillo brings us back to the basics: Prison City is a place where there is every opportunity for people who have made bad choices to continue doing so. Little in this place motivates anyone to change the thinking and behavior that brought them here. The weight of such change falls on the will and resolve of each incarcerated person who makes the choice to use the time to rethink the paths that brought them inside. But when such will and resolve meet basic (and highly cost-efficient) programming opportunities—such as formal education—then the last path out of Prison City is revealed. Castrillo's short meditation is a kind of amalgam of the abiding truths of the American prison: this is a bad and counterproductive institution, but it remains in part what its inhabitants make of it; and when individuals choose to make the best of a bad thing, *and they are aided by institutional support*, the results will always beat the low expectations we have become accustomed to believe are simply reflective of the low quality of the human beings inhabiting Prison City. The American prison's practical effect is to produce men and women of whom we can in fact expect little. Every morning that James Castrillo and thousands of others push back against such inertia is the morning of a day that every American should want to see reach an abiding high noon: a day that shrinks the shadow of America's fourth to the nation's fifth, then sixth, seventh, and eighth city . . . and finally to the smallest possible and most efficient community needed to heal and restore both the men and women who come there, and the families and communities to which they will return.

NOTES

1. Marc Mauer and Meda Chesney-Lind, eds., *Invisible Punishment: The Collateral Consequences of Mass Imprisonment* (New York: The New Press, 2002).

2. Chris Tracy and Cheryl Johnson, "Review of Various Outcome Studies Relating Prison Education to Reduced Recidivism," Windham School System, Texas Department of Criminal Justice, June 1994; see also "Fact Sheet: Education as Crime Prevention," The Wesleyan Center for Prison Education, http://www.wesleyan.edu/cpe/documents/CPEFactSheet2011.pdf; and Stephen J. Steurer and Linda G. Smith, "Education Reduces Crime, Three-State Recidivism Study—Executive Summary," Correctional Education Association, February 2003, http://www.ceanational.org/PDFs/EdReducesCrime.pdf.

3. "Overview of Prison Education Policies," The Prison Studies Project, http://prisonstudiesproject .org/overview-of-prison-education-policies/.

4. William J. Sabol and Heather C. West, "Prisoners in 2009 (Revised)," Bureau of Justice Statistics, http://bjs.ojp.usdoj.gov/content/pub/pdf/ac.pdf.

5. Ibid.

RANDALL LOUIS COLE, *Tennessee*

THE POWER OF EDUCATION

I was incarcerated in 1983 at the age of twenty-four and received a life sentence for murder. I didn't have any valid excuses for my criminal behavior, and certainly no excuse for killing another human being. My life was a disastrous mix of bad choices, criminal thinking, and ignorance. The ignorance was a result of moving around a lot as a kid and attending many different schools. I barely graduated and had no reason to believe in the power of education.

Because of bad behavior, I moved quickly through the prison system to the Tennessee State Prison in Nashville. Staff and inmates called it "The Walls" or "The Castle" because of the gothic-style architecture. To say it was a tough place is an understatement. A lot of bad things happened to both good and bad people. I learned many valuable lessons, but none of them were positive. One lesson I *never* expected to learn was the power of education.

To get away from the madness of the housing unit, I often went to the library. I did enjoy reading, and it was a pleasurable escape from that stressful life. There was a notice posted there about college classes. Tennessee State University was offering an extension program, and at that time prisoners were eligible for Pell grants. It was an interesting idea, but all my previous experiences with school were less than satisfying.

A few days later, I overheard some guys in the library talking about the college classes. They liked the idea of having somewhere to go at night other than the recreation yard or unit. They also thought college credits would help them get better prison jobs. I liked what I heard and signed up. There was only a few of us because most of the guys at the prison never finished high school or couldn't pass the GED test. I didn't really expect to finish a class, but I enrolled out of curiosity more than anything else.

Classes began and it was interesting to meet the professors. We expected them to be fearful of us and limited in their interaction. To our surprise, they treated us like normal people and clearly had a lot of expectations for the success of the class. Their approach was to involve us all in the learning process and to demand a certain level of participation. Our teachers made it clear. We weren't being *forced* to learn, and failure would be our *own* fault. That was a simple but powerful lesson for everyone. Education was there for us, but we had to *earn* it.

Time went by quickly and I passed my first two classes with A's. Some of the guys dropped out, but most passed and signed up again. It was hard to focus on learning with everything that was happening around us. The Tennessee prison system was under a federal court order to make reforms, and violence was common at our facility. One of our classmates was murdered by another prisoner. His unexpected death adversely affected us all.

Our English professor was shocked by the news, but showed great wisdom by instructing us to write about our thoughts on the event. I wrote a poem about the senseless act and was forced to examine my own self and the fact that I had killed someone. College had exposed me to thoughts and ideas that were starting to challenge my way of thinking. I had to be honest with myself about the terrible impact of violence and accept responsibility for the things I had done. I was starting to understand and feel the power of education.

Classes continued, and most of us did well in spite of our environment. It was never easy to find a good place to study, and a major riot at our facility interrupted class for several months. I was glad when classes resumed, and all of us discovered a surprising fact: we *liked* going to school. I don't know exactly when it happened, but learning was important to us now.

The most difficult class any of us encountered was the required credits in algebra. Up to that point, I had made nothing but A's. Now, I was in danger of failing! The algebra professor "felt our pain," so to speak, and began coming early to help us more. He was hard on us and worked everyone well beyond what we were used to in other classes. Slowly and painfully we actually began to learn something. I passed both algebra courses with a B. I also learned another important lesson about education: some teachers do care about their students and are willing to help more than they are paid for. I now knew that was true.

The Tennessee State program continued and I was close to obtaining an associate's degree. But part of the federal court order and settlement with the state was related to poor prison conditions, so our facility was scheduled to be closed. We all wondered what would happen to the college program. I decided to be thankful for the opportunity I had been given, and didn't worry about something that was out of my control.

One beautiful summer day, I was called to the counselor's office. I didn't have a clue what he wanted, so I was a little apprehensive, because people were getting shipped weekly to any prison with bed space. I went in, sat down, and prepared myself for the worst. The counselor got straight to the point. "Lake County Prison has a bachelor of science college program sponsored by the University of Tennessee at Martin. They're looking for students with enough credits to take some upper-level courses. I'll get you transferred if you're interested," he said. I didn't even know where Lake County was, but I quickly said, "Send me there."

There was a lot of fear and confusion at The Walls that summer. Guys were trying to request transfers to prisons they knew about, and the state was building a maximum-security prison called Riverbend. Less than a week after talking to the counselor, I was packed and on a bus to Lake County. I had a lot of time to think on the long ride. I realized how fortunate I was to be leaving such an awful place in one piece. I had learned that Lake County was a small regional prison with a reputation for good living conditions and quality programs. Normally, there was no way I would be going there with a life sentence. My participation in the college program was a ticket to relative freedom after living in chaos for so long. The powers I gained from education, in a very real sense, had sent my life in a totally new direction.

Lake County was a great place: good food, lots of outdoor time, and air conditioning. I was just in time for the fall semester of UTM, and all my TSU credits transferred. All the upper-level courses were in psychology. I liked the idea of learning about why people behave like they do. I met several of the other students and learned a lot about the program.

Classes started and I quickly discovered the work was a lot harder than I was used to. We were given piles of books to read and had to write papers every week. I had taken a full load of four classes and began to doubt my decision. I was also assigned a prison job of teacher's aide in a GED class, so my days were full. All I did was work and study for weeks at a time. It was really tough, but I made good grades and began to feel a sense of accomplishment. My intellectual world expanded, and I slowly started seriously considering the views of others. I was learning a completely different set of ideas about how people interact with their environment.

Our professors were a truly extraordinary group of people. Most were older men who had been front and center when psychology was developing as a science. Many had personally met and worked with several famous names in the field. I could tell they had a real passion for the subject, and to our amazement, they wanted to share their knowledge with *us*. I had always thought people like our professors were snobs. Some of the guys even joked that they were only here to study the "stupid convicts who think they're college students." It wasn't true. They were decent, intelligent people who had decided to teach us something important. I was in awe.

I made good progress over the years, and my grades were excellent. My personal life also changed in many positive ways. As my thinking changed, my behavior did also. I stopped associating with people who used drugs and broke the rules. Most of my own bad habits disappeared and I began to feel calmer and more in control of my life. Most importantly, I had learned to think for myself and to *trust* my thoughts and decisions. I learned to respect the rights and opinions of others, and my relationship with my family improved greatly. All these changes happened slowly, but they were a direct result of my education.

I graduated with honors in 1993. I received a bachelor of science degree in human relations. The warden was very pleased with the success of the college program. He did something for me I would never have dreamed possible. I was allowed to attend the actual graduation ceremony at the University of Tennessee at Martin campus. Of course, I was escorted by prison staff the entire time, but they were very discreet and I was allowed to visit with my family before the event. It was the best day of my life.

Before I got in the car on graduation day, the warden said, "Randall, if you even *try* anything wrong, it will cost me my job." "Don't worry, Warden," I replied, "I plan to spend the rest of my life doing the right thing." It was a truly remarkable day and I fully realized and appreciated the incredible power of education.

Myself and one other person were the last prisoners in Tennessee to graduate from a prison college program using a Pell grant. Before the next year, Congress abolished the grants for all prisoners. A lot of prisoners were deeply disappointed, and our professors found it hard to believe such a promising and beneficial program was over. All we could do was offer our thanks to the good teachers for their help and shake hands one last time. I knew how lucky I was to graduate before the program ended. I hope and pray the policy will change one day.

The greatest lesson I learned in college was the transformative power of education. Men like me and my fellow students would probably never have risen above the criminal mentality and self-centered thinking that dominated our lives without the positive influence of education. I personally know many prisoners, not just college students, who have altered their personalities, developed positive attitudes, and completely changed their outlook on life because of the power earned through education. Education gave all of us a rare and precious gift: hope for the future. We can only hope the leaders of our nation will one day recognize that education is the only real solution to the problem of crime and prison growth. The power of education is not just a concept or idea; it is a real and effective force, capable of producing positive results in *anyone's* life.

DESHAWN COOPER, *New York*

NOTES FROM THE UNDERGROUND

My experience in Bard College's Bard Prison Initiative[1] as an incarcerated student hasn't been anything like I expected, particularly after a despondent, forty-something heroin addict explained to me the wonders of taking college courses in prison. "It'll free you," he said, scratching the hallmarks of his trade that visibly lined his left arm. I wasn't sure if he was telling me the truth or simply pulling my leg. After all, he did tell me it was his second trip upstate in two years as we boarded the weather-beaten Department of Correction Services (DOCS) bus, ankle-bound in steel shackles, to Coxsackie Correctional Facility, to begin serving our respective sentences: two to four years for him, fourteen to thirty-one years for me. I was certain of only two things—fourteen years is a long time, and his monkey wasn't quite ready to let him go yet. It was 1995 and I had turned nineteen just a few months earlier.

Two hours and a swollen right ankle later, my travel companion concluded his diatribe by advising me to sign up for any college program our new residence provided.

"Remember what Malcolm said," he whispered to me, placing his hand on my right shoulder to steady himself as we prepared to step off the bus. "'Prison is the Black man's university.'" Unfortunately, I later learned that the "board of trustees" in Congress had other plans for the few hundred students walking Corrections' dreary university halls.[2]

Fast-forward through three years filled with countless tutoring sessions with *Hooked on Phonics*, a failed first attempt at the GED exam, and, finally, a diploma nine months later; members of Congress should have realized the potential good of someone carrying a resume rather than a gun when entering a retail store.

Fast-forward five more years and there's a bloated correctional officer standing at my cell gate in Easter Correctional Facility, pulling an acceptance letter from Bard College out of his mailbag.

Oddly enough, my experience as an incarcerated college student has been quite similar to that of traditional college students anywhere in the country, and it has remained that way since I received that letter in September of 2003. Like many traditional campus students, for example, I have enrolled in courses instructed by nutty professors whose course work seemed otherworldly. I have also had the distinct pleasure of drinking more cups of coffee than I would have liked in order to get those assignments completed and submitted on time—hence discovering the unique talent of drinking coffee and typing while half asleep.

As an incarcerated college student, however, I haven't had the luxury of utilizing the well-worn "the dog ate my homework" excuse for late papers, though there were times its use would have been fitting, and certainly analogous, to the pair of correctional officers who tossed my cell like a chef salad during a "random" cell inspection. But that's another story. On many occasions, however, I have found myself utilizing a more verbose approach when faced with demanding professors: "Excuse me, I have to go see my corrections counselor for my quarterly assessment of prison adjustment." Or, to another professor just before a lecture, "I cannot turn in my paper today because the facility's academic supervisor didn't feel up to printing any of our papers this morning." Or, my personal favorite to yet another professor, "I couldn't do the paper because the prison administration hasn't allowed the books for the course into the facility yet." It is these moments of disruption that remind me that this isn't Kansas, no matter how hard I try to imagine the classroom here being like others.

Another similarity that I share with traditional students is the undergraduate's affinity for chronic fits of anxiety during the semester. But unlike many of my campus counterparts, my anxiety lies not in my ability to pass an exam, write a quality research paper, or give a presentation on, say, the complex tug of war between traditionalism and modernity in Naguib Mahfouz's *Palace Walk*. It comes from knowing that I could be thrown into solitary confinement and shipped to another prison, where the BPI program does not exist, if I leave the mess hall with an extra slice of bread because I'm hungry.

Of course, there is the prison's instability to contend with every day, but there is also that ever dark, ominous cloud of the parole board that hangs suspended over my head every semester. An otherwise fascinating lecture about the devastating effects that social isolation has on Dostoevsky's Raskolnikov quickly loses its allure when my appearance before the parole board looms days, weeks, even months ahead. It becomes less fascinating when the sincerity of my remorse for hurting another human being, and my deep desire to be released wage war for undivided attention. It ultimately becomes inconsequential when the truth finally sets in: it just may be another two years before I can rejoin my family and friends, because the parole commissioners have no interest in what I have to say.

As an incarcerated college student, I too have the resources of Bard College readily at my fingertips—if only vicariously. If I want to research political theorist Hannah Arendt, for example, I have to ask one of three BPI administrators to either pull something from the academic research website JSTOR, or take out a book from the Annandale campus library for me. Then there is the waiting, a week's worth at best. In either case, I'm left with Encarta and the BPI prison library, which is slightly bigger than my 8 x 10 cell and usually devoid of anything I actually need. Thankfully, most, if not all of the professors who teach for BPI arrive with a degree of understanding that is certainly appreciated.

This is not to suggest that BPI faculty have taken it easy on me simply because I'm an incarcerated student. "I make the course hard," Tabetha Ewing, assistant professor of history at Bard, notes to *60 Minutes* correspondent Bob Simon, "because the inmates study harder."[3] Although I've never enrolled in any of her courses, I study "harder" because recidivism and failure are not an option for me, and it has been in that context that I have faced every densely written paragraph, revised every paper, and sweated through every oral presentation (sometimes with disastrous results).

The shared sense of community is another experience that I have in common with traditional college students, which is great because my brain tends to turn to mush when the subject turns to math. For the spring semester of 2005, for instance, I needed to pass a statistics course to fulfill the last portion of the associate degree requirements. I'm certain I wouldn't have passed without the help of a fellow incarcerated student who tutored the entire graduating class three nights a week for the whole semester. Thank God for math geeks.

Perhaps the experience I most share with traditional college students is the sense of pride and accomplishment one feels when graduating. My chest swelled, my head tilted further towards the sky, and my shoulders squared firmer with every step I made towards the podium to receive my degree from the college's president, Leon Botstein. And like they do for traditional college students, the tears that streamed down my grandmother's face told me everything I needed to know, for reasons that differed greatly from my campus counterparts: *I am capable of doing something good.*

In all, my experience as an incarcerated college student has been a six-year tour that continues to challenge me to use both imagination and experience to reach beyond myself, yet draw all the intensity possible from the self to reconnect with what was lost in the streets at such a young age: Hope. Faith. Compassion. Humanity. Community.

Unfortunately, it's going to take me just a little longer to share these things with everyone else. Maybe, just maybe, it will be with that disgruntled heroin addict. I just hope he's still alive out there, somewhere.

NOTES

1. The Bard Prison Initiative provides opportunities for higher education to nearly two hundred incarcerated students enrolled in a robust liberal-arts curriculum in three New York State maximum-security prisons (Eastern, Elmira, and Green Haven) and two medium-security prisons (Woodbourne and Bayview, a women's institution). In the past three years, Bard has awarded forty-two associate in arts degrees and eight bachelor in arts degrees.

2. In 1994, Congress eliminated the federally funded Pell education grant program for all prison-

ers with the passage of the Federal Crime Bill. New York Governor George Pataki followed suit that same year when he ended the state-sponsored Tuition Assistance Program (TAP) for New York State prisoners, seemingly closing every higher-education program in New York State prisons overnight. Politicians falsely argued that taxpayers shouldn't pay for prisoners' education when taxpayers struggled, and in most cases couldn't afford, to send their own children to college. However, studies by the Rand Corporation, the New York State League of Women Voters, and Robert Gangi from the Correctional Association of New York noted that it would have cost less than 1 percent of the total funds used to finance both Pell and TAP programs if all 72,000 New York State prisoners participated in higher-education programs. See also Jed Brown Tucker, "The Liberal Arts Unbound: Higher Education in an American Prison, 2005–2006" (PhD diss., Columbia University, 2009). ProQuest (UMI Number 3374087): "Of the total $5.3 billion budget for Pell in 1993, the penultimate year it could be tapped by prisoners, approximately 0.1% funded all the prison education programs." The BPI has been a privately funded program since its inception in 2001.

3. Bob Simon, "Maximum Security Education," *60 Minutes*, CBS News, posted September 19, 2007, http://www.cbsnews.com/video/watch/?id=2685517n.

EDWARD C. SHELLEY, *Washington*

ENDURING PRISON INSPIRES HOPE AND CHANGE

I am currently incarcerated in a Washington State correctional institution, serving a 129-month sentence of which I have just completed five years. I have spent eight of my last eleven years in incarceration.

Looking back over my life, it is hard to believe I have come to this point. Yet in retrospect, I can clearly see where my alcoholism and drug addiction led me to make some poor choices in my life, and I certainly didn't heed the warning signs that are so clear to me now. Prison seems to be one of those places where those of us fighting addiction and abuse often find ourselves. I say this because although I no longer have access to the source, I have read somewhere that probably 70–80 percent of those in prison are here due to chemical addictions or abuse. With figures such as those, it would seem prudent that today's prison system, if it is going to work on alleviating the source of the criminal and incarceration problem in this country, would focus on the apparent source, and statistics show that drug and alcohol abuse is the predominant precursor to criminal activity and, subsequently, prison.

I am of the opinion that drug and alcohol abuse is merely the symptom of a much deeper, complex problem. That problem I believe is buried somewhere deep within the person himself. There has been some damage to the personality and spirit of the person that leads to the chemical abuse. The reasons for the inner damage to the person can be varied. We can blame the slow deterioration of the family unit and its values, society's focus on the material instead of the emotional well-being of a child, some sort of childhood trauma, or the focus on material wealth rather than the strength or quality of a person's moral character, as society's indicator of personal success. The list of reasons can go on and on. I suggest, then, that prisons consider focusing more on the rebuilding and restorative development of the prisoner's inner self through mental health, group therapy, and addiction recovery programs.

My experience as an offender inside today's prison system has been illuminating, not only of the manner in which societal and political ideologies impact the managerial styles of administrative staff, but also of the ways in which I, myself, operate as a human being.

After numerous years without the fogging effects of alcohol and drugs, along with the elimination of what I call "the daily distractions of life"—for instance, the problems that arise with raising a family, holding down a job, or paying the bills, that come with trying to maintain a steady, solid lifestyle—I have actually had an opportunity to develop self-awareness and insight into who I am as a person, what my values are, my own character strengths, as well as those character weaknesses I need to work on improving. By peeling away the layers of my outside self, I've begun to learn what it is about me that is good, wholesome, and worth saving. In some respects, this prison experience has been like a monastic experience: becoming unplugged from so many outside influences, and reducing life to the lowest common denominator, which has given me the opportunity to focus on inner change. Yet I must say as well, some days or weeks have been hard for me to endure. It has been in my own psychological survival that I have been the most vulnerable these last years.

The people in prison come with varied stages of emotional and psychological maturity. My alcohol and drug addiction, in conjunction with early childhood traumas stunted my emotional and psychological growth. Also, my coping skills are limited and the psychological pressures I feel can be very intense, and because of this, my ability to make good choices during these times can be challenged. It is during these times that I am more likely to let my anger get the best of me, attempt suicide, or just make self-destructive decisions.

Being a very sensitive and emotional person, I can at times feel very out of place in this environment. I find a real craving for solitude or alone time. A quiet time which can be spent in reflection, or contemplation. A time to write or pray about my life experiences, my feelings, and my quest for spiritual growth, without the distractions of constant noise, people, traffic, etc. In prison, finding time to be alone, away from the negative energy, which can dominate the environment, can be close to impossible. Sometimes I will wake myself up at four or five in the morning, make a cup of coffee, and spend some quiet time with myself. I can then feel a certain healing going on within myself and I cherish these times. The most unfortunate thing about putting so many people in such a small place together is that the negativity tends to feed on itself. If I were to put a positive spin on this experience, it would be that through this hardest time in my life, I have learned to adapt, and in many ways the future looks brighter because of this.

This brings me to my real motivation for writing this essay. If society is going to continue to imprison people, why not make it a positive, life-changing experience that inspires people to be the best they can be?

It is apparent that over the last twenty years or so, the focus of the penal system in this country has been on punishment without much offering of acceptance, and until that need is met in some way, a person cannot achieve his potential. I suggest that if we help a person feel worthwhile, even good about himself, and develop a sense of purpose for his life, he will develop a sense of acceptance and belonging. In order to reach his potential, he will not subject himself to self-destructive behavior such as chemical abuse or criminal action.

Here, the State of Washington's Department of Corrections is supporting and implementing what they call therapeutic community recovery programs to help achieve this goal. In the Genesis Right Living Community, of which I am a member, it is emphasized that we are a community of people who desire change within our lives, and want to work on the goal of realizing rehabilitation. There is of course a value to the punishment aspect. It can and will be a deterrent for a lot of people. However, if we are aware that criminal behavior is learned behavior, then we must take the long view and focus some energies on helping the individual unlearn that behavior, rehabilitate the offender if we are going to reduce the recidivism rate, the prison population, and ultimately the amount of money spent on incarceration. Without helping that person unlearn his self-destructive behavior and rebuild from the inside, you are left with an individual no better able to deal effectively with society, life, or the community than when he entered prison. If you build the human being, you ultimately build the community.

Abraham Maslow spoke of the "hierarchy of needs," and of a human being's need for a sense of belonging; we as individuals are part of a greater community and must hold each other accountable for our individual actions, because ultimately our actions have an effect on the community as a whole, and in the process we have to become positive role models for each other. It is the hope that through working on inner change together, we develop a sense of self-acceptance as well as a sense of belonging. It is also the hope that through living in this therapeutic community 24/7, we will take these new skills into the community with us upon our release, and ultimately realize our potential and become contributing members of society.

Although the department hasn't gotten there yet, it is my hope that they will see the profound benefit of combining this recovery-based community program with some sort of vocational training program. By combining some sort of vocational trade education with rebuilding the inner self, we could have a profound effect on a person's successful transition into society.

The problem, of course, with investing time and money in this kind of endeavor is that we probably will not see the positive changes from these programs for a period of time, and as a society, along with government, we tend to want nearly instant, positive results or statistical data to support the success of our investment. But complex social problems are not solved with quick fixes. (One has no further to look than women's suffrage, civil rights, or the war on drugs or terror to see this.) We all know that financial independence doesn't often come from winning the lottery; it comes with the systematic discipline of saving, investing, putting off short-term wants for something better or greater in the long term. So it will most likely be with problems as complex as prison reform and the reduction of crime in the community. It is certainly apparent that what we have been doing hasn't worked.

For myself, anyway, it has been my years of incarceration, my forced clean-and-sober time, my steady emotional and spiritual maturation, the onset of age, the growing insight into myself as a person, and my participation in *a recovery-based program* that have begun to have a profound effect on the way in which I view life, society, and myself. It is my greatest hope that when I reenter society, I will bring the best parts of myself into the community.

JASON A. DAUGHERTY, *West Virginia*

MY GREATEST FEAR

Though I know it won't be easy, I hope to follow in the footsteps of those who have found success after prison. I am taking proactive steps now to prepare for the obstacles that I know await me on the outside. I have begun an extensive substance-abuse program to prepare for the temptations that I will face on a daily basis once I'm released. I have also begun working towards a college degree to better my chances of finding gainful employment. I realize that these steps will not guarantee me success upon reentering society, but they will greatly improve my chances of having a successful life after prison.

Why am I doing all this work inside?

One of my greatest fears in life is becoming a statistic. There are currently an estimated 7 million people under some form of custodial supervision (including probation and parole) in the United States. Of those, 2.3 million are in jail or prison.[1] Unfortunately, I am among them. It is another, far more disturbing statistic that worries me. Each year, six hundred and fifty thousand ex-offenders are sent back out into society. Of those, two thirds will return within three years.[2] This is the alarming reality that haunts my dreams of freedom. I cannot allow myself to become a part of that statistic.

One of the biggest problems faced by ex-offenders who are trying to reenter society successfully is finding a suitable place to live. Most inmates lose a significant portion of their material possessions during their incarceration. Some lose everything. I am one who has no place to go that will not lead to problems. The few opportunities available to me will all come with great pressure to relapse into the drug- and crime-fueled lifestyle that led me to prison in the first place. While other options do exist, such as halfway houses or rehab clinics, it is not easy to get into such places. It often requires extensive paperwork, long waiting lists, and the help of institutional staff, which is not always easy to get.

Another problem faced by ex-offenders is finding suitable and reliable transportation. For some, finding an affordable vehicle is the easy part. The hard part often comes when trying to get the vehicle road-legal, and in trying to get a valid driver's license. It can often cost thousands of dollars in fines and court fees before ex-felons can legally drive again. Again, there are other options, but they too have problems and limitations. A taxi can be expensive over a period of time, and a bus will only get you close to your destination.

The obvious solution to both of these problems would be to find a job, as this would provide the income necessary to acquire a home and vehicle. This is not as easy as it may seem, however, even in a healthy economy. Without a home, it is hard to list an address or phone number on a job application. Without transportation, it will be hard to get anywhere to complete a job application, to say nothing of the daily commute to and from work. Then there's the stigma attached to ex-felons. Few employers will hire a convicted felon for any type of meaningful work. The fear of theft or violence is an all too real threat in the workplace. Many employers fear that adding a felon to the mix would only add fuel to an already raging inferno.

The lack of home, transportation, or employment leads all too many people to relapse back into the drug habits or lifestyle that most criminals have become accustomed to. The trials and tribulations of trying to live right will cause many addicts to justify that first hit, just to relieve some stress. The pressure to pay bills and provide for their families will cause some to turn to criminal activity to get the money they need to meet their financial needs. I've heard many ex-felons say that they will "hustle" just long enough to get the money they need, and then they'll quit. The problem is, many never reach that goal. They are arrested long before they can get the money they intended to save. The ones who do reach their initial goal almost always continue in their criminal ways, stopping only once they've been arrested and joined the two thirds who return to prison in the first three years.

Despite the obstacles, many ex-felons have found success after prison. Nelson Mandela spent nearly twenty years in a South African prison before going on to become the country's first Black president. Michael B. Jackson was in and out of prison for ten years before becoming a successful author, motivational speaker, and businessman.[3] Stephen C. Richards spent nine years in federal prison for conspiracy to distribute marijuana, and is now a professor of criminal justice at the University of Wisconsin-Oshkosh.[4]

I'm working hard now, and upon my release I will continue to work to avoid the dangers and overcome the obstacles that I know will be waiting for me, so that I do not become a recidivism statistic.

NOTES

1. Jeffrey Ian Ross and Stephen C. Richards, *Beyond Bars: Rejoining Society after Prison* (New York: Alpha, 2009), xi.

2. Ron Krannich, *Best Jobs for Ex-Offenders: 101 Opportunities to Jump Start Your New Life* (Manassas Park, VA: Impact, 2001), 2.

3. Michael B. Jackson, *How to Do Good after Prison: A Handbook for Successful Reentry* (Willingboro, NJ: Joint FX, 2008), 9.

4. Ross and Richards, *Beyond Bars*, back cover.

CONNIE GIBBS, *Nebraska*

RECIDIVISM: THE NEED FOR TRANSITIONING GUIDANCE

The way I see it, the rate of recidivism is far beyond the limits of reason and acceptability. It could be reduced immensely by implementing a transitioning process before inmates are released back into the vicious cycle that landed them in prison in the first place.

The need to prepare these people to return to a society that has become foreign to them is urgent. This process should begin months prior to release and be maintained after transition out. My observations of how the mind responds to the dehumanization process that begins the minute a citizen becomes an inmate present a vivid picture of how and why "reform" doesn't seem to carry through after an inmate is released. If there were a viable transitioning program in place, with trained professionals who understand the dehumanization process, we would have a much better chance of stopping the cycle and thereby reducing recidivism.

During my search for an explanation for why "institutional rehabilitation" does not seem to stick once many inmates reenter society, I stumbled onto a similar situation in the attempts to offer spirituality inside. Many inmates who have never known spirituality, or have lost touch with it long ago, seem to take to it out of pure desperation in prison. Imagine giving a sandwich to a woman who is suffering from starvation. When she has finished gobbling it down, if you ask what it tasted like, she would not be able to give you a true account. To the starving person the taste, if any, was simply irrelevant. The sandwich was a means to an end. For many inmates, institutional spirituality is that sandwich. They are literally starved for unconditional love, acceptance, and forgiveness, which they are told is God. The message is not wrong; however, the people delivering it often do not understand that these individuals rarely consume it in a way that will exact actual change. The result is that the spiritual change or the "jail talk" change we hear articulated before release is no more substantial than carrying home a box that is empty, or full of packing materials. The ex-inmates grow weary of carrying around the empty box and simply stop carrying it. No one realized that the box had been empty all along; its contents faded away long before entering the hustle and bustle of the ex-offender life.

No one, including the former inmate, is aware that this is what is happening, so it goes uncorrected or there is no intervention. The former inmate takes the shortest route back into the prison system. The cycle begins again, and no one has even an inkling of what happened and how or where the former inmate got off on the wrong exit.

My own incarceration is only one year, and I have the good fortune of my own home, family, friends, and a job to return to. Yet I still foresee many major, difficult transitioning issues that I will need to face. The most pressing to me is the question "How will I fit into the space that I left behind, since I am virtually not the same person that I was when I left home?" I foresee that this will affect all aspects of my personal and professional life, in many ways. My loved ones have just begun to grasp the depth of the changes that have occurred within me. When I am able to furlough home, I am so much more sensitive than I was before, which I attribute to my feelings and emotions being suppressed for so long that when they have "freedom," I am much more sensitive. I believe both my family and I will need help with this transition because the woman coming home is simply not the same person as the one who left. I have the distinct advantage of some pretty powerful supports, which many inmates will not be so fortunate to have. I have been blessed with a keen foresight, and I have an amazing and dedicated therapist on the outside who has worked tirelessly with me throughout my incarceration via letter, homework assignments, telephone calls, and occasional visits. I arranged for this support coming from the outside myself. This is not programming offered to me by the system in which I am incarcerated. This contact from a therapist, who worked with me before, has been an invaluable part of my ability to process what has been happening. We have dedicated the last few months of my incarceration to preparing me psychologically for my transition from an inmate to a happy, healthy, productive citizen once again.

The professional guidance and influence of my therapist have thus far afforded me many precious advantages that I would otherwise not have had. I have put together a workable relapse-prevention plan that I will utilize on a daily basis. I have been gently guided through strengthening the bonds with my ever-devoted family and friends. I have been able to aid and direct my support group in becoming more familiar with my disease, recovery, and the transitioning process. I am working to prepare my family for the changes that have occurred in me because of the institutionalization and dehumanization that I have experienced. I have also been able to expand my support group with additions throughout the community. I have secured positive aftercare and transitioning therapy for when I return home, and I have held onto and strengthened my spirituality against some pretty forceful odds.

These are advantages that are mine to take with me as I walk out of these prison doors for the last time. I believe that I have the tools to be successful; however, I anticipate that it will be difficult. *The way I see it, all who desire this valuable, personalized programming should have the same potentially life-altering/saving opportunity.*

I am one of a very small percentage of inmates who are receiving programming guidance that has the potential to make the difference and reduce the rate of recidivism to the level that has some semblance of logic and reason.

I would be much more frightened if I faced being dropped in the middle of a "foreign society" all alone with absolutely no idea of what to expect or where to turn for help. Without a doubt, the frightened and lonely ex-inmate will latch onto the very first "familiar" that crosses her path. This would likely turn out to be in the same type of situation and circumstance that brought her to prison. If these inmates were taught, right here, at this stage, to recognize a positive "familiar" before their situation makes them frightened, alone, and even desperate, maybe, just maybe the first "familiar" they accept could be the one that makes a positive difference instead of the one that sends them back inside.

Because of this neglect, many inmates who are released *will* eventually re-offend. Near-release is a time in an inmate's incarceration when programming is needed and desired most, and in my case this has simply not been offered. Guided transitional programming could greatly improve the chances of success of individuals who are being discharged.

It saddens me deeply that this desperate need continues to go unacknowledged. This represents a tremendous disservice to those offenders whose true desire is never to re-offend and who wish to become healthy, productive citizens. Mere comprehension of this very challenging part of incarceration could very well make the difference for many.

With everything that I am, I wish that I could share the gifts that were given to me with all who are incarcerated and desire never to be so again, so that they too would have a real chance at prosperity and peace. Developing an understanding of the problem and increasing our support of programming that actually helps with the transition out would be well worth our time and effort.

INTELLIGENT ALLAH, *New York*

SMOOTHING THE ROAD: THE FORMERLY INCARCERATED GET A HELPING HAND

Seventeen-year-old Anthony Sheldon had chased fast cash until he ran into trouble with the law—and twenty-five years in prison. During decades of isolation, his friends vanished and he lost his parents to health problems. Anthony's forlorn journey to freedom culminated with the forty-two-year-old stepping out of prison and into a homeless shelter. In his pocket were forty dollars in personal savings, mandated by prison rules. In his heart was hope for a successful life. On his mind were thoughts of the first year of freedom, a period when approximately 75 percent of people released from prison remain jobless, and two-thirds are rearrested.

Anthony Sheldon is a fictional character in a hypothetical story that mimics the lives of men and women released from prison daily. The road to success after incarceration is filled with potholes and speed bumps that even experienced drivers may need help navigating.

But there is a roadmap: reentry. This is the process of helping prepare people to reenter and remain in society by attaining essentials like housing, employment, and drug treatment. Reentry programs span from pre-release efforts inside of prison to community-based organizations providing post-release assistance. Some comprehensive programs pair prison staff with community groups both inside and outside prisons.

BIRTH OF A MOVEMENT

Jeremy Travis, president of John Jay College of Criminal Justice, coined the phrase "reentry" in 1999 during his tenure as director of the National Institute of Justice. The term grew from then–Attorney General Janet Reno asking Travis, "What are we doing about all the people coming out of prison?" In October of that year, Travis and Reno held a press conference to publicize the concept of reentry. Travis further fueled the fervor in 2005 in his book *But They All Come Back: Facing the Challenges of Prisoner Reentry.*

Police officers lock up lawbreakers, but judges rarely throw away the key. According to the Bureau of Justice Statistics, 95 percent of all incarcerated people in state prisons will reenter society. Numbers present a clear picture for the eyes of politicians. During former President George Bush's 2004 State of the Union Speech, he stated, "Tonight I ask you to consider another group of Americans in need of help. This year, some 600,000 inmates will be released from prison back into society. We know from long experience that if they can't find work, or a home, or help, they are much more likely to commit crime and return to prison. So tonight, I propose a four-year, $300 million Prisoner Re-Entry Initiative. . . . America is the land of the second chance, and when the gates of the prison open, the path ahead should lead to a better life." Bush later formally introduced the Second Chance Act bill, calling for the reentry funding he proposed in his speech.

Bipartisan support for reentry radiated from the Oval Office and throughout the halls of Congress. Conservative Republican Senator Sam Brownback of Kansas and liberal Democrat Danny K. Davis of Illinois were central supporters of the Second Chance Act. The bill was endorsed unanimously by the U.S. Senate and received bipartisan approval of 347 to 62 in the

House of Representatives. Bush signed the Second Chance Act into law on April 9, 2008, allocating $326 million towards reentry programs.

This reentry effort echoed the sentiments of many presidential hopefuls prior to and during the race for the White House. Then-Senator Barack Obama was an early supporter of the Second Chance Act. He had proposed working towards ensuring that the formerly incarcerated gain employment. Senator John McCain supported reentry programs that focus on career training and job placement. Then-Senator Hillary Clinton had plans to address reentry through her Youth Opportunity Agenda. Ex-governor of North Carolina John Edwards and New Mexico Governor Bill Richards had both voiced a need for reentry programs.

HUMBLE BEGINNINGS

Before the word "reentry" became a catch phrase on Capitol Hill or in the media, and before cyberspace got wind of it, the concept was the foundation for many unpublicized community-based organizations. Since 1931, the Osborne Association has been aiding New Yorkers entangled within the criminal-justice system. With three external sites statewide, plus sites inside of jails, state prisons, and courts, the Osborne Association helps over five thousand people annually. They provide a broad spectrum of services, ranging from housing and health aid, to counseling and court advocacy.

Though parole is seen by many as purely supervisory, reentry has long been a hallmark of parole. In 1973, the National Advisory Commission on Criminal Justice Standards and Goals issued a report stating, "Parole staff has a specific task: to assist parolees in availing themselves of community resources." Despite parole's purpose, in many states its effectiveness in practice has been questioned. Devah Pager, associate professor of sociology at Princeton University, tackles the issue in her book *Marked: Race, Crime, and Finding Work in an Era of Mass Incarceration.* Pager reasons that the public's disenchantment with rehabilitation has fostered corresponding skepticism concerning the viability of parole.

REVITALIZING GOVERNMENTAL AID

The notion that failed rehabilitative efforts have dampened hope in reentry is debatable. Yet the current all-time high of people exiting prison and then returning proves that the most industrialized nation has missed its mark when aiming to reduce recidivism. The result is a $68 billion budget for 2.3 million men, women, and children behind bars—25 percent of the world's prisoners—making America the top nation for incarceration.

But recent advances in reentry have reinvigorated hope and shifted correctional policy towards innovative approaches for reducing recidivism. As the Second Chance Act's greenbacks swim through the red tape of Washington, scores of states are revitalizing their reentry efforts.

"It is on reentry that we as a state must hone our efforts to continue the historic reductions in crime and save taxpayer dollars," then-chairman of the New York State Division of Parole, George Alexander, writes in volume 1, issue 3 of the Division's newsletter. Under Alexander's leadership, Parole partnered with the Rensselaer County Re-entry Task Force and planned to assign special "reentry parole officers" for the Task Force initiative.

Arguably, the most celebrated endeavor involving parole in New York is a reentry program stationed inside of a state prison. Explaining the program, Alexander writes, "The Division of Parole, working with the Department of Correctional Services and the Office of Alcohol and Substance Abuse Services, this past August began a pilot program at Orleans Correctional Facility in western New York." Participants in the program are afforded services such as job training, anger management, and substance-abuse counseling, which Alexander stresses will "help them avoid returning to their old ways."

Other state programs are riding the rails of reentry. Michigan's $33 million Re-entry Initiative has expanded from fifteen metropolitan areas to cover the entire state. California is on the brink of developing thirty-two reentry centers in response to legislation signed by Governor Arnold Schwarzenegger. New Jersey has launched Another Chance, a program delivering health aid, job training, and other support to people incarcerated or on parole in Newark, Trenton, and Camden. The Next Door is a nonprofit reentry organization in Nashville, Tennessee, that has helped over 380 previously imprisoned women acquire housing, job training, and counseling.

COMMUNITY INTERVENTION

Reentry programs are frequently developed by nonprofit organizations in the same communities from which many people in prison come, and to which they will return. These programs are usually funded by charitable donations and government aid like the Second Chance Act. Staff run the gamut from volunteers to salaried workers. Further, a myriad of community-based organizations are managed partially or completely by men and women who have served time. The Osborne Association is one such organization. It is staffed predominantly by employees who do not have degrees in criminology. Nonetheless, a staff member's past life of crime and incarceration is the ultimate field study (from which he or she could easily pen a thesis).

Wahida Clark is a student of experience who champions reentry in her home state of New Jersey. She spent nearly a decade in federal penitentiaries. In the solace of a cell, Clark became a best-selling author of several books. She returned home and assumed the position of president of Prodigal Sons and Daughters, a nonprofit organization which provides various reentry services as well as support groups for the formerly incarcerated and for at-risk youth. Clark emphasizes that there is a need for formerly incarcerated people to work with reentry programs.

"My prison experience taught me there were more than two million inmates in state and federal prisons. It was then that I became convinced that the only ones who could solve the problem of recidivism of inmates were inmates themselves," says Clark. "I became the vice president of Prodigal Sons and Daughters after learning about their prison reentry program. Prodigal Sons and Daughters is the only reentry program that offers meaningful incentives for successful completion of its vocational and re-directional programs. We can boast of one-hundred successful ex-offenders."

There are a variety of positive effects of reentry assistance. The obvious effects are that the formerly incarcerated receive a collage of services that support responsible citizenship. Communities become safer, property values increase, and the quality of life soars when crime is reduced. Fewer bodies trickling back into prison equates to fewer dollars pulled from the pockets of taxpayers to finance prison construction and support the incarcerated. When individuals exhibit criminal behavior and serve time, but return home to live within the parameters of the law, they model redemption and hope to youth who skate on the thin ice covering crime-ridden streets.

Reentry programs are not a panacea for the countless problems plaguing the criminal-justice system and society. To reduce recidivism, the formerly incarcerated must possess the ambition, resilience, and discipline required to overcome societal hurdles that they once sidestepped through risky shortcuts. Individuals in society must be willing to empathize with people who are commonly stigmatized by virtue of the self-inflicted wounds of criminality. Successful reentry is a steppingstone towards raising the standards of society. Parole veterans like Alexander understand that reentry is predicated upon consistency and transcending norms: "We must continue to explore new strategies to drive down the number of individuals who re-offend" (*Alexander Newsletter*).

VALJEAN ROYAL, *Indiana*

POST-RELEASE PROGRAMS AND GENDER VARIANT PEOPLE

On Tuesday, January 20, 2004, President Bush called for the funding of programs to deal with some 600,000 inmates who would be released from prison that year—without work, without a home, without help. "America," he said, "is the land of second chances," and he added that "when the gates of the prison open, the path ahead should lead to a better life." The U.S. has a higher percentage of its citizens in prison than any other country in history, and accounts for an astonishing 25 percent of the world's inmate population. Americans are becoming increasingly concerned about what awaits communities that will have to absorb a disoriented and unprepared population of former inmates.

The President's funding of faith-based organizations' post-release programs became the only area in the federal budget where the government has merged church and state. Federal funding now allows faith-based organizations to play a key role as part of the states' efforts to reintegrate inmates into their communities, and to help them adjust to society. But before this act was put into place by the President—providing a chance for inmates to find success—funding for inmate education, drug counseling, and work programs designed to ease the transition from incarceration to freedom had been cut or remained stagnant. It is thus the hope of many that faith-based, post-release outreach ministries someday may be able to substantially diminish recidivism rates. However, I know from personal experience that for most transsexuals and other gender variant individuals, the process of reintegration will follow a rocky path: their families may not be willing to accept them, finding jobs will be difficult, and individuals in their old peer groups will be ready to support the resumption of criminal habits. Maintaining some tether to family is important for inmates being released. But the reality for trans people is that for most, that link does not exist or is often difficult to maintain. Going into a post-release program, also known as a transitional program, is a good idea. As with any change in life, a time of adjustment is essential. For inmates being released, adjusting to a drastically different society after having learned the regimented life of prison, it is crucial to be allowed a slow transition back into society; all need to learn virtually to start life over again: how to find employment, a home, to manage money, and to regain independence. Assisting, counseling, and monitoring inmates closely while they take these first steps towards reintegration into society is a way to ensure that they are learning the ropes again properly. I vote yes for any such programs.

However, transsexuals and other gender-variant individuals being released from prison are being excluded from the right to transitional programs provided by tax dollars funding the church and state programs promoted by President Bush. Could this be declared unconstitutional? Before answering, do keep in mind the following realities: in existing case law, the courts have found that transgendered people are not covered under anti-discrimination laws protecting persons on the basis of sexual/gender orientation or sex. Trans people were specifically excluded in the Americans with Disabilities Act of 1991, and they also are not covered under the disability laws of nearly all the states that have such laws. Both state and federal courts have almost uniformly held that transgendered people are outside the legal definitions and protections of existing anti-discrimination laws. Since changing gender is so readily apparent, trans people often lose their jobs and are denied employment, or become underemployed regardless of their experience or education. Trans people are frequently denied housing or even evicted from rented homes, and denied many public services. Trans people often must deal with transphobic administrators, directors, and law enforcement. This is a reality for many trans people that have never been to prison, or jail for that matter. Only a few jurisdictions, including the states of Minnesota (by statute), Oregon (by administrative decision), and a small but growing number of cities and counties offer trans people protection from discrimination. Thus, most transgendered activists have viewed inclusion in the Employment Non-Discrimination Act (ENDA) as absolutely critical.

Discrimination towards trans people in faith-based organizations cannot be denied. In her book *Crossing Over* (2001), Vanessa Sheridan suggests that a transphobic socio-religious attitude towards the transgendered is all too common: "Those who fear, hate, discriminate against, and exclude the transgendered often appear to be the routine and even rather predictable products of their culture." Vanessa offers insight into the transgender experience and confronts the harsh reality of the injustice prevalent in society and in the church towards those who are differently gendered. In *Trans-gendered: Theology, Ministry, and Communities of Faith* (2003), Justin Tanis writes:

> Trans people encounter a wide range of responses when entering a faith community. Many times, trans people choose not to attend in order to avoid what may be an uncomfortable experience and the judgment that they perceive will come from a community of faith. . . . In a number of different ways, a congregation can explicitly or unconsciously create an atmosphere that conveys to transgendered people that we are not welcome there. Communities of faith also need to be aware that they need to extend a welcome that bridges the fear of rejection that a transgender person may have that prevents them from seeking acceptance within the congregation. This one barrier is probably the single largest to the participation of transgendered people in communities of faith. . . . Barriers to participate: (1) Fear and unfamiliarity on the part of the congregation and the transgendered. (2) Language issues. (3) Physical layout that separates people by gender. (4) Programs that exclude or separate by gender. (5) Pathologizing or designating trans issues as sinful. (6) Overt hostility.

Most faith communities do make careful distinctions concerning gender, and show unjust disfavor towards transgender people. This spells discrimination to me, but remember, there are no laws protecting us from this injustice in most states. This scenario is tragic not only because of the ever-increasing number of gender variant people inside America's prison system, who are never mentioned (due to "trans" being excluded from U.S. Census reports, which include prisoners by sex, M or F), but also because no one knows how many transgendered are innocent, jailed because of selective harassment, planting of evidence, or inept defense. (For those who doubt the ability of police to abuse the law, the Mark Fuhrman tapes paint an evil picture of the police: unfettered by law, framing, beating, and even torturing people. In the Philadelphia police scandal, officers confessed to beatings, robbery, lying, and planting evidence resulting in jailing dozens, maybe hundreds, of innocent people.) Once there's no justice, crime, chaos, and the rate of recidivism increases. And that hurts everybody.

Reading the texts of Vanessa Sheridan and Justin Tanis, I realized that, as a Christian and transsexual seeking post-release assistance when released from prison, my primary source of help and support is likely to be from those who may not embrace me because of religious beliefs that ridicule the transgendered, and who view a trans lifestyle as sinful. Be ever mindful that in some cases such attitudes effectively subject transgendered people to a policy of "Don't Ask, Don't Tell," in order for us to be accepted into a post-release program that will provide some hope or promise of a successful transition back into society and its work force.

My personal experience was one of much pain and disappointment because I refused to acknowledge Don't Ask, Don't Tell, and for good reason. I, like many trans people, have been a victim of discrimination, social rejections, low self-esteem, and self-hatred, all of which caused emotional disorders. As a teen living as a male to female transsexual, I confessed to a crime that I had absolutely no knowledge of (my confession was the only thing that ever linked me to the crime), casting myself out of society, into the hell where my mental and emotional illness at the time made me feel I belonged. What happened next was more nightmarish than your wildest imagination. There was a crusade called "Save Our Children," founded by Anita Bryant. Ms. Bryant was a spokesperson for the Florida Sunshine Orange Juice manufacturers. "Save Our Children" was a crusade to ban gay and other alternative lifestyles from American communities in order to save the children of America from being affected by such lifestyles. During the height of that era, a correctional officer was murdered at the Indiana State Prison where I was housed. I was eventually charged, again, for a murder I knew nothing about. Not wanting to believe what was happening, I screamed that I was innocent. My screams were heard by uncaring hearts. Yet other inmates that knew I had never left my cell house on the morning of this murder stepped forward in an attempt to defend me. An inmate originally indicated my involvement. Even he eventually broke down and admitted that he manufactured his statements and accusations after receiving promises from state and prison officials for an early release from prison if he agreed to become a state witness in this murder. After his recantation, state officials went out and found three other inmates that they made promises to and deals with to testify to the fabrication. During an era when people of my lifestyle were already on trial—just for existing—I was placed on trial, convicted, and sentenced to life in prison. Again for a crime that today's technology would prove I did not commit. The state presented the false testimonies of the three inmates seeking early release. These fabrications were created by state and prison officials. The news media printed things like "Man Appears in Court as a Woman," "Makeup on Trial," "Anita Bryant vs. Valjean Royal," "The Two Faces of Justice," and "Justice Takes a Holiday." With no real evidence whatsoever to link me to the crime or the crime scene, I was sentenced and later received a life sentence while being housed on Indiana's death row, and was notified of this by way of the United States Postal Service. I have never murdered anyone. The only person that I have ever hurt has been myself, as well as the man whose murder I confessed to, which ultimately led to my initial incarceration. I have not been out of prison since. I was eighteen years old then; I'm fifty-six today. There is much more that I would like to share with you that will demonstrate how my journey was the cause and effect of being a transsexual whose nonacceptance by society and peer groups led to my incarceration and the lowest self-esteem imaginable. However, it would take some time to reveal the story of my life in its entirety—so I will get to the point: where I am now.

I've grown comfortably and gracefully into my womanhood, and I'm a very proud and dignified trans-woman despite the hard knocks life designed for me and my kind. I cannot begin to express the love and freedom in spirit I feel in just the total acceptance of myself as a trans-woman. It feels wonderful to know that you are God's precious jewel, just as you are. I only regret that I had to travel some of the paths that I have in order to find where I truly belonged. Paths of anger, rebellion, deceit, self-hatred, and self-sabotage all bear my footprints. No path is more important than the path to self-understanding and acceptance; it requires the ability to finally face a journey inside yourself, and confront all the pain and self-hatred—which has become your enemy number one—in all its reality, and slay a little of that self-hatred each day until this enemy no longer lives in you. Then the path into self can continue on, to reach a destination where you can love yourself and be loved. A place where the screaming stops and the Calm begins, a place where you can close your eyes and still find your way around because you are where you belong, a place of soulful acceptance of yourself, of your heart, of *your* life. So "Don't Ask, Don't Tell" would be like traveling back in time for me. Not an option!

In July of 2003 I went in front of the Indiana State Parole Board, as a model prisoner, after having served thirty years. I was placed into a six-month (nonresidential) transitional program. In this program I was disappointed that there did not exist any reference to post-release assistance for trans people, nor was there any representation from the transgender community among any of the guests scheduled to speak. I kept a journal throughout this program with thoughts of pursuing this same sort of program geared towards trans people. I hoped that this program could be implemented into the DOC transition programs everywhere. If implemented, my program would encourage, educate, and direct trans people, after their release, towards support groups that could accommodate the needs of trans people, assisting them toward the same success in their reintegration into communities as is afforded to others.

One of the inspirational speakers offering encouragement for those of us in the transitional classes I attended was a former inmate (heterosexual) who had succeeded in reaching goals that seemed unattainable at some points in his life. He gave very strong and powerful testimony. I gained a strong desire to be able to deliver the same sort of inspirational speaker for trans folks, to elevate and make a difference in these programs for trans people. My disappointment was replaced with determination to succeed. Six months later, after my successful completion of the transitional program, I returned to appear before the parole board. At this review I was given ninety days to come up with acceptable parole plans. The board members asked that I bring any community supporters that I might have to my next hearing, which was set for March 2004. I wrote hundreds of letters to churches and outreach missions for transitional post-release assistance. I never failed to mention my status as a MTF transsexual, and I never received any responses. I wrote to many people in the trans communities asking them to help me by networking on their computers to assemble a support system inside of the trans community—one able to attend my hearing so that a support system was present. I hoped that trans people would have packed the place! My mother and father were the only support I had, and they are both old and ill, so they could not be at my hearing. Gianna E. Israel, community counselor for the transgendered, supplied a statement of reference letter that I placed in every application and every appeal for support that I sent out. I began to feel sick inside, the closer my hearing date came. None of the faith community responded, and none of the trans community seemed interested at all. When I returned before the parole board on March the 26th, 2004, my heart was broken and I hurt to the core of my soul once again. No one at all was there for me, after all my efforts. No one but producer Dan Hunt of REID Productions, which had been granted permission at my request to film my parole hearing and follow my release after parole as part of a documentary that is being produced on PBS about transsexual life before, during, and after the prison experience.

My parole was denied, and as I lay in my bed, crying my heart out that evening, wanting to just die, I received a letter from the "first application" that I ever mailed to a faith community. The letter stated that I had been accepted into the "Jesus House," a post-release residential program for Christians. The letter came too late for my parole hearing, but for some reason that didn't matter. I felt good about it. So good, I dried my eyes, read it again, and I haven't cried since. Today, I'm okay. I'm still waiting, praying and waiting. There *is* a need for post-release assistance for trans-people, and I'm confident it's coming.

WORKS CITED

Sheridan, Vanessa. *Crossing Over: Liberating the Transgendered Christian.* Cleveland: Pilgrim Press, 2001.

Tanis, Justin. *Trans-Gendered: Theology, Ministry, and Communities of Faith.* Cleveland: Pilgrim Press, 2003.

JAMES CASTRILLO, *Maine*

EVERY MORNING

Every morning I find myself lying on my bunk, staring at the familiar ceiling, thinking. I've been doing that a lot lately, just thinking. At first it was hard—hard to concentrate with so much noise, the uncomfortable surroundings—but you get used to it. You get used to all of the noise: the jingle-jangle of keys, the bang of cell doors closing, the constant yelling. You learn to block it out. You get used to your surroundings: the concrete, the bars, the fences. You learn to live with them. What I haven't learned to live with yet is myself. Will I ever be able to again? I don't know.

The disappointment is almost unbearable. Like a giant net that I'm caught in, unable to escape. I think back to my past, high school, before this. I remember the things my teachers used to say to me: "James, you're special. Smarten up." "James, you have so much potential. Please, don't blow it." I wonder what they would say now. Have I blown it? I never took their comments seriously, never thought I had to. I was blind to the reality that the path I was on leads nowhere, and fast. That reality finally hit me, and when it did, it hit hard. I think to myself, is this the reason that I'm here, to be woken up? I don't believe in coincidence. I believe everything happens for a reason, but what is the reasoning behind this? Could there actually be some kind of good in coming to prison? Again an uncontrollable feeling of disappointment sweeps over my body. A feeling so incredibly cold and unforgiving that even underneath warm blankets, I can still feel an uncomfortable chill. What could possibly be good about this place? Not much. I think about my future and the uncertainty of it. Where will I be in the next five years? Who will still be there with me? Will anyone? Is this too great an obstacle to overcome? A part of me says, yes, there's no sense in trying; it's too hard, too late. The disappointment is too much to overcome. I don't want to get off this bunk. I want to just give in to the prison mentality that grips this place. A mentality that says the here and now is what's important, not the future. A mentality so dark and hopeless, only hatred can survive. It's a lot easier to be bad than good, so why should I try to change? Another part of me, the strongest part, won't quit. Won't give in. Wants to keep fighting. I think of how badly I want to be a success. How I want to make it in this world, the right way. That's what helps me to keep going, my drive to succeed. I know what I want; it's just having the strength to get it. Do I have strength enough to fight another day? Can I overcome this disappointment that tests my sanity? Am I going to allow it to win?

I can't. That's not me. I'm not a quitter. So, I get up off my bunk, brush myself off, and grab my books. On my way to the School Department, I walk by pool tables, card games, and television sets, all of which are occupied by the same people, day after day. I walk by hundreds of inmates, all doing the same thing: *nothing!* The looks on their faces when I tell them, "I can't talk right now; I'm late for class" could convey a thousand words, but only one comes to mind. Shock. With frayed brows and eyes the size of volleyballs, they stare as if I have two heads. They all seem to mutter the same thing: "What?" "Why are you going to school?" With their jaws on the floor, as if they have just seen Jennifer Lopez walking through the Pod naked. I leave them to answer their own moronic question. Why would I be going to school? Hmmm . . . that's a tough one.

Incarceration doesn't have to be the end of a life if you don't want it to be. You do have a choice. Everyone makes mistakes. That's part of being human. What separates the men from the boys, the winners from the losers, is how those mistakes are dealt with after they are made, if that disappointment is allowed to take over, to win. Disappointment is useless in a place like this because it gets you nowhere, and I'm tired of being nowhere. That's what helps me to keep fighting every day: my will to overcome that disappointment. My will to win.

As the morning's last thoughts of disappointment exit my mind, I enter my classroom. "Sorry I'm late. It won't happen again."

Epilogue

DANNER DARCLEIGHT, *New York*

GETTING OUT: NOTES FROM THE ROAD

> What's your road, man?—holyboy road, madman road, rainbow road, guppy road, any
> road. It's an anywhere road for anybody anyhow.
> —JACK KEROUAC

The prison wall stretches like a dark gray band in the van's rearview mirror. As we speed away, the gray line tapers down; in under a minute it's gone, and I've covered more distance than I have in a decade.

This is the first time I've been outside of a prison wall in all those years. I'm relieved that the feel of driving hasn't made me throw up farina into my shackles. My handcuffs are tethered to a waist chain (think praying, but at crotch level), the leg irons limit my gait to one-and-a-half-foot baby steps. The van's windows are tinted.

The transport officers are road guys, pros. Gunslingers. They get hazard pay and beaucoup overtime—and everyone likes leaving prison, even guards. The one riding shotgun, M, pushes aside the morning paper and turns to speak to me through the black metal cage. Chuckling, he says, "You really pissed someone off." He's fishing. Like most of the prison's population, he's been fed the tiniest morsels of my story and is hungry for intrigue. M knows I didn't do anything wrong . . . aside from entering into a relationship with a prominent woman from the community. Something like this happens often enough for the Department to have an unofficial policy in place: flick the inmate to the far end of the state so fast his fucking head spins. Luckily, the powers that be didn't hang a bogus charge on me and ship me out via the box.

Be that as it may, I'm not going to give either of them something that will anonymously appear in the local rag. I misdirect. "Get this," I tell him, "on my way out the door, I was told never to come back." The pair shake their heads, and laugh at the absurdity of it all. Darkest pit in the state and I've been barred from returning—admittedly, I'm wearing that with pride.

Two hours ago, I was in the mess hall when an odd hush fell over the place. A cop and a sergeant escorted me back to my cell, where I had forty minutes to pack everything I own—clothes, books, papers, toiletries, canned food, and assorted miscellany—into four duffels. I gave away practically half my cell in order to hew to the four-bag limit. Cops inventoried everything while I stayed moving in a thrumming frenzy of distraction. Fluff, my closest friend, carried the bags downstairs for me and put them in a cart. The effort left his flimsy white state undershirt absolutely drenched with sweat. This I learned when we hugged goodbye, natural, close. We'll likely never see each other again—that's what this prison life is all about. Impermanence and loss in an ongoing crash course. Walking out the door of the cellblock, I turned back. Oscar and Fluffy gave me sad waves. Under escort, I pushed the cart with my property through the halls. Waving goodbye to confused friends. Passing more than one checkpoint, I overheard a guard pick up a phone and report that I'd just walked by.

The fact is, we're driving away from this beef at fifty miles an hour, blowing the speed limit so they can get me to a deport prison in time for a large transport bus. The trouble is behind me, and I feel good, better than I have in a week.

The trip ahead promises to be sedate motoring through scenic countryside. There'll be a few stops as we spend the night at prisons along the circuitous route. Despite being shackled and under armed guard, I feel an exhilarating sense of freedom, traveling through *the world*, sharing the road with citizens.

We crest a large hill and I'm greeted by the slow waving arms of a cluster of wind turbines. How many times have I stared at the whitish blades from the distance of my window, the sun rising behind them as I sat in bed, penning quixotic paeans to their kinetic beauty. "Wonderful," I realize I just said aloud. P, behind the wheel, glances at me in the rearview. "The wind turbines," I say. "They're beautiful."

We make it to Prison B in just over an hour.[1] Since we're not allowed to travel with watches (or any personal effects), I catch the time where I can—the van's digital display, a hack's wrist as he removes my cuffs. It's just before noon. An inmate porter lugs my four heavy bags of property away to a staging area. P tells me that he worked for a time at Prison F, where I'm headed, that it's a shit hole, but that I'm a "smart kid" and will be "fine." I thank him for saying that.

They help me out of the van, flank me as I waddle indoors to the holding pens. Some forms are signed and custody of me is transferred to the locals. Standard operating procedure: rather than uncuff and unchain me, M claims a matching set of cuffs, chains, and leg irons. Like Jacob Marley, he leaves jangling keys and chains. Regarding this trade—me for trinkets—I vacillate between being amused and degraded.

The bullpen is the same one I sat in on my way upstate, ten years ago. Modern construction, heavy turquoise mesh instead of bars. Thick, blond-wood benches which haven't been burnt or scratch-tagged (we can do minimal damage when we're shackled and lacking toys). A Black con with designer frames and a red kufi stands in a corner, speaking sheistily to a Hispanic with perfectly coiffed waves. We don't acknowledge each other. I sit a few feet away from them. Straightening my back, I close my eyes and take good, deep breaths. Ever since *Silence of the Lambs*, the quiet white guy who doesn't seem to belong in prison can easily pass for someone who'll slip his cuffs and eat your fucking face off. I smile.

The gate opens and a couple more men shuffle in. One has a cast on his leg that goes up to the thigh; he's been shackled creatively to accommodate the crutches. The other is a slight Middle Easterner in his early forties with kind, dark eyes. He vibes "engineering student gone wrong," not "cabbie with a vehicular manslaughter." This man sits next to me and, after a time, asks what prison I've come from.

I've spent most of my time inside housed in the better areas of prison, working the better jobs, avoiding the riffraff. My instinct here is to play it cold and aloof. But on the road, we're all in it together, and life can get pretty boring when you give your peers the high hat.

With a smile, I tell him where I've been doing time, and inquire about him. We exchange names and abbreviated bios. Nassim was a med student who crashed and burned into the party scene in the early '90s. When he was twenty-three, I was thirteen, yet we partied at some of the same nightclubs.

Another man is brought into the pen. A small, mocha-skinned Black man in his late thirties. As soon as the guard walks away, he pulls out several cookies he managed to hide in his pocket. Sitting alone in the corner, he eats. In my head, I name him "Dusty," because he reminds me of a Dusty I knew in county.

It dawns on me—mainly from seeing men shackled to each other in an adjacent pen—that I'm with the special cases. The Hispanic with the waves in his hair volunteers that he escaped from juvie decades ago. The dude with the crutches can't be shackled to someone because of his limited mobility. Nassim's on the mental-health caseload. Who knows what Dusty's deal is. The Black kid in the red kufi is a high-ranking member of the Bloods. In describing a ticket he caught last night for a stolen TV in his cell, he mentions that the hacks doing the search could've written him up for his photos.[2] That and the fire-engine-red kufi badge him as a Blood, and high-rank—call that my intuition after being around these guys for so long.

Nassim has the minimal affect of a medicated depressive. He's really pissed at himself for catching another dirty urine and getting kicked out of a medium-security prison. I just listen quietly, letting him work through things. Mainly, he says, he's missing his partner, a smart, compassionate chap named Tom. I first hear "partner" as running, or crime partner, a friend he was getting baked with, breaking bread with. And that's when Nassim begins making vague, low-intensity passes. We're shackled, in a bullpen with other men, destined for different parts of the state. What's he hoping for? I guess it's just flirting. So as to stop Nassim before he gets too hot and bothered, I drop a non sequitur: "Fuckin' crazy, man. Three days ago I was eating a fantastic meal over a table with my mates—Fluff, Yas, and Doc. We had spaghetti. Normally, I'd bread and fry zucchini flowers, but they won't be ready till midsummer. So, I made this perfect, garlicky bruschetta."

With a watering mouth, he asks what I did to get the boot from Prison A.

I mention the girl. It feels good to talk of her during this tumult—and it lets Nassim know what team I play for. But now he's all abubble with questions. Rather than stopping his inquiry by saying something hurtful, I excuse myself, shuffle the few feet to the toilet, and have a piss.

When I return to my square of bench next to Nassim, I can tell he's about to resume his inquiry. "Hey, man," I say. "You were a med student, do an intake on me."

Immediately, his posture straightens, he's transported back to a time before everything went to shit. In this manner, he does a full workup: history, vital stats, chief complaint, symptoms.

This isn't entirely to misdirect Nas. I've been suffering from a bizarre food allergy for the past six months. The prison doctors haven't been any help. They ran blood and urine tests, tried different courses of powerful antibiotics, then threw up their hands: *The tests show nothing abnormal; come back in a few months if this is still bothering you.* By keeping a food journal, I learned that it was milk, whey, and lactic-acid starter cultures (found in virtually all processed meats) that produced not a traditional, gassy lactose intolerance, but debilitating lethargy, swollen tonsils, extreme mental fogginess, severe gut pain, and the entire spectrum of urinary problems (weak stream, dribbling, difficulty starting and stopping, frequent urination). The best I've been able to self-diagnose is that I'm suffering from some mutant non-bacterial prostatitis that has somehow commandeered my digestive tract from stem to stern. I'm thirty-three years old and this is hell. I know my condition is going to complicate this trip. On the road we're fed cold cuts and cheese, neither of which I can eat. I'm going to get ravenously hungry, then end up eating something that makes me ill and poorly suited to handle the complications of the road.

Nassim—willing to spend the time, but lacking the tests and tools of the trade—says it sounds like I have, go figure, non-bacterial prostatitis along with a severe allergy to milk products. I thank him and say it was fun.

Meanwhile, my attention has shifted to the Blood, standing a few feet away, leaning against the thick turquoise mesh. He's about my age, boyish face, very nice skin except for a thick scar that runs from the corner of his mouth back to his ear—the *de rigueur* battle scar of gang life. He's telling the Puerto Rican with waves about all the "books" he's written. Writing, like several other creative endeavors, is a latent talent that often gets nurtured only after someone finds him-or herself behind a wall. Guy like this probably reads and writes only when he's in the box; his stretches in general population are spent (gang) politicking. It's a shame, because there's definitely intelligence there. He could do something good. "Gentlemen, excuse me." They turn. I address myself to the Blood. "Are you getting your work out there?"

"How you mean?"

"Online." I talk of establishing an online presence, brand-building with blogs and social-networking sites—even mention a few sites that feature new talent. "You're a writer, man. You can't be creating in a vacuum. You need feedback."

He's accustomed to boasting about specifics, not discussing craft, and subjects me to the ending of what he's currently working on. It's *La Femme Nikita* meets *Kill Bill*, Pam Grier times Halle Berry. The story culminates with the protagonist taking a hyperviolent and ironic revenge on the man who raped her in the beginning.

"Okay," I say.

"Word. I always have some fucked up hate sex in my shit."

"Let the boys in marketing worry about it."

The gate opens and a beefy hack steps into the pen holding a garbage bag filled with our lunch. He drops the brown bags into our upturned hands, then leaves. I survey the contents: cheese sandwich, bologna sandwich, two chocolate chip cookies, a juice (Li'l Hugs, which come in a cute faux barrel). I can consume four slices of bread and sugar water—the rest will fuck me up. Nassim has miraculously gotten one sandwich with processed turkey, which he agrees to trade with me. I give him the cookies as a thank-you.

When the gate opens next, the beefy hack calls us out one at a time by our last names, in no apparent order. We drop our garbage in the larger bag from whence it came, and stand in front of a hack who's to apply our waist chains. My guy's all thumbs. Black, late thirties, wedding band, bad breath, glasses, uneven moustache. A new jack. He's doing it all wrong, but instead of being an asshole and yelling at me, he does this endearing, nerdy fumfurring: shifting his weight, shaking his head, furrowing his brow.

"It's okay, man," I whisper (we're less than a foot away from each other). "You'll get it." I make myself as pliant and unthreatening as possible. I feel for this guy, who probably takes shit from his wife, shit from his coworkers, and I can hear Black inmates calling him a "lame" or a "bird-ass n'ga." Sweat begins to pock his brow. "It's alright to ask a coworker. It gives them a teaching moment with you, and shows you're confident enough to ask for help."

He asks for help; a decent cop shows him how it's done, then steps off. Now that I'm chained properly, the new jack and I smile at each other. I decide against asking him to adjust my too-tight handcuffs; don't want him to think I had an ulterior motive all along.

At the next station, the trip sergeant asks my name and number, then confirms my mug against my mug shot. I get a cop to adjust my cuffs so they're not cutting into my wrists, then waddle outdoors into the drizzling rain and board the bus.

It's a Greyhound-type affair with a large state seal emblazoned along its exterior. A cage up front for the driver, sergeant, and another hack; similar cage in the back. The walls of the toilet have been replaced with plexi-glass and metal. The seats are hard plastic with a thin runner of padding. We're told where to sit. You don't have to worry about picking a riding partner—you're shackled to him. But not me and my band of special cases; we're boarded last, sit towards the front, and each has a bench to himself.

We get underway. The guy I named "Dusty" turns around and says I gave the Blood good advice on his writing back in the bullpen. He himself does some writing: illustrated books for his little girl.

I've heard of guys doing this; if you have a modicum of creativity, it's something nice you can do for your kid. I'm glad I don't have kids. All the storybooks and cards in the world can't make up for the fact that your child is growing up without a father on hand. "Keep on, man. Your kid must really appreciate it."

"Yeah," Dusty says wistfully.

The cop tells him to turn around.

As we leave the prison grounds and turn onto what passes for a major thoroughfare in this dusty patch of nowhere, the sergeant stands and addresses us from the other side of the cage. "Okay, men, we're now on the road. That means there's no talking. We'll be arriving at [Prison C] in approximately an hour and twenty minutes." When he turns to sit back down, I see his sidearm. A chunky, brushed-silver revolver luxuriating in a black leather holster. A cannon in a corset.

I don't know why his announcing our ETA tickles me so. Like we're paying customers—yet our flight attendant is packing heat. I'm grateful for the imposed silence. In a previous life, there was little my brain appreciated more than long drives alone, on some of the same roads I'll be traversing in the coming days. Those were the licentious road trips of college, the felonious drive to and from home, my Jeep's cabin awash in purple haze and drum and bass. But even now, shackled, I feel some of the same freedoms of the road. Until I touch down, all is possible. Pirsig was right: better to travel than to arrive.

In Prison C's reception room we have our cuffs and shackles removed. A pair of nurses stand behind a cart on the way to the cellblock. One is dour, one sweet. "Name?"

I give my last name. The call and response of the initial touch point.

"Number?"

Rattle it off.

"Take any meds?"

"No." Then, the lie I formulated five minutes ago: "My TMJ problem is acting up and my head is killing me." With a handful of aspirin packets, I'm on my way. Planning ahead to the evening, when the lack of caffeine begins to crack my skull. We're not provided coffee on the road—hopefully the aspirin sees me through the day or two of caffeine-withdrawal headaches.

In case one couldn't navigate himself to the cellblock door fifty feet across the lot, there are yellow boot prints in a line across the blacktop.

The cellblock is loud with the noise of hundreds of men, their TVs and radios, their taunts and tautologies. This is coming almost entirely from the three upper tiers, the guys who call this prison home. The ground floor (the "flats") is for transit. A guard is motioning to me from so far down the tier that he looks small. The far end, fifty cells away, is easily the length of a football field. Ten years ago I made this slow walk past the scores of double-bunk cells—nothing's changed. It's all the same chilly-dismal.

The cop radios to have the cell door closed after I step in. Quick scan of both bunks: there's only one blanket. I make the cop aware of this, request another blanket from the inmate porter. My calculus is thus: the eventual bunkie will punch me in the face and take my blanket; or, perhaps worse, he'll meekly shiver and I'll feel like a warm, heartless bastard.

The sink works, the toilet flushes. We each have a "mattress" and a pillow. There are half a dozen individually wrapped pink-foam lollipops with "dentifrice," i.e., toothbrushes. A porter wheels a cart past and tosses in a sheet, pillowcase, small towel, and a tiny bar of soap. I plead with him for something, anything, to read. He says he'll see what he can do, then moves on. The fluorescent is angled low; the cell is dark and dank and damn chilly for late spring. Washing up, I pay special attention to my bruised wrists that smell like dirty metal. Suck down some aspirin. Make up the bottom bunk, stretch out, and massage my temples. When I last passed through, I spent six miserable, mind-numbingly boring days here—delayed because of Memorial Day. As part of a cost-containment initiative, the Department keeps the buses off the road on Wednesdays. We were told we'd be back on the road Thursday. That means I've got tonight and tomorrow night at the least, and can't say anything more with certainty.

The sound of boots gets me to my feet. Outside the cell, flanked by a cop, is a Black guy roughly my age. Wild hair sticking straight up like a youthful Don King. Eyes behind large glasses with thick black frames stare back at me. The gate cracks, he steps in; it bangs closed, the cop walks away. "Waddup, kid?" I say.

"How you?"

These are vital moments—we're both sniffing each other out, assessing threat level. He just got out of the box. "Lemme guess," I say. "For stabbing a bunkie who asked too many questions."

Awkward silence. Then he erupts in genuine belly laughter, and I know we'll be okay. I extend my hand and offer my name. We shake and he says, "JT." JT is quiet for a moment, then says, "Fuck it. I'm going home. My name's Paul."

Paul takes off his glasses, says they're just for show. They make him look like a geek to the cops, and I can see why he'd want that. A porter comes by, tosses in a blanket, linens, and a book for me. A shitty murder mystery, dog-eared and greasy from countless readings, but I'm grateful to have something. Paul asks him, is anyone selling weed? The porter doesn't know.

"Have you tried to cop anything?" Paul asks me. "I've got stamps." (Translation: There are stamps snug in the finger of a latex glove secreted up his ass.)

"Nah." I'd smoke with him, but am not willing to do anything to make it happen.

After all that time in the box, Paul is mad for conversation. He's a likeable fellow—I oblige him. We each tell how we came to be on the road, where we've done time, volunteer very abridged versions of our lives prior to prison. He's shocked when I tell him I'm doing 25-to-life for murder. I tell him, "That's called 'cognitive dissonance,' man. Don't worry, I'm a pussycat."

He fishes for details.

"Heroin. I freaked the fuck out. Let's move on."

On we move. Paul tells of a string of bank robberies, claims to've been on the show *America's*

Most Wanted. He's now on his way to an immigration holding center; a Guyanese national here on a visa, Paul is being deported.

Still, the parole board hit him last week with two years. It's all a meaningless sham. When metrics of performance rest solely on the quantifiable, any bureaucracy will "juke the stats," as David Simon termed it. I've seen this same scenario several times in the past few years. The board denies parole knowing full well there's an "immigration hold." Someone—you, your consulate, or a parole officer—contacts Homeland Security, and the deportation process begins immediately. Parole keeps its release numbers down, while Corrections saves over sixty thou (the cost of housing an inmate for his two-year parole hit). Juking the stats . . . my country 'tis of thee, sweet land of chicanery.

Dinner arrives and the porter tells me it's around four-thirty. Chow is turkey tetrazzini, so I wash the cream sauce off a few gnarly pieces of lung meat and make a sandwich. Standing over the sink with my back to him, I can feel Paul looking askance. After I explain my horrible food allergy, he gives me his peas.

Day Two. Wednesday. I wake as the food cart stops in front of the cell. The air is bracing. I take the trays, hand Paul's up to him on the top bunk. The orange juice I use on the cornflakes alerts me to my sore throat. This mental fog isn't all early-morning haze—I consumed something that has made me sick. Ugh. Now I have this to deal with for the remainder of the trip. Headaches, lethargy, malaise, and mental fogginess, urinary stream like a showerhead. Aspirin, and back to sleep.

After lunch, I teach Paul "Ghost," a word game my grandmother taught me. He immediately takes to it and almost beats me. Now it's his turn to choose a game. Paul calls for box games—the drawn-out diversions of men who literally have nothing better to do. The most tedious is one in which the players agree on a category (animals, say), then take turns listing every example from each letter of the alphabet. After being in the box for a year, Paul got used to the dark, and I led a vampiric life in college. We lie in our bunks with the light off, dreamily reciting the names of people, places, and things. I fall asleep often.

Day Three. Thursday. After breakfast, the porter tells us we'll be leaving shortly. In the darkened cell, Paul and I take turns washing up with the dribbled cold water. No matter, we're happy to be getting out of this dungeon, back on the road. I'm conscious of leaving the cell nicer than I found it. The blanket is folded, there's aspirin and something to read.

The sound of cells cracking open grows closer. Paul and I shake hands. I wish him luck with the business ventures he has planned for Guyana. He tells me everything's going to work out fine with me and the girl—a throwaway pronouncement from a near-stranger in a dark prison cell. Yet it warms me, and I thank him.

Nassim sits next to me in the reception room's bullpen. Paul, destined for another part of the state, is in a different pen. It gets loud, the clock reads eight-fifteen, and my head feels like paper cuts. Nassim was bored shitless during our stopover because he didn't have a bunkie (almost certainly because *Homosexual* is indicated in his record). Several feet away sit fellow travelers Hoyt and Tattoo Lou, giggling to each other about how much fun they had during their stay. "Duuude," says Hoyt, a lazy eye fluttering in my direction.

"I know," says the heavily tattooed one. "We were blowin' it down the minute we locked in."

Blowing it down is the new slang for smoking pot; I've been hearing it a lot the past few days, as is the style with new slang. Two guesses as to coinage: "Blowing it up" becomes "down," like "beat up" morphs into "beat down"; or, it's named after the process of blowing a cloud of smoke down a flushing toilet to avoid detection.

"Blowing. It. Downnnnuh," echoes Hoyt.

There's something pathetic and desperate about it all. Did I really once sound like that? *Jerkoff.*

Nassim leans close: "You know, you're totally my type."

"You know, I'm totally straight."

He tells me about his last boyfriend, who I resemble.

Out of the blue, I go into journalist mode and ask all manner of questions. *Isn't it really hard to be openly gay in prison? What's it like to get split up from your partner? How do you know whom to hit on? How'd you know I wouldn't freak out and hurt you for an unwanted advance?*

This last gets Nassim talking. Not only does he like a long, protracted challenge, but he'll choose a tough, unlikely mark, then spend months trying to get in his pants. This modus operandi has, admittedly, earned him a few beatings; he chalks it up to the cost of doing business.

"C'mon, man," I say. "You're a smart guy, a good person. You've only got a few years left, don't risk your safety. Stick with sure things . . . go for the low-hanging fruit."

Nassim stares at me for a second, then we both crack up. "I hope we're shackled together on the bus," he says.

As luck would have it, the ankle eighteen inches from mine belongs to a big, friendly-seeming Black kid. In the moments before we get underway, he and I exchange names. Like many guys from the South (his family moved from Alabama when he was five), he goes by the handle "Country," but says I can call him J. J's a good-natured type who giggles at almost everything I say.

We pull away from Prison C and quiet is enforced. For kicks, I nudge J, who's in the window seat, and motion to the car next to us at the stoplight. A pudding of a woman talks on the phone while her Lhasa Apso frantically licks his balls in the passenger's seat. When J looks back at me, he sees my wildly contorted face, which sends him into a fit of snorting laughter. The cops look in our direction and we take it down to a mumbling titter. We'll be on the road until late afternoon. The sun is shining and I have good company.

After a couple hours, we pull off the highway and find ourselves rolling through a quaint little hamlet. Rather nice for a prison town. My peers crane their necks wildly and make raucous comments about asses as we pass them by. *Run!* I want to scream to these small-town folk, who stroll on Main Street completely oblivious to the busload of murderers, rapists, thieves, and derelicts in their midst.

Inside the wall of Prison D is a parking lot that serves as a bus depot for a few hours during the day. Buses pull in from the numerous prisons in this part of the state, lose some passengers, take on some more, swap baggage from cargo holds, serve a bag lunch, then get back on the road. The guards and driver disembark and mingle with the other crews on the blacktop. Sweaty, they suck down cigarettes, consult clipboards, compare notes, laugh.

I hear someone say, as if he's a paying customer, that the logistics of our trip "don't make no sense" because he's been taken completely out of the way on our roundabout journey. But it makes perfect sense if you view us as non-time-sensitive cargo. Pooling in centralized distribution hubs keeps transportation and labor costs down, while maintaining efficiency. UPS uses its Atlanta operation to just such ends.

Pairs of men shuffle by to use the toilet. I tell J I have to take a leak, and we clumsily move down the aisle. J's back is to mine as I stand before the smelly chemical toilet. With great relief, I begin peeing. J kicks our leg chain, and giggles as I splatter the floor. "Nice, asshole."

J can't understand why I give him my cookies, meat, and cheese in return for two slices of his bread. As I scarf down the bread and chase it with red-tinted sugar water, I'm forced to tell yet another person about my mysterious allergy. Explaining the condition, answering the questions (almost always the same), and responding to the recommendations is almost as tiring as the symptoms themselves.

The bus quiets as we eat.

J gets my attention by pulling on our leg chain. Apropos of nothing, he says, "You think everythin' happens for a reason?"

When I first went away, hearing volunteer Evangelicals spout such sentiments angered me no end; it implies that my victims were part of a divine plan, which I refuse to accept. Over the years of solitary meditation on this subject, I've cobbled together a *Weltanschauung* akin to that of Seneca, Viktor Frankl, and Voltaire—a happy cocktail of stoicism, existentialism, and optimism.

I tell J that a year ago, I would've answered this question differently. (Alas, with the miraculous appearance of the girl, I've grown somewhat Panglossian.) "I think *some* things may happen for a reason, even if we don't understand it at the time. So it's really on us to find the meaning in it, you know? To make the most of the path our life has taken."

J thinks about this for a moment, narrows his eyes, nods his head. "Mm-hmm, hell yeah. Thass deep, son."

"Eh," I say, "I read it on a Snapple bottle."

This earns J's hearty laughter. He leans over and we bump (cuffed) fists.

"Hey, look," Hoyt says to no one in particular. "Sergeant's getting his dick sucked by that dog."

And damned if a sergeant isn't leaning into the fence, a black tail wagging joyously from behind the white shirt. Everyone laughs. The sergeant turns to speak to a hack and we see that he's feeding the pooch not his dick, but the same sandwiches we just ate.

A handsome, happy, mid-sized dog, black with a splash of white on his chest, a year or two old. Home is a long patch of grass in between the prison wall and an inner fence; there's a brown doghouse and a smattering of toys. When I passed through here a decade ago, the dog was old and graying. Like the current iteration, it subsisted on bag lunches. The dog owes its existence to a tower guard's nostalgia, a remnant from the days before ground sensors and motion detectors made a guard dog obsolete. A guy says, "That dog ain't tough." A sociopath responds, "I'd kill that fuckin' dog if I had to."

The bus starts to back up, guards hop on, and we roll past the black dog smiling at us. "That's cruel and unusual," someone says. "Wah' did that dog do to deserve this?" says an old Black man. "He in jail just like we is."

> *I see trees of green,*
> *Red roses, too.*
> *And I say to myself . . .*

. . . is a song I hear as the driver scans between country stations.

We're motoring through a beautiful part of the state. Vineyards are beginning to cover the slow hills in bluish green. Garage sales, farmer's markets, open-air cafés hiring for the summer. A roadside lemonade stand operated by a fair-skinned boy and girl, smiling, squinting above their freckles. Rockwell couldn't have painted it truer.

The bus rumbles low, downshifts as we descend into the river valley. J is sleeping peacefully. The wide river teems with pleasure craft—sail and power, a crew team, wave runners—like slow-moving moths against a dark-blue screen. As we speed along the bridge's expanse, J's head lolls onto my shoulder. With the river moving slowly below, and the *faux dauphins* and scoundrels seated around me, I momentarily fancy myself Huckleberry Finn on an adventure with his good friend Jim (though if I try to jump from this raft, I'll wind up with a bullet through my neck).

Over the river and through some woods . . . and the air pumped into the bus begins to smell different. Greener, cleaner, more familiar. Not counting the trip upstate over a decade ago, I'm on roads that I haven't seen since my youth. Strings of memory are pulled taut, and clearly remembered scenes become bittersweet. The idyllic weekends spent with my brother: swimming, eating, exploring the woods. The spastically horny summers at sleep-away camp: sailing, lying, exploring the girls. I recognize road signs for old diners, local institutions that now offer free Wi-Fi.

Nestled into blast-carved shale are a few old trailer homes. In front of a silver capsule, a trio of lowlifes sit in flimsy lawn chairs nursing a midday beer buzz. They immediately recognize the bus's markings, and acknowledge its shackled passengers with a show of solidarity: a solemn nod, a raised beer can, the (index finger and pinky) rock n' roll salute. I promise myself that I'll remember this tableau. *Good gentlemen, how long has it been since you've ridden in such fashion? Have you laid your heads in some of the cellblocks I've called "home"? Does the sight of us make you shudder and drink in your freedom all the more?*

A dull ruckus a few rows ahead draws the aggravated attention of the sergeant. "It's real simple, guys. There's no talking. Keep it up and your property will never arrive." He fixes the offenders in a stare, then sits.

Absolute silence. The prospect of losing everything you own will have that effect. Flight attendants would be envious of the sergeant's ability to make that most credible threat.

At Prison E, J and I say goodbye as a guard removes our leg chain. He's led away, probably to disciplinary housing.

The bullpen—one of five—is very cold. The A/C is set as if the room were crammed tight with a hundred felons. Or, possibly, this pen is normally reserved for hard cases and the twenty or so of us are just unlucky. On the plus side, I now have a concrete example for the term "cooling my heels."

Opposite us, the pen is filled—easily seventy-five bodies, SRO—with guys who just got dropped off by the deputies from their county jails. Prison E is a Reception Center that processes roughly seven thousand men annually into the state prison system. Just like these men, ten years ago I had on the clothes from the day I was arrested (cargo pants and a ribbed sweater, musty from sitting in a property bag during my year in county); moving into the big leagues, I was scared and alone.

The managers of this human warehouse run a streamlined operation. These new jacks are about to get stripped of their clothes, assigned a number that will be their name for the remainder of the bid, marched naked into a cold shower for delousing, handed a small towel and boxers, put in a barber's chair and have their heads shaved, given three changes of clothes and a pair of boots, fingerprinted, photographed, fed, watered, and put to bed. In the coming weeks, they'll have their IQ tested, undergo a complete physical and psychological evaluation, and give up a vial of blood for the state's DNA databank (for which their inmate accounts will be encumbered to the tune of fifty dollars). If lucky, they'll be transferred within a couple months to a prison where they can put down roots, get a job, make some friends, find a groove in which to do their time.

The gate to our pen slides open; the guards call us out one at a time to remove our cuffs and waist chains. Nassim walks up to me and says, "God love you." I've never had anyone say that to me, let alone a gay Shiite Muslim convict. "Salaam," I say in response.

Prison E's cells are big and single occupancy and have hot water; trapezoidal with a window, a desk built into the wall. Over a stainless steel sink I bird-bathe, lathering up my bruised wrists. It never occurred to me how filthy handcuffs are, but there's a good reason the guards wear latex gloves to remove them. Inmates do all the scut work in any prison, but would no sooner be allowed to disinfect a pair of cuffs than a guard's nightstick.

Day Four. Friday. I've never done transit at Prison E; as opposed to Prison C, I'll be walking to the mess hall for meals and there'll be some time out of the cell. And showers. And phone calls!

When we get back from breakfast, the twelve of us sit on plastic chairs in the bright dayroom and watch garbage TV. Designed for thirty-six, the house feels empty. I'm told it'll fill up by tonight, which makes sense. A transit house turns over its inventory like a produce jobber.

The house officer gets off the phone and reads a list of all the guys who'll be leaving later today: everyone but me and an old Black Muslim called Shaheed. The prospect of spending the weekend here puts me at ease; it's a pleasurable delay of the inevitable.

Turns out the high-ranking Blood with the red kufi and D&G frames goes by "LS." This he tells me after lunch as we talk through portals in our cell doors. He's baked and excited to be going back to the City for a bullshit court case. LS thanks me for the advice I gave him on his writing three days ago, says how his homies just tell him "the shit's good," without offering any real comments. He floats a business idea for when he gets released: baby-safety products. Some woman his lawyer knows wants to help him get on the straight and narrow. I talk fervently about brand-building and leveraging free technology; suggest that he try to get a B-school marketing class to do some free work on his venture; stress the utility of exploiting the "bad kid gone good" story frame all the way to the bank. LS is sharp; he realizes I'm not full of shit. I think of my (dare I say?) lagniappe as community service—not so much for him as for the community he won't be terrorizing should he be successful in business. He wants to keep in touch, have me as a consultant. When he asks my name, I give a fake. LS gives me his "government" (the name on his birth certificate) and schools me on how to drop it if I ever get in trouble with his "people" (the Bloods). Though I'll probably never have to use it, I thank him for this underworld version of a PBA card.

His door opens and he comes over to shake hands. "Hold ya head, kid."

"You, too," I tell him. "Remember, he with the best narrative wins. Either you define yourself, or someone will come up with their own version of who you are."

It's not just Shaheed and I, so the cop deputizes us as porters for the house. The job is 20 percent work, 80 percent perk. In each cell we toss a roll of TP, soap, toothbrush, toothpaste, and a set of linens.

The cop is youngish, cool, ex-military. "What now?" I ask him.

"Watch TV, relax."

"Can I use the phone?"

It's good to hear my brother's voice, a constant amidst the change in scenery. I bring him up to speed, assure him that I'm safe, ask that he relay all this to the family.

Standing under the water of a hot shower is invigorating. It's my first since Monday night.

I lock in before the three o'clock shift change. It's been a productive day. I swept and mopped the cell's linoleum floor, so now I can walk around barefoot. On the desk are five sheets of paper, three envelopes, a pen, and T. C. Boyle's *Talk Talk*. The latter is a real gift from the gods. Behind the wall, schlock lit is the genre of choice—glossy covers featuring bloody weapons, foggy nights, or dragons. In transit houses especially, the Bible is wildly popular—its onion-skin pages can be used as rolling paper. Shaheed gladly handed me the book from his cell, and I hid my enthusiasm at encountering a proper author.

My pen hits the paper and I'm home. Journal entries couched within letters to loved ones. Prison E allows us five free letters a week.

In the evening, doors open and close, boots shuffle, and the house fills up, a few guys at a time. Toilets flush (think: staging area for the unloading of hidden cargo); tobacco smoke wafts into my cell. For homophobes, they sure manage to cram a lot of stuff up their asses. It's known as "slamming" or "stuffing," or the odd-sounding "boofing." To keep contents safe during shipping, the process entails using a latex glove, plastic bag, or condom. Tobacco, weed, dope, pills, stamps, matches, lighter, weapons; I've heard of guys slamming sensitive information on scraps of paper like spies in hostile territory. I'm really pleased with myself for giving up smoking two years ago. Otherwise, I'd be doing like the guys who didn't "pack" for their trip: frantically offering items from tomorrow's breakfast in return for a few measly shreds of loose tobacco and a match peeled in half.

Day Five. Saturday. After breakfast is cell cleanup. After lunch, the cop reads off all the cells that will be leaving Monday. I'm one of several who will be staying. The rule is you can't use the phone once you're told you'll be leaving (on the grounds of security risk)—so not only do I get on the phone first (another perk of portering), I won't have to worry about a long line of angry men behind me.

As the sun sets, I enjoy a session of yoga on the clean floor. Kick into a handstand supported by the cinder-block wall—good for seeing life differently. I do every restorative pose in the arsenal, easing away the aches that come from traveling in shackles, sitting on hard benches, and sleeping on pathetic mattresses. The two rolls of toilet paper liberated earlier from the supply closet, I now use as props under my sacrum; seated on the floor, I work on my breathing.

On the little desk I do much writing, nearly exhausting my replenished supply of paper (while most everyone hustled for something to smoke, I finagled another fifteen blank sheets). For Saturday night entertainment, I consume more than half of *Talk Talk*, carefully allotting enough reading to last me a few more days. This has always been me: more ant than grasshopper.

Day Six. Sunday. Another gorgeous afternoon spent indoors, in front of a television (not like we have the choice to go outside). Almost the entire house sits quietly watching *The Li'l Rascals* (the movie version from the '90s). It's the wildest thing: thuggish gangsters with gold teeth, neck tats, and bullet scars not only watching this movie, but delivering certain lines along with the actors.

I take a seat in the back next to a forty-something white guy who has a Hunter S. Thompson gestalt, and introduce myself. "Steven," I whisper, "what do you make of this?"

He simply shrugs. But I think I get it. Yesterday, after everyone locked in, I sat alone in the dayroom watching the *Puppy Hour* on WE, absolutely captivated by those impossibly cute, wriggling little fur balls. These men are pouring some artificial sweetener onto a sour patch in their bid.

Day Seven. Monday. Hearing my cell number over the PA springs me out of bed. The sun hasn't yet risen. A disembodied female voice says all the cells just called will be leaving in ten minutes. Is this a mistake? No, I quickly decide. The house officer did me a good turn by not telling me on Saturday, so I could continue using the phone—the best of all possible worlds. I seal the envelopes and hurriedly address them. Brush my teeth while I pee. Get dressed. Instinctively scan for something I'm forgetting. The next occupant will think he's hit the jackpot: extra TP, two pillows, a match, a good book, paper and pen. (Perhaps he too left his previous cell better than he found it and I'm an instrument of karma.)

There's yet another strip search. More waiting in bullpens.

One of the trip officers starts at the back of the bus and walks forward, asking our names and filling in a seating card (if they need to lose someone's luggage, this is how they know who's who). Well-built and friendly, he moves amongst us with an easy air; the ex-Marine jokes with us and we respect him. Cops and cons alike call him Pooch, a shortening of his surname. He's in his mid-to-late forties, but hasn't aged much over the decade since I last left Prison E. At the front of the rows, he props himself up on the back of a bench and addresses us, his accent sounding like home. "Mornin', fellas. Youse know the drill: tawk, but keep it down. We'll be on the road a little maw than three ow-ahs. Questions?"

A joker says: "Yeah, Pooch. Where we stoppin' to eat?"

"My mothuh's house. Hope you got strong stomachs. I'll cawl 'er right now."

This is the last leg of the trip. Cruising on the highway, I begin to feel anxious, uneasy. It's been awhile since I've had to establish myself in prison. The past seven or eight years have been spent in relative comfort, keeping time with friends, working good jobs, involved in various programs and activities. I miss my friends. We are barred from keeping in touch.

We blow past a billboard for a local tae kwon do dojo; a red and blue yin yang reminds me of a professor's televised lecture I took in my last weekend at Prison A. The topic was "embracing chaos." We suffer ennui, he said, when our lives are too ordered. Using a PowerPoint slide of a yin yang, he spoke of optimal experience. The dots within each paisley are to remind us that there is always a little chaos in order, and vice versa. Ideally, we should straddle each paisley: one foot in chaos, one in order. Hearing the lecture made me think back to my most stressful times over the preceding years; the cause of each instance was the fear of disruption to my established order. I was so content that I spent months at a time cringing, waiting for a shoe to drop.

The lecture also softened my mind state. Life is change, I realized, and I need to get on with it. Attachment to places kills the soul as surely as attachment to things. I vowed to flow with the current as it takes me to someplace new; to open myself to the universe, and learn from it.

Looking around at the faces on the bus, I realize that I have more time in than many of them. I'm no new jack; I paid my dues in the yards, crewing up with the heavy hitters, making the right moves, keeping my mouth shut when need be. I've met thousands of men, and helped many of them. I haven't an enemy in the state. My name, as they say, is golden.

As to navigating the local bureaucracy, the names will be different, but the rackets don't change. I know who to see, what to ask for, and how to ask for it. I've got a bachelor's degree, and in the land of the pre-GED, that makes me a fucking king. For almost my entire incarceration I've worked in offices, clerking for highly placed civilians. My security clearance is high, I'm not a sex offender, and I make people laugh. Climbing the ladder at Prison F will be almost too easy.

By tonight I'll be walking the yard, where I'll undoubtedly connect with old faces. I'll learn the best places to lock, the best jobs to have. They'll provide introductions to the right people, and I'll get juiced in with the quickness. That's how it goes for guys like me.

I'm tired of the road, tired of being shackled to strangers and dragged from one bullpen to another. I want to get my property, change into my clean clothes; sleep on my own sheets, dry with my own towels; cook a good meal and eat until I'm full; receive mail and make daily phone calls.

It is around noon when we pull off the highway and make our way onto smaller, more rural roads. Cresting a hill, the gray wall of Prison F rises to meet us. Everyone gets quiet, even those who've been here before. The wall stretches forever—more a feature of the landscape than one of architecture. Peering easily over it is a tan brick building, hundreds of yards long, four or five stories tall: the big house. It's like an old, dusky battleship floating on a sea of gray.

The bus hisses to a slow stop in front of the main gate: huge metal plates with chipped paint and rust spots. A tower guard steps out onto a crenellated turret, his assault rifle pointed at the sky.

NOTES

1. Allow me to letter the prisons. The names would likely mean nothing to you anyway.

2. The only way you can get written up for the content of your pictures is if the subjects are throwing gang signs.

EDITOR'S AFTERWORD

This volume began inside Attica Correctional Facility, where I initiated a creative writing workshop in November of 2006. Working with men inside Attica revealed to me the values and quality of thought that can be forged in men living under the daily heat of the prison environment—values and thinking that remain unknown to the public. As a teacher of writing for thirty years, I was also struck by the degree to which, in their early writing, the marks of the daily trauma of incarceration leveled out sizable differences in the educational backgrounds of the men in the class. These men's writing was more deeply marked by their experience of imprisonment than by their various levels of education (from GEDs earned inside to a master's degree earned outside). All struggled with keeping their focus true from the start to end of any piece of writing. As different as their backgrounds and experience with writing were, it was the chaotic, dehumanizing, and at times violent experience of the prison that marked every page of their work. I wondered if this were true of prison writing in general, or a trait peculiar to these men's work, or work coming out of Attica. This question led me to two summers of research at the Library of Congress, reading prison writing from the United States and around the world. There I found patterns similar to those I'd witnessed in the work produced by men inside Attica: the conditions of incarceration were consistently apparent in the style, tone, and structure of writing coming out of the UK, Ireland, South Africa, India, Australia, etc. This discovery led to the beginnings of a monograph on prison writing, and the decision to test my early theses in discussion with students.

In the process of developing an undergraduate course on prison writing, I discovered the dearth of in-print volumes of nonfiction essays by incarcerated Americans—particularly non-political, "common" criminals—writing today about their experience of the prison. At the same time, I began reading the work of, and attending conferences for, social scientists and legal scholars dealing with issues in criminal justice. In print and face-to-face, even amid critical discussions of the prison system, I found little thought given to what prisoners had said and were still saying about their condition. So *Fourth City* was born from multiple desires: to give more incarcerated writers a place to reflect publicly on their imprisonment; to create a text for teaching in relevant disciplines; and to make incarcerated writers' insights available to professionals in academia, as well as to prison administrators, policymakers, and the wider public.

After composing a Call for Essays, a student research assistant, Rory Pavach, compiled the addresses of correctional facilities in all fifty states. We also placed the Call in prison newsletters, on prisoner-support websites, and in a number of literary and pedagogical journals in hopes that prison teachers might pass the Call along. Several states responded in volume—California, New York, Illinois—while others offered a significant trickle of essays, or just one, or complete silence. Whether the absence of (usable) contributions from twenty-three states and Washington, DC, is more reflective of a flawed method of solicitation or of a reluctance by prison staff to see their wards writing about what they have witnessed inside should remain a question in the reader's mind, as it does in mine. One thing became very clear. Incarcerated Americans not only want to tell their stories, they want other incarcerated Americans to tell theirs as well. Dozens of essays came in with cover notes explaining that the authors knew nothing about the volume, but they had been passed our address and told that *someone* would read what they had written. (Several expressed surprise that the Call or our address had reached them at all, given the opposition by prison staff to these writers' attempts to get their stories out.) Clearly, imprisoned people were passing "kites" to other imprisoned people, feeling hope in the very idea that someone might read what they had written. It was the exceptional writer that did not thank us simply for being willing to read, to listen to their voices.

As the essays came in, I read and sorted them into three files: Yes, Maybe, No. In an effort to provide a holistic vision of prison life and personalities, I looked for complementarity—while avoiding redundancy—of subject, voice, and vision, and the widest possible demographic representation. As noted in the Introduction, the essays were also doing their own work: organizing themselves into the categories in which the reader finds them here, announcing the work of Americans living inside a nationwide institution that retains the complexity, differences, and likenesses of other cohesive communities, and on the scale of a major city. No doubt, different readers might debate these groupings, as I did in my own mind, with Rory, and with the other very fine readers I found among my prison-writing students. As far as possible I, and we, tried to facilitate a conversation among the voices in the essays themselves.

The initial sorting done, the next task was the hands-on hours of dealing with a deep file of hardcopy manuscripts: these ranged from clearly word-processed texts, to texts typed on ailing manual typewriters, to neat or barely decipherable handwritten pages of lined paper or blank sheets. In the fall of 2009, the twelve students enrolled in "English 442: Booked, Prison Writing"—all of whom would accompany me to my class at Attica—began volunteering to type these essays into Word files. They were instructed to type the essays exactly as they found them, including typos, misspellings, troubled syntax, and flawed grammar. In this process, one student, Olivia Wolfgang-Smith, emerged not only as a lightning-fast and accurate typist but an astute editorial commentator. Before the semester was over I had hired her as my research assistant, and she quickly became a working assistant editor (Rory Pavach having since graduated).

The process to this point had been fairly straightforward. Now, though, I faced the challenge of line-by-line editing. I had asked my students to type the essays exactly as they found them so that I would bear the full weight of responsibility for any interventions in style, grammar, syntax, spelling, or structure. My aim in every case was to respect and retain individual voices while making essays clear and readable, to achieve an ethical and practical balance between fidelity to voice and reader accessibility. (Many essays came with cover notes asking that the editors correct grammar and spelling; these writers knew that their skills were not complete.) A good number of essays required only corrections of obvious typos and occasional misspellings. Others presented moving, powerful, and important statements or stories, but in writing that few readers would have the patience to follow very far. Most fell between these ends. In the No file today there sit essays that have important things to say; but to make them accessible would require such drastic interventions in word-by-word style, grammar, or overall structure that the result would be a different essay than that written by the author. They are themselves a testament to the broad overlap between crime and the failures of public education.

This has been a difficult process, at times frustrating, maddening, and regularly heartbreaking. To read these essays is to vicariously suffer time inside, and then hold in one's hands a writer's dearest hope: to see her words in print—a hope made more poignant by the desperate desire that someone, anyone, listen to a voice caged in a world of shame, humiliation, and violent hopelessness.[1] To reject an essay felt like taking the side of the punishers, feeding a triumphant smirk that says, *No one will listen*, and closing yet another gate on a human being who has torn from despair and suffering the wherewithal to document his or her experience. My hope is that the essays printed here are as representative as they can be of all of those who submitted their writing, and that my editorial work at once respects the authors' intentions and singular voices, and allows readers to appreciate the quality and individuality of the thinking and reflection going on inside the American prison today.[2]

As in any other population, writers are just one segment of the prison's large and diverse set of men, women, and transgendered persons. So while this volume may be representative of the prison writers our Call reached, it is impossible for any single volume to map exactly today's prison population according to race, ethnicity, class, etc. Though their scattering among essays by male writers may make women writers seem underrepresented, women authors are in fact overrepresented relative to their percentage of the prison population (roughly 1/11) as a whole. That is little solace at a time when women are the fastest-growing part of the prison population, and are doubly invisible, as both prisoners and women.[3] Amid these inequities, the reader will also find repeat appearances by several authors (male, female, and transgendered; Black, white, and Hispanic). This last case of seeming inequity was one that was under my control. In the end, I decided that to strip the prison of evidence of its best and most prolific writers would be like gathering a collection that best represents Chicago but allots only one entry to Mike Royko, New York with only one entry by Jimmy Breslin or Elizabeth Hardwick, Philadelphia without both fiction and nonfiction by John Edgar Wideman, or Los Angeles without a strong sampling of the work of Joan Didion. By their committed thought and labor, these most prolific of our prison's observers have earned their space.

Finally, a word about the introductions to each section: these were suggested by the anonymous readers arranged by Michigan State University Press to review the manuscript. I was reluctant at first (the suggestion having been made before, and strongly resisted). I wanted these writers to speak for themselves. But over time I came to see that general readers and students might need some guidance in reading each grouping of essays. Yet I remained reluctant to present my readings alone, so I decided to draft the introductions and present them to the men in the writing workshop at Attica. It was with them, after all, that this project had begun. These short essays are in truth collaborative products in more than one sense: I reshaped these texts in the light of these men's readings of the relevant issues. More broadly, there is literally nothing I know, or think, or believe about the prison in America that has not been informed by my conversations, critical engagement, and seven-plus years of interaction and friendship with these men. *Fourth City* is of, by, and for them and the rest of the millions living inside cages in the United States.

NOTES

1. There were also essays pleading individual legal cases, or asking for legal help or for someone to correspond with, or describing egregious conditions and asking for aid in addressing these conditions. These messages are indicative of the despair housed inside our prisons, but were of course outside the range of work we could accept. In such cases, I referred writers to whatever appropriate organizations I could find in their area.

2. The editor is working now to construct the American Prison Writing Archive, an open-access digital depository that will scan, transcribe, and organize for research and general reading purposes non-fiction essays by incarcerated Americans, American corrections officers, staff, administrators, volunteers, the families of incarcerated people, and others affected by the prison system. The aim is to provide a comprehensive venue for those working and living inside the American prison to bear witness to their experience. See http://www.dhinitiative.org/projects/apwa/.

3. See Geneva Brown, "The Intersectionality of Race, Gender, and Reentry: Challenges for African-American Women," *American Constitution Society*, 10 November 2010, http://www.acslaw.org.

GLOSSARY

This is not a comprehensive glossary of all prison argot. It is a listing of definitions of the slang terms and prison jargon that appear in this volume. Many of the terms below are not peculiar to prison. Many prison-slang terms have entered into general circulation. Many are so commonly understood outside of prison (e.g., shiv, heist) as to seem not to require definition, and most of these terms are defined or explicable in the contexts in which they appear. They are offered here in one listing, both because they offer a study in their own right, and because they bring home the fact that Prison City has a language culture all its own (and that is heavily borrowed from by the free world). (There is a wealth of sources on "prison slang" on the Internet, from legitimate dictionaries to "tough guy" primers.) Whenever most useful, definitions are direct or modified quotations from the authors who first use any term in this volume. Many of these terms have more common usages, and retain these, of course: bread, for example, both indicates a baked good, and is slang for money. Many carry different nuances in different regions of the country, even from prison to prison, and in different periods of time.

The entire glossary, both its terms and its definitions, has been checked (and checked again) with Americans currently serving time. Sincere thanks to them all.

Ad-Seg	administrative segregation, isolation housing used for punishment or protection (see also *SHU, the hole, the box, 23/1*)
amping or **ampin' up**	encouraging someone to bad action, trying to get them riled into making trouble, as in "His homez might be ampin' him to do it, that's the word."
baked	intoxicated on marijuana
bang out	beat or, more often, kill
beef	in prison this can mean a criminal charge; more generally, it is used in prison as in free society to mean a problem, irritation, complaint, or conflict, as in "What's your beef with him?"
bid or **bit**	a prison sentence. (A nickel bid is a five-year sentence.)
block	segment of a prison complex, an independent building, or section of a larger building, such as in Attica Correctional Facility, whose four sides each constitute a lettered block, from A to D
blowing it down	blowing a cloud of (marijuana) smoke down a flushing toilet to avoid detection
the board	parole board, which determines whether prisoners will be released on parole, short of meeting their maximum sentence date. (To reach this date is to "max out.")
Blood or **Bloods**	originally an African American Los Angeles street gang, now national and more inclusive

boofing	using a latex glove, plastic bag, or condom as a skin around contraband inserted into the anus to avoid detection by prison staff (see also *slamming* and *stuffing*)
books	pornography (see also *short eyes*)
booster, boosting	shoplifter, shoplifting; thief, theft
the box	also called special housing unit (*SHU*), administrative segregation (*Ad-Seg*)—removal from the larger, general prison population, as punishment, into a more restrictive physical unit with more limited privileges (e.g., only one hour or half hour per day out of the locked cell; see also *the hole*, *23/1*)
boys	can mean one's *crew* as in "me and my boys"; boy or boys can also mean one or several openly homosexual (male) prisoners
bread	money
bubble	a protective observation booth used by correctional officers, with large windows facing multiple directions
bug or **bug-out**	a mentally damaged or unstable, wacky, weird prisoner; a bug can also indicate a prisoner on psychotropic medications
bugged out	gone crazy, or acting crazy, unstable
bullpen	used to refer to any number of types of temporary prisoner holding units
bunkie	cell mate (or "cellie")
burned	arbitrarily denied release from one's cell (for recreation, meals, programs, etc.) by a *CO* (see also *stalled*); cheated in any trade or sale of goods
cajones	(Spanish)—testicles, courage
call out	any list of prisoners approved to be released (called out) from their cells to attend programs, as in "I'm on the call out for the GED class."
chateauing (also called **"stretching out"**)	relaxing during one's sentence, being more concerned with personal comforts, food, and leisure than anything else
chicken hawk	an older man who seeks younger men or boys for sex
chow, chow hall	any meal, or the place where it is served to groups of prisoners
chrono	chronology of the series of programs a prisoner has completed to prove s/he has been rehabilitated, as in " . . . and gave me an 'attaboy' chrono for the parole board."
Chuck Chillout shit	critical characterization of the behavior of a prisoner who stays out of trouble, fights, etc.
chump	homosexual, coward, a weak man

civil confinement	a policy whereby, if deemed a continuing threat to the public, a sex offender can be held indefinitely
CO	corrections or correctional officer (see also *hack, Po-Po, police, screw, cops*)
coke	cocaine
company	a section of a block, gallery, or tier; a floor of a multi-floor or multi-tier housing unit
cooler	jail
cop, **cops**	correctional officers (see also *hack, Po-Po, police, screw, CO*)
cop out	in law, to plea bargain; in prison or elsewhere, to back down from a confrontation
crew	one's clique of closest friends, comrades, gang members, etc. (see also *boys*)
Crips	originally an African American Los Angeles street gang, now national and more inclusive
cutting	distinct from stabbing, this means slicing a victim's skin, as in the classic punishment for an unpaid debt—a cut from the corner of the mouth to the nearest ear, often bisecting the entire cheek with the aim of forming a profound scar
Dame esa pistola	(Spanish)—Give me the pistol (i.e., knife)
dirty case or **dirty crime**	sex crime—rape, child molestation, etc.
disciplinary hearing	meeting to investigate and determine punishment for a prison crime or a violation of prison rules
DOC	Department of Corrections; used to indicate prison administration and staff, this acronym is often matched with the initial(s) of a state: for example, the VADOC, for Virginia Department of Corrections
doing your own time	"this means an inmate is socially responsible to his peers, addresses the programs ordered by the court or recommended by the DOC, and serves his or her time without getting involved in any other inmates' business."
double bunked	housed in a cell with another prisoner, or in a cell holding twice the number of prisoners it was intended to hold
down	in jail or prison (e.g., "In the nearly five years I've been down . . .")
extract (extraction, cell extraction)	forced removal of a prisoner from his or her cell
fall, **to fall**	be sentenced to a prison term, as in "I fell two years ago at the age of fifty-six."
felony murder rule or **law**	a person involved in a murder, even if s/he did not carry out the actual

	killing (e.g., a driver, or someone who was part of a robbery in which someone else perpetrated the killing), is subject to the same penalties as the actual killer
fence	someone who buys and sells stolen goods
to fish, or **fishing**	a method used to transfer items from cell to cell; a line—often made from a sheet ripped into long strips—is anchored at one end with some kind of weight and thrown from one cell to another (with the help of convicts in between) until it reaches the intended destination; the desired item is then tied on and pulled back to the fisher's cell
fish line	line used for fishing
fish tank	temporary holding cell for convicted criminals as they are being processed into prison (from new prisoners being called "fresh bait")
Five Percenters	Nation of Gods and Earths, an offshoot of the Nation of Islam
flats or **the flats**	the first floor of an open-faced, multi-tier jail or prison block
fly	stylish, fancy, cool, as in "I know you looking all fly, you got your hair all slicked back, all flossed out with the flyest gear."
freestyling	altering one's history, padding one's past or present exploits, embellishing stories, lying (also called "fronting"); one who engages in this practice can be called a "stunter" or "truth-twister"; outrageous lies are sometimes said to cause "lip blisters"
friend	when it carries more than its standard meaning, a "friend" indicates a sex partner
full face	a woman in, and thus evidencing access to, full makeup
gallery	a section of a block or tier; a floor of a multi-floor or multi-tier housing unit (see also *company*)
game, **the game**	on the street, this often means handling (pimping) prostitutes; to play the game in prison means selling drugs and/or involvement in other criminal activities
gas booth	protective observation booth from which a CO can trigger the release of tear gas
gangbanger	a member of a criminal street gang, especially one who engages in armed violence against rival gang members; also used generically for gang members and (reductively and pejoratively) for youth of color more generally
gangster	someone whose life is fully involved in crime, by choice (whether or not s/he is actually a member of a street gang)
gat	gun, weapon

gate, **on the gate**	the gate is the set of bars fronting a prisoner's cell and facing and/or adjacent to other cell bars; to be on the gate is to lean on these bars to talk, whisper, or (more typically because of the number of other prisoners on the gate) to yell to other prisoners
gate etiquette	what one should or should not do while on the gate
general population (**GP**)	prisoners housed in standard conditions, with the majority of others in any prison facility, as distinct from those in *the box*, infirmary, an *honor block*, etc.
get one's name up	become known and respected (for violent/criminal exploits), or feared
get one's shit off	fight, as in "They decided to get their shit off," or "He got his shit off on X."
gladiator school	an especially violence-prone prison, indicating in particular an intake facility where young men first prove themselves able, ready, and willing to engage in violence against other prisoners
going down	to be killed in a fight, as in "Glances from men seem to say good luck, hold your head, or you're going down."
gold fronts	gold-capped or crowned front teeth
good time	time taken off one's sentence for a good or clean behavior record and/or successful completion of required programs
goon squad	corrections officers working in a group to extract prisoners from cells or impose other (official or unofficial) disciplinary measures
gun	when this does not mean an actual firearm, it indicates a prison-made knife or any device, of any material, used to stab another person (see also *shank* and *shiv*)
heavy	a person who provides a physical threat, as in "I even acted as the heavy in a few buys of coke."
heist	act of theft, robbery, or burglary (as in a "bank heist")
hack	corrections officer (see also *CO*, *Po-Po*, *police*, *screw*)
hang up, **hung up**	to commit suicide by hanging
hard time	a difficult prison sentence (for any reason—e.g., carrying a "dirty crime," inability to adjust to prison routine); to do hard time is also to be without access to basic amenities
hit	getting hit by a (parole) board means being turned down for parole release
hit the bricks	release from prison, as in "As soon as I hit the bricks after a jolt in the county cooler . . ."
hold down	help, look out for, supply; if, for example, a man or woman does not have

	money for commissary items, another prisoner might hold him or her down by giving or lending items
the hole	also called special housing unit (*SHU*), or administrative segregation (*Ad-Seg*)—a place for those removed from the larger prison population, as punishment, into a more restrictive physical unit with more limited privileges (e.g., only one hour or half hour per day [see *23/1*] out of the locked cell; see also *the box*)
to holler (or **holla**) **at you**	talk
homies, homez, homeboys	one's close friends or affiliates, often indicating fellow gang members
honor block	a housing unit in some prisons for men or women with clean prison-behavior records, and that offers privileges such as larger cells, more time out of cells, more showers per week, cooking facilities, refrigerators, a private yard, etc.
hoosegow	jail or prison
hophead	drug user/addict
horse	heroin (see also *scag* and *smack*)
institutionalized	this is a broadly used term, generally indicating that a person has become so deeply shaped by his or her life in prison that prison routine, culture, regulations, etc., have become their unquestioned norm; the result is that such persons are no longer accepted as peers by other prisoners; it is assumed unlikely that an institutionalized prisoner will ever be able to survive outside prison walls, and s/he shows no signs of recognizing a problem in this condition (which condition the prisoner may or may not be consciously aware of)
jail	this term is often used generically to refer to jail or prison, or it refers to a jail properly so-called—a county-level holding facility
jolt	jail or prison sentence, as in "after a jolt in the county cooler . . ."
junk	male genitalia; or heroin
juvie	juvenile detention
keep-locked	held in cell without regular movement, as punishment for, and/or pending an investigation of a crime or violation of rules
kite	a clandestine message passed between prisoners inside one facility, or between prisoners in different facilities; also used more generically to indicate any written prison communication
lace up	inform, tell, give information to, as in "I was not able to lace Cindy up on this situation"; can also mean to assault
Latin Kings	predominantly Puerto Rican street and prison gang

lay down	long-term segregation (*Ad-Seg*) status; to go with or adjust to the routine of such segregation by lying down for many hours each day
lock	to live in a cell; most often used to describe a person living in the same cell with, or in proximity to, the cell of the speaker, as in "Goldie, an African American named after a pimp, locks on my right side."
lockdown or **locked down**	restricted to cell for all but a minimum number of hours per day (typically imposed on individual prisoners as punishment, or on an entire population when violence threatens; or undergoing a *shakedown*)
lock-in-a-sock	a sock weighted with a lock or other heavy object and used as a cudgel to batter another human being
lockup	*noun*, typically a jail (versus prison), as in "the county lockup" (also used as a variation on *lockdown*); *verb*, lock up, used in the imperative: an order for prisoners to get into their cells and close their doors or gates
long and short con	a long con is a long-term scheme to cheat, rob, extort, or otherwise exploit someone for relatively high stakes (e.g., Bernard Madoff worked a long con); a short con seeks immediate, small returns (e.g., a few packs of cigarettes)
LWOP or **LWOPP**	life without parole, or life without possibility of parole (sometimes called "the other death penalty")
mainline	to shoot heroin or other drugs directly into one's veins (see *slam*).
the Man	police, official authority, security, and administration; for white prisoners this term is a generic reference; for African American prisoners it carries the traditional signification of established *white* power and authority expecting Black compliance; also used, as it is outside prison, as an indicator of (macho) respect, as in "He's the man."
meth	methamphetamine, a stimulant
'mos	homosexuals (openly so)
mule, to mule	*noun*, someone who smuggles drugs or contraband into prison; *verb*, the act of such smuggling
narc	undercover police narcotics agent
Ñetas	predominantly Puerto Rican prison and street gang, with international affiliations
new jack (or **new boot**)	anyone new to the prison system—officer, incarcerated, or administration
number, con numbers, DIN Number	each prisoner is designated by a prison or Department Identification Number (DIN), which identifies him or her through his/her prison sojourn; for example, in New York State, 03X772 indicates that a convict entered prison in 2003, was processed through facility X, and was the 772nd person processed through facility X in 2003.

off the chain	out of control, crazy
oíste	(Spanish)—"you heard" (see *you heard*)
packing a piece	carrying a firearm
peoples	friends or cohorts (see also *crew*, *homies*, *boys*), variously bound by family relations, race, language, gang, city of origin, etc.
piece	firearm
piss test	urinalysis
plotte (kooch)	sex, indicated by a metonymic reference to the vagina (as in "pussy")
pop a cap	shoot a bullet, as in "He was itching to pop a cap in my drug-dealing ass."
Po-Po	corrections officer(s) (see also *CO*, *cop*, *police*, *hack*, *screw*)
police	corrections officer(s) (see also *CO*, *hack*, *Po-Po*, *cop*, *screw*)
pop off	occur, happen, as in "Don't know who let you down. Who did you wrong. I can't answer why it had to pop off."
pulling a stunt	action taken in order to avoid a problem; instead of carrying out a threat or engaging in an expected act of violence (to defend life and/or honor), a prisoner willfully gets him- or herself caught by a *CO* for an infraction of prison regulations and put into *lockdown* or *the box* (*Ad-Seg*, *the hole*), thus avoiding the expected confrontation
punk	someone who has been (and can be) raped, and more generally, anyone identified as weak
pusher or **pusher man**	seller of illegal drugs
put it out	to say or do something in a public or semi-public setting; the term indicates that a prisoner has thus made an irrevocable gesture to which other prisoners are then entitled to respond, as in "If you didn't want to live with it, you shouldn't have put it out."
program or **programming**	required or voluntary programs aimed at rehabilitation, such as ART (Aggression Replacement Training), academic or vocational training, job assignments, etc.; used as a *noun-gerund*, "I participated in all available programming," or *verb*, "She's been programming."
protected	having protection by someone with authority or power (*CO*, another prisoner, etc.)
protective custody or **PC**	placement in a special and/or isolation unit, not as punishment but to protect a prisoner from anticipated assault; this can be voluntary on the part of the prisoner, or IPC (Involuntary Protective Custody)
quarter bag	twenty-five dollars' worth of any drug
rap sheet	the record of one's crimes

rat	someone who gives incriminating information about another prisoner or group of prisoners to prison security (see also *snitch*)
rec (recreation or **recreation yard)**	shorthand for allowed or mandated time in the recreation yard, as in "We're allowed to have one hour of rec at seven A.M. M–Friday," or "Soon I'll hear the dull, metallic clunk-clank signaling the opening of the cell gates for the evening rec."
reception	a facility where a man or woman is processed into the prison system
reds	barbiturates
ripper	rapist
sack	scrotum and testicles
scag	heroin (see also *smack* and *horse*)
score (*noun* or *verb*)	successful act of theft, robbery, etc., or purchase of drugs
screening or **hearing officer**	officer in charge of reviewing a charge against a prisoner
screw	corrections officer (see also *CO, police, Po-Po, cop, hack*)
sergeant, captain, etc.	corrections officer ranks, as in military organizations
serve out	completion of maximum sentence
shakedown	in the prison context, a cell-by-cell search of an entire prison for contraband, weapons, etc.; to shake down an individual is to rob him or her, typically by intimidating the victim with a show of aggression, a weapon, or some other form of threat
shank	prison-made knife, or any device, of any material, used to stab another person (see also *shiv* and *gun*)
shiv	prison-made knife or any device, of any material, used to stab another person (see also *shank* and *gun*)
short eyes	pornography; this term is taken from a film about a pedophile and so can also be used (though rarely) to indicate a pedophile
SHU	Special Housing Unit, isolation housing used for punishment or protection (see also *the hole, the box, 23/1*)
skin beef	sex crime
skinner	child molester
slam	shoot drugs into one's veins (see also *mainline*)
slamming	using a latex glove, plastic bag, or condom as a skin around contraband inserted into the anus to avoid detection by prison staff (see also *boofing* and *stuffing*)

smashed	severely beaten, by guards or other prisoners
smack	heroin (see also *scag* and *horse*)
snitch	someone who gives incriminating information about another prisoner or group of prisoners to prison security (see also *rat*)
solid crime	a crime respected by other prisoners (such as homicide [against a man] or armed robbery) as opposed to a *dirty crime*, such as rape or child molestation
solid prisoner	someone who has committed a *solid crime*, and has not otherwise damaged his reputation, for example, by working as a *snitch*
soul breaker	solitary confinement (see also *23/1*, *the hole*, *the box*, *Ad-Seg*)
sponsor	a prisoner that vouches for or protects another; "sponsor" can also mean someone approved by prison administration to oversee a prison program
stack, or **stacked**	adding charges to increase the possible sentence for a crime; district attorneys commonly stack charges (and years) in order to intimidate indicted people into plea bargaining; crimes committed inside prisons can stack years onto the perpetrator's existing sentence
stalled	delayed in release from cell, as in "We got burned on Saturday and stalled on Sunday." (see also *burned*)
strip search	being stripped naked to search for contraband, often with digital exploration of the anus and/or vagina
stuffing	sealing a latex glove, plastic bag, or condom (etc.) around contraband inserted into the anus to avoid detection by prison staff (see also *boofing* and *slamming*)
the system	the prison and/or judicial system—local, national, and often both
swag	money or goods taken by a thief
take a deal	bargain for a lesser sentence, often in exchange for information aiding in the conviction of another (or co-)defendant.
ticket	the written report of a rules violation by a prisoner, as in "He got a ticket for yelling at a CO" (see also *write-up*)
trannie	transvestite, transsexual, transgendered person
trippin' or **you trippin'**	you're wrong, you're misinformed, you're crazy
23/1, **23:1**, etc.	split of the time locked inside and allowed out of cell, indicating *lockdown*; the typical time-split in *the box*, *SHU*, *Ad-Seg*
upward, or **lower**,	refers to a judge's discretionary power (now largely evacuated by state

depart a sentence	legislatures) to set prison sentences above or below a recommended number of years, according to assessment of the circumstances of the crime and the criminal
Upside-down Kingdom	the prison world, and specifically that world's behavioral and moral code, based on the inversion of common values, as when violence is revered, friendship is seen as suspect, love as weakness, etc. (taken from the title of an essay by prison philosopher Eric Reid and circulated among prisoners in photocopies, mimeographs, and handwritten texts)
upstate, or **up the river**	these can mean, generically, sent to prison, as in "He got sent upstate" or "They sent her up the river"; these phrases are thought to come from New York state prison history, referring to New York City convicts shipped up the Hudson river to Sing Sing and other prisons located in the rural northern and northwestern parts of the state
wheelman	getaway-car driver for a robbery or other crime
wilyin', **wilyin' out**	acting up, acting wild, acting crazy, violating norms or codes
wing	a unit of prison housing; newer prisons are often built in wings (often from central control hubs); older prisons, built in rectangles, designate equivalent units as *blocks*
wing mate	a person serving time in the same wing
word to mother son	the truth, as in "'Word to mother son, dat's the way he is,' Toño explained."
the world	everywhere in the free world outside jail or prison
writ	used as in law, a legal motion, such as a writ of *habeas corpus*
write-up	the written form of a rules violation by a prisoner, as in "Write-ups are something that put us in the hole or prolong us from going home" (see also *ticket*)
the yard or **yard**	recreation yard, typically a space open to the sky with some athletic equipment, pay phones, TVs
yard birds	prisoners who go to the recreation *yard* whenever possible (for bad reasons and/or for lack of other interests or pursuits)
you heard	a phrase that can be tagged to any statement. It comes from prisoners yelling across prison halls to other prisoners, amid other yelling prisoners, and used to make sure the recipient has received one's message, as in "Well I ain't got unless you got somein' for me, you heard," much like pilots saying "Roger that" or "Ten Four." Also used for emphasis of a point, as in the example above.
Yo no se	(Spanish)—I don't know

FURTHER READING

These are by no means exhaustive lists, but an offering of direction to those newly interested in American prison writing, and in the history, effects, current operation of, and critical responses to mass incarceration in the United States. Note that many of the titles in prisoner writing are out of print but may be found through online booksellers and in libraries. Many more titles in prisoner writing can be found by searching WorldCat (click Advanced Search, and then, in the Keyword line, type Prison Writing).

SELECTED AMERICAN PRISONER WRITING

Abbott, Jack Henry. *In the Belly of the Beast*. New York: Knopf, 1991.

Abu-Jamal, Mumia. *Live from Death Row*. New York: Harper Collins, 1996.

Baxter, Carolyn. *Prison Solitary and Other Free Government Services*. Greenfield Center, NY: Greenfield Review Press, 1979.

Berrigan, Philip. *Widen the Prison Gates: Writing from Jails, April 1970 to December 1972*. New York: Simon and Schuster, 1973.

Betts, Dwayne R. *A Question of Freedom: A Memoir of Learning, Survival, and Coming of Age in Prison*. New York: Avery, 2010.

Braly, Malcolm. *On the Yard*. (Fiction). New York: New York Review Books, 2002.

Bruchac, Joseph, ed. *The Light from Another Country: Poetry from American Prisons*. Greenfield Center, NY: Greenfield Review Press, 1984.

Bunker, Edward. *Little Boy Blue*. (Fiction). New York: St. Martin's, 1997.

———. *No Beast So Fierce*. (Fiction). Harpenden, England: No Exit Press, 2008.

Carr, James. *Bad: The Autobiography of James Carr*. Oakland, CA: AK Press/Nabat, 2002.

Chevigny, Bell Dale, ed. *Doing Time: 25 Years of Prison Writing*. New York: Arcade, 1999.

Cleaver, Eldridge. *Soul on Ice*. New York: Delta, 1992.

Davis, Angela Y., and Bettina Aptheker. *If They Come in the Morning: Voices of Resistance*. New York: The Third Press, 1971.

Falkoff, Marc, ed. *Poems from Guantanamo: The Detainees Speak*. Iowa City: University of Iowa Press, 2007.

Franklin, H. Bruce, ed. *American Prisoners and Ex-prisoners, Their Writings: An Annotated Bibliography of Published Works, 1798–1981*. Westport, CT: L. Hill, 1982.

———. *Prison Writing in Twentieth-Century America*. New York: Penguin, 1998.

Furio, Jennifer, ed. *Letters from Prison: Voices of Women Murderers*. New York: Algora, 2001.

Grant, Joseph W. *Stop the Presses! I Want to Get Off! A Brief History of the Prisoners' Digest International*. East Lansing: Michigan State University Press, 2012.

Harris, Jean. *They Always Call Us Ladies: Stories from Prison*. New York: Scribner's, 1988.

Hartman, Kenneth E. *Mother California: A Story of Redemption Behind Bars*. New York: Atlas & Co., 2009.

Heard, Nathan. *House of Slammers*. (Fiction). New York: MacMillan, 1983.

Himes, Chester. *Yesterday Will Make You Cry*. (Fiction). New York: Norton, 1999.

Jackson, Bruce, ed. *Wake Up Dead Man: Afro-American Worksongs from Texas Prisons*. Cambridge, MA: Harvard University Press, 1972.

Jackson, George. *Blood in My Eye.* 1972; Baltimore: Black Classics Press, 1990.

———. *Soledad Brother: The Prison Letters of George Jackson.* Chicago: Lawrence Hill, 1994.

James, Joy, ed. *Imprisoned Intellectuals: America's Political Prisoners Write on Life, Liberation, and Rebellion.* New York: Rowman & Littlefield, 2003.

Jones, Hettie, ed. *Aliens at the Border: The [Poetry] Writing Workshop at Bedford Hills [Women's] Correctional Facility.* New York: Segue Books, 1997.

Kilgore, Deborah, ed. *My Mask Is: Prison Poems and Stories by Women.* Chicago: Small Garlic Press, 1999.

Knight, Etheridge. *The Essential Etheridge Knight.* (Poems). Pittsburgh: Pittsburgh University Press, 1986.

Martin, Dannie. *Committing Journalism: The Prison Writings of Red Hog.* New York: Norton, 1993.

Lamb, Wally, ed. *Couldn't Keep It to Myself: Wally Lamb and the Women of York Correctional Facility.* New York: HarperCollins, 2003.

———. *I'll Fly Away: Further Testimonies from the Women of York Prison.* New York: HarperCollins, 2007.

Mariah, Paul. *Personae Non Gratae.* (Poems). San Lorenzo, CA: Shameless Hussy, 1971.

Masters, Jarvis Jay. *Finding Freedom: Writings from Death Row.* Junction City, CA: Padma, 1997.

———. *That Bird Has My Wings: The Autobiography of an Innocent Man on Death Row.* New York: HarperOne, 2009.

McConnel, Patricia. *Sing Soft, Sing Loud.* (Fiction). Flagstaff, AZ: Logoria, 1995.

Melville, Samuel. *Letters from Attica.* New York: William Morrow, 1972.

Moody, Graham, ed. *Pelican's Progress: Anthology of Prison Writing from Pelican Bay State Prison.* Crescent City, CA: Pelican Bay State Prison, 2009.

Norfolk Prison Brothers. *Who Took the Weight? Black Voices from the Norfolk Prison.* Boston: Little, Brown and Co., 1972.

O'Hare, Kate Richards. *In Prison.* Seattle: University of Washington Press, 1976.

Pell, Eve, and members of the Prison Law Project, ed. *Maximum Security: Letters from California's Prisons.* New York: Dutton, 1972.

Peltier, Leonard. *Prison Writings: My Life Is My Sundance.* New York: St. Martins, 1999.

Prison Poetry. Trenton, NJ: New Jersey State Council on the Arts, 1973.

Rideau, Walter. *In the Place of Justice: A Story of Punishment and Deliverance.* New York: Knopf, 2010.

Salinas, Raul. *Un Trip through the Mind Jail y Otras Excursions.* Houston: Arte Publico, 1999.

Sanchez, Ricardo. *Selected Poems.* Houston: Arte Publico, 1985.

Scheffler, Judith, ed. *Wall Tappings: Women's Prison Writings, 200 A.D. to the Present.* New York: Feminist Press, 2002.

Seator, Lynette, ed. *Speaking through the Bars: Poems by Women.* Jacksonville, IL: End of Time Press, 1999.

Shakur, Assata. *Assata: An Autobiography.* New York: Lawrence Hill Books, 1988.

Slim, Iceberg. *The Naked Soul of Iceberg Slim.* Los Angeles: Holloway House, 2004.

Thomas, Piri. *Seven Long Times.* Houston: Arte Publico, 1994.

Tisdale, Celes, ed. *Betcha Ain't: Poems from Attica.* Detroit: Broadside Press, 1974.

Washington, Jerome. *Iron House: Stories from the Yard.* Fort Bragg, CA: QED Press, 1994.

Williams, Stanley "Tookie." *Life in Prison.* San Francisco: Chronicle Books, 2001.

Wozencraft, Kim. *Notes from the Country Club.* Boston: Houghton Mifflin, 1993.

X, Malcolm, (with Alex Haley). *The Autobiography of Malcolm X.* New York: Random House, 1987.

Zheng, Eddy, and Ben Wang. *Other: An Asian and Pacific Islander Prisoners' Anthology.* Hayward, CA: Asian Prisoner Support Committee, 2007.

HISTORY, EFFECTS OF, AND CRITICAL RESPONSES TO AMERICAN MASS INCARCERATION

Alexander, Michelle. *The New Jim Crow: Mass Incarceration in the Age of Colorblindness*. New York: The New Press, 2010.

Blackmon, Douglas A. *Slavery by Another Name: The Re-Enslavement of Black Americans from the Civil War to World War II*. New York: Anchor, 2009.

Bosworth, Mary. *Engendering Resistance: Agency and Power in Women's Prisons*. Aldershot, UK: Ashgate, 1999.

Brown, Michelle. *The Culture of Punishment: Prison, Society, and Spectacle*. New York: NYU Press, 2005.

Christianson, Scott. *With Liberty for Some: 500 Years of Imprisonment in America*. Boston: Northeastern University Press, 1998.

Curtin, Mary Ellen. *Black Prisoners and Their World, Alabama, 1865–1900*. Charlottesville: University of Virginia Press, 2000.

Davis, Angela Y. *Abolition Democracy: Beyond Empire, Prisons, and Torture*. New York: Seven Stories Press, 2005.

———. *Are Prisons Obsolete?* New York: Seven Stories Press, 2003.

Diaz-Cotto, Juanita. *Gender, Ethnicity, and the State: Latina and Latino Prison Politics*. Albany: State University of New York Press, 1996.

Garland, David. *Mass Imprisonment: Social Causes and Consequences*. New York: Sage, 2001.

Gilmore, Ruth Wilson. *Golden Gulag: Prisons, Surplus, Crisis, and Opposition in Globalizing California*. Los Angeles: University of California Press, 2007.

Hirsch, Adam J. *The Rise of the Penitentiary: Prisons and Punishment in Early America*. New Haven: Yale University Press, 1992.

James, Joy. *States of Confinement: Policing, Detention, and Prisons*. New York: St. Martin's, 2002.

Loury, Glenn C., Pamela Karlan, Loïc Wacquant, and Tommie Shelby, eds. *Race, Incarceration, and American Values*. Boston: MIT Press, 2008.

Loury, Glenn C., and Bruce Western, eds. "On Mass Incarceration." Special issue of *Daedalus* (Summer 2010).

Mauer, Marc. *Race to Incarcerate*. New York: New Press, 2006.

McBride, Keally. *Punishment and Political Order*. Ann Arbor: University of Michigan, 2007.

Page, Joshua. *The Toughest Beat: Politics, Punishment, and the Prison Officers Union in California*. New York: Oxford University Press, 2011.

Parenti, Christian. *Lockdown America: Police and Prisons in the Age of Crisis*. New York: Verso, 2000.

Patillo, Mary, David Weiman, and Bruce Western, eds. *Imprisoning America: The Social Effects of Mass Incarceration*. New York: Russell Sage, 2004.

Perkinson, Robert. *Texas Tough: The Rise of America's Prison Empire*. New York: Picador, 2010.

Schlosser, Eric. "The Prison-Industrial Complex." *Atlantic Monthly* (December 1998): 51–77.

Simon, Jonathan. *Governing through Crime: How the War on Crime Transformed American Democracy and Created a Culture of Fear*. New York: Oxford University Press, 2009.

Smith, Philip. *Punishment and Culture*. Chicago: University of Chicago Press, 2008.

Wacquant, Loïc. *Punishing the Poor: The Neoliberal Government of Social Insecurity*. Durham, NC: Duke University Press, 2009.

Western, Bruce. *Punishment and Inequality in America*. New York: Russell Sage, 2006.

CRITICAL PRISON WRITING STUDIES

Davies, Ioan. *Writers in Prison*. Oxford: Blackwell, 1990.

Franklin, H. Bruce. *Prison Literature in America: The Victim as Criminal and Artist*. New York: Oxford University Press, 1989.

Hames-Garcia, Michael. *Fugitive Thought: Prison Movements, Race, and the Meaning of Justice*. Minneapolis: University of Minnesota Press, 2004.

Harlow, Barbara. *Barred: Women, Writing, and Political Detention*. Hanover, NH: Wesleyan University Press, 1992.

———. *Resistance Literature*. New York: Methuen, 1987.

Haslam, Jason. *Fitting Sentences: Identity in Nineteenth- and Twentieth-Century Prison Narratives*. Toronto: University of Toronto Press, 2005.

Miller, D. Quentin, ed. *Prose and Cons: Essays on Prison Literature in the United States*. Jefferson, NC: MacFarland & Co., 2005.

Olguin, B. V. *La Pinta: Chicana/o Prison Literature, Culture, and Politics*. Austin: University of Texas Press, 2010.

Rodriguez, Dylan. *Forced Passages: Imprisoned Radical Intellectuals and the U.S. Prison Regime*. Minneapolis: University of Minnesota Press, 2006.

NOTES ON CONTRIBUTORS

Names of writers for whom no further information was available were omitted.

SUNDIATA ACOLI is a New Afrikan political prisoner of war, mathematician, and computer analyst who was born January 14, 1937, in Decatur, Texas, and was raised in Vernon, Texas. He graduated from Prairie View A&M College of Texas in 1956 with a BS in mathematics, and for the next thirteen years he worked for various computer-oriented firms, mostly in the New York area. During the summer of 1964 he did voter-registration work in Mississippi. In 1968 he joined the Harlem Black Panther Party and did community work around issues of schools, housing, jobs, child care, drugs, and police brutality.

STEVEN KING AINSWORTH's "Lessons in Stupidity" is autobiographical.

INTELLIGENT ALLAH's writings have been published in books, magazines, and online. He is a Bard College student, writing tutor, and editor of numerous books, including the *New York Times* bestselling novel *Justify My Thug*. He is also author of the *Don Diva Magazine* #1 Bestselling novel *Lickin' License*.

STEVEN G. AVALOY is a thirty-four-year-old African American who didn't take his family's advice when they saw him going down the wrong road. He's now paying for that.

MICHAEL B. BEVERLEY was born and raised in Massachusetts, the third of eight children. He has been a software engineer since graduating high school. He has a bachelor's degree in computer science, and spent eight years in the Air Force, six years as a missionary, and three years as an adjunct instructor for Franklin Pierce University, New Hampshire. He has four children—three boys and a daughter—and is currently nearing the end of his first of two 7½-to-15-year sentences running consecutively, in the New Hampshire state prison.

RAHASHEEM BROWN is currently enrolled in Bard College (BPI), working toward his AA in liberal arts. He is involved in and facilitates various experiential and therapeutic prison workshops—self-help and successful reentry programs (organizations). He also studies business and entrepreneurship, investing (stock and real property), and personal finances in his spare time.

DESHAWN COOPER was formerly a student in the Bard Prison Initiative (BPI) college program, and he has served as senior editor of BPI's literary magazine, *Rough Draft*.

MICHAEL CRAWFORD was born in Buffalo, New York, on July 10, 1980. He has about seven years left to complete a sentence of 22 years for robbery, auto theft, and homicide. During his time in prison, he has used his time wisely by accomplishing a number of educational and rehabilitative goals: He earned his GED in 1998; pursued legal research and law-library management in 2000; completed hospice aide training and served over one year as an aide at Ward Correctional Facility, 2005/2006; undertook Department of Labor apprenticeship training and one year service as a counseling aide, 2009; graduated in 2011 with an AA degree from Bard College Prison Initiative (BPI). Currently, he is working towards a BA degree with BPI at Eastern New York Correctional Facility.

DANNER DARCLEIGHT's essays have appeared in *Stone Canoe, the minnesota review*, and *Kenyon Review*. He has recently completed a book-length manuscript on the American prison experience.

JASON A. DAUGHERTY was born on July 21, 1982, and raised in Parkersburg, West Virginia. He is currently serving a 10-year sentence for accessory to bank robbery, and will discharge his sentence on April 26, 2016. While incarcerated, he has acquired 72 college credits with a 3.95 GPA. He hopes to complete a bachelor's degree in psychology once he is allowed back into society.

JOSE DI LENOLA's essay "The Years in Between" won a 2011 Honorable Mention from the PEN American Prison Writing contest and appeared in *Stone Canoe: A Journal of Arts, Literature and Social Commentary*. His passions include writing, music, teaching, and mentoring at-risk teens.

JANE DOROTIK is a registered nurse by education and has worked her whole life in the health-care/mental-health field. She was wrongfully convicted and is fighting for her rightful freedom. This experience has caused her to become a prison reform advocate and a jailhouse lawyer.

CURTIS L. DOWNING is the fourth child of Leon E. Downing and Edna M. Downing. He is an Afro-American, believed to be of Indian, Irish, and Scottish descent, and was born March 20, 1962. He fathered six children, though he was not present in their lives due to incarceration. He loves each and every one of them very much. He also loves and has truly deep respect for their mothers, who did the best they could to raise these children as single mothers. He is pleased to say that while incarcerated, he has taken opportunities to better himself, becoming a legal assistant/paralegal through BlackStone Paralegal Studies, Inc. in 2001. He has taken some college courses along the way and hopes to major in criminal justice with a minor in psychology. He is also pleased to write that he has decided not to blame others for situations or circumstances that occurred in his life, good or bad. He considers that all of these situations and circumstances have made him the person he is today, one who is giving, understanding, and helpful. He continues on work to overcome the injustice of his incarceration, and he is willing to take the "high road" because it's less traveled up there.

DEAN FAIELLO calls his prison writing a challenge. The simple acts of obtaining pen, paper, or typing ribbon can be a struggle. But the difficulties make seeing the finished product in print all the more satisfying. He writes inspired by espresso, seagulls, and the bumpy road that led him to Attica. He both thanks and curses the professor who introduced him to the craft of creative nonfiction, and to the frustrations and rewards of writing in prison.

LINDA FIELD is enjoying life since being released from prison. She speaks to anyone and every-one—including students, state representatives, and parents—about stopping domestic violence and childhood abuse. She knows there are many mothers in prison who only want to be reunited with their children and that many are there for trying to protect them. She advocates that unless you have walked in their shoes, no one can know their pain and suffering.

MARTIN G. GANN is a Native American of the Cherokee Nation.

MARISOL GARCIA served her time at York Correctional Institution. She has been released.

CONNIE GIBBS is passionate about becoming a strong and active participant in the solution rather than in the problems of society. She applies her knowledge of recovery to aid others in their difficult journey.

CHARLES HAMMER has been released.

LARRY G. "ROCKY" HARRIS is a prisoner activist trying to change a broken system. He is now fifty-three years old, and it has cost the taxpayer 347,904 dollars to house him. He wonders why he is not working at a job growing his food, teaching men to weld, or building wind turbines to offset the cost of his incarceration, now passed to the taxpayer. He wonders why he is placed in a cell all day long to rot while the taxpayer foots the bill.

KENNETH E. HARTMAN has served thirty-two years of a life-without-the-possibility-of-parole sentence in the California prison system. He is the award-winning author of *Mother California: A Story of Redemption Behind Bars* (2009), the editor of *Too Cruel, Not Unusual Enough*, and a founder of The Other Death Penalty Project.

ROBERT SALEEM HOLBROOK is a prisoner writer and social justice activist serving a life-without-parole sentence in Pennsylvania for a crime he was wrongly convicted of as a juvenile offender.

RONALD (RASHAWN) HUGHES has been incarcerated for twenty-two years. Throughout this time he has diligently worked to become a better man. He has received two college degrees, is a published author, and wants to demonstrate that there is no reason why life once set on its course cannot change.

JULIUS KIMYA HUMPHREY, SR. is a fifty-four-year-old Black man who has learned that his past actions and the conditions in which he was raised do not have to define him today. He believes that violence in his home, child abuse, social influences, and being raised in a single-parent home are things that he allowed to hinder his growth, but today he uses them as insight for his growth. He doesn't blame others for his disappointments in life, because he always had a choice. What he wants adults to understand is this: Thoughts are contagious, and when they turn into negative actions they become harmful to the development of our young people. Also, he didn't always understand the way he does now, but when he changed his way of thinking, he changed how he lives.

B. G. JACOBS is now thirty-one years old. He has been incarcerated since he was twenty-two. He is charged with Murder 2, and he believes that everything bad in his life stems from drug use. His earliest release date is 2021, when he will be forty. His latest release date is . . . never.

ROYAL GENE DOMINGO JONES, SR., was born in San Francisco, California, on September 2, 1967. He is the youngest of three children and has two beautiful sisters. He struggled in school as a child and had lots of trouble staying out of, and away from, trouble. As he got older he still managed to find trouble, but he did find also an appreciation for education. He finished his schooling and then enrolled in college. He is self-taught in French, Italian, Urdu, Swahili, Chinese, Japanese, and Arabic. He is currently working on a nonprofit organization, STOP (Start Trying Other Programs), that will help reduce the current juvenile incarceration population. He hopes only to be an inspiration for those who may have the struggles he has had, and those who are just in need of a story or two to take heed. He is due to be released from federal prison.

DORAN LARSON is Professor of English and Creative Writing at Hamilton College. He has led the Attica Writer's Workshop since 2006. He is the founder of the Attica-Genesee Teaching Project, which began delivering college-credit courses inside Attica Correctional Facility in January 2011. Larson's essays on prison writing and related issues have appeared in *Salmagundi*, *College Literature*, *English Language Notes*, *Radical Teacher*, and the *Chronicle of Higher Education*. He is the editor of "The Beautiful Prison," a special issue of *Studies in Law, Politics, and Society*, in which incarcerated writers, prison teachers, and prison critics try to imagine what the American prison would look like if it were a socially constructive institution. He is working now to create the American Prison Writing Archive—an open-access digital archive of nonfiction essays by American prisoners, prison staff, the families of incarcerated people, and prison volunteers. Larson has also published two novels, a novella, and over a dozen short stories, in addition to critical essays on American literature and film.

STEVEN F. LOMAS is part of the Soledad Prison Buddhist Meditation Community.

RICHARD ALAN ABOOD LYON grew up in rural Connecticut and attended public school. Upon graduation he attended the University of Massachusetts Amherst, and Amherst College, graduating with a BS in environmental design, and was accepted on full scholarship to Harvard University's three-year master's program in urban planning and real estate development. He is serving a life sentence for murder, and recently completed a second master's degree from the University of Houston. This essay is a true prison story, which he wrote for a class with Dr. Kathryn Peterson.

SHELLEY MAC believes that at times we all make bad choices. Choices can lead us to positive or negative places, and then we are faced with . . . another choice. Does this define us? Or, do we pick ourselves up, look back, learn, and thank God for another chance? She chooses the latter. We can never change what has been done, or predict what is to come. The only moment we have is NOW, which she willingly gives to the Creator. His plan is so much grander than hers ever was.

BRANDON MARTINEZ has devoted his life to change. With his prolific essays and poems, he constantly grasps the moral fortitude to make a difference. In spite of being in the midst of chaos and despair, he realizes that one's individual gesture of kindness, word of encouragement, or token of goodwill can have a significant impact in altering the course of another's life for the better. He believes that it is only by our contributions that we will ever save ourselves, and urges us to keep hope alive.

JARVIS JAY MASTERS is a widely published African American–Buddhist writer. He is the author of *Finding Freedom: Writings from Death Row*, and *That Bird Has My Wings: An Autobiography of an Innocent Man on Death Row*, nominated for a 2010 PEN USA Literary Award. Jarvis is the recipient of the 1991 PEN Award for Poetry, for his poem "Recipe for Prison Pruno."

PETER MEHMEL is an artist, architect, inventor, game designer, welder, teacher, and sometimes writer. He never could figure out who he wanted to be . . . and he still needs a job! Free in 2015.

SHAKKIR TALIB MUJAHID hopes that his writing may be of some service and inspiration, and that it may be informative of his prison experience.

COLLEEN O'BRIEN has currently done almost seven years of a 19-year sentence. She's working on reducing her sentence so she can go home to her mom, sisters, children, and grandchildren.

RICKY VINCENT PENDLETON II, a product of Charleston, West Virginia, is remorseful for the crimes he's charged with. He is going through atonement for those crimes. Even when the appeal is pending, he is still staying strong mentally, physically, emotionally, and hoping for release.

ROBERT F. PIWOWAR is a former educator from Hamburg, New York. He is an avid reader, musician, and golf enthusiast. His writing has appeared in *the minnesota review* and *Stone Canoe*.

ANTHONY POWERS has been incarcerated for 19 years. He has started a program titled "The Redemption Project," to create a system geared towards eliminating the negative cultures of prison. This project has had over 600 members and is currently in two prisons in Washington State with an additional two prisons expressing great interest in starting it there. For the Project, he and Mrs. Dawn Taylor co-authored a workbook on developing self-awareness.

KARTER KANE REED, serving a 15-to-life sentence for 2nd-degree murder, has been in prison since the age of sixteen. He was granted parole at his initial eligibility hearing in 2008, only to have that decision rescinded before his release. He has challenged the constitutionality of the parole rescission and is awaiting a decision by the court. He expects to be released.

MARKEITHIA R. REEVEZ's "Inmate Jane Doe" was awarded Second Place in the category of essay in the 2010 PEN American Prison Writing Contest.

COREY JOHN RICHARDSON has written widely about prison issues and sobriety for publications such as *Spotlight on Recovery*, *Cell Door Magazine* (the official publication of the National Death Row Assistance Network), *Kentuckiana News*, *Perspectives* (the official journal of the Association for Humanistic Psychology), *The Grapevine* (Alcoholics Anonymous's international publication), *The Long Term View: A Journal of Informed Opinion* (Massachusetts School of Law at Andover), *OUTlooks* (Canada's GLBT magazine), and others. He won 1st Prize in the Ford Foundation's 2009 National Writing Competition, has had "Think Outside the Cell" published in *Love Lives Here, Too* (2010), and has an Honorable Mention for his adaptation of *Gumbo* at the Kennedy Center for the Arts's Page-to-Stage Festival (September 3, 2011).

VALJEAN ROYAL: 2014, marks the 42nd year of captivity for this writer inside prison in America. African American, male to female pre-op transgender, Valjean Royal remains prayerful for liberty and justice. Valjean Royal is a past victim of teenage bullying, chronic depression (mental illness), countless sexual assaults, and finally self-sabotage, resulting in false imprisonment for crimes any real investigator would exonerate.

SANDY is fifty-four years old, an artist who enjoys drawing and painting. He is a jogger, and in addition to writing, he also enjoys writing and illustrating children's books. He is single, and enjoys the outdoors. He loves animals and people.

TERRENCE SAMPSON has been incarcerated for the past twenty-two years for a crime that he committed at the age of twelve. His accomplishments during incarceration include a bachelor's degree in psychology from Sam Houston State University (2003) and a master's degree in literature from the University of Houston–Clear Lake (2010).

JOHN H. SCHMIDT is studying to be a nationally certified compulsive-gambling counselor. He is responsible for giving gambling-awareness workshops in prison, and teaches gambling abstinence from a Biblical perspective. He is also a high school instructor for James H. Groves High School prison satellite program, and the recipient of the 2007 Volunteer Service Award for work with at-risk youth.

EDWARD C. SHELLEY served six years in the U.S. Navy, and worked for four years with the Federal Aviation Administration until alcohol abuse forced him to resign. He is now seven years clean and sober and working towards an associate degree in chemical-dependency counseling. He sincerely wants to share his experience with others in the hope of helping them.

ANDREW JACKSON SMITH was born on September 15, 1960. His education includes degrees in nursing and psychology. He has additional training as a cardiopulmonary technician, diagnostic medical sonographer, and as a minister and chaplain. He served in the U.S. military from 1982 to 1992. He was framed for the murder of his fiancée in 2001.

ANDREW R. SUMAHIT, JR.: Since writing "The Incarcerated Father," Andrew R. Sumahit, Jr., has been transferred from a maximum-security prison to a medium-security prison. He has established a relationship with his daughter, thus breaking the cycle of fatherlessness. To date, he has seen her eight times and is currently asking Family Court for increased visitation. He has also recently discovered that his own father is alive, and is trying to locate him. He continues to teach other incarcerated fathers about their parental rights, and is pursuing a degree in paralegal studies. He hopes his story will inspire others.

JON MARC TAYLOR received the Robert F. Kennedy and The Nation Institute/I.F. Stone journalism awards for his reporting on "Pell Grants for Prisoners," and he is the author of the *Prisoners' Guerrilla Handbook to Correspondence Programs in the United States and Canada* (2002).

DIANA WAGGY is in her early fifties. She is a grateful breast-cancer survivor and is in her 19th year of an 85-year sentence for murder. She has played brass and violin in the prison orchestra, and has trained seventeen dogs in the prison dog-training program. Diana is a practicing Zen Buddhist, and is also interested in the teaching of Ernest Holmes. She likes to encourage people to find their own spiritual paths. Diana was inspired and encouraged to write "Inspiration" by a wonderful teacher, Mary K., who taught a writing workshop at the prison in 2009–2010. Best advice: "It's never too late."

CHASTITY C. WEST's interests include literary classics and philosophy. She writes short stories, autobiographical reflections, poetry, and editorial pieces, but her passion lies in prison advocacy and social justice. Her goal is to earn a bachelor's degree in English with a minor in journalism. Chastity is currently pursuing post-conviction relief. She will use her education and incarceration experience to further her advocacy for society's downtrodden.

STEPHEN WHETZEL currently lives in Indianapolis, IN. He developed an interest in writing while participating in a college program through Ball State University. Mr. Whetzel continues to write and plans to publish more of his work. He works with Living Violence Free, an organization established to reduce abuse and violence in American society through education and training.

A. WHITFIELD has been incarcerated since 1985. During this time he has earned college degrees from Canisius College of Buffalo and Indiana University. He learned to "write" in a creative-writing workshop at Attica Prison. He has been published in *Stone Canoe* and *the minnesota review*.

GEORGE WHITHAM is fifty-nine years old; he came to prison when he was twenty-two years old. He describes himself as a very angry young man at the time, who had very little in the way of an education and very little respect for anyone. Now he is "older and a little wiser, as they say." In meeting his friend "Bill" his eyes were opened to so many good things; Bill helped him to attain these things. He has become a better human being because of their friendship. He is still in college; it's been a long road, but the end is in sight. He only needs 20 credits for his degree. When he gets that degree, he is planning to make a photocopy of it and send the original to Bill's wife, Patti. He feels that in a sense, they both have earned it.

INDEX